SAMS
Teach Yourself

Unix System Administration

in **24** *Hours*

Dave Taylor

SAMS   201 West 103rd St., Indianapolis, Indiana, 46290 USA

Sams Teach Yourself Unix System Administration in 24 Hours

Copyright © 2003 by Sams Publishing

International Standard Book Number: 0-672-32398-2

Library of Congress Catalog Card Number: 2001099557

Printed in the United States of America

First Printing: July 2002

05   04   03   02   4   3   2

Trademarks

Warning and Disclaimer

ACQUISITIONS EDITOR
Kathryn Purdum

DEVELOPMENT EDITOR
Heather Goodell

MANAGING EDITOR
Charlotte Clapp

PROJECT EDITOR
Elizabeth Finney

PRODUCTION EDITOR
Seth Kerney

INDEXER
Larry Sweazy

PROOFREADER
Suzanne Thomas

TECHNICAL EDITORS
Dee-Ann LeBlanc
David Ennis

TEAM COORDINATOR
Amy Patton

INTERIOR DESIGNER
Gary Adair

COVER DESIGNER
Alan Clements

PAGE LAYOUT
Stacey Richwine-DeRome

Contents at a Glance

Contents

Contents

HOUR 18 Running Your Own Name Server 353

HOUR 19 Running Internet Services 373

HOUR 20 Working with E-mail 391

About the Author

DAVE TAYLOR is a popular writer, teacher, and speaker focused on business and technology issues. The founder of The Internet Mall and iTrack.com, he has been involved with Unix and the Internet since 1980, having created the popular Elm Mail System and Embot mail autoresponder. A prolific author, his most recent books include *Learning Unix for Mac OS X, Sams Teach Yourself Unix in 24 Hours, Creating Cool HTML 4.0 Web Pages, Dynamic HTML Weekend Crash Course*, and *The e*Auction Insider*.

Previous positions include research scientist at HP Laboratories and senior reviews editor of *SunWorld* magazine. He has contributed software to the official 4.4 release of Berkeley Unix (BSD), and his programs are found in all versions of Linux and other popular Unix variants.

Dave has a bachelor's degree in computer science, a master's degree in educational computing, and is working on an MBA. He teaches business and technology-related courses both in the physical world through the University of Colorado at Boulder, and online with the University of Phoenix. His e-mail address has been the same for over 15 years: taylor@intuitive.com.

When not typing madly on the keyboard of his Mac, Dave's either playing with his wife Linda and two wonderful kids, Ashley and Gareth, or out bicycling around Boulder.

Dedication

To the three shining stars in my firmament...

Acknowledgments

This project has been quite complex, juggling multiple operating systems, installations, and configurations. Fortunately I was lucky to have a group of Unix and system experts helping me along. As a result, I'd like to thank Andy Lester for his help with my oft-inefficient Perl coding, Westley Annis for helping clarify the mysterious world of DNS, and Max Horn for his helpful corrections on the Darwin Fink project. Gideon Shaanan, Richard Blum, Cedric Higgins, Tim Hicks, Dave Ennis, Brian Bilbrey, Eugene Lee, and Tyler and Rima Regas were all also helpful with their comments and assistance.

I can't say enough wonderful things about Dee-Ann LeBlanc and David Ennis, the tech editors for this book. They're master nit-pickers, but ultimately any errors you encounter are probably mine. (But please, file an errata report so we can fix it in the next edition!) In particular, Dee-Ann was always available for late night IM sessions as my sanity started to slip. Thanks! I was also blessed to work with the same Sams team I've used on other books, notably Katie Purdum, Heather Goodell, and Elizabeth Finney. They're all ably led by my longtime friend Mark Taber.

Finally, I couldn't have done this book without the indulgence of my wife and kids. Thanks oodles to Linda, Ashley, and Gareth. It might not be entirely clear why Daddy's always on the computer, but there is an end-product occasionally!

We Want to Hear from You!

As the reader of this book, *you* are our most important critic and commentator. We value your opinion and want to know what we're doing right, what we could do better, what areas you'd like to see us publish in, and any other words of wisdom you're willing to pass our way.

You can e-mail or write me directly to let me know what you did or didn't like about this book—as well as what we can do to make our books better.

Please note that I cannot help you with technical problems related to the topic of this book, and that due to the high volume of mail I receive, I might not be able to reply to every message.

When you write, please be sure to include this book's title and author as well as your name, e-mail address, and phone number. I will carefully review your comments and share them with the author and editors who worked on the book.

E-mail: opensource@samspublishing.com

Mail: Mark Taber
             Associate Publisher
             Sams Publishing
             201 West 103rd Street
             Indianapolis, IN 46290 USA

Reader Services

For more information about this book or another Sams title, visit our Web site at www.samspublishing.com. Type the ISBN (excluding hyphens) or the title of a book in the Search field to find the page you're looking for.

Introduction

Welcome to *Teach Yourself Unix System Administration in 24 Hours*! This book has been designed so that it's helpful for both beginning system administrators and those with previous Unix experience. This text is helpful as a guide as well as a tutorial. The reader of this book is assumed to be intelligent, and to have at least a basic familiarity with Unix. If you would like to brush up on your Unix prior to delving into this book, I suggest the companion title *Teach Yourself Unix in 24 Hours*, a top-selling introductory title that'll get you up to speed with the intricacies of Unix faster than you can say "supercalifragilisticexpialidocious!" (or type it, for that matter!)

What This Book Isn't

I'd like to state my intent with this book up front, while you're still browsing in the bookstore: This book is not intended to be the only system administration material you ever study. Indeed, this book grew out of a course I taught, an *introduction* to Unix system administration. The reason for this distinction is because there are a number of very good reference works on administration (that typically run 800–1,100 pages) that offer a cookbook approach of "if this is wrong, do this to fix it." That's very helpful, and I have these titles on my reference shelf, but they don't teach you *how to approach, diagnose, and solve problems the Unix way*. That's a major goal for this book.

When you finish exploring this book, you will know how to think like a good system administrator, regardless of what variation of Unix you encounter. You'll learn how to hypothesize about problems, dig through man pages and configuration files, postulate solutions, then test and verify that they've worked. And have fun in the process too!

In the same vein, this book isn't 1,001 ways to fine-tune your Unix installation. In fact, we're going to gloss over the question of installation, because for most users the system is either already installed (like Mac OS X or Solaris), or has very good installation and configuration documentation. (Red Hat and Mandrake Linux distributions are standouts in this regard.)

What Flavors of Unix?

This book covers both the System V and BSD Unix worlds—the specific operating systems explored are Red Hat Linux 7.2 (with the 2.4.7 kernel), Solaris 8 (running on Intel, though it's identical to the SPARC version), and Darwin, the BSD OS hidden underneath Mac OS X (release 10.1.2).

Between them, these three represent the major families of Unix, with Red Hat representing the strong but anarchic Linux world; Solaris, the commercial Unix release; and Mac OS X, a direct descendant of the BSD school of Unix.

There are, of course, hundreds of different Unix distributions, ranging from free downloads to operating systems that only run on expensive, million-dollar supercomputers. That's why a major goal of *Teach Yourself Unix System Administration in 24 Hours* is to teach you how to work within the tools of generic Unix to diagnose and solve problems, rather than how to use vendor-supplied platform-specific tools.

Does Each Chapter Take an Hour?

You can learn the concepts in each of the 24 chapters in one hour. If you want to experiment with what you learn in each chapter, something I highly recommend, you might take longer than an hour. However, all the concepts presented herein are straightforward. If you are familiar with Windows applications or the Macintosh, you will be able to progress more quickly, and if you're already comfortable at the Unix command line, well, this book might well only be "12–16 hours" worth of studying!

What If I Take Longer than 24 Hours?

Since the publication of the first edition of my Unix book, I've received a considerable amount of praise and positive feedback, but the one message that's always been a surprise is "I finished your book, but it took me a lot longer than 24 hours." Now you can read here, direct from the author: It's okay! Take your time and make sure you try everything as you go along. Learning and remembering is more important than speed. Remember, too, that 24 hours doesn't necessarily mean 24 *consecutive* hours. And if you do finish it all in 24 hours, let me know!

How to Use This Book

This book is designed to teach you topics in one-hour sessions. All the books in the Sams *Teach Yourself* series enable you to start working and become productive as quickly as possible. This book will do that for you.

Each hour, or session, starts with an overview of the topic to inform you what to expect in each lesson. The overview helps you determine the nature of the lesson, and whether the lesson is relevant to your needs.

Main Section

Each lesson has a main section that discusses the lesson topic in a clear, concise manner by breaking the topic down into logical component parts and explaining each component clearly.

Interspersed in each lesson are special elements, called Notes, Tips, and Cautions, which provide additional information.

Notes are designed to clarify the concept that is being discussed. It elaborates on the subject, and if you are comfortable with your understanding of the subject, you can bypass them without danger.

Tips inform you of tricks or elements that are easily missed by most computer users. You can skip them, but often Tips show you an easier way to do a task.

A Caution deserves at least as much attention as a Tip, because Cautions point out a problematic element of the topic being discussed. Ignoring the information contained in the Caution could have adverse effects on the task at hand. These are the most important special elements in this book.

This book uses different typefaces to differentiate between code and regular English, and also to help you identify important concepts. Therefore, code lines, commands, statements, variables, and any text you see onscreen appear in a `computer typeface`. Additionally, any text you type as input appears in a **`bold computer typeface`**.

Tasks

This book offers another special element called a Task. These step-by-step exercises are designed to quickly walk you through the most important skills you can learn in different areas of Unix system administration.

Q&As and Workshops

A Q&A and Workshop section are at the end of each lesson. The Q&A section and Quiz questions reinforce concepts you learned in the lesson and help you apply them in new situations. You can skip this section, but it is advised that you go through the questions to see how the concepts can be applied to other common tasks.

The Online Component

There are lots of sample code listings, shell scripts, and other types of information throughout this book that you'll want to download from the official book Web site rather than type in:

```
http://www.intuitive.com/tyusa/
```

In addition, there's an errata area and an all-important errata report form on the site too: Any time you find any sort of hiccup or oddness with a command you try, please let us know! We'll keep an up-to-date errata list and make sure they're all fixed in the next edition of the book. Thanks!

PART I
Installing Unix

Hour

HOUR 1

Installing Unix

If you're reading this book, I bet that you already have a Unix operating system installed on a system you run. Whether it's a shared server that you're renting space on for your Web site, a file server in your office, or even a PC that you've used as a Unix test platform, this first hour will possibly be the least interesting one in this book.

However, it's also possible that you've read through some Unix books (perhaps even my own *Teach Yourself Unix in 24 Hours*), and are eager to learn more about the internals of Unix and how you can ensure that yours is stable.

This first hour, therefore, is going to go through a typical Red Hat Linux installation on a PC, with all the default configuration options specified. Then we'll look at some of the great online Unix and Linux help sites. If you have a different flavor of Unix you're interested in, your installation will doubtless be different (I have experimented with SuSE, Mandrake, Red Hat, Solaris, AIX, HP-UX, Mac OS X, FreeBSD and NetBSD, to name a few). The basic concepts, however, will prove similar in almost all cases.

And as a reminder, this is the *only* hour in this book where we'll only look at a single operating system. All subsequent material will explore Red Hat Linux, Solaris, and Mac OS X as the three reference flavors of Unix.

In this hour, you will learn about

- Unix installation options
- Basic Red Hat Linux installation
- Online installation resources

Unix Installation Options

The first issue of concern is whether your system meets the hardware requirements for a Unix installation. Although Linux (and Red Hat in particular) runs across a wide range of different hardware platforms, there are nonetheless certain requirements to have it run reasonably well:

- A minimum of 350MB of available disk space, and if you want to have the X Window System running, a Web server, developer software, and other standard Unix goodies, you'll find that the realistic minimum disk space requirement is 1.8–2GB.
- At least 64MB of RAM, though Unix is definitely an operating system where more RAM is always better. I always try for a minimum of 128MB, and if you have 256MB or more, you'll find greatly increased performance.
- A CPU. Should it be a specific minimum speed, like a 500Mhz Pentium III? Surprisingly, people have successfully run Linux on quite old and slow systems. Does it run well enough that you would enjoy using it? Well, you can answer that question for yourself. Generally, any computer sold since January 1, 2000, has plenty of horsepower to run a Linux *distro* (jargon for distribution) with good results.
- A CD-ROM drive (hopefully that is self-evident).
- A network card, ideally, so you can connect to the Internet. Be warned, it can be tricky to configure a modem and PPP (the Point-to-Point Protocol), though not at all impossible.
- A graphical display, display card, keyboard, and mouse.

It's worth noting that, armed with this book, you don't have to buy anything else to get a copy of Red Hat Linux and install it on your system. Start by going to the Red Hat download area and look for the latest version of their system. As of this writing, it's 7.2, so the download link is `http://www.redhat.com/download/rhlinux72.html`. On the other hand, by the time you read this, they'll likely be shipping 8.0, so your best bet is to start on the Red Hat home page to ensure you get the latest release.

There are good directions online about how to proceed. In general, you'll download ISOs (installation disk images) that are 650MB a pop, burned to a CD-ROM,[1] and used for the installation process. You'll need a minimum of two CD-ROMs for a good install, so that's a download of 2×650MB, and if you're on a 56K modem, you'll do much better to go to the computer store and buy the official Red Hat distribution box, with CD-ROMs, installation documents, and more, for about $60.

> There are also people who download the ISO files, burn CD-ROMs, then sell them online (and yes, it's legal). A quick search on eBay reveals "RH Linux 7.2 Brand New 4 CD-ROM Set Enigma" for a starting bid of only $8.95. Add $2 for shipping, and you can have a complete four-CD-ROM installation set—an exciting new operating system for your computer—for less than the price of a small pizza with anchovies and pineapple!

Other Linux distributors offer very low-cost CD-ROM distributions, if you are nervous about online auction venues. For example, the highly-rated Mandrake Linux (`www.mandrakesoft.com`) offers a three-CD-ROM Download Edition for $15, including shipping.

Other Unixes are priced differently, as you might suspect. Solaris Intel, from Sun Microsystems, can be downloaded for free from their Web site (`www.sun.com/solaris/`), or for $45 they have a very nice distribution package that includes 12 CD-ROMs and some (very sparse) documentation. However, there are some conflicting rumors about the long-term health of Solaris on Intel, so don't be surprised if at some point in the future Sun instead points you to a Linux distro.

Apple distributes Mac OS X on two CD-ROMS in a box with documentation and more. It's rather more expensive than the other distros discussed so far at $129 (`store.apple.com`), but if you have a recent Macintosh, you probably already have Mac OS X installed.

There are many other Unixes available, many of which are available as free downloads from online archive sites. You can start at `www.download.com`, for example. Select Linux, Distributions, and you'll have 36 matches from which to choose, including Phat Linux, Slackware Linux, Caldera OpenLinux, and the nifty Yellow Dog Linux for Mac systems.

---

[1]*Even better, it's legal. You are explicitly allowed to burn your own CD-ROM install disks from the downloaded ISOs on their site.*

Basic Red Hat Linux Installation

Let's assume that you want to install Red Hat Linux, as they have one of the best installation packages (called anaconda) out of all the Linuxes I've used.

1. The first step is to make sure you have a reliable backup of any information that you already have on your computer. Most likely, you'll want to just overwrite your entire disk with the new operating system, which will mean that all your existing files will be stomped, mutilated, and otherwise burned beyond recognition.

   Once you're sure you want to proceed, slip the first installation CD-ROM into the CD-ROM drive of your computer and boot up.

   It's not visually exciting, but the first thing you'll see is as shown in Figure 1.1, the boot-up screen options. I always choose the default by pressing Enter on the keyboard.

FIGURE 1.1

Red Hat Linux installation boot options.

```
                    Welcome to Red Hat Linux 7.2!
    -  To install or upgrade Red Hat Linux in graphical mode,
       press the <ENTER> key.

    -  To install or upgrade Red Hat Linux in text mode, type: text <ENTER>.

    -  To enable low resolution mode, type: lowres <ENTER>.
       Press <F2> for more information about low resolution mode.

    -  To disable framebuffer mode, type: nofb <ENTER>.
       Press <F2> for more information about disabling framebuffer mode.

    -  To enable expert mode, type: expert <ENTER>.
       Press <F3> for more information about expert mode.

    -  To enable rescue mode, type: linux rescue <ENTER>.
       Press <F5> for more information about rescue mode.

    -  If you have a driver disk, type: linux dd <ENTER>.

    -  Use the function keys listed below for more information.
    [F1-Main] [F2-General] [F3-Expert] [F4-Kernel] [F5-Rescue]
    boot:
```

2. Linux flashes into graphics mode, enabling your mouse, and the next screen you see lets you choose what language to use for the installation process. You'll probably choose English, in which case you can just click on the Next button on the bottom right.

   The next step, as illustrated in Figure 1.2, is to pick your keyboard configuration. Most likely, you can again select the default values and proceed to the next step.

   The mouse configuration is the third pre-installation step (these steps are just configuring anaconda, the installation application), and I've always had good results with the default 3 Button Mouse (PS/2).

FIGURE 1.2
Keyboard configuration.

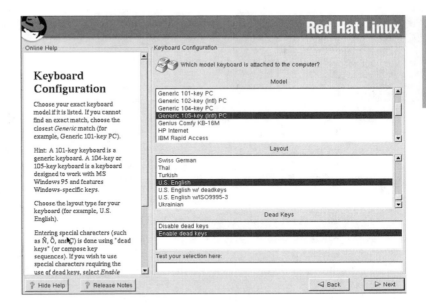

3. Now we're ready for the actual installation process to begin. The first selection—and perhaps the most important selection—is to decide what kind of installation you'd like. The choices are Workstation, Server, Laptop, and Custom.

   I recommend a workstation installation if you have sufficient disk space (about 2GB), because it's easier to install software and then not use it than to want to use it and find it wasn't installed. The server installation skips all the X Window System software packages, though you can add it back by going to the package groupings area.

4. The first major task during the installation process is to decide how you want to slice up your available disk space so that Linux can properly utilize it. In almost all cases, your best bet is to have the system figure out how much space you have and then partition it automatically. You can choose this with Have The Installer Automatically Partition For You.

   You'll probably see a dialog box similar to Figure 1.3. Don't panic. Remember, you've already done a complete backup, and we're planning on replacing the current OS on the computer with Linux.

   Next, choose Remove All Partitions On This System, unless you already had a previous Linux installed and want to use that existing partition space. Make sure that if you have multiple drives, it has picked the correct drive for the install we're about to start!

FIGURE 1.3

You need to confirm that you want to create new partitions.

The system automatically creates a reasonable partition strategy. For my system, with a 15GB disk available, it split it into /dev/hda1 (to mount as /boot) with 47MB of disk space, /dev/hda3 (to mount as swap space) with 188MB of space, and the remaining 15.1GB as /dev/hda2 (mounting as /).

Rather than accept this, I am going to split /dev/hda2 into two partitions, one that's 4.1GB and one that's 11GB. The latter will prove useful later in the book, when we explore disk formatting and the mount command. To accomplish this task, I select the partition in question and click Edit. This produces the dialog box shown in Figure 1.4. Notice that I've already specified a fixed size of 4100MB here.

FIGURE 1.4

Repartitioning to grab some space.

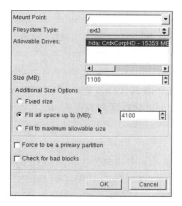

Once accepted (click OK), you'll now have a free space listed at 11029MB. Click on that, click Edit, and you can specify a mount point if you'd like. Or, leave it as free space and you can perhaps install Windows within and create a dual-boot configuration (see Hour 11, "Multiple Boot Configurations").

5. Now you need to pick a boot loader, if any. I prefer grub, but you might like lilo. I will say that there's really no reason *not* to pick one of these, just so you have flexibility in your configuration later on. Otherwise, leave all these options alone.

If you'd like, you can specify a grub password, which will mean that every time the system is rebooted, the password will be required to proceed with the boot process. Be thoughtful about this option: If you specify this and then have your system in a collocation rack, who will enter the password if it reboots?

The next step is to configure your network interface, as shown in Figure 1.5. If you have DHCP, you're in luck. Click that box and you're done! Otherwise, you'll want to fill out as much of the information specified as possible.

FIGURE 1.5

Configuring your network connection.

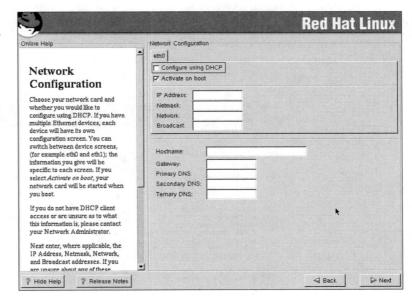

Almost done with the configuration questions. The last network configuration step is to pick a firewall configuration for security. Though the default is to customize your settings, I tend to select Use Default Firewall Rules and leave a security level of Medium.

6. If you want to make your system usable in multiple languages, you can specify them in the Additional Language Support screen that comes next. Even if you only want English (USA), spend a moment to scroll through this list and see just how many different choices there are. Quite impressive!

There are lots of languages listed, but it's worth highlighting that it's up to the individual application to support the language, so don't be surprised if you install Italian, just to find some *richiami del sistema in inglese*.

Your time zone should be specified next, and you can click on cities on the world map, select a regional map from the pull-down menu, or scroll until you find a city in your own time zone to select from the list. Living in the Mountain Time zone, I select Denver, Colorado, from the list.

The next screen is the Account Configuration screen. You don't need to create a number of accounts at this juncture, but if you know multiple people will be using the system, this is a very convenient place to add them. In Figure 1.6 you can see that I've created four user accounts, and also set the root password.

As a reminder, you *must* set a root password here, and it must be something that's simultaneously complex enough that it would be difficult for crackers to guess, and simple enough that you'll remember it. Don't forget what you specify here; it'll be critical to the long-term health of your Unix system down the road.

FIGURE **1.6**

Account
Configuration screen.

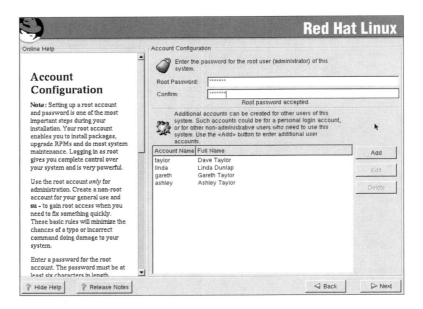

7. Finally, we are at the point where we need to select which packages we'd like to install. There are default packages already selected because of our workstation installation specification earlier, but additional material can be added.

   As Figure 1.7 shows, I recommend installing KDE in addition to Gnome and the Software Development Tools. Whether you want to include games is up to you.

   Notice in particular on the lower right corner the indicator of how big all the combined packages will be (here it's 1559MB, just about 1.6GB).

FIGURE 1.7
Selecting additional packages to install.

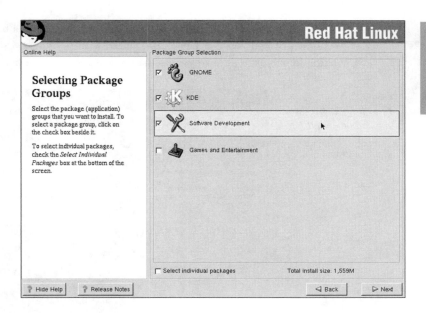

It's just about time to go and get a cup of tea and read the paper while anaconda slowly installs each of the hundreds of packages you've now selected.

8. The only task left is to configure the screen for X Windows System (which might seem a little weird, since we've already been working in a graphical environment with a mouse, but that's another story). Fortunately, I've found that anaconda does a very good job of analyzing hardware configurations, and just about always picks the best setup to match your physical system.

> At this point in the installation process, you can still back out, shut down your computer, eject the CD-ROM, and have your system just as it was prior to booting into the Red Hat world. Once we proceed beyond this, however, all the prior contents of the disk will be destroyed. Please, please ensure you have a good backup before going further!

Enough paranoia, let's install this baby!

The next screen shows you the progress of the installation process, as anaconda formats the file systems, transfers an install image (the ISO images we discussed earlier in this hour) to the disk, and then begins the actual transfer. Pay particular attention to the Total and Remaining package counts—they'll give you a very good idea of how much time you have left on the install.

Expect this step to take at least an hour, and possibly quite a bit longer, depending on how fast your system, CD-ROM, and disk are. Figure 1.8 shows how the installation looks just a little ways into the process (about 10 minutes).

FIGURE 1.8

Installing packages slowly but surely!

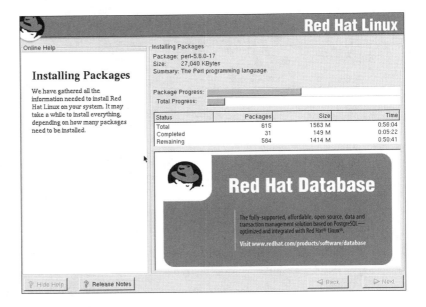

Once this process is done, you'll get a peppy Finished! screen and you can reboot and run your new Red Hat Linux installation on your computer. Congratulations!

The question of what to do after you've installed your system is, of course, the topic of the rest of this book. But one thing you might try is just logging in as a regular user, selecting either Gnome or KDE as your desktop environment, then launching a Web browser and surfing the Web. See how it is similar in some ways, and quite different in other ways, to Windows or Macintosh systems.

Installation Help Online

The documentation that's included with the Red Hat Linux distro is actually pretty good, particularly the *Installation Guide*, but you might find that there's useful information available online.

A good place to start your exploration is at the Red Hat Web site itself (www.redhat.com), where they have a complete documentation set available for searching and reading online (and, of course, printing, even if you're running Windows or Mac OS at the time).

Another valuable source of Linux installation and configuration information is Linux Planet (www.linuxplanet.com), where they also have a nice writeup comparing the different flavors of Linux available. Start by clicking on Tutorials when you visit this site.

A great source for all Unix documentation, though it's ostensibly focused on Linux, is the Linux Documentation Project (www.linuxdoc.org). It's out of date, but there's still helpful information in the *Installation and Getting Started Guide* in the Guides section of the LDP site. The HOWTO section offers some very specific information that you might find of use too, including a guide to installing Linux on an Acer laptop, booting a Compaq T1500 into Linux, and the useful Config-HOWTO.

The DMOZ Open Directory project has a very nice set of references that'll be worth a bookmark in your Web browser too, though the starting URL is rather long:

http://dmoz.org/Computers/Software/Operating_Systems/Linux/Support/Tutorials/

In particular, check out "Dancing with the Penguin," a good tutorial with a great title!

If you opted for a Unix other than Red Hat Linux, you'll find many of these Web sites quite useful. Also check out the vendor Web site, and you can also check out SlashDot (www.slashdot.com) for the latest gossip and discussion about Unix systems and distributions.

Summary

This hour has explored how to install and configure Red Hat Linux on a typical personal computer. Fortunately, the process is quite straightforward, and if you have the network information necessary to connect directly to the Internet prior to installation, you should be online by now, too. If you have another flavor of Unix, you'll find that the install varies quite a bit: Mandrake Linux is a breeze, Mac OS X Unix is even easier, but Solaris can prove to be tricky. We also discussed some of the top Web sites that can help with installation and configuration.

Q&A

This section contains common questions and answers about the topic covered in this hour. If you have additional questions that aren't covered, send me an e-mail and maybe it'll show up in the next edition!

Q Why are there so many different Unixes and Linuxes?

A That's a very good question. One of the main strengths and weaknesses of Unix has been that it's been widely distributed in both source and binary form, and that

it was built from the beginning for developers, by developers. The combination of these two, coupled with many years of legal wrangling over the ownership of the Unix code, trademarks, intellectual property, and so on, produces a veritable explosion of choices for the Unix-savvy computer user. Even Apple succumbed and made Unix the underpinning of Mac OS X.

Instead of seeing this as a point of confusion—though it is a bit confusing—think of it instead as a terrific advantage. You sure can't get 20 different free distributions of Windows, and there aren't even 20 total versions of Mac OS, even if you go all the way back to 1984 when it was released.

Q What Unix distributions do you run on your own systems?

A My main computer is a Mac OS X system with, of course, Darwin as the underpinnings. In addition, I have a PC that dual-boots Windows 2000 and Mandrake 8.1, and a collocated Web server that runs Red Hat Linux 7.2.

Workshop

Quiz

1. What's the most important first step in the installation process?
2. What's an ISO and why is it important?
3. If you can download the entire operating system installation data set from the net, why buy it?
4. If you do want prebuilt CD-ROMs for installation, where's a good place to get 'em cheap?
5. According to author Douglas Adams, what's the meaning of life?

Answers

1. Back up any pre-existing information on the disk. And ensure that the backup worked!
2. An ISO is an install system image, a single file that can be copied onto a CD-ROM, making that CD-ROM an instant install disk.
3. Buying it saves an immense amount of time, and as the cost is quite minimal, I think only people with a lot of patience actually download install images.
4. The eBay online auction site always has some Linux install CD-ROMs prebuilt and available for just a few dollars.
5. 42. (See the brilliant book *Hitchhiker's Guide to the Galaxy* to figure out what the heck it means!)

Now that we've got a Unix distro installed on your system, it's time to jump in and start looking at the job and responsibilities of Unix system administrator. Because it's impossible to instantly become a guru, we'll start next hour by exploring the unsung resource of online documentation and man pages.

1

PART II

Introduction to the Filesystem

Hour

HOUR 2

An Unsung Resource: Unix Documentation

The last hour discussed various nuances of Unix installation on smaller computers. This hour starts you toward becoming a Unix system administration expert. Our goal for this hour is to explore the valuable online documentation that's included with your Unix system. Along the way, we'll read through some shell scripts and Perl scripts, and fix a system bug, too.

In this hour you will learn the philosophy of digging, including

- How to use apropos to search through documentation
- How to find just the right command you need
- How to use the strings command to dig around binary files

The Philosophy of Digging

As promised in the Introduction, the fundamental approach to system administration I'd like to teach you in this book is what I call The Philosophy of Digging. It refers to the value of learning how to find things in the Unix world, and how it's ultimately more helpful than knowing commands themselves.

> There's an adage about the two types of sysadmins: A *wizard* is someone who knows how to do everything, and a *guru* is someone who knows how to find the answer to everything. Which do you think is a better model for you?

How can that be? Well, imagine this common scenario: You've been working with Mandrake Linux on your home computer to learn the Unix operating system, and your boss asks you to start maintaining a Red Hat Linux box. So far, so good. Three weeks later, a new Chief Technology Officer is hired and she announces, "All servers will be replaced with Sun Solaris systems forthwith!" Now you're going to move into a completely new Unix environment. Worse, your son hacks your home computer and replaces your trusty Mandrake Linux with FreeBSD, convinced that it's superior.

In a situation like this, having memorized all the Linux commands and flags is going to prove of limited value at best. But if you've learned a philosophy of digging, a strategy of exploring the system starting with the man pages themselves, you'll be able to get up to speed on the new Unix flavors in remarkably little time.

So let's see how that works in this chapter, as we begin to explore the online Unix documentation suite.

apropos: The Administrator's Secret Weapon

One of the classic dilemmas that a system administrator faces in the world of Unix, whether highly experienced or a neophyte, is to remember the name of the command that does *just what you want*. Then, once you recall the command, you must remember the exact sequence of flags and arguments that'll bend the system to your will and accomplish your task.

The secret weapon that smart sysadmins use is the apropros command (also known as man -k, because they're the same thing). apropos works with a database of one-line command summaries for the entire Unix system.

Task 2.1: apropos and the whatis Database

▼ TASK

To search for commands related to a specific topic, type apropos followed by the word you seek. It'll quickly search a prebuilt database of command summaries (more than 15,000 of 'em) and show you all the matches.

> The command apropos is available on most Unix systems, and is often just an alias to man -k. If it's not on your system, you can create it by adding the line alias apropos='man -k \!' to your .bashrc file.

1. Let's get started by looking for commands related to online documentation:

   $ apropos help
   help: nothing appropriate

   Hmmm...This is a little puzzling, because there are a number of Unix commands that contain the word "help" in their description, so there should be a number of matches. If you *do* get a list of possible matches, congratulations, your vendor set things up properly and you can skip the next few paragraphs, but don't. Read it instead; it's an informative journey into the recesses of Unix.

   Perhaps something's wrong with this system configuration. Let's dig around a bit, shall we?

2. A quick check of the apropos man page gives us a hint:

   $ man apropos
   ```
   apropos(1)                                              apropos(1)

   NAME
          apropos - search the whatis database for strings

   SYNOPSIS
          apropos keyword ...

   DESCRIPTION
          apropos  searches a set of database files containing short
   ➥descriptions of system commands
          for keywords and displays the result on the standard output.

   SEE ALSO
          whatis(1), man(1).

   (END)
   ```

   The critical part of this man page entry is the SEE ALSO section. Here it's pointing us to two other commands for more information: whatis and man. Because we already know the basics of the man command, let's have a peek at the whatis entry to see what it contains.

   $ man whatis
   ```
   whatis(1)                                               whatis(1)

   NAME
          whatis - search the whatis database for complete words.
   ```

```
SYNOPSIS
       whatis keyword ...

DESCRIPTION
       whatis  searches  a set of database files containing short
➥descriptions of system commands
       for keywords and displays the result on the standard output.
➥  Only complete  word  matches
       are displayed.

       The whatis database is created using the command /usr/sbin/
➥makewhatis.

SEE ALSO
       apropos(1), man(1).

(END)
```

There's the clue we're seeking: "The whatis database is created using the command /usr/sbin/makewhatis."

Rather than just run that command, however, let's dig into it and see if we can figure out the name of the database file itself.

3. To see the contents (instructions) within a system program, the first step is to use the file command, so we know what to expect:

```
$ file /usr/sbin/makewhatis
/usr/sbin/makewhatis: Bourne shell script text executable
```

Great! It's a shell script, so we can just step through it and see what's inside. Much easier to deal with than a compiled binary (but we'll look at digging through those in a little while).

```
$ head /usr/sbin/makewhatis
#!/bin/sh
# makewhatis aeb 010319 (from man-1.5i1)

program=`basename $0`

DEFMANPATH=/usr/share/man:/usr/man
DEFCATPATH=/var/cache/man:/usr/share/man/preformat:/usr/man/preformat:
➥/usr/share/man:/usr/man

# AWK=/usr/bin/gawk
AWK=/bin/gawk
```

Following these few definitions (which might be prefaced by lots and lots of comments or almost none, depending on your flavor of Unix) are many lines of shell script code, and about 75 lines into the script is the following snippet:

```
-u) if [ -e /var/cache/man/whatis ]; then
      findarg="-newer /var/cache/man/whatis"
      update=1
   fi
   continue;;
```

Here we can see that this is part of a section of code that parses starting arguments. The -u flag indicates that makewhatis should update the database with new commands (it's detailed in the script), so it's unsurprising to find the script testing for the existence of the whatis database.

And that's what we've been seeking: The name of the database that is used by makewhatis—and therefore by whatis and apropos—is /var/cache/man/whatis.

4. By contrast, Darwin (which, you'll recall, is the Unix underneath Mac OS X) is from the BSD Unix family, so it's a bit different. First off, the man page for apropos is more informative, with the following information included:

```
FILES
     whatis.db   name of the apropos database

SEE ALSO
     man(1),  whatis(1),  whereis(1),  makewhatis(8)
```

Not only does this establish the direct connection between apropos and the whatis command, but it also points to the tool needed to make the database, and even tells us that apropos uses the whatis.db file!

A quick man makewhatis reveals

```
SYNOPSIS
     /usr/libexec/makewhatis [manpath]
```

Now we have the location of the command in Darwin (note how different the file structure is!).

Interestingly, file reveals a surprising change:

```
$ file /usr/libexec/makewhatis
/usr/libexec/makewhatis: perl commands text
```

It's a Perl script, rather than a Bourne shell script. For the last step, let's look in the Perl script to find the name and location of the database file.

This proves to be tricky. The closest you can find in the script directly is the following (quite a ways down in the code!):

```
sub variables {
    $verbose = 0;               # Verbose
    $indent = 24;               # indent for description
    $outfile = 0;               # Don't write to ./whatis
    $whatis_name = "whatis.db"; # Default name for DB
    $append = 0;                # Don't delete old entries
```

```
# if no argument for directories given
@defaultmanpath = ( '/usr/share/man' );
```

From this, you can imply that the database will end up being saved as
/usr/share/man/whatis.db.

5. A smarter way to ascertain the output filename is to simply log in as root (or use
su to change to root), then rebuild the database with the -v flag specified.

```
$ makewhatis -v
Open /usr/share/man/whatis.db.tmp
open manpath directory ``/usr/share/man''
lots and lots of output as it lists each man page it finds and parses
sort -u > /usr/share/man/whatis.db.tmp
Rename /usr/share/man/whatis.db.tmp to /usr/share/man/whatis.db
2068 entries in /usr/share/man/whatis.db
```

Not only did this answer the question of "where's the database for apropos?" but it
also built it!

Contrast the preceding output from Darwin with the following output from Red
Hat Linux:

```
# /usr/sbin/makewhatis -v
about to enter /usr/share/man
adding ./uuidgen.1.gz
lots and lots and lots of output omitted
adding ./vacuum.1.gz
about to enter /usr/man
/usr/sbin/makewhatis: cd: /usr/man: No such file or directory
```

Ahhh...very interesting. The command failed on a stock RHL7.2[1] system. Having
to fix bugs and tweak the system just to get things to work in the first place is not
an uncommon occurrence in the world of Unix system administration.

So let's fix this bug, shall we?

6. First off, it's rather surprising that there isn't a /usr/man directory, because that's
part of standard (System V) Unix. Let's have a peek to ensure that we're reading
this properly:

```
$ ls -l /usr
total 152
drwxr-xr-x    2 root       root          36864 Nov 21 14:51 bin
drwxr-xr-x    2 root       root           4096 Feb  6  1996 dict
drwxr-xr-x    2 root       root           4096 Feb  6  1996 etc
drwxr-xr-x    2 root       root           4096 Nov 21 14:36 games
drwxr-xr-x   82 root       root           8192 Nov 21 14:51 include
drwxr-xr-x    8 root       root           4096 Nov 21 14:49 kerberos
```

---

[1]*RHL7.2 is shorthand for Red Hat Linux release 7.2. This type of shorthand is very common in the Unix
world, and you should try to get used to seemingly cryptic acronyms. Very much part of the Unix cul-
ture!*

```
drwxr-xr-x    71 root     root        45056 Nov 21 14:51 lib
drwxr-xr-x     7 root     root         4096 Nov 21 14:42 libexec
drwxr-xr-x    12 root     root         4096 Nov 21 14:33 local
drwxr-xr-x     2 root     root        16384 Nov 21 14:31 lost+found
drwxr-xr-x     2 root     root         8192 Nov 27 06:05 sbin
drwxr-xr-x   135 root     root         4096 Nov 21 14:51 share
drwxr-xr-x     3 root     root         4096 Nov 21 14:50 src
lrwxrwxrwx     1 root     root           10 Nov 21 14:33 tmp -> ../var/tmp
drwxr-xr-x     2 root     root         4096 Nov 22 09:14 web
drwxr-xr-x     8 root     root         4096 Nov 21 14:36 X11R6
```

Lots of stuff, but no man directory.

We have two ways of addressing this problem. The easy solution is to create /usr/man as a directory and leave it empty. The more sophisticated solution, however, is to dig through the makewhatis shell script to see why it looks in /usr/man in the first place, and teach it to ignore that directory.

The good news is that the more sophisticated solution is actually pretty easy. If you flip back a page or two, you'll see that at the very top of the script there's a variable DEFMANPATH that's defined as

DEFMANPATH=/usr/share/man:/usr/man

My guess is that if we simply rewrite this as /usr/share/man and nothing else, we'll be golden and it'll work.

> At this point you're doubtless thinking "Huh? We're just trying to find out what commands are on my Unix system! Why are we having to reprogram system shell scripts?" The answer to this conundrum is that, of course, the life of a Unix system administrator is divided into on-task activity and subsequent off-task sidetracks. For most sysadmins, it's probably about a 50/50 split between the two, but some days it's undoubtedly going to be more like 25/75 or, worst of all, 0/100.
>
> To some extent I'm leading you down the garden path here, too: It's entirely possible that your Unix system has the whatis database built and ready to use. But if this isn't broken, it's a sure bet that something else will be!

The change is simple, and because I like to leave a trail of comments for later reference, I'm not going to simply delete the :/usr/man suffix on the DEFMANPATH line, but instead change it as follows:

DEFMANPATH=/usr/share/man   # also used to include ":/usr/man"

Now, with this modification, I run the mkwhatis command again on the Red Hat Linux system and it works flawlessly! Hurray!

▼ 7. In contrast to both of these solutions, the Solaris system has a very different man
page for apropos, but the great news is that in the man page it states that "The
apropos utility displays the man page name, section number, and a short description for each man page whose NAME line contains a keyword. This information is
contained in the /usr/share/man/windex database created by catman(1M). If
catman(1M) was not run, or was run with the -n option, apropos fails."

A pointer to the command needed to fix things is always appreciated, and this even
details the exact filename in question, too! Let's pop over to catman and see what it
says on that man page:

```
$ man catman
NAME
       catman - create the formatted files for the reference manual

SYNOPSIS
       /usr/bin/catman [ -c ]  [ -n ]  [ -p ]  [ -t ]  [  -w  ]   [
       -M directory ]  [ -T macro-package ]  [ sections ]

DESCRIPTION
       The catman utility creates the preformatted versions of  the
       online  manual  from  the  nroff(1) or sgml(5) input files.
       This feature allows easy distribution  of  the  preformatted
       manual pages among a group of associated machines (for exam-
       ple, with rdist(1)), since it makes the directories of  pre-
       formatted manual pages self-contained and independent of the
       unformatted entries.

       catman also creates the  windex database file in the  direc-
       tories specified by the  MANPATH or the  -M option. The win-
       dex database file is a three column  list  consisting  of  a
       keyword,  the reference page that the keyword points to, and
       a line of text that describes the purpose of the utility  or
       interface  documented on the reference page. Each keyword is
       taken from the comma separated list of  words  on  the  NAME
       line before the  '-' (dash). The reference page that the key-
       word points to is the first word on the  NAME line. The text
       after  the - on the NAME line is the descriptive text in the
       third column. The NAME line must be immediately preceded  by
       the  page  heading  line created by the .TH macro (see NOTES
       for required format).

       Each manual page is examined and  those  whose  preformatted
       versions  are  missing  or out of date are recreated. If any
       changes are made, catman recreates the windex database.
```

Seems reasonable enough. To build the database, run the catman command with
the -w flag. If there are no problems, there's no output and everything should be
▼ installed and ready to run. Let's have a quick test:

▼
```
# apropos solaris | wc -l
    54
```

Great!

8. Now on any of our systems we can run the apropos command and find out what commands are related to the topic help:

```
$ apropos help
B::Stackobj          (3pm)  - Helper module for CC backend
consolehelper        (8)    - A wrapper that helps console users run
➥system programs
forum                (1)    - Interactive Help for MRTG users
help [builtins]      (1)    - bash built-in commands, see bash(1)
help [faq]           (1)    - How to get help if you have problems with MRTG
LDP                  (7)    - Intro to the Linux Documentation Project, with
➥help, guides and documents
mibhelp              (1)    - A Table of some interesting OIDs
Pod::ParseUtils      (3pm)  - helpers for POD parsing and conversion
QCharRef [qcharref]  (3qt)  - Helper class for
QToolTip [qtooltip]  (3qt)  - Tool tips (sometimes called balloon help)
➥for any widget or rectangular part of a widget
QXmlNamespaceSupport [qxmlnamespacesupport] (3qt)  - Helper class for XML
➥readers which want to include namespace support
smbmnt               (8)    - helper utility for mounting SMB filesystems
userhelper           (8)    - A helper interface to pam
```

This is from Linux, and you can see that there are a number of commands. Notice that they all have the letters h-e-l-p somewhere in their command or description text, but they don't all necessary relate to user-level help commands.

> As a reminder, the Unix man pages are broken into eight main categories: 1=user commands, 2=system maintenance commands, 3=system calls (for programmers), 4=administration files, 5=miscellaneous, 6=games, 7=special file formats, and 8=administrative commands.

Oftentimes you only want to see the interactive commands rather than the system maintenance commands, and so on. One simple way to do that is to use egrep:

```
$ apropos help | egrep '(1|8)'
consolehelper        (8)    - A wrapper that helps console users run
➥system programs
forum                (1)    - Interactive Help for MRTG users
help [builtins]      (1)    - bash built-in commands, see bash(1)
help [faq]           (1)    - How to get help if you have problems with MRTG
mibhelp              (1)    - A Table of some interesting OIDs
smbmnt               (8)    - helper utility for mounting SMB filesystems
userhelper           (8)    - A helper interface to pam
```
▼

▼
▲

A further nuance might be to feed this to sort such that it shows you all the section 1 commands, then the section 8 commands, but I'll leave that as an exercise for you!

What started out as a simple task of learning how to use the apropos command rapidly spun out of control, and ended up roaming far and wide as we found and fixed some system configuration problems. This is very typical of your day-to-day experience as a system administrator, as you'll find out as you spend more time learning Unix from the admin perspective.

Exploring the whatis Database

Now that we know how to build the whatis database, let's spend a few minutes digging inside of it to see what we can learn. Just a short additional sidetrack, I promise!

Task 2.2: What's Inside the whatis Database

TASK
▼

Being curious folk, we can't leave the database alone without a little exploration, so let's have a peek.

1. The database itself is a regular text file, so we can use head to see what's inside:

```
# cd /var/cache/man
# file whatis
whatis: ASCII English text
# head whatis
411toppm              (1)  - convert Sony Mavica .411 image to PPM
a2p                   (1)  - Awk to Perl translator
a2ps                  (1)  - format files for printing on a PostScript
printer
ab                    (8)  - Apache HTTP server benchmarking tool
abbrev [Text::Abbrev] (3pm)  - create an abbreviation table from a list
abort                 (3)  - cause abnormal program termination
ABORT [abort]         (1)  - Aborts the current transaction
abs                   (3)  - compute the absolute value of an integer
accept                (2)  - accept a connection on a socket
access                (2)  - check user's permissions for a file
```

Interesting, eh? This leads me to conclude that apropos is a synonym for grep -i, and sure enough, grep -i help whatis produces the exact same results we saw earlier. Try it!

2. More interestingly, we can now extract the different sections of the database and see how many commands there are in each section.

To accomplish this, I want to split the line at the beginning parenthesis, then again at the ending parenthesis, and leave just the value within. This can be done with

▼

two calls to cut, the first specifying the open paren delimiter, the second the closing paren. Here's what the first invocation does:

```
# cut -d\( -f2 < whatis | head -5
1)   - convert Sony Mavica .411 image to PPM
1)   - Awk to Perl translator
1)   - format files for printing on a PostScript printer
8)   - Apache HTTP server benchmarking tool
3pm) - create an abbreviation table from a list
```

and the second, added in the middle of the pipe:

```
# cut -d\( -f2 < whatis | cut -d\) -f1 | head -5
1
1
1
8
3pm
```

Now, finally, just a call to sort to sort them all, and uniq with the -c flag to get a final output count:

```
# cut -d\( -f2 < whatis | cut -d\) -f1 | sort | uniq -c
     14
   1405 1
      6 1m
     39 1ssl
    254 2
   8272 3
    400 3pm
    335 3qt
    657 3ssl
     77 3t
     61 3thr
   3603 3x
     36 4
    146 5
      1 5ssl
      3 6
     67 7
      1 7ssl
    380 8
     67 l
    446 n
      1 Paranoia release III
      1 xnmap
```

That's your answer. Ignore the odd ones (for example, Paranoia release III), and you can see that there are 1,405 section 1 commands, 380 section 8 commands, and over *13,000* different commands and functions for system programmers on a Linux system. No wonder it's not easy to program a Unix system!

It's interesting to note that there are only 1,324 section 1 commands and a grand total of 6,689 commands in Solaris, and an even more paltry 478 section 1 commands and a grand total of 2,068 commands documented in the whatis.db file on Darwin.

This section is not only a good example of how you can combine Unix commands to produce useful results, but how you can also get quite sidetracked. Even the author finds it occasionally difficult to avoid poking around and learning more about the system!

Finding Commands

The apropos command offers a very helpful way to navigate through the man commands based on the one-line command summaries, but there are other ways to explore the commands available on your Unix system. Most notably, which will search your path and tell you what file is to be executed for a given command name, and locate is a fast way to try to match a pattern against a list of all filenames on your system.

The latter, however, is really a special purpose variation of the powerful general purpose find command, which we'll cover in greater detail later in the book.

Task 2.3: Which Command Are You Running?

The first step in debugging any problem in Unix is to ensure that your PATH is correct, then to make sure that the version of the command you think you're running is the version that is being invoked.

All command shells build what's called a *hash table* of commands, a quickly-searched list of filenames located in each of the directories specified in the PATH environment variable. If there are collisions (for example, two directories have the same filename), the directory referenced earlier in the PATH wins.

The characteristic of earlier PATH matches overriding later PATH entries is exactly why having a PATH set up like PATH=.:*other stuff* is so dangerous: If you're in a directory where there's a fake version of, say, ls, you could execute it without even realizing it. Why is that dangerous? Because the fake ls could do something sneaky, like make a secret copy of the shell, then chmod it to have it setuid for your account. The cracker comes along some time later, and any time she wants to masquerade as you, she simply runs that shell. This is what's called a *trojan horse hack*.

▼   1. Let's start by finding out what our PATH is, and then seeing what version of man
      we're running when we use the man command:

```
# echo $PATH
/usr/local/bin:/bin:/usr/bin:/usr/X11R6/bin:/home/taylor/bin
# which man
/usr/bin/man
```

   You can see that our Linux path consists of /usr/local/bin, /bin, /usr/bin,
   /usr/X11R6/bin (the X Window System files), and /home/taylor/bin (my personal additions to the Unix command world). Notice there's no . entry, and that
   my personal version of any command will *not* supplant the standard version
   because my directory comes last in the PATH. To have it supplant built-in commands, I'd need to have it appear first in the PATH instead.

   2. Some versions of which know about aliases, whereas others don't. Both Linux
      and Darwin have an alias of ll="ls -l", but the difference in which output is
      interesting:

   Linux:

```
# alias ll
alias ll='/bin/ls -l'
# which ll
which: no ll in (/usr/local/bin:/bin:/usr/bin:/usr/X11R6/bin:
➡/home/taylor/bin)
```

   Darwin:

```
# alias ll
ls -lag !* | more
# which ll
ll:      aliased to ls -lag !* | more
```

   Some of this output is directly related to what shell the user is running—often
   C Shell (csh) will include alias parsing, whereas the Bourne-Again Shell (bash)
   won't.

   Solaris behaves exactly like Linux in this example, happily displaying the alias for
   ll, but with a which command that is unaware of shell aliases.

   The puzzle here is that if we're using Linux, we now have an example of a command that works—ll—but isn't in our path. Most mysterious if you don't remember the alias command, too.

   3. But then again, maybe there *is* an ll command, and we're just not seeing it with
      the which command. To search quickly through all the filenames on the system, the
      locate command is our choice; though like much of Unix, it takes a little bit of
      thinking to figure out how to use it most appropriately:

```
# locate ll | wc -l
   4021
```
▼

2

Alright, more than 4,000 filenames match the double-l sequence. Of course, you might well have a different number due to the specific packages you opted to install on your system. No worries! Instead, let's try prefixing it with a slash:

```
# locate /ll | wc -l
    11
```

Eleven is a much more manageable number, so let's see what they are:

```
# locate /ll
/usr/share/doc/HTML/en/kdevelop/reference/C/CONTRIB/SNIP/ll_msort.c
/usr/share/doc/HTML/en/kdevelop/reference/C/CONTRIB/SNIP/ll_qsort.c
/usr/share/man/man2/llseek.2.gz
/usr/share/man/man3/llabs.3.gz
/usr/share/man/man3/llrint.3.gz
/usr/share/man/man3/llrintf.3.gz
/usr/share/man/man3/llrintl.3.gz
/usr/share/man/man3/llround.3.gz
/usr/share/man/man3/llroundf.3.gz
/usr/share/man/man3/llroundl.3.gz
/usr/share/man/mann/llength.n.gz
```

Interesting, but there's no sign of an `ll` command in the entire system.

The `locate` command can also show you where commands you suspect are part of Unix are located. For example:

```
# locate chess
/usr/share/ghostscript/6.51/examples/chess.ps
/usr/share/licq/qt-gui/icons.computer/chess.xpm
# locate cribbage
/home/taylor/bin/cribbage
/home/taylor/DEMO/Src/cribbage.c
```

Neat! As you can see, `locate` casts a net across the entire file system, including individual user files. Very helpful.

> Of course, there's a security hole: I wasn't user `taylor` when I did this `locate` search, but it told me the names of files and directories within the `taylor` account, even if they were otherwise shut off to me. That's why `locate` isn't included with Solaris. Something to consider if you make `locate` available on your system.

One of the first tasks of any system administrator is to be able to figure out what's going on when a user complains of a problem (or when encountering your own problem). To do that, it's critical to ascertain what command the user is invoking and whether that's the correct version for the system. That's the province of the helpful `which` command.

When that fails, `locate` can be used to see if there's a match, and if you really need to roll out the power tools, `find` is a lifesaver, as you'll see throughout this book.

Digging Around in Executable Binaries

The combination of `which` to identify commands, `file` to ascertain what kind of command it is, the `man` page, and even viewing the file itself (if it's a script) can reveal a lot about your system. Sometimes, though, the file in question might be a compiled binary, and the source might not be handy. That's where the `strings` command can be very helpful.

Task 2.4: The `strings` Command

The `strings` command is an unsung hero of sysadmins, just as the `file` command is such a winner, even though it's rarely mentioned in system administration books. What `strings` does is read through the contents of any file, looking for printable ASCII sequences. If it finds one, it displays it on the screen.

Given this behavior, it's quite easy to feed the output to `grep` and extract useful information from the executable binary itself, including what configuration files it uses, and more.

1. Let's have a look at the `man` command itself. To start, I'll use `which` to see where the command lives, then I'll use `file` to see whether it's a script or executable:

```
# which -a man
/usr/bin/man
# file /usr/bin/man
/usr/bin/man: ELF 32-bit LSB executable, Intel 80386, version 1,
➥dynamically linked (uses shared libs), stripped
```

> In the world of Darwin, this same program is reported as `Mach-O executable ppc`, whereas Solaris also uses the ELF (Executable and Linking Format) binary format for executables.

Now that we know it's a binary, let's peek inside with the `strings` command:

```
# strings /usr/bin/man | head
/lib/ld-linux.so.2
__gmon_start__
libc.so.6
strcpy
ioctl
getgid
```

▼

```
printf
stdout
vsprintf
geteuid
```

Not too exciting, but if we grep this for the sequence conf...

```
# strings /usr/bin/man | grep conf
[no configuration file]
/usr/share/misc/man.config
/usr/share/misc/man.conf
/usr/lib/man.config
/usr/lib/man.conf
/etc/man.conf
/etc/man.config
Reading config file %s
   C file   : use `file' as configuration file
man-config.c: internal error: string %s not found
Unrecognized line in config file (ignored)
but the configuration file does not define COMPRESS.
Warning: cannot open configuration file %s
is not in the config file
is in the config file
Line too long in config file
Error parsing config file
```

This is the kind of output that can prove very useful. Here you can see that the man command uses a configuration file, and that it can appear in any of a number of different places:

```
/usr/share/misc/man.config
/usr/share/misc/man.conf
/usr/lib/man.config
/usr/lib/man.conf
/etc/man.conf
/etc/man.config
```

It would be a matter of a quick ls or two to find out which is the actual file on this system; then we'd be learning how to configure man, even though the man page only mentions the configuration file in passing.

▲

Although the Unix documentation can reveal quite a bit about how to work with different commands, sometimes popping open the proverbial hood to tinker on the engine is necessary. With shell and Perl scripts, that's easy, but if you encounter a compiled binary, the strings command can be an invaluable addition to your toolbox!

Summary

This hour has focused on demonstrating how to use common Unix tools like grep, cut, and head to fine-tune the online documentation tools. You have also seen how SEE ALSO and FILES sections in man pages offer great assistance in figuring out how commands work and how to configure them.

As somewhat of a sidetrack, you saw how commands rely on each other within Unix, and how specifically the apropos command relies on the database that the whatis command uses, and is created by makewhatis. Building that database, we encountered an error condition, diagnosed the problem, postulated a couple of possible solutions, and implemented the best of them, permanently fixing the command.

Finally, the other important aspect of this chapter is that it demonstrates how this book is focused on teaching you how to explore Unix and find solutions for yourself, rather than listing all the command flags for each command, or even ensuring that every possible use of every possible command has been enumerated.

This problem-solving orientation will prove a great boon as you go through these 24 hours' worth of material, and you'll have a much greater degree of comfort on new and alien Unixes than if you memorized lots of Unix flavor-specific commands.

Q&A

Q Is it a wizard or a guru who knows how to find the answer to everything?

A A guru. A wizard is someone who can *do* things as if they're magic, but can't ever teach anyone else what they're doing.

Q Why do some Unix systems have a command apropos if it's really just an alias to the grep command?

A As is common with Unix, some development teams err on the side of offering maximal usability, enabling users to just start typing and go, whereas others prefer the simple elegance of core commands and nothing else.

Workshop

Quiz

1. No cheating now: What do you think the whatis command does?
2. Write an equivalent of whatis using grep. Think carefully about the transformation you want to make to the given pattern before searching through the whatis database.

3. Are system administrators more likely to get sidetracked if they're working on an OS like Windows? Why, or why not?

4. What command is in the man pages section "Paranoia"?

5. How many section 1 commands do you have on your system? Can you think of another way to figure that number out?

Answers

1. `whatis` summarizes in a single line of output the purpose of any Unix command specified on the command line.

2. The equivalent of `whatis floppy` would be `grep -iE '^floppy\('` `/usr/man/whatis.db` (the exact syntax might change based on where your system stores the `whatis` database). Note that you need to construct a regular expression that ensures `whatis cp` doesn't match `uucp` or other commands containing the letters `cp`. The `-i` flag ignores case, and the `-E` indicates that a regular expression will follow.

3. Well, you can probably be sidetracked on any operating system if you're the sort to poke around and explore, but generally there's so much power underneath the hood on a typical Unix system that I think you're more likely to get sidetracked than if you're in the constrained and confined world of Windows.

4. On Red Hat Linux 7.2, searching for Paranoia in the `whatis.db` database reveals that it's the `cdparanoia` command, which is described as "an audio CD-reading utility which includes extra data verification features."

5. One obvious strategy for this is `grep '(1)' /usr/man/whatis.db | wc -l`, but there are a variety of commands that are officially in section 1, but end up listed as `1L` or `1B` or some other such cryptic subsection. The best strategy, therefore, if you want to exploit the `whatis` database, is to use `grep '(1' /usr/man/whatis.db |` `wc -l`. Another way to ascertain this number that's even more direct is to `ls /usr/man/man1 | wc -l` (though you'll end up with more than you expect, because some man pages are symbolically linked to more than one command name for historical reasons).

In the next hour, you'll learn how to explore the file allocation information within Unix through use of the `du` and `df` commands. We'll also look at how to create a simple shell script that will report the size of every user's home directory, sorted from largest to smallest.

Hour **3**

Disk Usage

One of the most common problems that system administrators face in the Unix world is disk space. Whether it's running out of space, or just making sure that no one user is hogging all your resources, exploring how the hard disks are allocated and utilized on your system is a critical skill.

In this hour, you learn:

- How to look at disk usage with df and du
- How to simplify analysis with sort
- How to identify the biggest files and use diskhogs

Physical Disks and Partitions

In the last few years, hard disks have become considerably bigger than most operating systems can comfortably manage. Indeed, most file systems have a minimum size for files and a maximum number of files and/or directories that can be on a single physical device, and it's those constraints that slam up against the larger devices.

As a result, most modern operating systems support taking a single physical disk and splitting it into multiple virtual disks, or *partitions*. Windows and Macintosh systems have supported this for a few years, but usually on a personal desktop system you don't have to worry about disks that are too big, or worse, running out of disk space and having the system crash.

Unix is another beast entirely. In the world of Unix, you can have hundreds of different virtual disks and not even know it—even your home directory might be spread across two or three partitions.

One reason for this strategy in Unix is that running programs tend to leave *log files*, *temp files*, and other detritus behind, and they can add up and eat a disk alive.

For example, on my main Web server, I have a log file that's currently growing about 140K/day and is 19MB. Doesn't sound too large when you think about 50GB disks for $100 at the local electronics store, but having big disks at the store doesn't mean that they're installed in your server!

In fact, Unix is very poorly behaved when it runs out of disk space, and can get sufficiently corrupted enough that it essentially stops and requires an expert sysadmin to resurrect. To avoid this horrible fate, it's crucial to keep an eye on how big your partitions are growing, and to know how to prune large files before they become a serious problem.

Task 3.1: Exploring Partitions

Enough chatter, let's get down to business, shall we?

1. The command we'll be exploring in this section is df, a command that reports disk space usage. Without any arguments at all, it offers lots of useful information:

```
# df
Filesystem           1k-blocks      Used Available Use% Mounted on
/dev/sda5               380791    108116    253015  30% /
/dev/sda1                49558      7797     39202  17% /boot
/dev/sda3             16033712     62616  15156608   1% /home
none                    256436         0    256436   0% /dev/shm
/dev/sdb1             17245524   1290460  15079036   8% /usr
/dev/sdb2               253871     88384    152380  37% /var
```

Upon first glance, it appears that I have five different disks connected to this system. In fact, I have two.

2. I'm sure you already know this, but it's worth pointing out that all devices hooked up to a computer, whether for input or output, require a specialized piece of code called a *device driver* to work properly. In the Windows world, they're typically hidden away, and you have no idea what they're even called.

Device drivers in Unix, however, are files. They're special files, but they show up as part of the file system along with your e-mail archive and login scripts.

That's what the /dev/sda5 is on the first line, for example. We can have a look at this file with ls to see what it is:

```
# ls -l /dev/sda5
brw-rw----   1 root     disk       8,   5 Aug 30 13:30 /dev/sda5
```

The leading b is something you probably haven't seen before. It denotes that this device is a block-special device.

> If you ever have problems with a device, use ls -l to make sure it's config-ured properly. If the listing doesn't begin with a c (for a character special device) or a b (for a block-special device), something's gone wrong and you need to delete it and rebuild it with mknod.

Here's a nice thing to know: The device names in Unix have meaning. In fact, sd typically denotes a SCSI device, and the next letter is the major device number (in this case an a), and the last letter is the minor device number (5).

From this information, we can glean that there are three devices with the same major number but different minor numbers (sda1, sda3, and sda5), and two devices with a different major number and different minor numbers (sdb1 and sdb2).

In fact, the first three are partitions on the same hard disk, and the second two are partitions on a different disk.

3. How big is the disk? Well, in some sense it doesn't really matter in the world of Unix, because Unix only cares about the partitions that are assigned to it. If the second disk is 75GB, but we only have a 50MB partition that's available to Unix, the vast majority of the disk is untouchable and therefore doesn't matter.

If you really want to figure it out, you could add up the size of each partition (the Available column), but let's dissect a single line of output first, so you can see what's what:

```
/dev/sda5           380791   108116   253015  30% /
```

Here you're shown the device ID (sda5), then the size of the partition (in 1K blocks within Linux). This partition is 380,791KB, or 380MB. The second number shows how much of the partition is used—108,116KB—and the next how much is available—253,015KB. This translates to 30% of the partition in use and 70% available.

Those purists among you will realize the error of this calculation: 380,791/1024 is not a simple division by 1,000. So everyone is happy, that reveals that this partition is exactly 371.8MB.

The last value is perhaps the most important because it indicates where the partition has been connected to the Unix file system. Partition sda5 is the root partition, as can be seen by the /.

4. Let's look at another line from the df output:

```
/dev/sda3          16033712     62616   15156608    1% /home
```

Notice here that the partition is considerably bigger! In fact, it's 16,033,712KB, or roughly 16GB (15.3GB for purists). Unsurprisingly, very little of this is used—less than 1%—and it's mounted to the system as the /home directory.

In fact, look at the mount points for all the partitions for just a moment:

```
# df
Filesystem           1k-blocks      Used Available Use% Mounted on
/dev/sda5               380791    108116    253015  30% /
/dev/sda1                49558      7797     39202  17% /boot
/dev/sda3             16033712     62616  15156608   1% /home
none                    256436         0    256436   0% /dev/shm
/dev/sdb1             17245524   1290460  15079036   8% /usr
/dev/sdb2               253871     88389    152375  37% /var
```

We have the topmost root partition (sda5); then we have additional small partitions for /boot, /usr, and /var. The two really big spaces are /home, where all the individual user files will live, and /usr, where I have all the Web sites on this server stored.

This is a very common configuration, where each area of Unix has its own sandbox to play in, as it were. This lets you, the sysadmin, manage file usage quite easily, ensuring that running out of space in one directory (say, /home) doesn't affect the overall system.

5. Solaris 8 has a df command that offers very different information, focused more on files and the file system than on disks and disk space used:

```
# df
/                 (/dev/dsk/c0d0s0   ):  827600 blocks   276355 files
/boot             (/dev/dsk/c0d0p0:boot):  17584 blocks       -1 files
/proc             (/proc            ):       0 blocks     1888 files
/dev/fd           (fd               ):       0 blocks        0 files
/etc/mnttab       (mnttab           ):       0 blocks        0 files
/var/run          (swap             ): 1179992 blocks    21263 files
/tmp              (swap             ): 1179992 blocks    21263 files
/export/home      (/dev/dsk/c0d0s7  ): 4590890 blocks   387772 files
```

It's harder to see what's going on, but notice that the order of information presented on each line is the mount point, the device identifier, the size of the device in 1K blocks, and the number of files on that device.

There's no way to see how much of the disk is in use and how much space is left available, so the default df output isn't very helpful for a system administrator.

Fortunately, there's the -t *totals* option that offers considerably more helpful information:

```
# df -t
/                       (/dev/dsk/c0d0s0    ):   827600 blocks   276355 files
                              total:  2539116 blocks   320128 files
/boot                   (/dev/dsk/c0d0p0:boot):    17584 blocks       -1 files
                              total:    20969 blocks       -1 files
/proc                   (/proc          ):        0 blocks     1888 files
                              total:        0 blocks     1932 files
/dev/fd                 (fd              ):        0 blocks        0 files
                              total:        0 blocks      258 files
/etc/mnttab             (mnttab          ):        0 blocks        0 files
                              total:        0 blocks        1 files
/var/run                (swap            ):  1180000 blocks    21263 files
                              total:  1180008 blocks    21279 files
/tmp                    (swap            ):  1180000 blocks    21263 files
                              total:  1180024 blocks    21279 files
/export/home            (/dev/dsk/c0d0s7    ):  4590890 blocks   387772 files
                              total:  4590908 blocks   387776 files
```

Indeed, when I've administered Solaris systems, I've usually set up an alias df="df -t" to always have this more informative output.

> If you're trying to analyze the df output programmatically so you can flag when disks start to get tight, you'll immediately notice that there's no percentile-used summary in the df output in Solaris. Extracting just the relevant fields of information is quite tricky too, because you want to glean the number of blocks used from one line, then the number of blocks total on the next. It's a job for Perl or awk (or even a small C program).

6. By way of contrast, Darwin has a very different output for the df command:

```
# df
Filesystem              512-blocks       Used    Avail Capacity  Mounted on
/dev/disk1s9              78157200   29955056 48202144    38%    /
devfs                          73         73        0   100%    /dev
fdesc                           2          2        0   100%    /dev
<volfs>                      1024       1024        0   100%    /.vol
```

```
/dev/disk0s8              53458608 25971048 27487560    48%    /Volumes/
➥Macintosh HD
automount -fstab [244]           0        0        0   100%    /Network/
➥Servers
automount -static [244]          0        0        0   100%    /automount
```

About as different as it could be, and notice that it suggests that just about everything is at 100% capacity. Uh oh!

A closer look, however, reveals that the devices at 100% capacity are devfs, fdesc, <volfs>, and two automounted services. In fact, they're related to the Mac OS running within Darwin, and really the only lines of interest in this output are the two proper /dev/ devices:

```
/dev/disk1s9   78157200 29955056 48202144    38%    /
/dev/disk0s8   53458608 25971048 27487560    48%    /Volumes/    Macintosh HD
```

The first of these, identified as /dev/disk1s9, is the hard disk where Mac OS X is installed, and it has 78,157,200 blocks. However, they're not 1K blocks as in Linux, they're 512-byte blocks, so you need to factor that in when you calculate the size in GB:

$78,157,200 \div 2 = 39,078,600$ 1K blocks

$39,078,600 \div 1024 = 38,162.69$MB

$38,162.69$MB $\div 1024 = 37.26$GB

In fact, this is a 40GB disk, so we're right on with our calculations, and we can see that 38% of the disk is in use, leaving us with $48202144 \div (2 \times 1024 \times 1024) = 22.9$GB.

Wondering what happened to the 2.78GB of space that is the difference between the manufacturer's claim of a 40GB disk and the reality of my only having 37.26GB? The answer is that there's always a small percentage of disk space consumed by formatting and disk overhead. That's why manufacturers talk about "unformatted capacity."

Using the same math, you can calculate that the second disk is 25GB, of which about half (48%) is in use.

7. Linux has a very nice flag with the df command worth mentioning: Use -h and you get:

```
# df -h
Filesystem          Size  Used Avail Use% Mounted on
/dev/sda5           372M  106M  247M  30% /
/dev/sda1            48M  7.7M   38M  17% /boot
```

```
/dev/sda3              15G    62M    14G    1% /home
none                  250M     0    250M    0% /dev/shm
/dev/sdb1              16G   1.3G    14G    8% /usr
/dev/sdb2             248M    87M   148M   37% /var
```

A much more human-readable format. Here you can see that /home and /usr both
have 14GB unused. Lots of space!

This section has given you a taste of the df command, but we haven't spent too much
time analyzing the output and digging around trying to ascertain where the biggest files
live. That's what we'll consider next.

A Closer Look with du

The df command is one you'll use often as you get into the groove of system administration work. In fact, some sysadmins have df e-mailed to them every morning from cron
so they can keep a close eye on things. Others have it as a command in their .login or
.profile configuration file so they see the output every time they connect.

Once you're familiar with how the disks are being utilized in your Unix system, however,
it's time to dig a bit deeper into the system and ascertain where the space is going.

Task 3.2: Using du to Ascertain Directory Sizes

The du command shows you disk usage, helpfully enough, and it has a variety of flags
that are critical to using this tool effectively.

1. There won't be a quiz on this, but see if you can figure out what the default output
   of du is here when I use the command while in my home directory:

```
# du
12        ./.kde/Autostart
16        ./.kde
412       ./bin
36        ./CraigsList
32        ./DEMO/Src
196       ./DEMO
48        ./elance
16        ./Exchange
1232      ./Gator/Lists
4         ./Gator/Old-Stuff/Adverts
8         ./Gator/Old-Stuff
1848      ./Gator/Snapshots
3092      ./Gator
160       ./IBM/i
136       ./IBM/images
10464     ./IBM
76        ./CBO_MAIL
```

```
52       ./Lynx/WWW/Library/vms
2792     ./Lynx/WWW/Library/Implementation
24       ./Lynx/WWW/Library/djgpp
2872     ./Lynx/WWW/Library
2880     ./Lynx/WWW
556      ./Lynx/docs
184      ./Lynx/intl
16       ./Lynx/lib
140      ./Lynx/lynx_help/keystrokes
360      ./Lynx/lynx_help
196      ./Lynx/po
88       ./Lynx/samples
20       ./Lynx/scripts
1112     ./Lynx/src/chrtrans
6848     ./Lynx/src
192      ./Lynx/test
13984    ./Lynx
28484    .
```

If you guessed that it's the size of each directory, you're right! Notice that the sizes are cumulative because they sum up the size of all files and directories within a given directory. So the `Lynx` directory is 13,984 *somethings*, which includes the subdirectory `Lynx/src` (6,848), which itself contains `Lynx/src/chrtrans` (1112).

The last line is a summary of the entire current directory (`.`), which has a combined size of 28484.

And what is that pesky unit of measure? Unfortunately, it's different in different implementations of Unix so I always check the man page before answering this question. Within RHL7.2, the man page for `du` reveals that the unit of measure isn't specifically stated, frustratingly enough. However, it shows that there's a `-k` flag that forces the output to 1KB blocks, so a quick check

```
# du -k | tail -1
28484    .
```

produces the same number as the preceding, so we can safely conclude that the unit in question is a 1KB block. Therefore, you can see that `Lynx` takes up 13.6MB of space, and that the entire contents of my home directory consume 27.8MB. A tiny fraction of the 15GB `/home` partition!

Of course, I can recall when I splurged and bought myself a 20MB external hard disk for an early computer. I couldn't imagine that I could even fill it, and it cost more than $200 too! But I'll try not to bore you with the reminiscence of an old-timer, okay?

2. The recursive listing of subdirectories is useful information, but the higher up you go in the file system, the less helpful that information proves to be. Imagine if you were to type du / and wade through the output:

```
# du / | wc -l
   6077
```

That's a lot of output!

Fortunately, one of the most useful flags to du is -s, which summarizes disk usage by only reporting the files and directories that are specified, or . if none are specified:

```
# du -s
28484    .
# du -s *
4        badjoke
4        badjoke.rot13
412      bin
4        browse.sh
4        buckaroo
76       CBO_MAIL
36       CraigsList
196      DEMO
48       elance
84       etcpasswd
16       Exchange
3092     Gator
4        getmodemdriver.sh
4        getstocks.sh
4        gettermsheet.sh
0        gif.gif
10464    IBM
13984    Lynx
```

Note in the latter case that because I used the * wildcard, it matched directories *and files* in my home directory. When given the name of a file, du dutifully reports the size of that file in 1KB blocks. You can force this behavior with the -a flag if you want.

> The summary vanishes from the bottom of the du output when I specify directories as parameters, and that's too bad, because it's very helpful. To request a summary at the end, simply specify the -c flag.

▼ 3. While we're looking at the allocation of disk space, don't forget to check the root
level, too. The results are interesting:

```
# du -s /
1471202 /
```

Oops! We don't want just a one-line summary, but rather all the directories contained at the topmost level of the file system. Oh, and do make sure that you're
running these as root, or you'll see all sorts of odd errors. Indeed, even as root the
/proc file system will sporadically generate errors as du tries to calculate the size
of a fleeting process table entry or similar. You can ignore errors in /proc in any
case.

One more try:

```
# du -s /*
5529     /bin
3683     /boot
244      /dev
4384     /etc
29808    /home
1        /initrd
67107    /lib
12       /lost+found
1        /misc
2        /mnt
1        /opt
1        /proc
1468     /root
8514     /sbin
12619    /tmp
1257652 /usr
80175    /var
0        /web
```

That's what I seek. Here you can see that the largest directory by a significant margin is /usr, weighing in at 1,257,652KB.

Rather than calculate sizes, I'm going to use another du flag (-h) to ask for human-
readable output:

```
# du -sh /*
5.4M     /bin
3.6M     /boot
244k     /dev
4.3M     /etc
30M      /home
1.0k     /initrd
66M      /lib
12k      /lost+found
▼ 1.0k     /misc
```

```
2.0k    /mnt
1.0k    /opt
1.0k    /proc
1.5M    /root
8.4M    /sbin
13M     /tmp
1.2G    /usr
79M     /var
0       /web
```

Much easier. Now you can see that /usr is 1.2GB in size, which is quite a lot!

4. Let's use du to dig into the /usr directory and see what's so amazingly big, shall we?

```
# du -sh /usr/*
121M    /usr/bin
4.0k    /usr/dict
4.0k    /usr/etc
40k     /usr/games
30M     /usr/include
3.6M    /usr/kerberos
427M    /usr/lib
2.7M    /usr/libexec
224k    /usr/local
16k     /usr/lost+found
13M     /usr/sbin
531M    /usr/share
52k     /usr/src
0       /usr/tmp
4.0k    /usr/web
103M    /usr/X11R6
```

It looks to me like /usr/share is responsible for more than half the disk space consumed in /usr, with /usr/bin and /usr/X11R6 the next largest directories.

You can easily step into /usr/share and run du again to see what's inside, but before we do, it will prove quite useful to take a short break and talk about sort and how it can make the analysis of du output considerably easier.

5. Before we leave this section to talk about sort, though, let's have a quick peek at du within the Darwin environment:

```
# du -sk *
5888      Desktop
396760    Documents
84688     Library
0         Movies
0         Music
31648     Pictures
0         Public
32        Sites
```

▼   Notice that I've specified the -k flag here to force 1KB blocks (similar to df, the default for du is 512-byte blocks). Otherwise, it's identical to Linux.

The du output on Solaris is reported in 512-byte blocks unless, like Darwin, you force 1KB blocks with the -k flag:

```
# du -sk *
1          bin
1689       boot
4          cdrom
372        dev
13         devices
2363       etc
10         export
0          home
8242       kernel
1          lib
8          lost+found
1          mnt
0          net
155306     opt
1771       platform
245587     proc
5777       sbin
32         tmp
25         TT_DB
3206       users
667265     usr
9268       var
0          vol
9          xfn
```

This section has demonstrated the helpful du command, showing how -a, -s, and -h can be combined to produce a variety of different output. You've also seen how successive du commands can help you zero in on disk space hogs, foreshadowing the diskhogs shell script we'll be developing later in this hour.

Simplifying Analysis with sort

The output of du has been very informative, but it's difficult to scan a listing to ascertain the four or five largest directories, particularly as more and more directories and files are included in the output. The good news is that the Unix sort utility is just the tool we need to sidestep this problem.

Task 3.3: Piping Output to `sort`

▼TASK

Why should we have to go through all the work of eyeballing page after page of listings when there are Unix tools to easily let us ascertain the biggest and smallest? One of the great analysis tools in Unix is `sort`, even though you rarely see it mentioned in other Unix system administration books.

1. At its most obvious, `sort` alphabetizes output:

```
# cat names
Linda
Ashley
Gareth
Jasmine
Karma
# sort names
Ashley
Gareth
Jasmine
Karma
Linda
```

No rocket science about that! However, what happens if the output of `du` is fed to `sort`?

```
# du -s * | sort
0       gif.gif
10464   IBM
13984   Lynx
16      Exchange
196     DEMO
3092    Gator
36      CraigsList
412     bin
48      elance
4       badjoke
4       badjoke.rot13
4       browse.sh
4       buckaroo
4       getmodemdriver.sh
4       getstocks.sh
4       gettermsheet.sh
76      CBO_MAIL
84      etcpasswd
```

Sure enough, it's sorted. But probably not as you expected—it's sorted by the ASCII digit characters! Not good.

3

2. That's where the `-n` flag is a vital addition: With `-n` specified, `sort` will assume that the lines contain numeric information and sort them numerically:

```
# du -s * | sort -n
0       gif.gif
4       badjoke
4       badjoke.rot13
4       browse.sh
4       buckaroo
4       getmodemdriver.sh
4       getstocks.sh
4       gettermsheet.sh
16      Exchange
36      CraigsList
48      elance
76      CBO_MAIL
84      etcpasswd
196     DEMO
412     bin
3092    Gator
10464   IBM
13984   Lynx
```

A much more useful result, if I say so myself!

3. The only thing I'd like to change in the sorting here is that I'd like to have the largest directory listed first, and the smallest listed last.

The order of a sort can be reversed with the `-r` flag, and that's the magic needed:

```
# du -s * | sort -nr
13984   Lynx
10464   IBM
3092    Gator
412     bin
196     DEMO
84      etcpasswd
76      CBO_MAIL
48      elance
36      CraigsList
16      Exchange
4       gettermsheet.sh
4       getstocks.sh
4       getmodemdriver.sh
4       buckaroo
4       browse.sh
4       badjoke.rot13
4       badjoke
0       gif.gif
```

One final concept and we're ready to move along. If you want to only see the five largest files or directories in a specific directory, all that you'd need to do is pipe the command sequence to `head`:

```
# du -s * | sort -nr | head -5
13984   Lynx
10464   IBM
3092    Gator
412     bin
196     DEMO
```

This sequence of sort|head will prove very useful later in this hour.

A key concept with Unix is understanding how the commands are all essentially Lego pieces, and that you can combine them in any number of ways to get exactly the results you seek. In this vein, sort -rn is a terrific piece, and you'll find yourself using it again and again as you learn more about system administration.

Identifying the Biggest Files

We've explored the du command, sprinkled in a wee bit of sort for zest, and now it's time to accomplish a typical sysadmin task: Find the biggest files and directories in a given area of the system.

Task 3.4: Finding Big Files

The du command offers the capability to either find the largest directories, or the combination of the largest files and directories, but it doesn't offer a way to examine just files. Let's see what we can do to solve this problem.

1. First off, it should be clear that the following command will produce a list of the five largest directories in my home directory:

```
# du | sort -rn | head -5
28484   .
13984   ./Lynx
10464   ./IBM
6848    ./Lynx/src
3092    ./Gator
```

In a similar manner, the five largest directories in /usr/share and in the overall file system (ignoring the likely /proc errors):

```
# du /usr/share | sort -rn | head -5
543584  /usr/share
200812  /usr/share/doc
53024   /usr/share/gnome
48028   /usr/share/gnome/help
31024   /usr/share/apps
# du / | sort -rn | head -5
1471213 /
1257652 /usr
543584  /usr/share
```

▼
```
436648  /usr/lib
200812  /usr/share/doc
```

All well and good, but how do you find and test just the files?

2. The easiest solution is to use the `find` command. `find` will be covered in greater detail later in the book, but for now, just remember that `find` lets you quickly search through the entire file system, and performs the action you specify on all files that match your selection criteria.

    For this task, we want to isolate our choices to all regular files, which will omit directories, device drivers, and other unusual file system entries. That's done with `-type f`.

    In addition, we're going to use the `-printf` option of `find` to produce exactly the output that we want from the matched files. In this instance, we'd like the file size in kilobytes, and the fully qualified filename. That's surprisingly easy to accomplish with a `printf` format string of `%k %p`.

> Don't worry too much if this all seems like Greek to you right now. Hour 12, "Managing Disk Quotas," will talk about the many wonderful features of `find`. For now, just type in what you see here in the book.

Put all these together and you end up with the command

```
find . -type f -printf "%k %p\n"
```

The two additions here are the ., which tells `find` to start its search in the current directory, and the `\n` sequence in the format string, which is translated into a carriage return after each entry.

3. Let's see it in action:
```
# find . -type f -printf "%k %p\n" | head
4 ./.kde/Autostart/Autorun.desktop
4 ./.kde/Autostart/.directory
4 ./.emacs
4 ./.bash_logout
4 ./.bash_profile
4 ./.bashrc
4 ./.gtkrc
4 ./.screenrc
4 ./.bash_history
4 ./badjoke
```
▼

You can see where the sort command is going to prove helpful! In fact, let's preface head with a sort -rn to identify the ten largest files in the current directory, or the following:

```
# find . -type f -printf "%k %p\n" | sort -rn | head
8488 ./IBM/j2sdk-1_3_0_02-solx86.tar
1812 ./Gator/Snapshots/MAILOUT.tar.Z
1208 ./IBM/fop.jar
1076 ./Lynx/src/lynx
1076 ./Lynx/lynx
628 ./Gator/Lists/Inactive-NonAOL-list.txt
496 ./Lynx/WWW/Library/Implementation/libwww.a
480 ./Gator/Lists/Active-NonAOL-list.txt
380 ./Lynx/src/GridText.c
372 ./Lynx/configure
```

Very interesting information to be able to ascertain, and it'll even work across the entire file system (though it might take a few minutes, and, as usual, you might see some /proc hiccups):

```
# find / -type f -printf "%k %p\n" | sort -rn | head
26700 /usr/lib/libc.a
19240 /var/log/cron
14233 /var/lib/rpm/Packages
13496 /usr/lib/netscape/netscape-communicator
12611 /tmp/partypages.tar
9124 /usr/lib/librpmdb.a
8488 /home/taylor/IBM/j2sdk-1_3_0_02-solx86.tar
5660 /lib/i686/libc-2.2.4.so
5608 /usr/lib/qt-2.3.1/lib/libqt-mt.so.2.3.1
5588 /usr/lib/qt-2.3.1/lib/libqt.so.2.3.1
```

Recall that the output is in 1KB blocks, so libc.a is pretty huge at more than 26MB!

4. You might find that your version of find doesn't include the snazzy new GNU find -printf flag (neither Solaris nor Darwin do, for example). If that's the case, you can at least fake it in Darwin, with the somewhat more convoluted

```
# find . -type f -print0 | xargs -0 ls -s | sort -rn | head
781112 ./Documents/Microsoft User Data/Office X Identities/Main Identity/
➥Database
27712 ./Library/Preferences/Explorer/Download Cache
 20824 ./.Trash/palmdesktop40maceng.sit
 20568 ./Library/Preferences/America Online/Browser Cache/IE Cache.waf
 20504 ./Library/Caches/MS Internet Cache/IE Cache.waf
 20496 ./Library/Preferences/America Online/Browser Cache/IE Control
➥Cache.waf
 20496 ./Library/Caches/MS Internet Cache/IE Control Cache.waf
 20488 ./Library/Preferences/America Online/Browser Cache/cache.waf
 20488 ./Library/Caches/MS Internet Cache/cache.waf
 18952 ./.Trash/Palm Desktop Installer/Contents/MacOSClassic/Installer
```

Here we not only have to print the filenames and feed them to the `xargs` command, we also have to compensate for the fact that most of the filenames will have spaces within their names, which will break the normal pipe. Instead, `find` has a `-print0` option that terminates each filename with a null character. Then the `-0` flag indicates to `xargs` that it's getting null-terminated filenames.

> Actually, Darwin doesn't really like this kind of command at all. If you want to ascertain the largest files, you'd be better served to explore the `-ls` option to `find` and then an awk to chop out the file size:
>
> `find /home -type f -ls | awk '{ print $7" "$11 }'`
>
> Of course, this is a slower alternative that'll work on any Unix system, if you really want.

5. To just calculate the sizes of all files in a Solaris system, you can't use `printf` or `-print0`, but if you omit the concern for filenames with spaces in them (considerably less likely on a more traditional Unix environment like Solaris anyway), you'll find that the following works fine:

```
# find / -type f -print | xargs ls -s | sort -rn | head
55528 /proc/929/as
26896 /proc/809/as
26832 /usr/j2se/jre/lib/rt.jar
21888 /usr/dt/appconfig/netscape/.netscape.bin
21488 /usr/java1.2/jre/lib/rt.jar
20736 /usr/openwin/lib/locale/zh_TW.BIG5/X11/fonts/TT/ming.ttf
18064 /usr/java1.1/lib/classes.zip
16880 /usr/sadm/lib/wbem/store
16112 /opt/answerbooks/english/solaris_8/SUNWaman/books/REFMAN3B/index/
➥index.dat
15832 /proc/256/as
```

Actually, you can see that the memory allocation space for a couple of running processes has snuck into the listing (the `/proc` directory). We'll need to screen those out with a simple `grep -v`:

```
# find / -type f -print | xargs ls -s | sort -rn | grep -v '/proc' | head
26832 /usr/j2se/jre/lib/rt.jar
21888 /usr/dt/appconfig/netscape/.netscape.bin
21488 /usr/java1.2/jre/lib/rt.jar
20736 /usr/openwin/lib/locale/zh_TW.BIG5/X11/fonts/TT/ming.ttf
18064 /usr/java1.1/lib/classes.zip
16880 /usr/sadm/lib/wbem/store
16112 /opt/answerbooks/english/solaris_8/SUNWaman/books/REFMAN3B/index/
➥index.dat
12496 /usr/openwin/lib/llib-lX11.ln
```

```
12160 /opt/answerbooks/english/solaris_8/SUNWaman/books/REFMAN3B/ebt/
➡REFMAN3B.edr
9888 /usr/j2se/src.jar
```

The find command is somewhat like a Swiss army knife. It can do hundreds of different tasks in the world of Unix. For our use here, however, it's perfect for analyzing disk usage on a per-file basis.

Keeping Track of Users: diskhogs

Let's put all the information in this hour together and create an administrative script called diskhogs. When run, this script will report the users with the largest /home directories, and then report the five largest files in each of their homes.

Task 3.5: This Little Piggy Stayed Home?

This is the first shell script presented in the book, so a quick rule of thumb: Write your shell scripts in sh rather than csh. It's easier, more universally recognized, and most shell scripts you'll encounter are also written in sh. Also, keep in mind that just about every shell script discussed in this book will expect you to be running as root, since they'll need access to the entire file system for any meaningful or useful system administration functions.

In this book, all shell scripts will be written in sh, which is easily verified by the fact that they all have

```
#!/bin/sh
```

as their first line.

1. Let's put all this together. To find the five largest home directories, you can use

   ```
   du -s /home/* | sort -rn | cut -f2 | head -5
   ```

   For each directory, you can find the largest files within by using

   ```
   find /home/loginID -type f -printf "%k %p\n" | sort -rn | head
   ```

   Therefore, we should be able to identify the top home directories, then step one-by-one into those directories to identify the largest files in each. Here's how that code should look:

   ```
   for dirname in `du -s /home/* | sort -rn | cut -f2- | head -5`
   do
     echo ""
     echo Big directory: $dirname
     echo Four largest files in that directory are:
     find $dirname -type f -printf "%k %p\n" | sort -rn | head -4
   done
   exit 0
   ```

3

▼   2. This is a good first stab at this shell script. Let's save it as `diskhogs.sh`, run it and
         see what we find:

```
# sh diskhogs.sh
Big directory: /home/staging
Four largest files in that directory are:
423 /home/staging/waldorf/big/DSCF0165.jpg
410 /home/staging/waldorf/big/DSCF0176.jpg
402 /home/staging/waldorf/big/DSCF0166.jpg
395 /home/staging/waldorf/big/DSCF0161.jpg

Big directory: /home/chatter
Four largest files in that directory are:
1076 /home/chatter/comics/lynx
388 /home/chatter/logs/access_log
90 /home/chatter/logs/error_log
64 /home/chatter/responding.cgi

Big directory: /home/cbo
Four largest files in that directory are:
568 /home/cbo/financing.pdf
464 /home/cbo/investors/CBO-plan.pdf
179 /home/cbo/Archive/cbofinancial-modified-files/CBO Website.zip
77 /home/cbo/Archive/cbofinancial-modified-files/CBO Financial
➥Incorporated .doc

Big directory: /home/sherlockworld
Four largest files in that directory are:
565 /home/sherlockworld/originals-from gutenberg.txt
56 /home/sherlockworld/speckled-band.html
56 /home/sherlockworld/copper-beeches.html
54 /home/sherlockworld/boscombe-valley.html

Big directory: /home/launchline
Four largest files in that directory are:
151 /home/launchline/logs/access_log
71 /home/launchline/x/submit.cgi
71 /home/launchline/x/admin/managesubs.cgi
64 /home/launchline/x/status.cgi
```

As you can see, the results are good, but the order of the output fields is perhaps
less than we'd like. Ideally, I'd like to have all the disk hogs listed, then their
largest files listed. To do this, we'll have to either store all the directory names in a
variable that we then parse subsequently, or we'd have to write the information to a
temporary file.

Because it shouldn't be too much information (five directory names), we'll save the
directory names as a variable. To do this, we'll use the nifty backquote notation.

> Unix old-timers often refer to backquotes as *backticks*, so a wizened Unix admin might well say "stick the dee-ewe in backticks" at this juncture.

Here's how things will change. First off, let's load the directory names into the new variable:

```
bigdirs="`du -s /home/* | sort -rn | cut -f2- | head -5`"
```

Then we'll need to change the for loop to reflect this change, which is easy:

```
for dirname in $bigdirs ; do
```

Notice I've also pulled the do line up to shorten the script. Recall that a semicolon indicates the end of a command in a shell script, so we can then pull the next line up without any further ado.

3. Now let's not forget to output the list of big directories before we list the big files per directory. In total, our script now looks like this:

```
echo "Disk Hogs Report for System `hostname`"

bigdirs="`du -s /home/* | sort -rn | cut -f2- | head -5`"

echo "The Five biggest home directories are:"
echo $bigdirs

for dirname in $bigdirs ; do
  echo ""
  echo Big directory: $dirname
  echo Four largest files in that directory are:
  find $dirname -type f -printf "%k %p\n" | sort -rn | head -4
done

exit 0
```

This is quite a bit closer to the finished product, as you can see from its output:

```
Disk Hogs Report for System staging.intuitive.com
The Five biggest home directories are:
/home/staging /home/chatter /home/cbo /home/sherlockworld /home/launchline

Big directory: /home/staging
Four largest files in that directory are:
423 /home/staging/waldorf/big/DSCF0165.jpg
410 /home/staging/waldorf/big/DSCF0176.jpg
402 /home/staging/waldorf/big/DSCF0166.jpg
395 /home/staging/waldorf/big/DSCF0161.jpg

Big directory: /home/chatter
Four largest files in that directory are:
```

3

```
1076 /home/chatter/comics/lynx
388 /home/chatter/logs/access_log
90 /home/chatter/logs/error_log
64 /home/chatter/responding.cgi

Big directory: /home/cbo
Four largest files in that directory are:
568 /home/cbo/financing.pdf
464 /home/cbo/investors/CBO-plan.pdf
179 /home/cbo/Archive/cbofinancial-modified-files/CBO Website.zip
77 /home/cbo/Archive/cbofinancial-modified-files/CBO Financial
➥Incorporated .doc

Big directory: /home/sherlockworld
Four largest files in that directory are:
565 /home/sherlockworld/originals-from gutenberg.txt
56 /home/sherlockworld/speckled-band.html
56 /home/sherlockworld/copper-beeches.html
54 /home/sherlockworld/boscombe-valley.html

Big directory: /home/launchline
Four largest files in that directory are:
151 /home/launchline/logs/access_log
71 /home/launchline/x/submit.cgi
71 /home/launchline/x/admin/managesubs.cgi
64 /home/launchline/x/status.cgi
```

This is a script you could easily run every morning in the wee hours with a line in
cron (which we'll explore in great detail in Hour 15, "Running Jobs in the
Future"), or you can even put it in your .profile to run automatically each time
you log in.

4. One final nuance: To have the output e-mailed to you, simply append the
following:

```
| mail -s "Disk Hogs Report" your-mailaddr
```

If you've named this script diskhogs.sh like I have, you could have the output e-
mailed to you (as root) with

```
sh diskhogs.sh | mail -s "Disk Hogs Report" root
```

Try that, then check root's mailbox to see if the report made it.

5. For those of you using Solaris, Darwin, or another Unix, the nifty -printf option
probably isn't available with your version of find. As a result, the more generic
version of this script is rather more complex, because we not only have to sidestep
the lack of -printf, but we also have to address the challenge of having embedded
spaces in most directory names (on Darwin). To accomplish the latter, we use sed
and awk to change all spaces to double underscores and then back again when we
feed the arg to the find command:

```
#!/bin/sh
echo "Disk Hogs Report for System `hostname`"

bigdir2="`du -s /Library/* | sed 's/ /_/g' | sort -rn | cut -f2- | head
➥ -5`"

echo "The Five biggest library directories are:"
echo $bigdir2

for dirname in $bigdir2 ; do
  echo ""
  echo Big directory: $dirname
  echo Four largest files in that directory are:
  find "`echo $dirname | sed 's/_/ /g'`" -type f -ls | \
    awk '{ print $7" "$11 }' | sort -rn | head -4
done

exit 0
```

The good news is that the output ends up being almost identical, which you can verify if you have an OS X or other BSD system available.

Of course, it would be smart to replace the native version of find with the more sophisticated GNU version, but changing essential system tools is more than most Unix users want!

> If you want to explore upgrading some of the Unix tools in Darwin to take advantage of the sophisticated GNU enhancements, then you'd do well to start by looking at http://www.osxgnu.org/ for ported code. The site also includes download instructions.
>
> If you're on Solaris or another flavor of Unix that isn't Mac OS X, check out the main GNU site for tool upgrades at http://www.gnu.org/.

This shell script evolved in a manner that's quite common for Unix tools—it started out life as a simple command line; then as the sophistication of the tool increased, the complexity of the command sequence increased to where it was too tedious to type in directly, so it was dropped into a shell script. Shell variables then offered the capability to save interim output, fine-tune the presentation, and more, so we exploited it by building a more powerful tool. Finally, the tool itself was added to the system as an automated monitoring task by adding it to the root cron job.

Summary

This hour has not only shown you two of the basic Unix commands for analyzing disk usage and utilization, but it's also demonstrated the evolution and development of a useful administrative shell script, `diskhogs`.

This sequence of command-to-multistage command-to-shell script will be repeated again and again as you learn how to become a powerful system administrator.

Q&A

Q **Why are some Unix systems built around 512-byte blocks, whereas others are built around 1024-byte blocks?**

A This is all because of the history and evolution of Unix systems. When Unix was first deployed, disks were small, and it was important to squeeze as many bytes out of the disk as possible. As a result, the file system was developed with a fundamental block size of 512 bytes (that is, the space allocated for files was always in 512-byte chunks). As disks became bigger, millions of 512-byte blocks began to prove more difficult to manage than their benefit of allowing more effective utilization of the disk. As a result, the block size doubled to 1KB and has remained there to this day. Some Unix systems have stayed with the 512-byte historical block size, whereas others are on the more modern 1KB block size.

Q **Do all device names have meaning?**

A As much as possible, yes. Sometimes you can't help but end up with a `/dev/fd13x4s3`, but even then there's probably a logical explanation behind the naming convention.

Q **If there's a flag to `du` that causes it to report results in 1KB blocks on a system that defaults to 512-byte blocks, why isn't there a flag on 1KB systems to report in 512-byte blocks?**

A Ah, you expect everything to make sense? Maybe you're in the wrong field after all....

Workshop

Quiz

1. Why do most Unix installations organize disks into lots of partitions, rather than a smaller number of huge physical devices?

2. When you add up the size of all the partitions on a large hard disk, there's always some missing space. Why?

3. If you see devices /dev/sdb3, /dev/sdb4, and /dev/sdc1, what's a likely guess about how many physical hard disks are referenced?

4. Both Solaris and Darwin offer the very helpful -k flag to the df command. What does it do, and why would it be useful?

5. Using the -s flag to ls, the -rn flags to sort, and the -5 flag to head, construct a command line that shows you the five largest files in your home directory.

6. What do you think would happen to our script if a very large file was accidentally left in the /home directory overnight?

Answers

1. By dividing a disk into multiple partitions, you have created a more robust system because one partition can fill without affecting the others.

2. The missing space is typically allocated for low-level disk format information. On a typical 10GB disk, perhaps as much as two to four percent of the disk space might not be available after the drive is formatted.

3. This probably represents two drives: /dev/sdb and /dev/sdc.

4. The -k flag makes a system that defaults to 512-byte blocks report file sizes in 1KB block sizes.

5. ls -s $HOME | sort -rn | head -5.

6. The script as written would flag the very large file as one of the largest home directories, then would fail when it tried to analyze the files within. It's an excellent example of the need for lots of error condition code and some creative thought while programming.

The next hour will continue to build the foundations of sysadmin knowledge with the oft-convoluted file ownership model. This will include digging into both the passwd and groups files and learning how to safely change them to create a variety of different permission scenarios.

HOUR 4

File Ownership

After you've wrestled with how to figure out how much disk space you have and how to manage it (Hour 3, "Disk Usage"), the next logical topic is how to change the ownership of files and directories. Although this might seem like a simple topic, this hour demonstrates some of the nuances of file management necessary for a Unix file and system administrator.

In this hour, you will learn

- To use commands like ls and chmod to work with file and directory ownership
- The intricacies of the /etc/passwd file
- The concepts of Unix groups and /etc/group

Starting at the Beginning: Permission Strings

Any discussion of file and directory ownership must begin with a primer on how to use the ls command to ascertain the owner, group, and permissions associated with a specific file. A discussion of permission strings, however,

naturally expands to cover a variety of additional topics, including umask, chmod, and
more.

Task 4.1: The Basics of File Permissions

To start at the beginning, all directories in Unix are treated as if they were files. Similar
to files, directories also have a user owner and group owner, and similar to files, groups
have a finite number of possible permissions. Both files and directories have their permissions split into three categories: user, group, and others.

1. To start, here's a long-format listing of a few files and directories:

    ```
    $ ls -laF
    total 172
    drwxrw----    3 taylor    coders      4096 Jan  7 21:35 ./
    drwxr-x---   13 taylor    coders      4096 Jan  7 21:35 ../
    -rw-rw----    1 taylor    coders       263 Dec  5 05:12 snapshot.sh
    -rw-rw----    1 taylor    coders    153600 Dec  5 05:12 sourcefiles.cpio
    drwxrw----    2 taylor    coders      4096 Dec  5 05:12 Src/
    ```

    The permission string is, of course, the sequence of dashes, r, w, and x at the
    beginning of each file listed. The owner of each file (or directory) is listed, then the
    group. In this case, notice that all files are associated with account taylor and
    group coders.

    The .. (parent) directory is an interesting example of permission strings because it
    offers read, write, and execute permission (rwx) to the owner of the directory (tay-
    lor), read and execute permission to other members of the group coders, and no
    access to anyone else on the system.

2. To change file permissions, use the chmod command. Although you can specify a
    target octal permission (for example, 0750), it's probably easiest to use mnemonic
    change notation instead. To fix the peculiar permissions of the current directory, for
    example:

    chmod u+x .

    says "user plus execute" (user = file owner, but the o notation is for others, con-
    fusingly).

3. To be able to experiment, two useful Unix commands should be highlighted: touch
    and mkdir. touch updates the last-modified-time of a specific file or directory, but
    if the file doesn't exist, touch creates an empty file. mkdir, of course, makes direc-
    tories.

    A quick example. Note the default permissions for the new file and directory that
    are set up:

```
$ ls
snapshot.sh  sourcefiles.cpio  Src/
$ touch testfile
$ mkdir testdir
$ ls -alF
total 176
drwxrw----    4 taylor   coders     4096 Jan  7 21:47 ./
drwxr-x---   13 taylor   coders     4096 Jan  7 21:35 ../
-rw-rw----    1 taylor   coders      263 Dec  5 05:12 snapshot.sh
-rw-rw----    1 taylor   coders   153600 Dec  5 05:12 sourcefiles.cpio
drwxrw----    2 taylor   coders     4096 Dec  5 05:12 Src/
drwxrwxr-x    2 taylor   coders     4096 Jan  7 21:47 testdir/
-rw-rw-r--    1 taylor   coders        0 Jan  7 21:47 testfile
```

4. The default permissions for files and directories are specified by the value of the umask setting. As a user you probably don't have to worry too much about your umask setting, but as a system administrator, you'll probably want to figure out a preferred value, and then set that in a shared configuration file like /etc/profile.

A quick peek in /etc/profile shows that there's no explicit setting for umask, so we're getting the default, as is every other user who logs in to the system. To ascertain your own default value, simply type umask at the shell prompt:

```
$ umask
002
```

If through analysis of your user base, it makes sense to have the default permission be read + write + execute for the owner, read + execute for the group, and nothing for everyone else, it would be time to modify the umask setting.

5. You'll need to stick with me for this explanation, because umask values are the exact octal opposite of the permissions you seek. Octal values range from 0–7, and each value represents a unique permission, as shown in Table 4.1.

TABLE 4.1 Octal Permission Values

Octal Value	Permission	umask *Opposite*
0	no access allowed	7
1	execute only	6
2	write only	5
3	write + execute	4
4	read only	3
5	read + execute	2
6	read + write	1
7	read + write + execute	0

▼ Working with this, the permission represented by the permission string `-rwx r-x --- ` can also therefore be conveyed as `750`. The umask to produce this default permission is its inverse: `027`.

 The most common `umask` values are `002`, `022`, and `027`, which translate (thanks to Table 4.1) as "rwx for owner and group, r-x for others," "rwx for owner, r-x for group and others," and "rwx for owner, r-x for group, and no access for others."

It's worth noting also that although most files don't need execute permission, your best bet is to specify a umask that allows it, and let the individual file creation programs (`vi`, for example) figure out what settings they need. These umasks are
▲ changed with, simply enough, `umask` *newvalue*, as in `umask 022`.

File ownership in Unix is really most akin to a multifaceted diamond. One facet is file permission, with its `umask` settings and `chmod` values. Other facets are the owner and group settings, and that's what we'll explore next.

Ownership and `/etc/passwd`

The next concept we need to explore is how file ownership works in Unix. Fortunately, this is straightforward and it all revolves around the entries in the `/etc/passwd` file.

Task 4.2: Understanding `/etc/passwd`

All files and directories have a pair of integer values associated with them representing the owner ID and group ID. In fact, your account itself has two similar numeric IDs associated with it (your so-called user ID, or UID, and your group ID or GID). Those are the numbers that are used to tag all the files that you own so the system knows what's what.

1. To start, find out not only what your user ID and group ID are, but what groups you're in as well. You can use `id` to do so:
```
$ id
uid=502(taylor) gid=502(coders) groups=502(coders),4(adm)
```

In this output you can see that my account has a UID of 502, and a GID of 502. In addition, it shows me that I am not only a member of the group `coders` but also
▼ have been added to `adm`, group 4.

2. User accounts are defined in the /etc/passwd file, and here's what they look like:

```
$ tail /etc/passwd
radvd:x:75:75:radvd user:/:/bin/false
postgres:x:26:26:PostgreSQL Server:/var/lib/pgsql:/bin/bash
apache:x:48:48:Apache:/var/www:/bin/false
squid:x:23:23::/var/spool/squid:/dev/null
named:x:25:25:Named:/var/named:/bin/false
pcap:x:77:77::/var/arpwatch:/bin/nologin
mthorne:x:500:500:Matt Thorne:/home/mthorne:/bin/bash
mdella:x:501:501:Marcos R. Della:/home/mdella:/bin/csh
taylor:x:502:502:Dave Taylor:/home/taylor:/bin/bash
```

We'll examine each of these fields in the next hour, but for the purposes of file permissions, it's important that we recognize that fields are separated by colons, and that the first field is the account name, the third is the UID, and fourth is the GID.

To split those out is a quick task for awk:

```
$ awk -F: '{print $1" has UID="$3" and GID="$4}' < /etc/passwd
root has UID=0 and GID=0
bin has UID=1 and GID=1
daemon has UID=2 and GID=2
adm has UID=3 and GID=4
lp has UID=4 and GID=7
sync has UID=5 and GID=0
shutdown has UID=6 and GID=0
halt has UID=7 and GID=0
mail has UID=8 and GID=12
news has UID=9 and GID=13
uucp has UID=10 and GID=14
operator has UID=11 and GID=0
games has UID=12 and GID=100
gopher has UID=13 and GID=30
ftp has UID=14 and GID=50
nobody has UID=99 and GID=99
mailnull has UID=47 and GID=47
rpm has UID=37 and GID=37
xfs has UID=43 and GID=43
ntp has UID=38 and GID=38
rpc has UID=32 and GID=32
gdm has UID=42 and GID=42
rpcuser has UID=29 and GID=29
nfsnobody has UID=65534 and GID=65534
nscd has UID=28 and GID=28
ident has UID=98 and GID=98
radvd has UID=75 and GID=75
postgres has UID=26 and GID=26
apache has UID=48 and GID=48
squid has UID=23 and GID=23
named has UID=25 and GID=25
pcap has UID=77 and GID=77
```

4

```
mthorne has UID=500 and GID=500
mdella has UID=501 and GID=501
taylor has UID=502 and GID=502
```

By convention, UIDs lower than 100 are system accounts or system IDs and should be ignored. The only exception is UID=0, which is the `root` or `superuser` account. You want to keep track of that because anyone with that ID can ignore all file permissions and edit, change, and even delete any file they'd like.

3. A simple `awk` command to use occasionally to keep track of these UID=0 accounts—since a sysadmin can always set up any number of different accounts with a given UID, and UID=0 is obviously the most important to watch—is

```
awk -F: '{ if ($3 == '0') print $0 }' /etc/passwd
```

Your output should be a single line: the `root` account. If there are other matches, you need to immediately look into it and ascertain why there's another superuser account. (We'll explore this issue further in Hour 5, "Working with User Accounts.")

4. To change the owner UID of a file or directory, use the `chown` command. To demonstrate, let's try to change the ownership of the `testfile` file created earlier to `games` (which you can see in the earlier listing is UID=12):

```
$ chown games testfile
chown: changing ownership of `testfile': Operation not permitted
```

This error is good news, in fact. This means that Red Hat Linux 7.2 is one of the Unix systems available that prevents users from changing the ownership of their own files. Why? Because otherwise there's a really sneaky way that users can circumvent quotas. They could change the ownership of a very large file (an MP3 archive, for example) to a+rwx (giving everyone read, write, and execute access), then changing ownership to another user ID. When the quota system analyzes disk usage by UID, the huge file shows up as being owned by someone else. When the user wants to return to their ownership, they copy it into a new filename (which they own by default), and delete the version that had been recorded as owned by the other user. Tricky, eh?

> Both Solaris and Darwin have a similar restriction on `chown` usage by regular users, so this sneaky trick must be more popular than I thought!

Good news or not, this means that it's time to become `root` to be able to change ownership. This can be done a variety of different ways, but I typically use `su`, which, without any arguments, spawns a subshell as UID=0, after prompting for the `root` account password.

```
$ su
Password:
bash-2.05# chown games testfile
bash-2.05# ls -laF
total 176
drwxrw----     4 taylor    coders     4096 Jan  7 21:47 ./
drwxr-x---    13 taylor    coders     4096 Jan  7 22:27 ../
-rw-rw----     1 taylor    coders      263 Dec  5 05:12 snapshot.sh
-rw-rw----     1 taylor    coders   153600 Dec  5 05:12 sourcefiles.cpio
drwxrw----     2 taylor    coders     4096 Dec  5 05:12 Src/
drwxrwxr-x     2 taylor    coders     4096 Jan  7 21:47 testdir/
-rw-rw-r--     1 games     coders        0 Jan  7 21:47 testfile
```

As you can see, as root I can change ownership of a file with nary a complaint or warning.

5. An interesting observation is that although the Unix system displays the UID by account *name*, it's really only storing it by account *ID*. Which means, if user mdella were to ask me, as sysadmin, to change his login account name to marcos, all I'd have to do is change the first word of the account-information line in /etc/passwd, and all the file listings would magically change as well.

For example, if I change taylor to davet in the password file:

```
davet:x:502:502:Dave Taylor:/home/taylor:/bin/bash
```

then the very same ls command has different results:

```
# ls -laF
total 176
drwxrw----     4 davet     coders     4096 Jan  7 21:47 ./
drwxr-x---    13 davet     coders     4096 Jan  7 22:27 ../
-rw-rw----     1 davet     coders      263 Dec  5 05:12 snapshot.sh
-rw-rw----     1 davet     coders   153600 Dec  5 05:12 sourcefiles.cpio
drwxrw----     2 davet     coders     4096 Dec  5 05:12 Src/
drwxrwxr-x     2 davet     coders     4096 Jan  7 21:47 testdir/
-rw-rw-r--     1 games     coders        0 Jan  7 21:47 testfile
```

Working with account IDs in Unix is fairly straightforward, and if you're already working on a Unix system, it was doubtless a simple review. Unix handles groups in a way that is quite helpful, but understood much less. That's what we'll explore next.

Understanding Unix Groups and /etc/group

To fully understand Unix groups, it's helpful to take some time to talk about the historical roots of the Unix operating system. Unix was developed at AT&T Bell Telephone Labs (also known as Bell Labs, now a core part of Lucent Corporation) during a period when all computers were shared by multiple users. In the jargon of the time, Unix is a multiuser, multitasking operating system.

One of the challenges of multiuser systems is file permission, and a popular research operating system at the time that had gained considerable attention at Bell Telephone Labs (BTL) was Multics. Developed originally by BTL, the Massachusetts Institute of Technology, and General Electric (BTL later dropped out of the project), Multics was an astonishingly complex multiuser system that had a highly sophisticated security model, based on concentric circles of access to files, peripherals, and applications.

Brian Kernighan and Ken Thompson, the inventors of the Unix system, had helped with Multics before BTL quit, and although they liked many of its capabilities, they disliked its complexity. The Unix security model, therefore, has an approximately similar concept of circles of access, but in a much simpler manner.

It's worth mentioning that the name Unix is a bit of a poke at Multics. UN-IX, MULT-ICS. The saying at Bell Labs used to be "Unix is one of whatever Multics was many of." Learn more, if you're curious, at `http://www.multicians.org/`

On first glance, the Unix security model seems to be three levels of access: owner, group, and everyone else. A glimmer of how this can be more complex was suggested earlier when I used the `id` command and learned that I was in two groups, not one. Therefore, although files, programs, or directories can only have a single owner and group, a user can be a member of many groups and thereby end up with access privileges that represent the union of all the individual permissions.

It's not entirely true that files can only have one owner and group. Creating a *hard link* to a file can enable the new name to be assigned a different owner and/or group. Yet there's still only one file on the system, so no additional disk space has been consumed. This is a very important concept for system administrators who are going to develop more sophisticated access control methods on their system.

For our purposes, let's start by exploring standard Unix groups, then go from there.

Task 4.3: Groups and the `/etc/group` file

Every user account is assigned what's called a default group. On many modern Unix systems, the use of groups has become so uncommon that by default every user gets his own group, effectively negating a powerful characteristic of the Unix operating system itself.

1. Look at the last ten lines of the /etc/passwd file for a moment, running it through the awk filter, shown earlier in this hour:

```
$ awk -F: '{print $1" has UID="$3" and GID="$4}' < /etc/passwd | tail
radvd has UID=75 and GID=75
postgres has UID=26 and GID=26
apache has UID=48 and GID=48
squid has UID=23 and GID=23
named has UID=25 and GID=25
pcap has UID=77 and GID=77
mthorne has UID=500 and GID=500
mdella has UID=501 and GID=501
taylor has UID=502 and GID=502
```

Notice that every UID has a corresponding GID, and that no two accounts share a default group.

I think this is somewhat silly. It's akin to buying a Ferrari and never putting it in high gear, or a multifunction stereo and only listening to AM radio. (Well, maybe that's a bit of an exaggeration!)

Since mthorne and taylor are both administrators, it would actually make more sense to have them in the same administrative group on this system. mdella, by contrast, is a regular user and should not be included in the sysadmin group.

2. To change who is in what group, it's time to delve into the /etc/group file. Let's start by examining the file (which does have a tendency to vary in format from flavor to flavor, in case yours isn't exactly the same):

```
$ head /etc/group
root:x:0:root
bin:x:1:root,bin,daemon
daemon:x:2:root,bin,daemon
sys:x:3:root,bin,adm
adm:x:4:root,adm,daemon,taylor
tty:x:5:
disk:x:6:root
lp:x:7:daemon,lp
mem:x:8:
kmem:x:9:
```

As you can see, the file format is quite similar to the /etc/passwd file examined earlier. In this case, the format for each line is

```
account name : encrypted password : group ID : member list
```

The first thing to notice is that an encrypted password value of x denotes that there's a shadow password file stored elsewhere on the system—for security reasons—that has the actual encrypted password string. The next hour explores the password's /etc/shadow file, but for groups, the relevant group file is

4

▼   /etc/gshadow. Before we look at that, however, just observe that the first group—root—is group ID=0, and has one member: account root. The second, group bin, has three members, adm has four, and so on.

3. A user can be moved from one default group to another by changing the number associated with his default group in the /etc/passwd file, as you might expect.

Adding a user to additional groups is most efficiently done by editing the group file itself. On Linux, there's a simple tool vigr (vi group) that enables you to safely edit the /etc/group file without worrying about another sysadmin making changes underfoot. If you have that on your system, I recommend using it. Otherwise, you can directly edit the file with the editor of your choice and if you're the only admin, you should be safe.

To demonstrate, I'm going to add user taylor to the administrative group wheel by simply appending the login ID taylor to the line.

Before the change, wheel looks like this:

```
# grep wheel /etc/group
wheel:x:10:root
```

and after the change:

```
# grep wheel /etc/group
wheel:x:10:root,taylor
```

Now, when user taylor logs in, the id command reports something slightly different:

```
$ id
uid=502(taylor) gid=502(coders) groups=502(coders),4(adm),10(wheel)
```

Voilà! Now taylor is a member of three groups.

> The wheel group is an interesting one: On most Unixes, only users who are part of the group wheel can use the su command to switch user accounts without logging out.

Users can temporarily join a group with the newgrp command, though they'll need to know the group password if one has been set. (Groups have random, impossible-▲   to-guess passwords by default, by the way.)

A good philosophy to follow is to create mnemonic groups for the teams in your organization, and add and delete members of the group to reflect the current membership. Then, the group members are free to create directories and allow limited access to programs and files without worries about unauthorized access.

Using Groups to Control Access

As a demonstration of how to work with groups in Unix, let's control access to the printer on this system. We're going to change permissions on the printing application to only allow access to members of the lp group. To do this, we're going to add a password to the lp group, then change the permissions of the lp binary to match.

Task 4.4: Access Control with Groups

▲ TASK

Using groups to control access to the lp command proves an informative and illustrative example. I should let you know up front that a more common solution to this problem is to rename the lp command something like lp.authorized, then create a shell script called lp that checks user ID against a list of valid, authorized users.

The downside of the authorization list, of course, is that it must be maintained. Creating an lp group is more elegant in many ways because the administrator needs simply to give out the password and a user is authorized. If you want to disable a single user, however, it's a bit of a problem.

1. The first step is to make sure that there's an lp group in the /etc/group file. Easily done with grep, fortunately:

   ```
   # grep lp /etc/group
   lp:x:7:daemon,lp
   ```

   Looks good. Now let's add user mdella to the list to ensure that he can print whenever he wants without fuss. This can be done in a variety of ways, but the group editing utility vigr is really the optimal solution. So, that'll let me change the line above (in the non-shadow groups file) to

   ```
   # grep lp /etc/group
   lp:x:7:daemon,lp,mdella
   ```

2. Setting the password for a group can be a very hard task on most Unix systems. Linux has the helpful gpasswd program that enables you to specify the password for a group, but most Unixes have no equivalent. As a result you are left changing the password of a regular user account, then copying-and-pasting the encrypted password string into the group file. Ugh.

   Making this even more complex, modern Unixes use a *shadow password file*, meaning that the passwords themselves (encrypted) are kept in a different file than the account information. With the group file, passwords are stored in /etc/gshadow. By default, the lp group password is left blank (unmatchable):

   ```
   # grep lp /etc/gshadow
   lp:::daemon,lp
   ```

4

We'll want to edit this file by hand to add the new group member. Then, rather than try to add the new encrypted password by hand—a tricky proposition—and since we have the gpasswd command, let's use it to set the password for the lp group:

```
# gpasswd lp
Changing the password for group lp
New Password:
Re-enter new password:
# grep lp /etc/group
lp:x:7:daemon,lp,mdella
```

Notice that there are no changes in the /etc/group file. The shadow password file looks a bit different, however:

```
# grep -C lp /etc/gshadow
tty:::
disk:::root
lp:0UexIr.hI7TDY::daemon,lp,mdella
mem:::
kmem:::
```

> A really handy flag for grep is -C (on most modern Unixes), causing the command to show you the context of your matches. By default two lines before and after the line that matched are included in the output.

3. Time to modify the lp command itself. I'll use the which command to ensure that I'm finding the official copy:

```
# which lp
/usr/bin/lp
# ls -l /usr/bin/lp
lrwxrwxrwx   1 root     root            3 Nov 21 14:36 /usr/bin/lp -> lpr
```

Aha! Turns out that the lp command is symbolically linked to lpr. So, it's the lpr command that really must be changed.

```
# which lpr
/usr/bin/lpr
# ls -l /usr/bin/lpr
-rwxr-xr-x   1 lp       lp         408536 Aug 10 18:32 /usr/bin/lpr
```

Conveniently, the command is already owned by the group lp, so the change required is simply a matter of the permissions.

A moment's thought should reveal that the desired permissions are read + execute for members of group lp, and no access permission for anyone else. The chmod command can make this change in one easy step:

```
# chmod o-rx /usr/bin/lpr
# ls -l /usr/bin/lpr
-rwxr-x---   1 lp          lp          408536 Aug 10 18:32 /usr/bin/lpr
```

Done!

4. To test this new configuration, let's see if user mdella can execute the lp command:

```
$ ls | lp
$
```

Looks like it worked with nary a hitch.

How about user taylor, who isn't part of the lp group?

```
$ id
uid=502(taylor) gid=502(coders) groups=502(coders),4(adm),10(wheel)
$ ls | lp
bash: /usr/bin/lp: Permission denied
```

That's what we want to have occur—the system rejected the print request because user taylor isn't part of the lp group, and therefore doesn't have permission to run the lpr program.

5. To get permission, the user has to know the password and change to the lp group by using the newgrp command:

```
$ newgrp lp
Password:
$ id
uid=502(taylor) gid=7(lp) groups=502(coders),4(adm),10(wheel)
```

As you can see, newgrp spawns a new subshell for the user that has the requested group as the primary GID. This does not, however, mean that taylor is part of group lp permanently. Just temporarily. Dangerously, any files or directories created while in this subshell *will* have lp as the group owner, however. Beware so that doesn't trip you up.

```
$ ls | lp
$
```

That's exactly the solution we were hoping to create.

Using groups to control access to applications is a great demonstration of the unheralded power of Unix group permissions. The actual implementation of groups within the various programs that comprise the Unix system varies, however. If you find that your explorations come to an occasional dead end, I encourage you to focus on using groups for file and directory access instead. It's a much more common approach.

Summary

This hour has focused on how file and directory permissions relate to the contents of the /etc/passwd and, especially, /etc/group files. You've seen how you can use groups to compartmentalize information on the Unix system you administer through thoughtful use of group membership for users. Finally, the extensive example of using the lp group to control access to the printer through changes to the group and application permission modifications.

Groups are a surprisingly under-utilized feature of Unix. When I've administered Unix boxes, I've always tried to model the group and team membership of my colleagues with groups on the computer itself.

Q&A

Q Unix essentially has three concentric circles of access as its permission model (owner, group, and other). Did Multics really have more?

A Yes indeed. In fact, Multics was the first computer operating system awarded the B2 security level certification from the United States government.

Q Why use vigr to edit the /etc/group file, rather than just regular old vi?

A Because it's always dangerous to edit an underlying system file in case someone else is editing it or otherwise tries to alter it simultaneously. Imagine if you're editing the file while another sysadmin unknowingly runs gpasswd to change a group password. You then save your edit session and their password change is lost. The vigr program creates a lock file that prevents gpasswd from writing to the file while you're editing it.

Workshop

Questions

1. Why do most modern Unixes automatically place each new user in his own private group?

2. What umask value would create files with read permission for the owner, read + write for the group, and read + write + execute for everyone else? Would this make sense as a umask?

3. I want to end up with an octal directory permission of 754. What umask would I specify?

4. How many accounts do you have on your Unix system with user IDs greater than 100? Less than 100?

5. Changing the spelling of the account name in /etc/passwd has what far-reaching effects?

Answers

1. As best as I can figure, modern Unix systems figure that sysadmins will forget to manage groups. The easiest way to sidestep that possible security problem is to drop each user into their own group, effectively eliminating the entire capability of groups in Unix.

2. Read for owner, read+write for group, and read+write+execute for everyone else is r--rw-rwx, which can be expressed as 467. The umask is the opposite: 310. This would be a really weird umask value, of course, because the person with the least permissions is the owner!

3. If you want to end up with 754, you need the opposite for the umask: 023.

4. On my systems I have 20–30 accounts under UID=100, and no more than five or ten actual user accounts.

5. Changing the spelling of the account not only changes the owner information shown in file listings, but it also forces the user to use the new name when he logs in, and it might also affect his e-mail address on the system.

4

Next hour will focus on the creation and management of user accounts. We touched on the /etc/passwd file in this hour, but in the next hour we'll dig deep into the file and learn how to manage and modify the content to implement security and usage policies.

PART III

User & Package Management

Hour

HOUR 5

Working with User Accounts

One of the most common tasks facing a Unix system administrator is the management of user accounts. Whether it's helping someone change a login shell, adding new users, or promptly closing an account when someone is given "walking papers," you'll constantly find yourself fiddling and tweaking these settings. That's what this hour and the next are all about: working with user accounts. This hour focuses specifically on adding new users, which is more involved than you might think....

In this hour, you learn about

- Exploring the /etc/passwd file
- Using NetInfo to manage user accounts in Mac OS X
- Adding users and the adduser script
- Adding users in an NIS world

Understanding the `/etc/passwd` File

The best place to start this hour is with the `/etc/passwd` file, as it's the central hub of all user accounts and information. Seems like an unlikely database, but it's true: The `/etc/passwd` file is the core account database on every Unix system.

Task 5.1: Exploring `/etc/passwd`

When Unix was first developed, databases were considered massive applications on custom hardware, appropriately used for heavy-duty information analysis like the census or tax data, but not for something as trivial as keeping track of what home directory is associated with a specific user account.

However, the need for some sort of database that could track

- Account name
- User ID
- Default group ID
- Login shell
- Home directory

remained, and was solved with the creation of the `/etc/passwd` file.

Fortunately, it's easy to understand this seemingly cryptic file. Let's have a look!

1. First off, let's get the line of the `/etc/passwd` file associated with your own account. To do this, simply `grep` for the value of `$USER`:

   ```
   # grep $USER /etc/passwd
   taylor:x:502:502:Dave Taylor:/home/taylor:/bin/bash
   ```

   The entry is divided by colons, as we learned in the last hour, and the information therein is

   ```
   account name : password placeholder : user ID : default group ID :
   ➡    comment : home directory : login shell
   ```

   The password is only stored encrypted in Unix, and modern Unixes all use the shadow password file to avoid having even that displayed to users. Why? Because if a cracker has an encrypted password string, she can encrypt words in a dictionary and compare the two encrypted strings. Given enough time, it's remarkable how many passwords can be cracked. Hide the encrypted strings and the system is just that much more secure.

   Indeed, notice the permissions of the `/etc/passwd` file compared to the encrypted password-containing `/etc/shadow` file:

```
# ls -l /etc/passwd
-rw-r--r--    1 root       root           1583 Jan  8 17:32 /etc/passwd
# ls -l /etc/shadow
-rw-------    1 root       root           1155 Jan  8 17:32 /etc/shadow
```

2. Knowing how this file is organized, it's a simple task to see which login shells are in use. For example:

```
# cut -d: -f7 /etc/passwd | sort | uniq -c | sort -rn
     16 /sbin/nologin
      6 /bin/false
      6 /bin/bash
      2 /dev/null
      1 /sbin/shutdown
      1 /sbin/halt
      1 /bin/sync
      1 /bin/nologin
      1 /bin/csh
      1
```

The blank match defaults to the standard shell of /bin/sh, which is replaced in Linux with the more capable /bin/bash. The other shells listed are all intended to prevent users from logging on using those accounts. Let's have a peek at what accounts have /bin/false as their login shell:

```
# grep /bin/false /etc/passwd
xfs:x:43:43:X Font Server:/etc/X11/fs:/bin/false
rpc:x:32:32:Portmapper RPC user:/:/bin/false
nscd:x:28:28:NSCD Daemon:/:/bin/false
radvd:x:75:75:radvd user:/:/bin/false
apache:x:48:48:Apache:/var/www:/bin/false
named:x:25:25:Named:/var/named:/bin/false
```

Quite reasonable. None of these accounts should have login privileges.

> Why have accounts that can't log in? To organize files and directories and set access permissions properly. Consider the example at the end of Hour 4: the lp account isn't a login account (in RHL7.2 its default shell is /sbin/nologin), but it's very helpful for having a single owner of all printer-related files and applications. Accounts with a UID under 100 are usually administrative accounts of this nature.

Notice that there are also some command shortcuts accessible from a direct login:

```
# egrep '(shutdown|halt|sync)' /etc/passwd
sync:x:5:0:sync:/sbin:/bin/sync
shutdown:x:6:0:shutdown:/sbin:/sbin/shutdown
halt:x:7:0:halt:/sbin:/sbin/halt
```

5

▼   If you know the password for sync, shutdown, or halt, you can perform the asso-
    ciated command right at the login prompt, without having to even log in as root.
    Helpful in case of emergencies, but potentially dangerous if others can access these
    administrative functions remotely.

3. One really useful script that will help illustrate how to work with the /etc/passwd
    file is checkhomes.sh—it extracts all the home directories in the password file,
    then verifies that each exists, flagging any errors.

    Sound difficult to write? It's easy!

```
$ cat checkhomes.sh
#!/bin/sh

# Checkhomes.sh - Scan /etc/passwd for all home directories, then make
#                 sure that each exists.

pw=/etc/passwd

for homedir in `cut -d: -f6 /etc/passwd`
do
  # echo checking home directory $homedir
  if [ ! -d $homedir ] ; then
    echo Warning: home directory $homedir does NOT exist
  fi
done

exit 0
```

    The cut in the for loop pulls out all the home directories; then one by one they're
    assigned to $homedir and checked to see whether they're a directory. If they're not
    ("! -d" returns true), then an error message is output.

    Surprisingly, the stock RHL7.2 configuration has some problems:

```
$ sh checkhomes.sh
Warning: home directory /var/adm does NOT exist
Warning: home directory /var/spool/news does NOT exist
Warning: home directory /var/spool/uucp does NOT exist
Warning: home directory /var/gopher does NOT exist
Warning: home directory /home/root does NOT exist
```

4. To be fancy, it'd be nice if each of these errors also listed the account name itself,
    but that's quite a bit more complex: You'd want to use read to load two variables at
    a time from the cut command. Extracting them both is easy, though: cut -d:
    -f1,6 would do it.

    Here's the much improved script:

```
$ cat checkhomes.sh
#!/bin/sh
```

▼

```
# Checkhomes.sh - Scan /etc/passwd for all home directories, then make
```

```
#                    sure that each exists.
cut -d: -f1,6 /etc/passwd  | sed 's/:/ /g' | \
(while read acct homedir
do
   # echo checking home directory $homedir
   if [ ! -d $homedir ] ; then
     echo Warning: home directory $homedir for account $acct is missing
   fi
done )

exit 0
```

Although this might look considerably different from the previous version, a closer
glance will confirm that the only significant refinement to this version of the script
is that we're using surrounding parentheses around the test and output. The paren-
theses spawn a subshell that then has the output of the cut|sed command as its
standard input, so we can use the built-in read shell command.

```
$ sh checkhomes.sh
Warning: home directory /var/adm for account adm is missing
Warning: home directory /var/spool/news for account news is missing
Warning: home directory /var/spool/uucp for account uucp is missing
Warning: home directory /var/gopher for account gopher is missing
Warning: home directory /home/root for account taylorsu is missing
```

The output is definitely more user friendly!

> Solaris has a very nifty utility pwck that does a number of these /etc/passwd
> consistency checks. It's well worth knowing.

5

5. An equally important test is whether there's more than one UID 0 (root) account,
   and whether there are any accounts without a password.

   The first test can be done with a very simple awk invocation:

```
$ awk -F: '$3 == 0 { print $0 }' /etc/passwd
root:x:0:0:root:/root:/bin/bash
```

   The $3 == 0 is a conditional test: If it is true, then the entire line is printed.

> If you ever have a change in the number of accounts with UID 0, it's time
> to **IMMEDIATELY** investigate. Remember, anyone with UID 0 access can do
> anything they want, including replacing login with their own version that

> e-mails account/password pairs to an e-mail address surreptitiously, or
> worse!

The test to see whether there are any accounts without passwords is a bit more
tricky, because we need to check not only the /etc/passwd file, but also the
/etc/shadow file. The trick is that only root can access the /etc/shadow file in
the first place, so this command will have to be run by root:

```
# cat /etc/passwd /etc/shadow | awk -F: 'length($2) < 1 { print $0 }'
#
```

No output. Phew! What a relief!

To make this more interesting, however, I'll create a new account and omit the
password:

```
# cp /etc/passwd /etc/passwd.save
# echo "taylorsu::0:502:Dave as Superuser:/home/root:/bin/bash" >>
➥/etc/passwd
```

> The >> is a *very* dangerous command, so either don't do it at all, or do it
> very, very carefully. If you were to accidentally use > instead of >>, for exam-
> ple, you'd have just deleted your entire /etc/passwd file, which could have
> catastrophic results! That's why you can see that I'm also saving a copy of
> the /etc/passwd file as /etc/passwd.save, just in case....

Now running the zero-password test is more interesting:

```
# cat /etc/passwd /etc/shadow | awk -F: 'length($2) < 1 { print $0 }'
taylorsu::0:502:Dave as Superuser:/home/root:/bin/bash
```

Got it! How about checking for more than one UID 0 account?

```
# awk -F: '$3 == 0 { print $0 }' /etc/passwd
root:x:0:0:root:/root:/bin/bash
taylorsu::0:502:Dave as Superuser:/home/root:/bin/bash
```

Good. That flagged it, too. To fix it, I'll use passwd to set the password for this
account, and we're done with this task.

There are a number of ways that the /etc/passwd file can be analyzed and tested in an
automated fashion, as we've seen in this first task. The most important thing isn't to
come up with super-fancy analysis tools, but to do some sort of analysis frequently. If
someone hacks into your system, they're not going to wave a flag or send you an e-mail
message, so your vigilance with the accounts in the /etc/passwd file is critical!

Password Files in BSD/Mac OS X

Darwin has a completely different approach to managing user accounts. For single-user mode, the standby /etc/passwd is available, but in normal multiuser mode, the system uses a considerably more sophisticated (and very complex) system called NetInfo.

Task 5.2: Accounts and the Password File in Darwin

▼ TASK

In addition to the standard Unix /etc/passwd file, BSD also works with a system called NetInfo, which has both an attractive graphical interface and a crude but powerful command-line interface available.

1. A simple glance at /etc/passwd shows just how different things are. Notice that I'm logged in as taylor, but that my account information doesn't even show up here!

```
$ who am i
taylor    ttyp1      Jan  9 12:29
$ cat /etc/passwd
##
# User Database
#
# Note that this file is consulted when the system is running in single-
user
# mode.  At other times this information is handled by lookupd.  By
default,
# lookupd gets information from NetInfo, so this file will not be consulted
# unless you have changed lookupd's configuration.
##
nobody:*:-2:-2:Unprivileged User:/nohome:/noshell
root:*:0:0:System Administrator:/var/root:/bin/tcsh
daemon:*:1:1:System Services:/var/root:/noshell
www:*:70:70:World Wide Web Server:/Library/WebServer:/noshell
unknown:*:99:99:Unknown User:/nohome:/noshell
```

As the comment indicates, most user account information is stored in the cryptic NetInfo database, and can most easily be accessed from the graphical NetInfo application within the world of Mac OS X.

2. There are a number of different command line utilities for NetInfo too, fortunately:

```
$ man -k netinfo
netinfo(3)         - library routines for NetInfo calls
netinfo(5)         - network administrative information
netinfod(8)        - NetInfo daemon
nibindd(8)         - NetInfo binder
nicl(1)            - NetInfo command line utility
nidomain(8)        - NetInfo domain utility
nidump(8)          - extract text or flat-file-format data from NetInfo
nifind(1)          - find a directory in the NetInfo hierarchy
```

5

```
nigrep(1)          - search for a regular expression in the NetInfo
▸hierarchy
niload(8)          - load text or flat-file-format data into NetInfo
nireport(1)        - print tables from the NetInfo hierarchy
niutil(1)          - NetInfo utility
```

To see the full NetInfo database, the proper command is `nidump`:

```
$ nidump passwd .
nobody:*:-2:-2::0:0:Unprivileged User:/dev/null:/dev/null
root:c8bkMtK6Wlth2:0:0::0:0:System Administrator:/var/root:/bin/tcsh
daemon:*:1:1::0:0:System Services:/var/root:/dev/null
unknown:*:99:99::0:0:Unknown User:/dev/null:/dev/null
www:*:70:70::0:0:World Wide Web Server:/Library/WebServer:/dev/null
taylor:fse2juv3k6JiE:501:20::0:0:Dave Taylor:/Users/taylor:/bin/tcsh
```

You can see that it's similar to the `/etc/passwd` file, with the exception of the `tay-lor` account. A closer look will reveal that there are more information fields listed than are in `/etc/passwd`.

> Note that `nidump` is a user-level command, and that it shows encrypted password strings rather than just a placeholder, while hiding the actual encrypted password in a shadow file. A potential security consideration, if you're paranoid about guest users!

3. The `nidump` command lists all the entries in the `/etc/passwd` file along with all the additional accounts set up in the NetInfo database, so modifying the earlier tests and scripts isn't too difficult. Every time we simply had `"/etc/passwd"` referenced, we'll instead need to stream in the output of `nidump`, and we'll have to modify the field count to compensate for the additional information output:

```
# nidump passwd . | cut -d: -f10 | sort | uniq -c | sort -rn
   4 /dev/null
   3 /bin/tcsh
```

However, there's a much more sophisticated way to work with NetInfo: the `nireport` command. This way of accessing the NetInfo information requires that you know the names of the fields in the `users` area of the NetInfo database. They are summarized in Table 5.1.

TABLE 5.1   NetInfo `/users` Property Names

Property Name	Explanation
name	The login name of the user
passwd	The encrypted password of the user

▼ **TABLE 5.1** continued

Property Name	Explanation
uid	The user ID of the user
gid	The default group ID of the user
realname	The real name of the user
home	The home directory of the user
shell	The login shell of the user

To see this in action, here's how I could extract a report that lists the account names and password strings:

```
$ nireport . /users name passwd
nobody  *
root    c8bkMtK6Elth9
daemon  *
unknown *
www     *
taylor  fse2juv5k6JiA
```

You can see that four of these accounts (the ones with the /dev/null login shell, as reported earlier) have login capability disabled, while two have explicit encrypted passwords.

4. To make this more interesting, I created a UID 0 account with no password called badguy, appropriately enough. I can't just append the information to the /etc/passwd file this time, however; I need to use a script called niadduser to add the information to the NetInfo database. (We'll develop this script a bit later in this hour.)

   With this new account in place, let's see how nireport can be combined with some regular Unix utilities to create some useful analysis filters:

```
$ nireport . /users name uid | awk '$2 == 0 { print $0 }'
root    0
badguy  0
```

   That reports that there are two accounts that have UID=0.

   The test for missing passwords is a bit more subtle:

```
$ nireport . /users name passwd | awk 'NF==1 { print $0 }'
badguy
```

   In this instance, the variable NF is the *number of fields*, so the awk test is, in essence, "if there's only one field in the output line."

5. Finally, before we leave, let's change the password for the badguy account, to ensure we don't leave this gaping security hole!

▼
```
$ passwd badguy
Changing password for badguy.
New password:
Retype new password:
$ nireport . /users name passwd | grep badguy
badguy  Hk4IS.3eeh69.
```
▲   Looks like things are safe again!

In some sense, NetInfo is a great application, managing the various databases that comprise the Unix system world, including printers, Internet services, user accounts, and network connections. It also has a venerable pedigree, coming from the Network Information Service (NIS) and Yellow Pages (YP) services originally developed by Sun Microsystems. (More in a minute about those services.)

However, NetInfo is also a bit of an oddball in the Unix world. Not only is it not a part of the popular Linux distributions, it's also not included in any of the major commercial Unix distributions either (other than Mac OS X). NetInfo is therefore very incompatible and platform- and version-specific.

Ordinarily, I'd recommend that you shy away from using the utility for just this reason, but if you're running Darwin or another NIS/YP-enabled (NetInfo) Unix system, you *must* go through the NetInfo facility or your changes will be ignored. As an example, the /etc/passwd file on the test Darwin platform includes the following few lines at its end:

```
$ tail -3 /etc/passwd
www:*:70:70:World Wide Web Server:/Library/WebServer:/noshell
unknown:*:99:99:Unknown User:/nohome:/noshell
testme::0:0:Unknown Root User:/var/root:/bin/tcsh
```

Yet you'll notice that the testme account never showed up in the NetInfo listings if you flip back and look. That's because it was added to the password file, but not to the NetInfo database.

Adding Users and the adduser Script

Putting Darwin, BSD, and the NetInfo weirdness aside for a bit, let's breathe some fresh air and go back to "regular Unix" (whatever *that* means!), okay?

There are a couple of steps required for creating a new user account, more than just creating a new entry in the /etc/passwd file. These steps are as follows:

1. Add the user to the /etc/passwd file.
2. Add the user to the /etc/group file.
3. Create their home directory.

4. Optionally copy default `.profile`/`.login` files.

5. Ensure that the directory and its contents are all owned by the new user.

6. Set their initial password to a known value.

A fair number of steps, which can all be done by hand, but why do that? Instead, let's build a script that will automate it all and add the user to the system in one simple step.

> There is an `adduser` command already built into both Solaris and Red Hat Linux 7.2, but as you work with multiple flavors of Unix, you'll find that `adduser` is not widely available, and that the syntax varies from system to system. A smarter solution is to understand what the command does and then duplicate it for your own needs. With your own script, you can fine-tune it for your preferred configuration and then move it from system to system as your administrative responsibilities expand. Many of the top sysadmins have an entire toolkit that they bring with them.

Task 5.3: Adding Users in a Conventional Unix World

▲ TASK

If you're using a standard Unix system, adding a user is a straightforward sequence of adding them to the password file and the group file, then creating a home directory and setting an initial password.

1. To start out, we'll need to collect the information from the sysadmin before we can begin to build the account. This is most easily done with the `read` function built into the shell. Here's a demonstration of how it can work:

```
echo "Add new user account to `hostname`"
echo -n "login: "      ; read login
echo -n "uid: "        ; read uid
echo -n "gid: "        ; read gid
echo -n "full name: "  ; read fullname
echo -n "home dir: "   ; read homedir
echo -n "shell: "      ; read shell

echo "Setting up account:"
echo "    " ${login}:x:${uid}:${gid}:${fullname}:${homedir}:${shell}
```

As practice, if you run this script, you can see how it simplifies collecting the necessary data and emitting an `/etc/passwd`-format line:

```
Add new user account to staging.intuitive.com
login: astaire
uid: 211
gid: 211
full name: Fred Astaire
```

5

▼
```
home dir: /home/astaire
shell: /bin/bash
Setting up account:
    astaire:x:211:211:Fred Astaire:/home/astaire:/bin/bash
```

That's the core functionality of the script. Now it's time to refine things....

2. To start, let's recognize that home directories are always in the same folder on a system, and that their name is always the same as the account name:

```
$homedir=$defaulthome/$account
```

Furthermore, it's difficult to prompt the admin for a UID without any further information. At the same time, by convention, UIDs go in ascending order in the /etc/passwd file, so if you were to automatically extract the last UID and increment it, you could use that as the default new UID:

```
currentUID="`tail -1 /etc/passwd | cut -d: -f3`"
newUID="`expr $currentUID + 1`"
```

The problem with this approach is that if for some reason the password file does *not* have the highest UID as the last line, you could get into significant trouble. Instead, a smarter approach is to use awk to extract the *highest* UID (plus one):

```
uid="`awk -F: '{ if (big < $3) big=$3 } END { print big + 1 }'
➥/etc/passwd`"
```

This is a very elegant and quite typical Unix solution.

> Many Unix sysadmins prefer to work with Perl rather than awk, but I still lean toward awk because I can be 100% certain it'll be included in the standard distribution of all Unixes, whereas some exclude Perl, letting users install it after the fact.

3. There are two approaches to assigning the default group, as we've already seen. Some sites give each user his own personal group by default, which is always the same value as the UID. Others have a standard group that all users are dropped into by default. These can be modeled in the code quite easily:

```
# if your site policy is for all users to get their own group
gid =$uid
# otherwise, add them to the default group
gid=$defaultgid
```

There's an additional tweak needed when we automatically modify the /etc/group file to include the new account, but we're getting ahead of ourselves!
▼

4. Here's our first full version of the script, including an additional test to ensure that only user root can run it:

```
$ cat adduser.sh
#!/bin/sh

# ADDUSER - add a new user to the system, including building their
#           home directory, copying in default config data, etc.

progname="`basename $0`"
pwfile="/etc/passwd"
gfile="/etc/group"
hdir="/home"

if [ "`whoami`" != "root" ] ; then
  echo "$progname: Error: You must be root to run this command."
  exit 0
fi

echo "Add new user account to `hostname`"
echo -n "login: "      ; read login

uid="`awk -F: '{ if (big < $3) big=$3 } END { print big + 1 }'
/etc/passwd`"
homedir=$hdir/$login

# we are giving each user their own group, so gid=uid
gid=$uid

echo -n "full name: " ; read fullname
echo -n "shell: "     ; read shell

echo "Ready to set up account:"
echo "   " ${login}:x:${uid}:${gid}:${fullname}:${homedir}:${shell}
exit 0
```

When it's run, there are only three fields required:

```
$ sh adduser.sh
Add new user account to staging.intuitive.com
login: testdude
full name: The Test Dude
shell: /bin/csh
Ready to set up account:
    testdude:x:503:503:The Test Dude:/home/testdude:/bin/csh
```

The next step is, obviously, to have the script start *doing things* rather than just demonstrating how to prompt for input! That can be done by adding the following lines:

```
echo ${login}:x:${uid}:${gid}:${fullname}:${homedir}:${shell} >> /etc/passwd
mkdir $homedir
```

▼
```
chmod 755 $homedir
chown $login $homedir
echo "Please enter a default initial password for $login now:"
passwd $login
```

In a small nutshell, those six lines accomplish almost all that the adduser command requires. In a bit, you'll see how we can deal with the shadow file issue. The only two steps missing are to manipulate the /etc/group file appropriately (which many adduser scripts skip), and copy across any default cshrc, login, or profile files.

5. Adding the new user in the /etc/group file is easy if each user gets her own group. It's accomplished with one line:

```
echo "${login}:x:${gid}:${login}" >> /etc/group
```

Where things get more difficult is if we're adding the new user to an existing group. Then we need to extract the group line from the /etc/group file, append the user name, then write it back to the file:

```
grep -v "${groupname}:" /etc/group > /tmp/group.tmp.$$
groupline="`grep "${groupname}:" /etc/group`"
echo "$groupline,$login" >> /tmp/group.tmp.$$
mv /tmp/group.tmp.$$ /etc/group
chmod 644 /etc/group
```

This no doubt looks odd, but we copy every line but the matching group line to a temp file; then set groupline to the matching line that's been extracted, append the new login, and then move the temp group file to the master group file and change its mode to our required default (644).

6. Finally, to copy default configuration files across, Linux includes the standard /etc/skel directory, which contains prototypical default files for new home directories:

```
$ ls -la /etc/skel
total 15
drwxr-xr-x    3 root     root         1024 Nov 21 14:48 ./
drwxr-xr-x   50 root     root         4096 Jan 10 06:12 ../
-rw-r--r--    1 root     root           24 Jul  9  2001 .bash_logout
-rw-r--r--    1 root     root          191 Jul  9  2001 .bash_profile
-rw-r--r--    1 root     root          124 Jul  9  2001 .bashrc
-rw-r--r--    1 root     root          820 Jul 30 03:03 .emacs
-rw-r--r--    1 root     root          118 Aug  9 17:15 .gtkrc
drwxr-xr-x    3 root     root         1024 Nov 21 14:40 .kde/
-rw-r--r--    1 root     root         3511 Aug  3 09:53 .screenrc
```

Because there's a subdirectory (for KDE, the K Desktop Environment) we'll want
▼   to use the -R flag to cp when we copy these files across.

▼   Now, with all that, here's the complete second half of the script, built with the
     assumption that every user gets his own group.

```
echo "Setting up account $login for $fullname..."

echo "${login}:x:${uid}:${gid}:${fullname}:${homedir}:$shell" >> /etc/passwd
echo "${login}:*:11647:0:99999:7:::" >> /etc/shadow

echo "${login}:x:${gid}:$login" >> /etc/group
#uncomment below if your system is using group shadow files too
#echo "${login}:!::" >> /etc/gshadow

mkdir $homedir
cp -R /etc/skel/.[a-zA-Z]* $homedir
chmod 755 $homedir
find $homedir -print | xargs chown $login

echo "Please enter a default initial password for $login now:"
passwd $login

exit 0
```

Notice that because this version of Unix is working with shadow password files,
we need to include new entries for the account in /etc/shadow, and for the group
in /etc/gshadow.

> Solaris doesn't use the gshadow file. Instead the encrypted passwords for
> groups are saved in the /etc/group file regardless of whether shadow pass-
> words are enabled on the system overall.

5

```
# sh adduser.sh
Add new user account to staging.intuitive.com
login: testdude
full name: The Test Dude
shell: /bin/bash
Setting up account testdude for The Test Dude...
Please enter a default initial password for testdude now:
Changing password for user testdude
New password:
Retype new password:
passwd: all authentication tokens updated successfully
```

     That's all that's required. Simple, succinct, and the resultant account is ready to go
▲   with default files from /etc/skel and everything.

This has been a long and involved script that has demonstrated a variety of sophisticated shell script techniques. It also is written in a completely portable fashion, can be run easily on any system that supports shadow passwords, and, with a few small tweaks, even on systems that don't have /etc/shadow enabled.

To have the adduser script work with an NIS-compatible system like Solaris, I'd recommend making the adduser script a front end to the built-in useradd utility. Darwin, with NetInfo, is a proverbial horse of a different color, as the next section will succinctly detail.

Adding Users in a NetInfo World

The earlier shell script for adding users directly manipulated the /etc/passwd file, but as was demonstrated earlier, systems running NetInfo or another NIS descendant require new users to be added to the NIS database. This sounds harder than it is, though, because that's exactly what the niutil command does.

Task 5.4: The Darwin Version of adduser

The world of NetInfo not only changes how we need to examine the user account data, but also forces significant changes on how new accounts are created. That's the bad news. The good news is that Darwin includes a variety of different command-line NetInfo utilities, most notably including the general purpose niutil.

There are two modes to niutil that we're interested in for this task: -create specifies that a new entry should be made in the database, then -createprop adds specific properties and assigns the specified values within the specified record.

1. To start out, we'll have to recode the section that calculates the highest UID in use. To do this, we'll use nireport and sort -n:

   ```
   uid1="`nireport . /users uid | sort -n | tail -1`"
   uid="`expr $uid1 + 1`"
   ```

   The next step is to actually create a new user account record. This can be done with niutil, using the -create option:

   ```
   niutil -create . /users/$login
   ```

2. Each individual property of the user record must be defined and have a value assigned to it. It's a bit more work than a single line output to /etc/passwd:

   ```
   niutil -createprop . /users/$login passwd
   niutil -createprop . /users/$login uid $uid
   niutil -createprop . /users/$login gid $gid
   niutil -createprop . /users/$login realname "$fullname"
   niutil -createprop . /users/$login shell $shell
   niutil -createprop . /users/$login home $homedir
   ```

▼ There shouldn't be any surprises in the name/value pairs but it's worth highlighting that `fullname` is the only variable that might have spaces, hence the quotes in the script.

3. For the Darwin version of the script, we're also going to add all users to the `hometeam` group rather than give them each unique groups. This is done by using the `niutil` command to modify the field `users` for the specified group:

```
niutil -appendprop . /groups/hometeam users $login
```

Other than those changes, the rest of the script is identical to the Linux version.

Here's the entire Darwin `adduser` script:

```
#!/bin/sh

# ADDUSER - add a new user to the system, including building their
#           home directory, copying in default config data, etc.

progname="`basename $0`"
dgroup="hometeam"
dgid=101
hdir="/Users"

if [ "`whoami`" != "root" ] ; then
  echo "$progname: Error: You must be root to run this command."
  # exit 0
fi

echo "Add new user account to `hostname`"
echo -n "login: "     ; read login

uid1="`nireport . /users uid | sort -n | tail -1`"
uid="`expr $uid1 + 1`"
homedir=$hdir/$login

# we are putting all users into the "$dgroup" group, which has a fixed GID
gid=$dgid

echo -n "full name: " ; read fullname
echo -n "shell: "     ; read shell

echo "Setting up account $login for $fullname..."

niutil -create     . /users/$login
niutil -createprop . /users/$login passwd
niutil -createprop . /users/$login uid $uid
niutil -createprop . /users/$login gid $gid
niutil -createprop . /users/$login realname "$fullname"
niutil -createprop . /users/$login shell $shell
niutil -createprop . /users/$login home $homedir
```

5

▼
```
niutil -createprop . /users/$login _shadow_passwd ""

# adding them to the $dgroup group...
niutil -appendprop . /groups/$dgroup users $login

mkdir $homedir

if [ -d /etc/skel ] ; then
  cp -R /etc/skel/.[a-zA-Z]* $homedir
fi

chmod 755 $homedir
find $homedir -print | xargs chown $login

echo "Please enter a default initial password for $login now:"
passwd $login

exit 0
```

4. Let's test it out by creating an account!

```
$ adduser
adduser: Error: You must be root to run this command.
```

Oops! Use the su command to switch to root (you'll need to enter your adminis-trative password) and try again:

```
# adduser
Add new user account to dsl-132.dsldesigns.com
login: tintin
full name: Tintin, Boy Reporter
shell: /bin/tcsh
Setting up account tintin for Tintin, Boy Reporter...
Please enter a default initial password for tintin now:
Changing password for tintin.
New password:
Retype new password:
```

And verify its existence and proper creation:

```
# nireport . /users name realname
nobody   Unprivileged User
root     System Administrator
daemon   System Services
unknown  Unknown User
www      World Wide Web Server
taylor   Dave Taylor
badguy   Test Account
tintin   Tintin, Boy Reporter
```

▲   Welcome to the world of Darwin, Mr. Tintin! All looks good.

Many systems include some sort of utility for adding new users, but as a system administrator, you never really know exactly what they're doing, and what is or isn't accomplished by the application. Further, some Unixes do half the job: The best `adduser` utility available for Darwin I could find neglected to add the user to any group.

Summary

This has been the first hour that has focused more on common daily system administration tasks. Whether you're learning more about how to work with your own personal Unix box, or whether you're responsible for an entire computing facility, managing user accounts is something you can't avoid.

Fortunately, building your own custom utilities lets you subsequently hide the oddities, peculiarities, and quirks of each Unix system; then you're done forever. That's one of the greatest reasons to build your own tools in my opinion: If you learn all the Red Hat Linux account management tools, for example, that's not going to help you one iota if you suddenly find yourself managing an HP-UX or AIX system.

We'll explore this topic in greater detail as we proceed throughout the lessons in this book.

Q&A

Q Can you add new users such that the first time they log in, they're forced to pick a password, rather than you choosing a password for them and having to write it down for them?

A Yes. Most Unix systems support either password aging or a similar mechanism. This is an important concept that's covered in greater detail in the next hour.

Q Isn't having the `/etc/passwd` file readable to anyone logged in a bit of a security risk?

A Well, yes and no. It's risky because someone can get a lot of information about user accounts by reading it (home directories, valid login names, and so on), but it's just about impossible to hide this information and still be running Unix. Whether it's the output of `ls  /home` or the results of typing **who**, it's very hard to completely hide the password and account information from curious eyes.

Q Why would I ever have more than one UID 0 account on my system?

A While at first it might seem kinda wacky, I have always been a proponent of each administrator having a different UID 0 login account. I'd be set up as `taylorsu` (su for super user), for example. The advantage of this approach is that you can more easily manage access for these admins. If you have three UID 0 admins, for example, and one no longer needs access, it's considerably easier (and safer) to delete the account than to constantly be changing the root password on a system.

Workshop

Quiz

1. There are a variety of additions to the adduser command that would improve it, not the least of which is checking to see whether the specified account name already exists in the database. How would you do that?

2. Jump onto the Web for this question: Go to Google (www.google.com) and see if you can find a program that advertises its capability to crack encrypted password strings, or even an entire /etc/passwd file.

3. Throughout the last hour or two we've used basename. Use the man system to ascertain what it actually does.

Answers

1. To ensure you're not creating two accounts with the same name, immediately after the prompt for the account name grep for that account name in the password file. This can be done with

   ```
   egrep '^${account}:' /etc/passwd
   ```

   though you'd want to capture the output and analyze the results in a conditional test of some sort.

2. I hopped onto Google and used the following search string:

   ```
   +UNIX +password +cracker +download
   ```

   (The + forces Google to ensure that all the words appear in each match it presents.) It returned more than 9,000 matches. More interestingly, Google also has some categorization of a subset of their enormous database, and a link to Computers -> Security -> Unix -> Exploit Software shows up on the results page, too. That proves the best area to explore, and it's distressingly easy to find a half dozen programs available for download that promise to crack Unix-encrypted passwords[1].

---

[1]*It's worth noting that none of these programs really crack any passwords. The encryption used for Unix passwords is one-way: You can encode it, but you can't decode it. The programs work by guessing a password, encrypting it, and then comparing that encryption key to the encrypted password itself. If they match, it's "cracked" the password. A good reason for picking weird and impossible-to-guess passwords, if you ask me!*

3. The useful `basename` command strips all the directory information from a fully qualified filename. If you specify `basename /usr/sbin/bash`, it'll return `bash`.

The next hour will add to your sysadmin toolbox by creating suspend and delete user account commands. It will also more closely examine the `passwd` command and the `/etc/shadow` file, and explore password aging and acceptable use policies for organizations.

5

HOUR **6**

Account Management

The last hour explored the steps involved in adding a new user to a Unix system, whether through NetInfo or with additions to /etc/passwd and /etc/shadow. This hour will present the additional tools needed for complete account management, tools that will let you suspend user accounts and delete them.

Additionally, if you are running with shadow passwords, there are some interesting techniques you can use to enable password aging on your Unix system.

In this hour you will learn about

- Suspending user accounts
- Deleting user accounts
- Linux account management tools
- Solaris account management tools
- Password aging

Ways to Suspend User Accounts

There are three basic account management tasks that you'll perform frequently: account creation, account suspension, and account deletion.

Creating new accounts can be done with the handy but rather long adduser script we've already built in the previous hour. Fortunately, suspending and deleting accounts are quite a bit easier.

Task 6.1: Suspending Users

Perhaps your company works with contractors who come and go as projects demand. Or perhaps your school likes to suspend student accounts during breaks to ensure that they really take time off and not get obsessed with modern technology. Then again, the police might have just served a subpoena and you are required to lock down an account to avoid anything changing. Whatever the reason, it's helpful to know the super-simple trick for suspending user accounts—change the password.

> To suspend a user account in case of an emergency, simply change the password!

A smart way to either suspend or remove an account starts by ensuring that the user isn't actually logged in. If he is logged in, you'll probably need to immediately kick him out. Change the user's password first, though, or he'll just log in again.

1. The first step on any suspension or deletion is to change the account password. That's easily done with passwd. For ease of use, I always just enter my own account password: No one knows it, I'm very used to typing it in, and it's just about impossible to guess or crack.

   Then it's time to check whether the user is logged in, and log him out if necessary. If he's logged in, the process ID of his login shell must be obtained, and that can be done with the ps processor status command:

   ```
   # ps -jU testdude
     PID  PGID   SID TTY          TIME CMD
   11259 11259 11259 pts/1     00:00:00 bash
   11380 11380 11259 pts/1     00:00:00 vi
   ```

   You can see that testdude is running a vi session. Probably not good.

2. To log him out, you want to extract the session ID (or, in BSD terms, the parent process ID, or PPID) and use it as an argument to the kill command. If the script has been called with the account name as its argument ($1), then

```
if [ "`who | grep $1`" != "" ] ; then
   sid="`ps -jU $1 | awk '{print $3}' | tail -1`"
   kill -HUP $sid
   echo "$1 was logged in. Just logged $1 out."
fi
```

If you force the logout of a user while he's logged in, be prepared for an emotional response! A better way to code this is to have the script warn him, then give him a few seconds to promptly exit his apps before being booted off.

To send a message to a user on the system, there's a faster solution than sending e-mail that might be ignored: Write information directly to the user's terminal device. Consider the second field in the output of the who command:

```
$ who
taylor     pts/0     Jan 14 05:09 (dsl-132.dsldesigns.com)
testdude   pts/1     Jan 14 05:11 (dsl-132.dsldesigns.com)
```

That's the terminal device address if you preface it with /dev/ (so testdude is logged in to /dev/pts/1). Obtain that information and you can write a message to the user's screen directly (then sleep $secs seconds):

```
tty="`who | grep $1 | tail -1 | awk '{print $2}'`"
cat << "EOF" > /dev/$tty

*************************************************************
URGENT NOTICE FROM THE ADMINISTRATOR:

This account is being suspended by the request of management.
You are going to be logged out in $secs seconds. Please
shut down any processes you have running immediately.

If you have any questions, please contact your supervisor or
Jane Mansmith, director of corporate computing.
*************************************************************
EOF
   echo "(Warned $1, now sleeping $secs seconds)"
   sleep $secs
```

Another step I like to take when suspending accounts is to close off the user's home directory. This is also easy:

```
chmod 000 $homedir/$1
```

3. In total, and with some useful comments added, the suspend script looks like this:

```
#!/bin/sh

## Suspend - suspend a user account for the indefinite future

secs=10 # seconds before user is logged out (if logged in)
homedir="/home"   # home directory for all users
```

```
if [ "$1" = "" ] ; then
   echo Usage: `basename $0` account
   exit 0
fi
if [ "`whoami`" != "root" ] ; then
   echo `basename $0`: Error. You must be 'root' to run this command.
   exit 0
fi

passwd $1

# Now, let's see if they're logged in, and if so, boot 'em

if [ "`who | grep $1`" != "" ] ; then

  tty="`who | grep $1 | tail -1 | awk '{print $2}'`"

  cat << "EOF" > /dev/$tty

*****************************************************************
URGENT NOTICE FROM THE ADMINISTRATOR:

This account is being suspended by the request of management.
You are going to be logged out in $secs seconds. Please shut down
any processes you have running immediately.

If you have any questions, please contact your supervisor or
Jane Mansmith, director of information technology.
*****************************************************************
EOF

  echo "(Warned $1, now sleeping $secs seconds)"

  sleep $secs

  sid="`ps -jU $1 | awk '{print $3}' | tail -1`"
  kill -HUP $sid
  echo "$1 was logged in. Just logged $1 out."
fi

# Finally, let's close off their home directory from prying eyes:

chmod 000 $homedir/$1

echo "Account $1 has been suspended."

exit 0
```

4. When we're ready to shut testdude out of his account, it's now easy:

```
$ suspend testdude
Changing password for user testdude
```

```
New password:
Retype new password:
passwd: all authentication tokens updated successfully
(Warned testdude, now sleeping 10 seconds)
testdude was logged in. Just logged testdude out.
Account testdude has been suspended.
```

The user `testdude` would have seen the following pop up on his screen:

```
*************************************************************
URGENT NOTICE FROM THE ADMINISTRATOR:

This account is being suspended by the request of management.
You are going to be logged out in 10 seconds. Please shut down
any processes you have running immediately.

If you have any questions, please contact your supervisor or
Jane Mansmith, director of information technology.
*************************************************************
```

And, sure enough, ten seconds later `testdude` would be logged out and unable to log back in.

> Compatibility-wise, the third field of the `ps` output on BSD systems is the parent process ID (PPID) rather than the session ID. The good news is that it'll work just as well for this task, so the script works across platforms, with but one small change necessary: `homedir` must be defined as appropriate for each server.

4. To re-enable an account after you've suspended it is sufficiently straightforward enough that I'll just show you the snippet of the shell script (unsuspend) that does the work:

```
passwd $1               # change their password back to a known value
chmod 750 $homedir/$1   # and open their home directory back up
```

There are other ways to suspend accounts on some Unix systems that are worth mentioning. If you're running Linux, for example, there's usermod, which lets root change the status of a user account. With the -L flag, it locks the account, disabling the password by prefacing the encrypted password string with a !, and with -U it removes that ! and enables the account again.

Solaris uses the passwd command to enable suspension: passwd -l acct will lock the specified account (specifying a new password with the standard passwd acct will unlock the account again).

6

On BSD systems, it's a bit more tricky, because there isn't a command as accessible as usermod by default. That's why it's easier just to change the user's password to something else, as shown in the script.

Deleting User Accounts

Suspending accounts is helpful, but often you'll need to completely remove the account from the system, including deleting all the files. Another relatively simple task, but if you want to do everything properly, you might find that there are more nuances than initially expected.

Task 6.2: Deleting User Accounts

▼ TASK

The most important step in deleting a user account is to remove the entry from the /etc/passwd file. With that done, the user ceases to exist as far as the Unix system is concerned. However, the user still has files in the system, a home directory, and perhaps also e-mail coming into the system and more. But let's take one step at a time.

1. It's time to delete accounts once the word has come down that the person no longer needs, and will never again need, access to the system. This is most easily done by deleting the user's entry from the /etc/passwd file (or the NetInfo database), then using the dangerous '-rf' flags to the rm command to force a recursive deletion of all files and folders within the user's home directory.

   Deleting a line from the password file is superficially easy within a script:
   ```
   grep -vE "^${1}:" /etc/passwd > /tmp/newpasswd
   mv /tmp/newpasswd /etc/passwd
   chmod 655 /etc/passwd
   ```

The problem with this solution is that you need to prevent any other system administrator from touching or changing the /etc/passwd file while you're doing this. In Unix terms, it's called *locking the file*, and there's no easy solution to this dilemma overall.

On some Unix systems—including RHL7.2—there's a user-level command lockfile, but although it will help you ensure that two accounts aren't deleted at the same time, it only works for scripts that you've written. The danger, however, is with all the other commands that might alter the file (including the passwd command on a non-shadow password system).

A better solution is to use vipw, a special file-locking version front end to vi that locks the password file, lets you edit it, then unlocks it when done. Fortunately, vipw is available on Red Hat Linux, Solaris, and Darwin.

▼

2. The second step required is to remove the user's home directory and all its contents within a script, assuming that $1 is the user's account name:

```
rm -rf $homedir/$1
```

There's a nuance to this, however, because the user might very well have files elsewhere on the system.

3. Finding these stray files is a job for the find command, which will search throughout the file system for any remaining files or directories that are owned by the user. For example:

```
$ find / -uid 501 -print
/var/spool/mail/mdella
```

In this case, you can see that though you've stripped all the files in the /home directory, there was still an e-mail mailbox lingering in the spool directory.

One ramification of adding this check for files outside the user's home directory is that you need to grab the UID of the account before deleting it. This is done with the line

```
uid="`egrep "^${1}:" /etc/passwd | cut -d: -f3`"
```

4. Here's the full script with the exception of stripping the account information out of shadow files. Notice that the first step is to call the suspend script to ensure that the user can't log in and is logged out if needed. No reason to duplicate that code here!

```
#!/bin/sh

## Delete - delete a user account without a trace...

homedir="/home"

if [ "$1" = "" ] ; then
  echo Usage: `basename $0` account; exit 0
fi
if [ "`whoami`" != "root" ] ; then
  echo `basename $0`: Error. You must be 'root' to run this command.
  exit 0
fi

suspend $1     # suspend their account while we do the dirty work

uid="`egrep "^${1}:" /etc/passwd | cut -d: -f3`"

egrep -v "^${1}:" /etc/passwd > /tmp/newpasswd
mv /tmp/newpasswd /etc/passwd
chmod 655 /etc/passwd

rm -rf $homedir/$1
```

6

```
echo "Files still left to remove (if any):"
find / -uid $uid -print

echo "Account $1 (uid $uid) has been deleted, and their /home "
echo "directory has been removed."
exit 0
```

5. Upon reflection, however, it seems smarter to move the user's /home directory to a different, temporary staging area, just in case a request comes the next day for some of the files. To do this, replace the rm -rf call with

   ```
   mv $homedir/$1 $holdingarea
   ```

   The variable $holdingarea should be somewhere secure, with minimal access. A good location would be /home/root/pending_deletion or someplace similar.

6. The Darwin version of deleteuser is a bit different, because instead of extracting the line from the /etc/passwd file, you can use the much safer niutil command:

   ```
   niutil -destroy . /users/$1
   ```

   One significant advantage to the Darwin version is that there's no worry about the potential danger from not using a file locking protocol—NetInfo itself automatically ensures that commands don't step on each other.

It would be wise to include a test in the deleteuser script to flag and refuse to delete the root account. If you accidentally deleted that account, the results would be very bad. It's recoverable (boot in single-user mode and fix the password file or NetInfo database), but very, very bad.

Deleting accounts proves to be more than just deleting a line from the /etc/passwd file. Indeed, there's an additional step necessary for a deleted account that we won't address until Hour 18, "Running Your Own Name Server"—setting up an automatic e-mail response informing people that the user is no longer accessible through this system.

Rather than fall too far into the trap of the "not invented here syndrome," however, let's spend the rest of this hour looking at some of the platform-specific account management tools available in Linux, Solaris, and Darwin.

Linux Account Management Tools

Lurking under the hood of the simple passwd command in Linux (and Solaris, for that matter) is a powerful set of options that can significantly simplify your administrative tasks. They're different on each platform, alas, but if you're in a relatively homogeneous environment (or just managing a single Unix system), a thorough knowledge of these options will prove to be a great boon.

There are other administrative commands, too, so let's examine them all while we're here.

Task 6.3: Linux Admin Tools

Based on the material discussed last hour and earlier in this hour, you might think that there aren't any tools available to help you administer user accounts in any of the flavors of Unix available. That would be wrong. As indicated earlier, the problem isn't that there aren't any tools, the problem is that there are too many different tools and nothing that exists—in the same form—across all the major platforms.

As a case in point, if you're running on a Linux system, you can add users with the `useradd` command, a program that seems to offer much of the power of the shell script developer earlier. Indeed, here's the synopsis of the command from the Linux man pages:

```
SYNOPSIS
        useradd [-c comment] [-d home_dir]
                [-e expire_date] [-f inactive_time]
                [-g initial_group] [-G group[,...]]
                [-m [-k skeleton_dir] | -M] [-p passwd]
                [-s shell] [-u uid [ -o]] [-n] [-r] login
```

That's all well and good, but without being able to see what's going on inside, it's impossible to know what's really happening. How does the program pick the UID, and will it work if you have a password file where entries aren't in ascending numeric order? Nonetheless, there are built-in commands that are worth exploring if you only have to worry about Linux boxes, or if you have the luxury of being able to learn the nuances of each Unix flavor you manage.

The most useful of the built-in account management commands is `passwd`. Let's have a look.

1. The first stop is always the man page, where it'll no doubt surprise you to learn how many options there are. The command synopsis is

   `passwd [-k] [-l] [-u [-f]] [-d] [-S] [username]`

   The meanings of these flags are summarized in Table 6.1.

TABLE 6.1 Command Flags for Linux `passwd`

Flag	Meaning
-k	Update should only apply to expired authentication tokens (relevant only if you're running Kerberos or another token-generating authorization system. For a vanilla Linux, this won't have any effect).

▼

TABLE 6.1 continued

Flag	Meaning
-l	Lock the specified account out by prefacing the encrypted password string with a ! character, thereby making it impossible for the user to match. Note that this method of suspending an account would still allow the user to have previously set her home directory permission to be world-readable, and therefore accessible from another account. The partner option is -u.
-u	This unlocks the specified account by stripping out the ! prefix from the encrypted password string. The partner to -l.
-f	By default, passwd won't let you unlock an account if the ! is the only character in the encrypted password string, because unlocking it would then leave the account without a password. If you know what you're doing and really want to do this anyway, add the -f flag to force the unlocking of the account.
-d	Disables the password protection for an account. I'm not sure why you'd ever want to use this, but passwd -d testdude will instantly strip out the password from the testdude account and let anyone log in.
-S	Shows the status of an account. Lists the password status of a specific account.

Many of these options are very helpful shortcuts, particularly if you haven't already typed in the suspend script discussed earlier in this hour.

The -S summary is interesting:

```
# passwd -S taylor
Changing password for user taylor
Password set, MD5 encryption
```

The output is a bit awkward, however, because the Changing password line shouldn't be output. No worries; we're in Unix, so you can modify the output! Let's wrap this command in a loop and see the status of some the accounts on the system.

```
# for name in `cut -d: -f1 /etc/passwd`
> do
>   echo Status of account $name is `passwd -S $name|tail -1`
> done
Status of account root is Password set, MD5 encryption
Status of account bin is No Password set.
Status of account daemon is No Password set.
Status of account adm is No Password set.
Status of account lp is No Password set.
Status of account sync is No Password set.
```

▼ *... lots of output removed ...*

▼
```
Status of account apache is Locked password.
Status of account squid is Locked password.
Status of account named is Locked password.
Status of account pcap is Locked password.
Status of account mthorne is Locked password.
Status of account mdella is Password set, MD5 encryption
Status of account taylor is Password set, MD5 encryption
Status of account taylorsu is Password set, MD5 encryption
Status of account testdude is Empty password.
```

Lots of output, but the important thing is to be aware of any account that's similar to operator or ftp where the status is No Password set. In fact, screening all the Locked password lines (which should be the state of all admin daemons) will make this output considerably clearer:

> Notice that when you type in a multiline command, the shell automatically recognizes the continuation and prompts you for subsequent lines with the > prompt. Very helpful!

```
# for name in `cut -d: -f1 /etc/passwd`
> do
>   echo Status of account $name is `passwd -S $name|tail -1` | grep
-v Locked
> done
Status of account root is Password set, MD5 encryption
Status of account bin is No Password set.
Status of account daemon is No Password set.
Status of account adm is No Password set.
Status of account lp is No Password set.
Status of account sync is No Password set.
Status of account shutdown is No Password set.
Status of account halt is No Password set.
Status of account mail is No Password set.
Status of account news is No Password set.
Status of account uucp is No Password set.
Status of account operator is No Password set.
Status of account games is No Password set.
Status of account gopher is No Password set.
Status of account ftp is No Password set.
Status of account nobody is No Password set,
Status of account mdella is Password set, MD5 encryption
Status of account taylor is Password set, MD5 encryption
Status of account taylorsu is Password set, MD5 encryption
```
▼
```
Status of account testdude is Empty password.
```

6

This is another output that would be very useful to monitor! In particular, notice that some accounts have no password set, and the testdude account has an empty password string (functionally the same as having no password set).

> Any account that doesn't have a password set is a security hole. If someone can get to you via telnet, for example, she could log in using any of the accounts that don't have a password. Fortunately most of them have /bin/nologin as their shell, but it's worth checking that very closely. And, needless to say, testdude needs to have a password!

2. The testdude account is the most glaring security problem here, so let's lock the account:

```
# passwd -l testdude
Changing password for user testdude
Locking password for user testdude
passwd: Success

# passwd -S testdude
Changing password for user testdude
Locked password.
```

Much better. When you try to unlock it, notice what happens:

```
# passwd -u testdude
Changing password for user testdude
Unlocking password for user testdude
Warning: unlocked password for testdude is the empty string.
Use the -f flag to force the creation of a passwordless account.
passwd: Unsafe operation
```

A very helpful warning and something that would cause a savvy sysadmin to sit up and take notice!

3. Before we leave this, let's create a quick script that checks to ensure that any account that's flagged as No Password set has a shell that prevents interactive use:

```
#!/bin/sh

# CHECKPW - Check the status of all accounts on the system, checking
#      to ensure that any account without a password has a shell that
#      prevents interactive use. Any others will be flagged in output.
```

```
# This only runs on Linux systems with the '-S' flag to 'passwd'

temp="/tmp/tocheck.$$"

trap "/bin/rm -f $temp" 0  # remove the file upon exit

for name in `cut -d: -f1 /etc/passwd`
do
  echo "$name" `passwd -S $name|tail -1` | \
    egrep -v "(Locked|encryption)" | awk '{print $1}'  >> $temp
done

for account in `cat $temp`
do
  shell="`egrep \"^${account}:\" /etc/passwd | cut -d: -f7`"
  if [ "$shell" != "/sbin/nologin" ] ; then
    echo "*** WARNING: Account $account has no password and login
shell $shell"
  fi
done

exit 0
```

Nothing too fancy in this script, but notice that we've had to resort to a temporary file for intermediate output. The results are quite helpful and could easily become part of a daily system status report:

```
# checkpw.sh
*** WARNING: Account sync has no password and login shell /bin/sync
*** WARNING: Account shutdown has no password and login shell
/sbin/shutdown
*** WARNING: Account halt has no password and login shell /sbin/halt
*** WARNING: Account news has no password and login shell
*** WARNING: Account testdude has no password and login shell /bin/bash
```

The shells sync, shutdown, and halt are indicative of shortcuts available at the login prompt. Type in **shutdown** as the account name and—remember that there's no password—the system will probably be shut down. You might want to disable those accounts if you don't think you'll ever need them.

In more than 20 years of working with Unix systems, most of which had these three administrative logins, I've never used them in this manner. I always shut these accounts off when I install a new system.

▼   When there's no shell listed, that means that the system will default (usually) to
         /bin/sh as the shell, so news is just as much a security risk as testdude. Both
         need to be closed, and

         passwd -l testdude

         does the trick for testdude, but locking the other accounts requires that an initial
         password be set. That can be done with passwd news . Then use the passwd -l
         news to lock it.

3. The final command worth viewing is the userdel command, the built-in Linux
    command to delete users. Scan the man page and you'll see that it's straightforward
    and useable, though it doesn't log the user out if she's logged in (instead, the com-
    mand fails), and it leaves you, the system administrator, on your own trying to fig-
    ure out how to identify what other files the user might have.

```
# man userdel
USERDEL(8)                                                        USERDEL(8)

NAME
       userdel - Delete a user account and related files

SYNOPSIS
       userdel [-r] login

DESCRIPTION
       The  userdel  command  modifies  the system account files,
       deleting all entries that refer to login.  The named  user
       must exist.

       -r      Files  in the user's home directory will be removed
               along with the home directory itself and the user's
               mail  spool.   Files  located in other file systems
               will have to be searched for and deleted  manually.

FILES
       /etc/passwd - user account information
       /etc/shadow - secure user account information
       /etc/group - group information
```

▲   A reasonable solution to the problem, but if you looked for an equivalent command
         in the Darwin/BSD world, you'd be stymied—there is no equivalent command in
         Darwin. Hence the script that we created earlier in this hour.

There are a lot of smart people who have contributed to the evolution and growth of Unix
over its 25+ year life. Many of them have been system administrators who have sought to
simplify their lives through the development of sophisticated tools. Unfortunately,
because of the erratic and chaotic development of the many different flavors of Unix, no
account administration tools have ended up as standard and common across all systems.

Indeed, the greatest challenge as a Unix system administrator isn't how to accomplish sysadmin tasks on a particular system, but rather how to do those tasks on *any system that you're responsible for maintaining*. It's the bane of all admin people, but an unpleasant fact of life: Installations are much more likely to be heterogeneous than homogeneous. That is, you're more likely to find that your data center has a legacy IBM AIX system, three Solaris servers, a dozen Linux servers, all but one of which is running Red Hat Linux, and a separate Darwin-based file and print server that doubles as the workstation for the department secretary. In that sort of environment, knowing that userdel is available on Red Hat Linux 7.2 isn't going to make your life that much easier, alas.

Indeed, there's no section in this hour entitled "The Darwin Account Management Tools" because, frankly, there are none, other than the rather primitive niutils or graphical NetInfo application.

Solaris Account Management Tools

Solaris is quite similar to Linux, fortunately. Well, let me rephrase this to better reflect the evolution of Unix: Linux has been inspired by many of the Solaris utilities. This means that the passwd command in Solaris includes a summary option and the capability to lock accounts, and that most of the scripts presented in the Linux section will work for Solaris.

However, it's not exactly the same, and that's a bit of a problem. For example, in Linux passwd -S taylor would show a summary of the password status for account taylor, but Solaris doesn't know the -S flag and instead uses -s for this function. And did I mention the output is different?

Task 6.4: Solaris Account Administration Tools

TASK

The differences between Solaris and Linux are more subtle nuances than dramatic variations with command-line account administration tools. It's no surprise, then, that the scripts already discussed just need minor tweaks to work within the Solaris world.

1. Adding a user can be done with the useradd command, though the syntax is a little different than the Linux command of the same name:

```
# man useradd | head -18
Maintenance Commands                                        useradd(1M)

NAME
        useradd - administer a new user login on the system

SYNOPSIS
        useradd [ -c comment  ]  [  -d dir  ]  [  -e expire  ]  [
```

6

```
     -f inactive  ]  [ -g group ]  [   -G group  [  ,  group ...   ]
     ]  [   -m   [ -k skel_dir ]   ]   [    -u uid   [  -o  ]   ]    [
     -s shell   ]  [ -A authorization  [ ,authorization... ]  ]  [
     -P profile  [ ,profile... ]  ]  [ -R role  [ ,role...  ]   ]
     login

     useradd -D  [ -b base_dir ]  [ -e expire ]  [ -f inactive  ]
     [ -g group ]
```

Sharp eyes will notice the addition of the -A, -P, and -R flags for authorizations, profiles, and roles, respectively. We don't have space to get into the Solaris security model, but if you're running a Solaris system, you'll find time spent reading the auth_attr(4), exec_attr(4), and user_attr(4) man pages very worthwhile.

> Standard Unix nomenclature with man page entries is to specify the command followed by the section in the man page database where that command can be found. So auth_attr(4) indicates that it's the auth_attr man page in section four (file formats). You would read this page with man 4 auth_attr at your command line.

2. The real difference in Solaris appears when you look at the passwd man page:

```
# man passwd
User Commands                                                passwd(1)

NAME
     passwd - change login password and password attributes

SYNOPSIS
     passwd [ -r files | -r ldap  | -r nis  | -r  nisplus ]  [
     name ]

     passwd [   -r files   ]  [ -egh ]  [ name ]

     passwd [   -r files   ]  -s  [ -a ]

     passwd [   -r files   ]  -s  [ name ]

     passwd [   -r files   ]  [ -d | -l ]  [ -f ]  [  -n min  ]   [
     -w warn ]  [ -x max ]  name

     passwd  -r  ldap  [ -egh ]  [ name ]

     passwd  -r  nis  [ -egh ]  [ name ]

     passwd  -r  nisplus  [ -egh ]  [ -D domainname ]  [ name ]
```

```
passwd   -r  nisplus  -s  [ -a ]

passwd   -r  nisplus  [ -D domainname ]  -s  [ name ]

passwd   -r  nisplus  [ -l ]  [ -f ]  [ -n min ]  [ -w warn ]
[ -x max ]  [ -D domainname ]  name
```

There are a bewildering number of different possible ways to work with the `passwd` command in Solaris, but if you're not running LDAP (Lightweight Directory Access Protocol), NIS (Network Information Service) or NIS+ (an improved NIS architecture), you can thankfully ignore them.

To clarify the differences, here's my own synopsis of the Solaris `passwd` command, minus all the confusing NIS stuff:

```
passwd [  -s  ]  [ -d | -l ]  [ -f ]  [  -n min  ]
       [ -w warn ]  [ -x max ]  name
```

Quite similar to Linux, but with two notable differences: The `-S` summary flag is now `-s`, and although there's a `-l` for locking accounts, notice that there isn't a `-u` to unlock them.

Indeed, to lock an account in Solaris, you can use the familiar `passwd –l` *account*, but to unlock an account there's no `-u` flag that resets the password to its original state (as there is in Linux). Instead, to unlock an account, simply set the password to a known value with `passwd` *account*.

3. The output of the `-s` summarize command is a bit more succinct:

```
# passwd -s taylor
taylor   PS
```

Checking the `man` page for `passwd` reveals that there are three possible values for this flag, as summarized in Table 6.2.

TABLE 6.2 Output States for the `passwd` Account Summary in Solaris

Value	Meaning
PS	Password set
NP	No password associated with this account
LK	Account is locked

Armed with this, let's use the `-a` (show all entries) flag in combination with the `-s` flag to analyze the different accounts on the Solaris system. First, here's the `passwd –sa` command in action:

```
# passwd -sa
root   PS
```

```
daemon  LK
bin  LK
sys  LK
adm  LK
lp  LK
uucp  LK
nuucp  LK
listen  LK
nobody  LK
noaccess  LK
nobody4  LK
taylor  PS
testtdude  LK
testdude  NP
```

Notice that these are shown in the order that they're listed in the /etc/passwd file.

Screening out the locked accounts is simple:

```
# passwd -sa | grep -v LK
root  PS
taylor  PS
testdude  NP
```

It's not particularly easy to read when compared to the Linux output, but you could fix that if you want to, of course.

5. Another nifty utility in Solaris is the terrific pwck command, which performs a variety of consistency checks against the information in the /etc/passwd file. It will catch a nonexistent home directory, but it doesn't check to see if no-password accounts have login shells, so you'll still have to do that by hand.

```
# pwck

testtdude:x:101:1:::/home/testtdude:/bin/sh
        Logname too long/short
        Login directory not found

testdude:x:102:1:::/home/testdude:/bin/sh
        Login directory not found
```

To accomplish the task, you can substantially simplify the shell script that performed the checking in Linux, checkpw.

```
# cat checkpw.sh
#!/bin/sh

# CHECKPW - Check the status of all accounts on the system, checking
#    to ensure that any account without a password has a shell that
#    prevents interactive use. Any others will be flagged in output.

# This only runs on Solaris systems with the '-sa' flags to 'passwd'
```

```
for account in `passwd -sa | grep NP | awk '{print $1}'`
do
   shell="`egrep \"^${account}:\" /etc/passwd | cut -d: -f7`"
   if [ "$shell" != "/sbin/nologin" ] ; then
      echo "*** WARNING: Account $account has no password and login
shell $shell"
   fi
done

exit 0
```

When it's run, the results are what you would hope:

```
# checkpw.sh
*** WARNING: Account testdude has no password and login shell
/bin/sh
```

5. Let's lock testdude out with the passwd –l option:

```
# passwd -l testdude
# passwd -s testdude
testdude  LK
```

No feedback was given on the first command, but the -s summarizes the new state as LK (locked), which is correct. To unlock the account again, use passwd test-dude, then enter an appropriate new password value.

6. One more quick examination of the userdel command for comparison's sake proves that it's 100% identical to the Linux version shown earlier. Hurray!

```
# man userdel
Maintenance Commands                                          userdel(1M)

NAME
      userdel - delete a user's login from the system

SYNOPSIS
      userdel [ -r ]  login

DESCRIPTION
      The userdel utility deletes a user account from  the  system
      and  makes  the  appropriate  account-related changes to the
      system file and file system.

OPTIONS
      The following options are supported:

      -r    Remove the user's home directory from the system. This
            directory  must exist. The files and directories under
            the home directory will no longer be  accessible  fol-
            lowing successful execution of the command.
```

▼

▲

Again, notice that although it can remove the user's home directory, it does not explore the rest of the file system to identify what additional files might be owned by the user.

Solaris has traveled a very different path of development. Growing originally from the Stanford University Network (that's where "Sun" comes from), where Scott McNealy had the savvy to take the idea of a networked workstation and build a company around it, Solaris (originally SunOS) started out much more like BSD Unix—their head scientist is Bill Joy of UC Berkeley, after all—but ironically is much more like Linux now.

Being yet another flavor of Unix, however, it has differences that mean it's yet another variant, and although a command might work perfectly well on Linux, it doesn't in fact work on Solaris, too. It's the never-ending challenge of modern Unix systems, and should probably be our mantra for this book.

Password Aging

One more topic before we wrap up this hour, okay? Last hour, we peeked into the /etc/shadow file and found out that there were a bunch of new and intriguing field values associated with a user account. To wit (from the shadow(5) man page):

```
DESCRIPTION
        shadow  contains  the  encrypted  password information for
        user's accounts and optional the password  aging  informa?
        tion.  Included is

            Login name
            Encrypted password
            Days since Jan 1, 1970 that password was last changed
            Days before password may be changed
            Days after which password must be changed
            Days before password is to expire that user is warned
            Days after password expires that account is disabled
            Days since Jan 1, 1970 that account is disabled
            A reserved field
```

The capability that the shadow password system enables that we're interested in is called *password aging*. It's a way to force users to change their password on a given schedule, and to automatically enforce a policy of disabling accounts after a certain period during which users don't log in.

Task 6.5: Tools for Managing Password Aging

The mechanism for specifying a password aging policy varies by operating system, but that's probably no surprise! Solaris neatly tucks the options into the passwd command,

▼

▼ while Linux uses the command `chage`. There's no equivalent mechanism in Mac OS X/Darwin, nor does Darwin support the shadow password file mechanism.

1. Let's start with `chage`, because it makes the various possible settings quite obvious:

```
# man chage | head -12
CHAGE(1)                                                    CHAGE(1)

NAME
        chage - change user password expiry information

SYNOPSIS
        chage [-m mindays] [-M maxdays] [-d lastday] [-I inactive]
              [-E expiredate] [-W warndays] user
chage -l user
```

The `-l` flag is a good place to start, as it generates a report of password aging information for the specified account and can be used by anyone:

```
$ chage -l taylor
Minimum:          0
Maximum:          99999
Warning:          7
Inactive:         -1
Last Change:              Jan 14, 2002
Password Expires:         Never
Password Inactive:        Never
Account Expires:          Never
```

As you can see, `taylor` is in luck; the password never expires, and the account never expires, either. The first four fields deserve an explanation, however.

The Minimum and Maximum fields are the minimum and maximum number of days between password changes—quite literally. If the minimum was two days and user `taylor` changed his password early one morning, he couldn't change it again until the minimum number of days value had elapsed.

The Warning field indicates the number of days before the password expires that the user will be warned during the login process, and, finally, the Inactive field indicates how many days after a password expires that the account will automatically be locked (similar to `passwd -l`).

2. Remember our friend `testdude`? It's time to make some changes to his account to match the account password policy implemented at our site.

The first update is that passwords must be changed every 30 days, and that if the user doesn't log in within 14 days of the expiration date of their password, the account should be automatically locked out. The `testdude` account should have a two-day warning before being forced to change the password upon login, and it's
▼ also due to expire on August 3, 2003, so that'll be specified too.

6

Here's the command needed:

```
# chage -M 30 -W 2 -I 14 -E 2003-08-03 testdude
```

If all is well, there's no output, in a typical Unix manner. To verify that it worked:

```
# chage -l testdude
Minimum:           0
Maximum:           30
Warning:           2
Inactive:          14
Last Change:               Jan 12, 2002
Password Expires:          Feb 11, 2002
Password Inactive:         Feb 25, 2002
Account Expires:           Aug 03, 2003
```

Perfect, and quite simple, once you learn the magic incantation—or refer to Table 6.3 for details of all the flags to chage.

TABLE 6.3   Command Flags to Linux's chage Command

Flag	Meaning
-m	Minimum number of days between password changes (0 = no minimum)
-M	Maximum number of days between password changes
-E	Expiration date, specified in number of days since January 1, 1970, or in YYYY-MM-DD format
-I	Number of days of inactivity after a password expires before the account is automatically locked
-W	Number of days prior to password expiration that the user will be presented with a warning message

3. By contrast, Solaris slips these flags into the passwd command, as highlighted in Table 6.4.

TABLE 6.4   Password Aging Flags in Solaris passwd Command

Flag	Meaning
-f	Forces the password to expire immediately; user will be prompted for a new password upon next login
-n	Minimum number of days between password changes
-x	Maximum number of days between password changes
-w	Number of days prior to password expiration that the system should generate a warning message to the user

▼

As you can see, to set a specific account expiration date, you need to use the Solaris usermod command, with a -e flag. To accomplish the same task as shown in Linux with the chage command, therefore, requires two steps:

```
# passwd -x 30 -w 2 testdude
# usermod -e 08/03/2003 testdude
```

Notice that there's no way to automatically lock accounts after a certain number of days of inactivity (the -I flag in the Linux chage command).

Checking the settings is yet another Solaris command: logins. There are lots of flags to this useful utility (see the man page for details), but to see the settings for a specific account, use the -x extended output flag:

```
# logins -xl testdude
testdude              102        other                  1
                                 /home/testdude
                                 /bin/sh
                                 NP 011802 0 30 2
```

The output is a bit cryptic, but remember that NP means "no password," and much of the rest of the information can be inferred by peeking at the /etc/passwd entry:

```
# grep testdude /etc/passwd
testdude:x:102:1::/home/testdude:/bin/sh
```

The output of logins shows us that account testdude has UID 102, and a default group of other, which has a GID of 1. The home directory is /home/testdude, the login shell is /bin/sh, and the password expiration information is, in order: date the password last changed, number of days required between changes, number of days allowed before a change is required, and the pre-expiration warning value.

Do you see what's missing? There's no clue that the account itself is scheduled to automatically turn off in August of 2003.

▲

Linux offers a succinct and sophisticated password aging capability through its chage command. Solaris offers a similar capability, but the interface is considerably more awkward, split across three different commands. And Darwin—well, as of yet, Darwin doesn't support password aging.

Regardless of whether it's easy or difficult, however, the password aging capability is a very good addition to your Unix sysadmin toolkit if it's available on the systems you administer.

Summary

This hour has explored many facets of account management, with a focus on working with recalcitrant users and shutting them down as needed. It also highlights how much

6

difference there can be between different flavors of Unix. Just because they all have the same OS name doesn't mean that they're identical!

Q&A

Q Why is it so important to make sure that someone isn't logged in if you're going to disable their account?

A Oftentimes you'll find that you need to suspend an account because of inappropriate activity by the user, or because the user's been furloughed temporarily. In those situations, it's best to avoid any potential copying of confidential files, attempts to sabotage the system, or what have you by simply giving the user the boot.

Q The whole idea of file locking seems pretty critical to the design of a multiuser operating system. Is it?

A Absolutely, and even with file locking, it's still not uncommon for multiple admins to override each others' changes (what I'd call "stepping on each other"). The best policy is to have one person who is empowered to make changes to critical files, then let everyone else feed change requests to them.

Workshop

Quiz

1. What's the super-fast less-than-a-minute technique for suspending a user account?

2. The `passwd` command on most Unix systems has heuristics (a fancy word for rules) defining what is an acceptable password. Find out what the rules are on your main system.

3. The built-in `usermod -L` mechanism for locking accounts consists of simply sticking an ! in front of the encrypted password string. Will that work for any system? Try it.

4. Why might you use `passwd -d` on a Linux or Solaris system?

Answers

1. Suspending a user account can be done very quickly by changing the password as `root`.

2. The easiest way to find out what rules the passwd command uses is to check the passwd man page. Here's the relevant excerpt from the Solaris man page:

```
Passwords must be constructed to meet the following require-
    ments:

        o   Each password must have PASSLENGTH  characters,  where
            PASSLENGTH  is  defined  in /etc/default/passwd and is
            set to 6. Only the first eight characters are signifi-
            cant.

        o   Each password must contain  at  least  two  alphabetic
            characters and at least one numeric or special charac-
            ter. In this case, "alphabetic" refers to all upper or
            lower case letters.

        o   Each password must differ from the user's  login  name
            and  any reverse or circular shift of that login name.
            For comparison purposes, an upper case letter and  its
            corresponding lower case letter are equivalent.

        o   New passwords must differ from the  old  by  at  least
            three  characters.  For  comparison purposes, an upper
            case letter and its corresponding  lower  case  letter
            are equivalent.
```

3. Prefacing an encrypted password string with a new character will definitely make the password unmatchable, effectively turning the account off. It's another trick you can use if there's no locking mechanism available.

4. If you set up an account with a shell of, say, lpq or something similar, you might make it general access by informing users that they can log in to the lpq account from any login prompt to see the state of the printer queue.

In the next hour, we'll have a close look at backup and archiving tools with Unix, focusing specifically on gzip and tar, two tools that every Unix system administrator should know like the proverbial back of the hand. We'll also compare compression packages to see which does the best job of saving disk space and making transfers more speedy.

6

HOUR 7

Large File Management and Backups

The last few hours have concentrated on tools and techniques for managing user accounts on your Unix system. However, users have expectations of you as a system administrator in much the same way you have expectations of them. Chief among their expectations is that the file system has a high level of integrity. Put another way, you'd better be doing backups!

This hour will concentrate on managing large files and archives, and then talk about common methods of backing data up onto an archival device.

In this hour you'll learn about

- Managing big files with `compress`
- The `gzip` alternative
- A zippy tour of `zip`
- Copying directory trees with `tar`
- Dump and system backups

Shrinking Big Files with compress

If you've picked up the newspaper in the last few years or walked into a computer shop, you know that the price of hard disks has been decreasing at a rather astonishing rate. Today I can walk into the local electronics store and buy a 40 gigabyte hard disk for under $100. When I remember how much my first 20 megabyte disk cost years ago… well, I promised I wouldn't bore you with reminisces, so I'll stop there.

The point is that it's hard to imagine filling up disks, or having files on a Unix system that are so large that it's necessary to worry about coming up with a technique that will let you shrink them down.

Until, that is, your users start to explore multimedia files. A four minute MP3-encoded music file can easily be 50MB or more, a JPEG image from a digital camera can sprawl across 1MB or more, and even Word documents have been known to grow at a surprising rate once editing and reviewing begins.

That's why one of the foundational topics for system administration is managing large files. Like it or not, you have some on your computer, and you're bound to have more as more users are added (or as you use it more yourself).

Task 7.1: Working with compress

The primary cross-platform tool for managing large files is a program called compress, which uses an adaptive Lempel-Ziv encoding that shrinks files down 20% to 30% on average.

1. To start out, I've been exploring how my users are using their disk space, and found that that pesky taylor guy has all sorts of large files in his directory. Here's a representative sampling:

```
$ ls -l
total 5036
-rw-r--r--    1 taylor    coders       1113 Jan 10 08:12 adduser.sh
-rw-rw----    1 taylor    coders         56 Dec  5 05:10 badjoke
-rw-rw----    1 taylor    coders         56 Dec  5 05:10 badjoke.rot13
drwxrw----    2 taylor    coders       4096 Dec  5 05:48 bin/
-rw-rw----    1 taylor    coders        739 Dec  5 05:11 browse.sh
-rw-rw----    1 taylor    coders        276 Dec  5 05:11 buckaroo
drwxrwxr-x    2 taylor    coders       4096 Dec 18 21:26 CBO_MAIL/
-rw-r--r--    1 root      coders        537 Jan  9 22:39 checkhomes.sh
-rw-r--r--    1 root      coders        756 Jan 14 21:31 checkpw.sh
drwxrw----    2 taylor    coders       4096 Dec  5 05:12 CraigsList/
-rw-r--r--    1 root      coders        693 Jan 14 06:40 delete.sh
drwxrw----    4 taylor    coders       4096 Jan  7 21:47 DEMO/
-rw-rw-r--    1 taylor    coders        373 Jan  7 20:22 diskhogs.sh
drwxrw----    2 taylor    coders       4096 Dec  5 05:12 elance/
```

```
-rw-rw----    1 taylor   coders     81491 Dec  5 05:12 etcpasswd
drwxrw----    2 taylor   coders      4096 Dec  5 05:12 Exchange/
drwxrw----    5 taylor   coders      4096 Dec  5 05:16 Gator/
-rw-rw----    1 taylor   coders       605 Dec  5 05:21 getmodemdriver.sh
-rw-rw----    1 taylor   coders       569 Dec  5 05:21 getstocks.sh
-rw-rw----    1 taylor   coders       593 Dec  5 05:21 gettermsheet.sh
-rw-rw----    1 taylor   coders         0 Dec  5 05:21 gif.gif
drwxrw----    4 taylor   coders      4096 Dec  5 05:28 IBM/
drwxrwxr-x   12 10185    root        4096 Dec 18 05:07 Lynx/
-rw-r--r--    1 taylor   coders   4303501 Jan 21 12:41 Nice Work.mp3
-rw-r--r--    1 taylor   coders    130048 Jan 21 12:42 proposal.doc
-rw-r--r--    1 taylor   coders    522970 Jan 21 12:43 rowing-w-jasmine2.jpg
-rw-r--r--    1 root     coders      1290 Jan 14 04:15 suspend.sh
```

There are a number of large files, including the more than four megabyte MP3 audio file `Nice Work.mp3` and the 522KB JPEG image `rowing-w-jasmine2.jpg`. These don't seem too out of control, but imagine if instead of having this one file, the user actually had the entire Ella Fitzgerald discography online? If each song is roughly 4MB, that would be many, many gigabytes of space, space that other users can't use.

The solution is to compress the files to minimize the disk space used and maximize the utility of the drive itself.

2. The standard Unix command for compressing files is `compress`, and it has a number of different starting arguments:

```
$ compress --help
Unknown flag: '-'; Usage: compress [-dfvcVr] [-b maxbits] [file ...]
       -d   If given, decompression is done instead.
       -c   Write output on stdout, don't remove original.
       -b   Parameter limits the max number of bits/code.
       -f   Forces output file to be generated, even if one already.
            exists, and even if no space is saved by compressing.
            If -f is not used, the user will be prompted if stdin is.
            a tty, otherwise, the output file will not be overwritten.
       -v   Write compression statistics.
       -V   Output vesion and compile options.
       -r   Recursive. If a filename is a directory, descend
            into it and compress everything in it.
```

You can see a lazy sysadmin's shortcut to remembering how to work with a specific Unix command: Use the `--help` flag. Either the command will understand the flag and output some help, or it'll parse the flag and find it isn't known and output a `Usage` error that includes the help information anyway. Either way, it's easy and works 99% of the time.

The most interesting flag is `-v`, which shows the results of the compression activity. Let's try it!

```
$ compress -v *mp3
Nice Work.mp3: No compression -- Nice Work.mp3 unchanged
```

An interesting first test: Because of the way that the information is laid out in this file, `compress` tried to compress it, but found that the compressed file wasn't significantly smaller than the original, so it refused to complete the compression task.

Let's try it on some other files instead:

```
$ compress -v *jpg *doc
rowing-w-jasmine2.jpg: No compression -- rowing-w-jasmine2.jpg unchanged
proposal.doc:  -- replaced with proposal.doc.Z Compression: 62.31%
```

Here you can see the results: the `proposal.doc` file compressed down more than 60%—it was originally 130K, but it's now only 49K, as shown:

```
$ ls -l p*
-rw-r--r--     1 taylor    coders       49010 Jan 21 12:42 proposal.doc.Z
```

However, the file itself is no longer usable without being uncompressed first, which is the purpose of the `uncompress` command.

3. One super-useful utility that lets you work with compressed files without hassle is `zcat`, which acts exactly like the `cat` command, but can uncompress compressed files on the fly. Among other things, this is how many `man` systems work on Unix: All the `man` pages are stored in a compressed form, and their contents are uncompressed on the fly, with `zcat` feeding its output to the `nroff` formatter.

For our purposes, let's use `zcat` to sneak a peek at the first few lines of a compressed mail log file, without uncompressing it:

```
$ zcat maillog.txt.Z | head -2
Dec 24 04:02:09 staging sendmail[16202]: fBOC29k16202: from=root, size=186,
class=0, nrcpts=1, msgid=<200112241202.fBOC29k16202@staging.intuitive.com>,
relay=root@localhost
Dec 26 04:02:09 staging sendmail[19880]: fBQC29D19880: from=root,
size=1315, class=0, nrcpts=1,
msgid=<200112261202.fBQC29D19880@staging.intuitive.com>,
relay=root@localhost
```

The `zcat` command on Linux is actually part of the `gzip` utility, which we'll explore a bit later in this hour.

5. It turns out that in the world of Red Hat Linux, there are a number of utilities that can work directly with compressed files, as summarized in the following listing:

```
zcat [compress]      (1)  - compress and expand data (version 4.1)
zcat [gzip]          (1)  - compress or expand files
zcat [uncompress]    (1)  - compress and expand data (version 4.1)
zcmp [zdiff]         (1)  - compare compressed files
zdiff                (1)  - compare compressed files
zgrep                (1)  - search possibly compressed files for expression
zless                (1)  - file perusal filter for viewing compressed text
zlib                 (3)  - compression/decompression library
zmore                (1)  - file perusal filter for viewing compressed text
znew                 (1)  - recompress .Z files to .gz files
```

6. It's also fun and illustrative of the subtle differences between Unix flavors to see how the same command compressing the same original files has different results on different Unix platforms.

Red Hat Linux 7.2:

```
$ compress -v Nice* maillog* prop* rowing*
Nice Work It.mp3: No compression -- Nice Work.mp3 unchanged
maillog.txt:  -- replaced with maillog.txt.Z Compression: 90.65%
proposal.doc:  -- replaced with proposal.doc.Z Compression: 62.31%
rowing-w-jasmine2.jpg: No compression -- rowing-w-jasmine2.jpg unchanged
```

Solaris 8:

```
$ compress -v Nice* maillog* prop* rowing*
Nice Work.mp3: Compression: -29.87% -- file unchanged
maillog.txt: Compression: 90.60% -- replaced with maillog.txt.Z
proposal.doc: Compression: 62.31% -- replaced with proposal.doc.Z
rowing-w-jasmine2.jpg: Compression: -30.28% -- file unchanged
```

Darwin/Mac OS X:

```
$ compress -v Nice* maillog* prop* rowing*
Nice Work.mp3: file would grow; left unmodified
maillog.txt.Z: 9% compression
proposal.doc.Z: 38% compression
rowing-w-jasmine2.jpg: file would grow; left unmodified
```

Amazingly, the resultant size of the maillog.txt file is different on each of the platforms, as summarized in Table 7.1.

TABLE 7.1 Variation in Compressed File Size

Filename	Original Size	Linux	Solaris	Darwin
maillog.txt	39,350,440	3,677,629	3,696,761	3,696,039

As you spend more time digging around on your Unix system, you'll inevitably find huge files that are rarely accessed. Perhaps an old development project saved in an archival format? A set of MP3s residing on the server for a garage band? A streaming video that's not part of a Web site any more? Archival log files that are kept for long-term system usage analysis?

Regardless of the reason for little used files, compress is a terrific tool to help maximize the availability of your disk space. Not only that, it's also a great command to teach your users so they can manage their own disk space more wisely, too.

The gzip Alternative

Although compress has a long, venerable history, it's not the only utility available on Unix systems that knows how to compress files. There are two others worthy of note, zip and gzip. They sound like the same program, but they're definitely not.

The zip utility lets you build a package of files and directories, then automatically compresses them. What's most helpful about this utility is that it's completely compatible with the very popular PKZIP and WinZip utilities on Windows. Even better, Aladdin System's very successful StuffIt system for Mac OS also knows how to work with ZIP archives, so it's a completely multiplatform solution.

> In fact, ZIP archives are compatible across Unix, VMS, MSDOS, OS/2, Windows, Macintosh, Amiga, Atari, and even Acorn systems.

The gzip utility is intended to be a replacement to compress, as is stated explicitly by the program's author in the documentation: "We developed this program as a replacement for compress because of the UNISYS and IBM patents covering the LZW algorithm used by compress. These patents made it impossible for us to use compress, and we needed a replacement. The superior compression ratio of gzip is just a bonus."

> A bit of history: The "GNU" project (which stands for, and I'm not kidding, GNU's Not Unix) was born out of a dissatisfaction in the developer community with the strongarm tactics of AT&T, the patent holder and owner of the original Unix system. GNU's purpose in life was to offer a free version of Unix that was clear of all patents and other corporate intellectual property, and it succeeded astonishingly well. It's a fascinating read and can be found online at http://www.gnu.org/.

There is one other common compression program available with some flavors of Unix: pack. The pack command, which uses a Huffman encoding compression algorithm, is available on Solaris 8, but not Linux or Darwin. I expect that no one uses it, however, because of the widespread availability of compress and gzip.

Task 7.2: Working with gzip

There are alternative compression utilities, but gzip is worth significant attention because it has become the de facto compression utility of choice for the Unix community.

1. To start, let's see if using the --help flag will produce some useful information:

```
$ gzip --help
gzip 1.3
(1999-12-21)
usage: gzip [-cdfhlLnNrtvV19] [-S suffix] [file ...]
 -c --stdout      write on standard output, keep original files unchanged
 -d --decompress  decompress
 -f --force       force overwrite of output file and compress links
 -h --help        give this help
 -l --list        list compressed file contents
 -L --license     display software license
 -n --no-name     do not save or restore the original name and time stamp
 -N --name        save or restore the original name and time stamp
 -q --quiet       suppress all warnings
 -r --recursive   operate recursively on directories
 -S .suf --suffix .suf    use suffix .suf on compressed files
 -t --test        test compressed file integrity
 -v --verbose     verbose mode
 -V --version     display version number
 -1 --fast        compress faster
 -9 --best        compress better
 file...          files to (de)compress. If none given, use standard input.
Report bugs to <bug-gzip@gnu.org>.
```

Notice that there are two forms of each command flag: the single-letter traditional Unix flag (for example, -f, -v) and the double-dash full-word flag (for example, --force, --verbose). Only GNU versions of Unix commands have the full-word flag options, so although it might be tempting to use them, I will counsel you to learn the single-letter flags instead. It's less typing, and you won't subsequently get frustrated when you're working with a non-GNU command that thinks --help is a request for the five flags -, -h, -e, -l, and -p.

2. Armed with this summary, here's the first demonstration of gzip's use:

```
$ gzip -v Nice* maillog* prop* rowing*
Nice Work.mp3:          2.4% -- replaced with Nice Work.mp3.gz
```

7

```
maillog.txt:              92.3% -- replaced with maillog.txt.gz
proposal.doc:             79.9% -- replaced with proposal.doc.gz
rowing-w-jasmine2.jpg:     0.2% -- replaced with rowing-w-jasmine2.jpg.gz
```

It did an outstanding job compressing the `maillog.txt` file: Compared to the 3.6MB average for `compress`, `gzip` has shrunk it down to 2.9MB. However, one annoying characteristic of `gzip` is that it compresses just about everything, even if the savings are pointless (the JPEG image has been compressed 0.2%, and the original file that was 522Kb has been replaced with its `gzipped` version that's 521Kb.

Here's how our four files compressed with the regular `gzip` invocation:

```
-rw-r--r--   1 taylor   coders   2992332 Jan 21 16:08 maillog.txt.gz
-rw-r--r--   1 taylor   coders   4197440 Jan 21 12:41 Nice Work.mp3.gz
-rw-r--r--   1 taylor   coders     26159 Jan 21 12:42 proposal.doc.gz
-rw-r--r--   1 taylor   coders    521565 Jan 21 12:43 rowing-w-jasmine2.
➥jpg.gz
```

To uncompress them is a simple matter of invoking `gunzip`

```
$ gunzip *.gz
```

and compressing them with a higher requested compression ratio (the `-9` flag):

```
$ gzip -v9 Nice* maillog* prop* rowing*
Nice Work.mp3:             2.4% -- replaced with Nice Work.mp3.gz
maillog.txt:              93.3% -- replaced with maillog.txt.gz
proposal.doc:             80.1% -- replaced with proposal.doc.gz
rowing-w-jasmine2.jpg:     0.2% -- replaced with rowing-w-jasmine2.jpg.gz
```

The result files are just a tiny bit smaller:

```
-rw-r--r--   1 taylor   coders   2604313 Jan 21 16:08 maillog.txt.gz
-rw-r--r--   1 taylor   coders   4197118 Jan 21 12:41 Nice Work.mp3.gz
-rw-r--r--   1 taylor   coders     25850 Jan 21 12:42 proposal.doc.gz
-rw-r--r--   1 taylor   coders    521565 Jan 21 12:43 rowing-w-jasmine2.
➥jpg.gz
```

Better, but probably not enough to worry about whether you remember to use the `-9` flag or not!

3. One great capability of `gzip` is its ability to recursively compress every file in the current directory and any subdirectory from a given point:

```
$ cd ~testdude
$ gzip -rv9 *
adduser.sh:               46.3% -- replaced with adduser.sh.gz
browse.sh:                57.1% -- replaced with browse.sh.gz
checkhomes.sh:            50.4% -- replaced with checkhomes.sh.gz
checkpw.sh:               38.8% -- replaced with checkpw.sh.gz
delete.sh:                43.7% -- replaced with delete.sh.gz
```

```
DEMO/testfile:              0.0% -- replaced with DEMO/testfile.gz
DEMO/Src/cribbage.c:       69.0% -- replaced with DEMO/Src/cribbage.c.gz
DEMO/snapshot.sh:          28.8% -- replaced with DEMO/snapshot.sh.gz
DEMO/sourcefiles.cpio:     72.8% -- replaced with DEMO/sourcefiles.cpio.gz
diskhogs.sh:               37.2% -- replaced with diskhogs.sh.gz
getmodemdriver.sh:         37.0% -- replaced with getmodemdriver.sh.gz
getstocks.sh:              39.1% -- replaced with getstocks.sh.gz
gettermsheet.sh:           37.0% -- replaced with gettermsheet.sh.gz
rowing-w-jasmine2.jpg:      0.2% -- replaced with rowing-w-jasmine2.jpg.gz
suspend.sh:                47.3% -- replaced with suspend.sh.gz
```

> In case you haven't seen it before, the *~acct* notation is a convenient short-
> cut for the home directory of user *acct*. Without any account specified, ~
> itself expands to your home directory in just about every worthwhile shell.

The gzip program has automatically replaced each file in the directory (and subdirectories below it) with compressed versions, and, as usual, each has been given a
.gz suffix.

This behavior is terrific for system administrators. In particular, this can be a great
additional step taken when an account is suspended—automatically compress all
the files in the user's home directory to maximize available disk space for active
users.

4. The gunzip command is another name for the gzip program, through a hard link.
   The nuances of symbolic versus hard linking is a bit beyond the scope of this book
   (check out *Sams Teach Yourself Unix in 24 Hours* for a good explanation), but
   when you see a man page that starts similar to gzip (with a list of commands), it
   implies that the file system is set up a certain way.

   Because ensuring that commands are installed properly is an important sysadmin
   task, let's have a quick sidetrack to learn how this is done! Besides, I love these
   sidetracks, don't you?

```
$ man gzip | head
GZIP(1)                                                    GZIP(1)

NAME
       gzip, gunzip, zcat - compress or expand files

SYNOPSIS
       gzip [ -acdfhlLnNrtvV19 ] [-S suffix] [ name ...  ]
       gunzip [ -acfhlLnNrtvV ] [-S suffix] [ name ...  ]
       zcat [ -fhLV ] [ name ...  ]
```

7

Any time you see a set of different command names in the SYNOPSIS of a man page, it means that the same executable binary has multiple names in the file system. This should be revealed with ls:

```
$ which gzip
/bin/gzip
$ cd /bin
$ ls -l gzip gunzip zcat
-rwxr-xr-x   3 root     root          51228 Aug 23 20:02 gunzip*
-rwxr-xr-x   3 root     root          51228 Aug 23 20:02 gzip*
-rwxr-xr-x   3 root     root          51228 Aug 23 20:02 zcat*
```

Perfect. They're all the same size, and all three have the same *link count* (the second column of the -l long output format).

Notice anything surprising in that last output? Flip back a few pages for a clue.... The zcat command is supposed to be associated with the compress utility, but you can see that it's clearly part of the gzip family of compression commands instead. What's going on here?

The solution to this puzzle is that one of the unheralded features of gzip is that it can not only uncompress its own compressed file formats, but it can also uncompress compressed files from compress, zip, and pack!

6. If you're perpetually encountering disk space problems and can't afford to buy bigger disks, you can combine gzip with find to automatically comb through user files and autocompress any exceptionally large ones:

```
$ find /home -type f -size +1000k -print
/home/taylor/Gator/Snapshots/MAILOUT.tar.Z
/home/taylor/IBM/fop.jar
/home/taylor/IBM/j2sdk-1_3_0_02-solx86.tar
/home/taylor/Lynx/src/lynx
/home/taylor/Lynx/lynx
/home/taylor/maillog.txt.gz
/home/taylor/Nice Work.mp3.gz
```

This particular command lists all files (-type f) that are greater than 1000Kb. There are a number of steps required to turn this into a fully usable shell script, but let's skip straight to the end product this time:

```
# cat autocompress.sh
#!/bin/sh

#  AUTOCOMPRESS - automatically find and compress excessively large files
#      in the /home directory tree, sending email to the user so they know
#      what's happened.

homedir="/home"
threshold="+1000k"        # files must be bigger than this to compress
```

```
compressed=0

# clean up our temp files before we start
/bin/rm -f /tmp/autocompress.*

for fname in `find $homedir -type f -size $threshold -print | \
  egrep -v '(.Z$|.gz$|.tgz$)'`
do
  owner="`ls -l $fname | awk '{print $3}'`"
  if [ $owner = "root" ] ; then
    echo "... skipping file $fname (owned by root)"
  else
    echo "autocompressing file $fname (owned by $owner)"
    gzip $fname
    echo "    $fname" >> /tmp/autocompress.$owner
    compressed="`expr $compressed + 1`"
  fi
done

# now send out email reports to any users who has had files compressed

if [ $compressed -gt 0 ]; then
  for report in `ls /tmp/autocompress.*`
  do
    recipient="`echo $report | sed 's/\/tmp\/autocompress\.//'`"
    echo ""
    echo "Sending autocompress report to ${recipient}:"
    cat $report
    (
      echo "In an effort to save disk space, files larger than $threshold"
      echo "are automatically compressed on this system. On a regular sweep"
      echo "through the disk, the following file or files of yours have been"
      echo "identified and auto-compressed:"
      cat  $report
      echo "To learn how to work with compressed files, please see the "
      echo "gzip man page. You can do this with the command"
      echo "    man gzip"
    ) | mail -s "Notice: Compressed your big files" $recipient

    /bin/rm -f $report
  done
  echo ""
  echo "$compressed file(s) compressed."
else
  echo ""
  echo "autocompress: no files compressed, no report generated"
fi

exit 0
```

7

▼   This is a considerably more sophisticated shell script than those presented in earlier hours, so I encourage you to spend some time reading it line by line. Note particularly how the $compressed variable keeps count of how many matches there are, and how parentheses spawn a separate subshell and let you compose a very friendly e-mail message to the user with various Unix commands. The use of temp files to store intermediate information is also worthy of study.

7. Let's run the script to see what happens:

```
# autocompress.sh
autocompressing file /home/taylor/IBM/fop.jar (owned by taylor)
autocompressing file /home/taylor/IBM/j2sdk-1_3_0_02-solx86.tar
➥(owned by taylor)
... skipping file /home/taylor/Lynx/src/lynx (owned by root)
... skipping file /home/taylor/Lynx/lynx (owned by root)

Sending autocompress report to taylor:
    /home/taylor/IBM/fop.jar
    /home/taylor/IBM/j2sdk-1_3_0_02-solx86.tar

2 file(s) compressed.
```

Two files have been compressed, and two potentially large files were skipped because they're owned by root (suggesting that they are perhaps more important). The second half of the script ensures that these changes don't occur silently. Instead, the user will receive an e-mail message notifying him of the autocompression:

```
From: root
Subject: Notice: Compressed your big files

In an effort to save disk space, files larger than +1000k
are automatically compressed on this system. On a regular sweep
through the disk, the following file or files of yours have been
identified and auto-compressed:
    /home/taylor/IBM/fop.jar
    /home/taylor/IBM/j2sdk-1_3_0_02-solx86.tar
To learn how to work with compressed files, please see the
gzip man page. You can do this with the command
    man gzip
```

▲

The two commands compress and gzip perform the same function on a Unix system— they replace a large file with a smaller file that has the same information, albeit in a slightly less useable format. The difference in compression quality is important, but not critical, so if you've long since wired compress into your brain as the way to shrink files, you're probably okay without learning any new tricks.

If you're coming at this for the first time, however, gzip is the way to go. If you want a strong motivation, have a peek inside /usr/share/man and notice that all the man pages are stored with .gz suffixes—they're all stored by default in the gzip compressed format. In the next hour we'll explore the various Unix package mechanisms, and you'll see again that gzip is the compression system of choice in the software development community.

A Zippy Tour of zip

Although zip sounds like it's the direct relative of gzip, it's actually quite a different program. Yes, it does file compression (though zip calls it *deflation* and *inflation*, rather than compression and decompression), but the primary purpose of the zip utility is to create an archive file that contains multiple files and folders within.

Historically, zip was developed by Phil Katz of PKWare (makers of PKZIP) in 1989, and has since been adopted as an archive format by a wide variety of vendors and most major computing platforms. The zip command on Linux was developed over many years and is *not* a part of the GNU project, so it doesn't support those peculiar --*word* command arguments.

Task 7.3: Working with zip

Enough talk, let's see what zip does!

1. Just before he left, our pal testdude asked if we could build a Windows-friendly archive of files and folders in his home directory and e-mail it to him. This is a perfect job for zip!

> It's worth pointing out that you probably do *not* want to send all the files from a user's home directory without checking if it's okay. I recommend you get approval—in writing—from either human resources or the legal departments before you let users have their e-mail archive, project directory, or any file that's at all questionable.

If you check out the zip man page, you'll doubtless be a bit overwhelmed, but fortunately typing zip without any arguments will give you a (very) concise summary of use:

```
$ zip
Copyright (C) 1990-1999 Info-ZIP
Type 'zip "-L"' for software license.
Zip 2.3 (November 29th 1999). Usage:
zip [-options] [-b path] [-t mmddyyyy] [-n suffixes] [zipfile list] [-xi list]
  The default action is to add or replace zipfile entries from list, which
```

TASK

7

```
can include the special name - to compress standard input.
If zipfile and list are omitted, zip compresses stdin to stdout.
  -f   freshen: only changed files  -u   update: only changed or new files
  -d   delete entries in zipfile    -m   move into zipfile (delete files)
  -r   recurse into directories     -j   junk (don't record) directory names
  -0   store only                   -l   convert LF to CR LF (-ll CR LF to LF)
  -1   compress faster              -9   compress better
  -q   quiet operation              -v   verbose operation/print version info
  -c   add one-line comments        -z   add zipfile comment
  -@   read names from stdin        -o   make zipfile as old as latest entry
  -x   exclude the following names  -i   include only the following names
  -F   fix zipfile (-FF try harder) -D   do not add directory entries
  -A   adjust self-extracting exe   -J   junk zipfile prefix (unzipsfx)
  -T   test zipfile integrity       -X   eXclude eXtra file attributes
  -y   store symbolic links as the link instead of the referenced file
  -R   PKZIP recursion (see manual)
  -e   encrypt                      -n   don't compress these suffixes
```

To build a PKZIP-compatible archive, you want to ensure that you use the following flags: -r causes the program to recurse into subdirectories and include that content too, -9 requests the best possible compression, and -v offers verbose output:

```
$ zip -r -9 -v testdude.zip *
  adding: adduser.sh     (in=1113) (out=597) (deflated 46%)
  adding: browse.sh      (in=739) (out=317) (deflated 57%)
  adding: checkhomes.sh  (in=537) (out=266) (deflated 50%)
  adding: checkpw.sh     (in=756) (out=462) (deflated 39%)
  adding: delete.sh      (in=693) (out=390) (deflated 44%)
  adding: DEMO/ (in=0) (out=0) (stored 0%)
  adding: DEMO/testfile (in=0) (out=0) (stored 0%)
  adding: DEMO/Src/    (in=0) (out=0) (stored 0%)
  adding: DEMO/Src/cribbage.c   (in=26150) (out=8081) (deflated 69%)
  adding: DEMO/snapshot.sh    (in=263) (out=187) (deflated 29%)
  adding: DEMO/sourcefiles.cpio...    (in=153600) (out=41688) (deflated 73%)
  adding: DEMO/testdir/ (in=0) (out=0) (stored 0%)
  adding: diskhogs.sh    (in=373) (out=234) (deflated 37%)
  adding: getmodemdriver.sh    (in=605) (out=381) (deflated 37%)
  adding: getstocks.sh   (in=569) (out=346) (deflated 39%)
  adding: gettermsheet.sh     (in=593) (out=373) (deflated 37%)
  adding: rowing-w-jasmine2.jpg.......   (in=522970) (out=521525) (deflated 0%)
  adding: suspend.sh     (in=1290) (out=679) (deflated 47%)
total bytes=710251, compressed=575526 -> 19% savings
```

Neatly done, and the file testdude.zip is now ready to e-mail to the user. Notice that the compressed value shown on the last line is in fact the size of the resultant archive file: 575,526 bytes.

▼   2. If you want to check that the contents of the package are correct, you can use the
         companion `unzip`, which also tells you how it works if you omit arguments:

```
$ unzip
UnZip 5.42 of 14 January 2001, by Info-ZIP.  Maintained by C. Spieler.  Send
bug reports to the authors at Zip-Bugs@lists.wku.edu; see README for details.

Usage: unzip [-Z] [-opts[modifiers]] file[.zip] [list] [-x xlist] [-d exdir]
  Default action is to extract files in list, except those in xlist, to exdir;
  file[.zip] may be a wildcard.  -Z => ZipInfo mode ("unzip -Z" for usage).

  -p  extract files to pipe, no messages     -l  list files (short format)
  -f  freshen existing files, create none    -t  test compressed archive data
  -u  update files, create if necessary      -z  display archive comment
  -x  exclude files that follow (in xlist)   -d  extract files into exdir

modifiers:                                   -q  quiet mode (-qq => quieter)
  -n  never overwrite existing files         -a  auto-convert any text files
  -o  overwrite files WITHOUT prompting       -aa treat ALL files as text
  -j  junk paths (do not make directories)   -v  be verbose/print version info
  -C  match filenames case-insensitively     -L  make (some) names lowercase
  -X  restore UID/GID info                   -V  retain VMS version numbers
                                             -M  pipe through "more" pager
Examples (see unzip.txt for more info):
  unzip data1 -x joe   => extract all files except joe from zipfile data1.zip
  unzip -p foo | more  => send contents of foo.zip via pipe into program more
  unzip -fo foo ReadMe => quietly replace existing ReadMe if archive file
newer
```

         To check that the ZIP archive is correct, simply use the -l flag:

```
$ unzip -l testdude.zip
Archive:  testdude.zip
  Length     Date   Time    Name
 --------    ----   ----    ----
     1113  01-21-02 23:19   adduser.sh
      739  01-21-02 23:19   browse.sh
      537  01-21-02 23:19   checkhomes.sh
      756  01-21-02 23:19   checkpw.sh
      693  01-21-02 23:19   delete.sh
        0  01-21-02 23:17   DEMO/
        0  01-21-02 23:17   DEMO/testfile
        0  01-21-02 23:17   DEMO/Src/
    26150  01-21-02 23:17   DEMO/Src/cribbage.c
      263  01-21-02 23:17   DEMO/snapshot.sh
   153600  01-21-02 23:17   DEMO/sourcefiles.cpio
        0  01-21-02 23:17   DEMO/testdir/
      373  01-21-02 23:19   diskhogs.sh
      605  01-21-02 23:19   getmodemdriver.sh
```

7

```
       569  01-21-02 23:19   getstocks.sh
       593  01-21-02 23:19   gettermsheet.sh
    522970  01-21-02 23:19   rowing-w-jasmine2.jpg
      1290  01-21-02 23:19   suspend.sh
--------                     -------
    710251                   18 files
```

Although no rational Unix system administrator uses zip as a mechanism for moving archives around or backing them up onto other media (that's what tar or tar + gzip are for, as you'll learn shortly), there are plenty of users who need portable archives for their non-Unix system, and that's where zip shines.

In many years of system administration, I have only built one or two ZIP archives myself, but it's really great to know that the capability is available on Unix systems.

> There is no command-line zip utility in Darwin, so you'll need to use StuffIt Deluxe or another graphically-oriented ZIP utility if you must create a ZIP-format archive for a user. You could also install a zip port through fink or similar, as discussed in the next hour.

On the Windows side, there are a bunch of different ZIP-friendly utilities available. The two most popular are WinZip and PKZIP. WinZip features built-in support for CAB files and popular Internet file formats such as tar, gzip, uuencode, BinHex, and MIME. PKZIP also supports the uuencode, BinHex, MIME, tar, gzip, CAB, and JAR formats. The Mac-equivalent super-utility is the wonderful—and completely free—StuffIt Expander, and it not only supports the ZIP format, but also the BinHex, tar, MIME, gzip, ARC, uuencode, and even the .Z files from the Unix compress. (StuffIt Expander is also available for Windows, Linux, and Solaris, if you want to improve your own working environment.)

All these applications are available on the Web for any users who request your assistance with this process. Send them to http://www.winzip.com/ for WinZip, http://www.pkware.com/ for PKZIP, or http://www.aladdinsys.com/ for the StuffIt application suite.

Copying Directory Trees with tar

When it comes to building Unix-friendly archives of files and directories, the command of choice is tar. Amazingly, tar started out life as a way to write files onto a backup tape device so that you could later restore them, retaining any subdirectory information.

Zoom forward a few years, and `tar` is the most common utility for creating snapshots of file sets and directory structures. Sure, you can use something like `cp -R` to recursively copy a directory tree elsewhere on your system, but what if you need to transfer it via `ftp` to a second machine? That's a great use of `tar`, and that's where we'll start exploring this powerful utility.

Task 7.4: Working with `tar`

On first glance, you might be thinking, "As a sysadmin, why would the capability to create archival files be so useful?" In fact, it's remarkable to me how often I find myself working with the `tar` command, whether it's to transfer directory trees from one system to another, copy files from one spot on the disk to another, or even to take quick "snapshots" of a development directory so I have a backup copy.

The most popular use for `tar` is transferring files and directories in bulk from one system to another.

1. The `tar` command has oodles of options, but there are three core uses of `tar` that are a good starting point: creating archives, extracting files from archives, and examining the contents of archives. These are `-c`, `-x`, and `-t`, respectively. Other useful flags are summarized in Table 7.2.

TABLE 7.2 Useful Flags to `tar`

Flag	Meaning
`-c`	Create a new archive.
`-f` *file or device*	Save output as specified filename, or write to the specified device. The default output device varies by system, but on Linux it's `/dev/rmt0`, which is usually a tape drive or similar streaming backup media.
`-N` *date*	Only archive files newer than the specified date. Date formats can include `2003-08-03` (year-month-day), and `3 Aug 2003` (day month-name year). *This flag is only available in GNU `tar`.*
`-p`	Preserve file information. Ensures that, if possible, the UID, GID, file permissions and access and modification times are restored along with the file itself.
`-t`	Show the contents of a `tar` archive.
`-v`	Verbose output. Applies to all three modes of `tar` usage.
`-x`	Extract a file or files from a `tar` archive.
`-Z`	Filter the archive through `compress`.
`-z`	Filter the archive through `gzip`.

7

▼   There are at least 20 different flags to the `tar` command, and more than double that in the GNU version, so check the `man` page if you really want to have your head start swimming! Instead, let's just start using the `tar` command.

  2. Having just set up a new OS X system, why don't we create a compressed `tar` archive of all the files in my Linux account, `ftp` them to the Mac, then unpack them with `tar`? This is a very common task!

     The first step is to create the archive on the Linux system. Because I want to also pick up the dot-files (those that start with `.`), I'll use a sophisticated file matching pattern:

```
$ cd ~taylor
$ tar -cvzf /tmp/taylor-dir.tar.gz .[a-zA-Z]* *
.bash_history
.bash_logout
.bash_profile
.bashrc
.emacs
.gtkrc
.kde/
.kde/Autostart/
.kde/Autostart/Autorun.desktop
.kde/Autostart/.directory
.mc/
.mc/tmp/
.mc/ini
.mc/history
.mc/Tree
.screenrc
1
CBO_MAIL/

... lots of output removed ...

elance/getquotes-txt.sh
etcpasswd
getmodemdriver.sh
getstocks.sh
gettermsheet.sh
gif.gif
mail.log
proposal.doc.gz
rowing-w-jasmine2.jpg.gz
suspend.sh
```

     Notice what `file` reports for the archive:

```
$ file *gz
taylor-dir.tar.gz: gzip compressed data, deflated, last modified: Tue Jan
22
➥12:06:33 2002, os: Unix
```
▼

▼ 3. To transfer the file to the Mac system, I'll use `ftp`, a program that isn't elegant, but
   works great:

```
$ ftp g4.intuitive.com
Connected to g4.intuitive.com (198.76.82.132).
220 g4.intuitive.com FTP server (Version 6.00LS) ready.
Name (g4.intuitive.com:taylor): taylor
331 Password required for taylor.
Password:
230 User taylor logged in.
Remote system type is Unix.
Using binary mode to transfer files.
ftp> binary
200 Type set to I.
ftp> lcd /tmp
Local directory now /tmp
ftp> cd /tmp
250 CWD command successful.
ftp> put taylor-dir.tar.gz
local: taylor-dir.tar.gz remote: taylor-dir.tar.gz
227 Entering Passive Mode (198,76,82,132,195,54)
150 Opening BINARY mode data connection for 'taylor-dir.tar.gz'.
226 Transfer complete.
3064316 bytes sent in 125 secs (24 Kbytes/sec)
ftp> quit
221 Goodbye.
```

It took just barely more than two minutes to transfer the 3MB of data from a Linux
server at a remote location to my Mac server in my office, through a slow DSL
line. Not bad.

4. To unpack the archive on the Darwin box, let's start by checking its contents with
the `-t` flag, and let's also specify a pattern against which the filenames will be
matched:

```
 $ tar -tzf *gz DEMO
DEMO
DEMO/testfile
DEMO/Src
DEMO/Src/cribbage.c
DEMO/snapshot.sh
DEMO/sourcefiles.cpio
DEMO/testdir
```

This shows all the files and directories that match the specified pattern DEMO.
Another quick example lists all the C program source files:

```
$ tar -tzf *gz \*.c
DEMO/Src/cribbage.c
bin/fixit.c
elance/filter.c
```

7

To extract specific files, simply change the `-t` flag to an `-x` flag. Here's how you would unpack the DEMO directory in Darwin:

```
$ tar -xzvpf /tmp/*gz DEMO
DEMO
DEMO/testfile
DEMO/Src
DEMO/Src/cribbage.c
DEMO/snapshot.sh
DEMO/sourcefiles.cpio
DEMO/testdir
```

Like most `tar` archives, this one assumes that you're already in the directory you want to install into, so the DEMO directory has been added to the current working directory.

5. One very common usage of `tar` is to copy a directory tree from one spot to another while retaining the original file ownership and permissions.

The standard solution for this is to specify `-` as the output device, because all the information will be streaming into standard output. Simply have another `tar` on the receiving end that's expecting information from standard input:

```
cd olddir; tar -cf - . | (cd newdir; tar -xpf -)
```

The parentheses, recall, spawn a subshell which inherits the `stdin`, `stdout`, and `stderr` of the parent shell. In this case, the subshell changes to the new directory, then the `tar` begins to unpack what's being given to it from the first `tar` command.

> One warning related to using `tar` to move directory trees without an intermediate file. Because `tar` tries to intelligently rebuild symbolic links as it unpacks an archive, it's a good habit to always specify *newdir* as an absolute directory name (for example, one that begins with /).

Archiving a directory, moving the archive elsewhere, and unpacking it selectively in another location is probably the quintessential use of `tar` in the Unix world. It's a sophisticated task done quite easily with standard Unix tools.

dump and System Backups

The `tar` command can also be used for system backups, but unless you have the sophisticated GNU `tar` with its helpful `-N` *date* flag, you'll probably find `tar` too primitive for standard system backups. You could back up pieces of your system, but is that sufficient?

In fact, the standard Unix approach for system backups is the `dump` command, and its partner, `restore`.

Task 7.5: Incremental Backups

In the world of system administration, there are two types of backups that are necessary—full backups, in which every file in the file system is copied or archived, and incremental backups, in which only those files that have changed since the previous backup are saved.

A full backup is easy, and can even be accomplished by `tar -cf /dev/st0 /`, where `/dev/st0` is the name of a SCSI backup device, perhaps a DAT tape or similar.

> A common backup device is a tape drive added to the SCSI chain. If that's your configuration, your tape drive is probably best referenced as `/dev/st0` for Linux, `/dev/rsa0` for Darwin (though you'll have to `mknod` it before you can use it), and `/dev/rmt/0` for Solaris. There are nuances regarding whether the device will rewind or not too, so double-check with your system documentation to verify the exact device name. For example, although `/dev/st0` works for Linux, the nonrewinding device name for the same SCSI tape drive would be `/dev/nst0`.

The more interesting situation is when you want to do an incremental backup. How do you find the files that have changed since the previous backup (either a full or incremental backup, depending on what happened the previous night) and copy just those to the archival device?

You can identify files that have changed with `find`, using its super-helpful `-newer` flag, but let's focus instead on the standard Unix `dump` command, because it has this capability built in and lots more besides.

1. The `dump` command is built on the concept of multiple backup levels: a level 0 dump is a full backup, whereas a level 1-9 backup will only save files that have changed since the last backup of a similar, or higher level. That's confusing, I admit, so instead just use two levels like most people: 0 for full backups, 1 for incremental backups.

> The dump command on Solaris is for programmers who want to analyze the contents of binary executables. The equivalent backup command is called `ufsdump` (and `ufsrestore`), which otherwise work completely identically to what's demonstrated here.

▼

7

The last-backed-up timestamp is stored in the file /etc/dumpdates, and a somewhat annoying characteristic of dump must be considered: it can only back up one partition or disk at a time. A quick glance at the output of df shows

```
# df
Filesystem              1k-blocks      Used Available Use% Mounted on
/dev/sda5                  380791    102093    259038  29% /
/dev/sda1                   49558      7797     39202  17% /boot
/dev/sda3                16033712     40416  15178808   1% /home
none                       256436         0    256436   0% /dev/shm
/dev/sdb1                17245524   1310620  15058876   9% /usr
/dev/sdb2                  253871     86739    154025  37% /var
```

Ignore /dev/shm because it's part of the virtual memory system, and you can see that there are five different partitions on this system. This means that you'll need to invoke dump five times to successfully backup the entire system.

2. To do a full backup within the Linux environment to a nonrewinding SCSI tape drive would therefore look like this:

```
dump -0uf /dev/nst0 /
dump -0uf /dev/nst0 /boot
dump -0uf /dev/nst0 /home
dump -0uf /dev/nst0 /usr
dump -0uf /dev/nst0 /var
```

Somewhat tedious, admittedly, but backup utilities are fairly crude in the world of Unix, even after 30 years of development.

The dump command has many starting flags, of which the most critical are highlighted in Table 7.3.

TABLE 7.3   Critical Flags for dump

Flag	Meaning
0-9	Dump level. Level 0 is always a full dump.
-b *size*	Block size of the output device.
-f *file*	Send output to specified file or device.
-S	Estimate the amount of tape needed, without actually doing the backup itself.
-T *date*	Calculate what files to dump based on whether they're newer than the specified date. See ctime(3) for correct date format.
-u	Update the /etc/dumpdate file after a successful dump.
-W	Show which file systems need to be backed up, and when the last backup of each system was, if ever.

▼   3. To experiment with dump, we can write output to /dev/null, a device that's the
       "bit bucket" of Unix—you can write as much as you want to it, and it never fills
       up. Everything just vanishes:

```
# /sbin/dump -0uf /dev/null /boot
  DUMP: Date of this level 0 dump: Wed Jan 23 12:58:11 2002
  DUMP: Dumping /dev/sda1 (/boot) to /dev/null
  DUMP: Exclude ext3 journal inode 8
  DUMP: Label: /boot
  DUMP: mapping (Pass I) [regular files]
  DUMP: mapping (Pass II) [directories]
  DUMP: estimated 3726 tape blocks.
  DUMP: Volume 1 started with block 1 at: Wed Jan 23 12:58:23 2002
  DUMP: dumping (Pass III) [directories]
  DUMP: dumping (Pass IV) [regular files]
  DUMP: Closing /dev/null
  DUMP: Volume 1 completed at: Wed Jan 23 12:58:24 2002
  DUMP: Volume 1 3720 tape blocks (3.63MB)
  DUMP: Volume 1 took 0:00:01
  DUMP: Volume 1 transfer rate: 3720 kB/s
  DUMP: 3720 tape blocks (3.63MB) on 1 volume(s)
  DUMP: finished in 1 seconds, throughput 3720 kBytes/sec
  DUMP: Date of this level 0 dump: Wed Jan 23 12:58:11 2002
  DUMP: Date this dump completed:  Wed Jan 23 12:58:24 2002
  DUMP: Average transfer rate: 3720 kB/s
  DUMP: DUMP IS DONE
```

As a second experiment, let's dump all the files in /home that have been changed
since January 21, 2002 (two days prior to the creation of this example):

```
# /sbin/dump -0f /tmp/homedump -T "Mon Jan 21 00:00:00 2002" /home
  DUMP: Date of this level 0 dump: Wed Jan 23 13:10:09 2002
  DUMP: Date of last level ? dump: Mon Jan 21 00:00:00 2002
  DUMP: Dumping /dev/sda3 (/home) to /tmp/homedump
  DUMP: Exclude ext3 journal inode 8
  DUMP: Label: /home
  DUMP: mapping (Pass I) [regular files]
  DUMP: mapping (Pass II) [directories]
  DUMP: estimated 2649 tape blocks.
  DUMP: Volume 1 started with block 1 at: Wed Jan 23 13:10:26 2002
  DUMP: dumping (Pass III) [directories]
  DUMP: dumping (Pass IV) [regular files]
  DUMP: Closing /tmp/homedump
  DUMP: Volume 1 completed at: Wed Jan 23 13:10:26 2002
  DUMP: Volume 1 2680 tape blocks (2.62MB)
  DUMP: 2680 tape blocks (2.62MB) on 1 volume(s)
  DUMP: finished in less than a second
  DUMP: Date of this level 0 dump: Wed Jan 23 13:10:09 2002
  DUMP: Date this dump completed:  Wed Jan 23 13:10:26 2002
  DUMP: Average transfer rate: 0 kB/s
  DUMP: DUMP IS DONE
```

▼   This backup image took 2.6MB, or 2,744,320MB of disk space.

7

4. Let's have a look at what file systems do and don't need to be backed up:

```
# /sbin/dump -W
Last dump(s) done (Dump '>' file systems):
  /dev/sda5     (       /) Last dump: never
  /dev/sda1     ( /boot) Last dump: Level 0, Date Wed Jan 23 12:58:11 2002
  /dev/sda3     ( /home) Last dump: never
  /dev/sdb1     (  /usr) Last dump: never
  /dev/sdb2     (  /var) Last dump: never
```

Surprisingly, the /home partition still lists as never being backed up. This is because the -T flag is mutually exclusive with the -u flag necessary to update the incremental backup data file /etc/dumpdates.

5. The partner command for dump is restore, which lets you extract one or more files from a dump archive. To list what's in a dump archive, the -t flag should be familiar:

```
# /sbin/restore -tf /tmp/homedump
Dump   date: Wed Jan 23 13:10:09 2002
Dumped from: Mon Jan 21 00:00:00 2002
Level 0 dump of /home on staging.intuitive.com:/dev/sda3
Label: /home
        2        .
   326401        ./taylor
   326408        ./taylor/.bash_history
  1256641        ./taylor/bin
  1256671        ./taylor/bin/autocompress.sh
   326425        ./taylor/mail.log
   326427        ./taylor/sentinel.file
   326428        ./taylor/proposal.doc.gz
   326423        ./taylor/rowing-w-jasmine2.jpg.gz
  1844161        ./testdude
  1893121        ./testdude/DEMO
  1909441        ./testdude/DEMO/Src
  1909443        ./testdude/DEMO/Src/cribbage.c.gz
  1925761        ./testdude/DEMO/testdir
  1893123        ./testdude/DEMO/testfile.gz
  1893124        ./testdude/DEMO/snapshot.sh.gz
  1893125        ./testdude/DEMO/sourcefiles.cpio.gz
  1844169        ./testdude/adduser.sh.gz
  1844179        ./testdude/browse.sh.gz
  1844171        ./testdude/delete.sh.gz
  1844173        ./testdude/getmodemdriver.sh.gz
  1844174        ./testdude/getstocks.sh.gz
  1844175        ./testdude/gettermsheet.sh.gz
  1844176        ./testdude/rowing-w-jasmine2.jpg.gz
  1844177        ./testdude/suspend.sh.gz
  1844180        ./testdude/checkhomes.sh.gz
  1844170        ./testdude/checkpw.sh.gz
  1844172        ./testdude/diskhogs.sh.gz
```

Although you can specify which files to restore directly from the command line, restore has a nifty interactive mode that is considerably easier to work with. You get there with the -i flag:

It's a bit different than the way tar handles things, because restore is actually an interactive program of its own, as demonstrated in this example:

```
# /sbin/restore -if /tmp/homedump
/sbin/restore > what
Dump    date: Wed Jan 23 13:10:09 2002
Dumped from: Mon Jan 21 00:00:00 2002
Level 0 dump of /home on staging.intuitive.com:/dev/sda3
Label: /home
/sbin/restore > ls
.:
taylor/    testdude/

/sbin/restore > cd testdude
/sbin/restore > ls
./testdude:
DEMO/                      checkpw.sh.gz            getstocks.sh.gz
adduser.sh.gz              delete.sh.gz             gettermsheet.sh.gz
browse.sh.gz               diskhogs.sh.gz           rowing-w-
jasmine2.jpg.gz
checkhomes.sh.gz           getmodemdriver.sh.gz     suspend.sh.gz

/sbin/restore > cd DEMO
/sbin/restore > ls
./testdude/DEMO:
Src/                 sourcefiles.cpio.gz  testfile.gz
snapshot.sh.gz       testdir/

/sbin/restore > add testfile.gz
/sbin/restore > add snapshot.sh.gz
/sbin/restore > ls
./testdude/DEMO:
 Src/                 sourcefiles.cpio.gz  *testfile.gz
*snapshot.sh.gz       testdir/

/sbin/restore > extract
You have not read any tapes yet.
Unless you know which volume your file(s) are on you should start
with the last volume and work towards the first.
Specify next volume #: 1
set owner/mode for '.'? [yn] y
/sbin/restore > quit
```

The concept here is that you're interactively exploring the archive and marking each file that you'd like to have added to the restore list (extracted). When you're done, extract begins the actual work. If your backup is in multiple volumes, you'll need to specify which, or 1 for a single-volume dump.

7

Backups are difficult to implement safely and reliably on Unix systems because the commands and utilities are relatively primitive. Nonetheless, ignoring backups is a dangerous practice, and at any time your system could crash and potentially burn. And then what would your users say about you?

Explore the information about different backup devices and their tradeoffs online—one good place to start is `http://www.backupcentral.com/`—then ensure that the device is supported by your flavor of Unix before you buy and install it. Once you have everything running smoothly, immediately establish a tape rotation regimen and add the `dump` commands to your `crontab` file. (We'll cover `cron` in great detail in Hour 15, "Running Jobs in the Future.")

Summary

This hour has explored the nuances of compression and file system backup. We've seen how different compression tools can produce surprisingly varied results on Unix systems, and that there are a variety of non-tape-backup uses for these utilities, too. One final comment: If you're going to create a backup regimen, remember to rotate your tapes, so you always have a safe backup from a few days ago in addition to the tape you're using for the latest backup.

Q&A

Q Why are the backup solutions so poor on Unix?

A That's a good question with no good answer. With thousands of Unix servers powering the Internet, you'd think that there are better backup solutions than `dump` and expensive commercial solutions. The only other interesting backup applications I know of are Kbackup (X Window System-based), BURT (based on Tcl/Tk), and Amanda (Advanced Maryland Automatic Network Disk Archiver).

Q How do you do backups on your own server?

A Um, err, next question?

Q What's your favorite compression program?

A I always use `gzip -9` if it's available, to get the maximum compression possible. On the other hand, the command `compress` is certainly more mnemonic, so perhaps an alias...?

Workshop

Quiz

1. Why do you think that `compress` had different results on different platforms?

2. When compressing lots of different types of files, what's the main difference—other than compression efficiency—between `compress` and `gzip`?

3. How do you view the contents of compressed files without uncompressing them?

4. Where will `cd ~` take you?

5. What does `tar -xvZpf /dev/st0` do?

Answers

1. Actually, that's a really good question. Logically, if they're using the same algorithm, they should all have the same results. I'd be interested in hearing your own theory on this puzzling variation.

2. The main difference is that `gzip` likes to compress everything, even if the resultant file is a tiny bit *bigger* than the original. This rarely occurs, because `gzip` does a great job of compression, but it's still peculiar.

3. Use `zcat`, or if you have them, `zmore`, `zgrep`, or something similar.

4. To your home directory, exactly as `cd $HOME` and `cd` would do.

5. Extract commands from the `dev/st0` device, uncompressing them with verbose output, and try to retain ownership and permission information from the archive.

The next hour explores the nifty world of package management—the mechanism by which administrators can obtain, install, and uninstall new software on their computer. This hour will offer a basic overview of package management functionality, and explore basic package functionality with RPM and `fink`, the Mac OS X package management system.

7

Hour **8**

Unix Package Management

In the world of personal computers, if you want to add a software package to your system, you buy it (or download it, perhaps) and run an installer program that does lots of behind-the-scenes magic and eventually pops up with an "installed!" message. What it did, and indeed what you have installed on your system, can be a mystery.

Rising from more egalitarian roots, the Unix system for many years was saddled with packages that were distributed as source code along with very complex instructions on how to build and install the program when (alright, *if!*) it compiled.

Over the last half dozen years, however, Unix has caught up and in many ways surpassed the installation strategies of the personal computer world. However, there's no standard. Red Hat Linux, for example, uses RPM, the Red Hat Package Manager system. Darwin uses the still-evolving fink system, and Solaris has its own solution—pkg.

In this hour you will learn about

- Working with RPM on Linux
- Adding RPM packages from the Internet
- Working with `fink` on Darwin
- Working with `pkg` on Solaris

Red Hat Package Manager and Linux

The Red Hat Package Manager (RPM) system is one of the most sophisticated available in the Unix marketplace, and is the result of years of development by contract programmers (and eventually employees) of Red Hat Linux Corporation. Indeed, some sysadmins stick with Red Hat because RPM is so easy to work with.

The concept behind RPM is the same as with all package managers: They encapsulate all the files and configuration details needed to install and enable the specified package, including tracking version numbers of libraries, installing relevant documentation, and even checking automatically to ensure that the installation won't step on files needed by a different package.

The interface to RPM is a bit baffling, however, so let's jump right in and see how it works.

> If you are using a GUI, the good news is that there's an RPM front end for both of the popular window managers in Linux—GnoRPM for GNOME, and Kpackage for KDE.

Task 8.1: Working with RPM

There are basic tasks that you'll want to know how to do in your package manager: query what packages are installed, install (or update) a specific package, list what files are included with a given package, and delete a package from the system.

1. The most basic RPM command is to query all packages. This is done with `-qa`, and you'll probably have 400–600 packages installed on your system. When we first installed Red Hat Linux (see Hour 1, "Installing Unix"), recall that we opted for the "workstation" configuration, and that it took forever because it was installing package after package. RPM is how you can go back and query exactly what it did.

```
$ rpm -qa | head
redhat-logos-1.1.3-1
glibc-2.2.4-13
```

```
cracklib-2.7-12
dosfstools-2.7-1
gdbm-1.8.0-10
ksymoops-2.4.1-1
mktemp-1.5-11
perl-5.6.0-17
setserial-2.17-4
netconfig-0.8.11-7
$ rpm -aq | wc -l
    638
```

There are more than 600 packages installed, so typing `rpm -qa` without feeding it to a pager or something similar would result in a phenomenal wave of information!

Each package is identified by its name, version number, and the package version number. For example, the Perl package is identified as `perl-5.6.0-17`, which means that it's the `perl` package for version 5.6.0 of Perl, and that this is the 17th version of the RPM package for this particular distribution of Perl.

> Why is this the *seventeenth* version of this package? Because when packages are large, include lots of files, and have lots of dependencies, it can often take package developers quite a few tries to get things just right for all platforms and possible configurations. Nothing to worry about!

2. To learn more about a specific package, use `rpm -qi`, either by specifying the full package name, or just the base name instead:

```
$ rpm -qi setserial
Name        : setserial              Relocations: /usr
Version     : 2.17                        Vendor: Red Hat, Inc.
Release     : 4                       Build Date: Sun 24 Jun 2001
➥11:59:21 PM PDT
Install date: Wed 21 Nov 2001 02:34:04 PM PST      Build Host: elliot.
➥devel.redhat.com
Group       : Applications/System     Source RPM: setserial-2.17-4.
➥src.rpm
Size        : 31113                      License: GPL
Packager    : Red Hat, Inc. <http://bugzilla.redhat.com/bugzilla>
Summary     : A utility for configuring serial ports.
Description :
Setserial is a basic system utility for displaying or setting serial
port information. Setserial can reveal and allow you to alter the I/O
port and IRQ that a particular serial device is using, and more.
```

3. One of the features I really like about other package systems that isn't a part of RPM is the capability to provide a summary listing of packages and their descriptions.

And yet, if you look at the output, there's a Summary line. So a little bit of judi-cious shell script coding produces showrpms:

```
$ cat showrpms.sh
#!/bin/sh

# SHOWRPMS - List all the RPM packages on the system in a friendly manner

count=0

for package in `rpm -qa`
do
  summary="`rpm -qi $package | grep '^Summary' | cut -d: -f2-`"
  echo ${package}: $summary
  count="`expr $count + 1`"
done

echo ""
echo "Listed $count RPM packages"

exit 0
```

In a nutshell, this loops through all packages reported by rpm –qa, querying each for its information, then extracts the summary line and outputs the package name and summary on the same line:

```
$ showrpms.sh | head
redhat-logos-1.1.3-1: Red Hat-related icons and pictures.
glibc-2.2.4-13: The GNU libc libraries.
cracklib-2.7-12: A password-checking library.
dosfstools-2.7-1: Utilities for making and checking MS-DOS FAT filesystems
➥on Linux.
gdbm-1.8.0-10: A GNU set of database routines which use extensible hashing.
ksymoops-2.4.1-1: Kernel oops and error message decoder
mktemp-1.5-11: A small utility for safely making /tmp files.
perl-5.6.0-17: The Perl programming language.
setserial-2.17-4: A utility for configuring serial ports.
netconfig-0.8.11-7: A text-based tool for simple configuration of ethernet
➥devices.
```

An attractive and much more sysadmin-friendly output!

> There is actually a way to convince RPM to output information in this for-mat, if you really dig into it. There's a command option --queryformat that lets you specify exactly what information you want presented, and in what form. If you use
>
> ```
> rpm -qa --queryformat '%{NAME}: %{SUMMARY}\n'
> ```
>
> your output will be the same as the showrpms script.

4. Now we can more effectively search to see, for example, what command line shells are installed:

```
$ showrpms.sh | grep -i shell
sharutils-4.2.1-8: The GNU shar utilities for packaging and unpackaging
➥shell archives.
mc-4.5.51-36: A user-friendly file manager and visual shell.
docbook-utils-0.6.9-2: Shell scripts for managing DocBook documents.
bash-2.05-8: The GNU Bourne Again shell (bash) version 2.05.
ash-0.3.7-2: A smaller version of the Bourne shell (sh).
tcsh-6.10-6: An enhanced version of csh, the C shell.
sh-utils-2.0.11-5: A set of GNU utilities commonly used in shell scripts.
```

The RPM package is a powerful way to manage packages on your system, but where it really gets exciting is when you can grab different packages from the Internet and extend the capabilities of your system with ease!

Adding New RPM Packages from the Internet

There's no capability within the rpm command to reach out to a Net archive and search for available packages, so you'll need to pop into your graphical Web browser (perhaps Kommando, a popular Linux browser) and poke around a bit.

Task 8.2: Installing New Web-Based RPM Packages

To install new packages on your system, you need to explore the Web and identify the specific package desired.

> A great place to start your RPM package search is the Pbone Web site at http://rpm.pbone.net/. You can also make sure you have the latest version of RPM by checking http://www.rpm.org/.

1. Because the network isn't always available, I like to have copies of relevant documentation on my own system for backup purposes. I popped over to Pbone and learned that the great Linux FAQ set is available as an RPM package called faq-7.2-1.noarch.rpm. On the site, it also lists the full URL of the specific package at a variety of servers around the world.

I'll pick a link from the University of Oklahoma and feed it to the RPM package with the -i to install, -v for more verbose output, and -h to show a sequence of hash marks as the file downloads:

```
# rpm -ivh ftp://ftp.ou.edu/mirrors/linux/redhat/redhat-7.2-
en/doc/RedHat/RPMS/faq-7.2-1.noarch.rpm
Retrieving ftp://ftp.ou.edu/mirrors/linux/redhat/redhat-7.2-
en/doc/RedHat/RPMS/faq-7.2-1.noarch.rpm
Preparing...                 ######################################### [100%]
   1:faq                     ######################################### [100%]
```

2. Looks like it installed just fine. Let's double-check with the `-qi` flag:

```
# rpm -qi faq
Name         : faq                       Relocations: (not relocateable)
Version      : 7.2                             Vendor: Red Hat, Inc.
Release      : 1                           Build Date: Thu 30 Aug 2001
➥12:10:48 PM PDT
Install date: Sat 26 Jan 2002 11:31:11 AM PST      Build Host: stripples.
➥devel.redhat.com
Group        : Documentation             Source RPM: faq-7.2-1.src.rpm
Size         : 1596478                       License: distributable
Packager     : Red Hat, Inc. <http://bugzilla.redhat.com/bugzilla>
Summary      : Frequently Asked Questions (FAQ) about Linux.
Description :
The faq package includes the text of the Frequently Asked
Questions (FAQ) about Linux from
http://metalab.unc.edu/pub/Linux/docs/faqs/.  These FAQs are a great source
of information (sometimes historical) about Linux.

Install the faq package if you'd like to read the Linux FAQ off your own
machine.
```

There's another useful flag to RPM that will show you the exact names of all the files installed with a package—the `-l` flag:

```
# rpm -ql faq | wc -l
   121
```

You can see that more than 120 files were installed with this simple `rpm` install. To have a peek, let's use `head`:

```
# rpm -ql faq | head -20
/etc/X11/applnk/Documentation
/etc/X11/applnk/Documentation/Linux Community
/etc/X11/applnk/Documentation/Linux Community/faq.desktop
/usr/share/doc/FAQ
/usr/share/doc/FAQ/html
/usr/share/doc/FAQ/html/AfterStep-FAQ
/usr/share/doc/FAQ/html/AfterStep-FAQ/AfterStep-FAQ-1.html
```

▼
```
/usr/share/doc/FAQ/html/AfterStep-FAQ/AfterStep-FAQ-10.html
/usr/share/doc/FAQ/html/AfterStep-FAQ/AfterStep-FAQ-2.html
/usr/share/doc/FAQ/html/AfterStep-FAQ/AfterStep-FAQ-3.html
/usr/share/doc/FAQ/html/AfterStep-FAQ/AfterStep-FAQ-4.html
/usr/share/doc/FAQ/html/AfterStep-FAQ/AfterStep-FAQ-5.html
/usr/share/doc/FAQ/html/AfterStep-FAQ/AfterStep-FAQ-6.html
/usr/share/doc/FAQ/html/AfterStep-FAQ/AfterStep-FAQ-7.html
/usr/share/doc/FAQ/html/AfterStep-FAQ/AfterStep-FAQ-8.html
/usr/share/doc/FAQ/html/AfterStep-FAQ/AfterStep-FAQ-9.html
/usr/share/doc/FAQ/html/AfterStep-FAQ/AfterStep-FAQ.html
/usr/share/doc/FAQ/html/AfterStep-FAQ/new.gif
/usr/share/doc/FAQ/html/AfterStep-FAQ/next.gif
/usr/share/doc/FAQ/html/AfterStep-FAQ/prev.gif
```
▲

The preceding example of the FAQ package is a great place to start, because it has no dependencies. One of the great frustrations of working with RPM is that there are inconsistencies in the dependencies listed, so an attempt to install one package often causes you to install a half dozen updated library and support packages first. It can be most frustrating!

Being able to quickly and easily install RPM packages from the Web is one of the true luxuries of working with Linux. It's just as easy to update your installed software against a newly downloaded RPM, too (use `rpm -Uvh` *package* rather than `-ivh`, for example). To delete a package, use `rpm -e` *packagename*. The most helpful `rpm` flags are summarized in Table 8.1.

TABLE 8.1 Helpful Flags to `rpm`

Flag	Meaning
-e	Eliminate the specified RPM package from the system.
-h	Show progress of any downloads as hash marks (#) on the screen.
-i	Install. (Use with -v to see what's going on.)
-p	Query an uninstalled package. Quite helpful!
-q	Query the RPM database: -qa queries all packages, or you can specify a package by name.
-U	Upgrade whatever parts of the specified package have changed since the last install.
-v	Verbose—RPM usually only lists errors, which can be disconcerting. Use -v to see what it's doing.

Package Management in Darwin

There is no built-in default package manager in Darwin, and while Mac OS X has a very sophisticated installation system for Mac applications, it's not accessible from the command line, nor does it particularly help you extend the Unix side of things.

The good news is that the open source community has banded together and built a very sophisticated alternative package management system called `fink`.

 Wondering what `fink` means? From the original developer: "Fink is the German name for Finch, a kind of bird. I was looking for a name for the project, and the name of the OS, Darwin, led me to think about Charles Darwin, the Galapagos Islands, and evolution. I remembered a piece about the so-called Darwin Finches and their beaks from school, and well, that's it...." You can read more at the great `fink` FAQ at `http://fink.source-forge.net/faq/`.

To get started with `fink`, you need to download the initial `fink` distribution package, which is packaged as a standard Mac OS X application binary.

Task 8.3: Installing and Working with `fink`

▲ TASK

The first step toward using `fink` on your OS X Macintosh is to make sure that you've installed Developer Tools, which was included with your Mac OS X distribution. If you don't have it, you can always download it from Apple at `http://developer.apple.com/tools/macosxtools.html`.

Once you're ready, pop over to `http://fink.sourceforge.net/` and click on the Downloads link. Then you'll want to choose the Binary Installer, which is a bit less than 8MB.

Once that's downloaded, click on the `.pkg` opened box icon to install the `fink` system. Remember that you'll need your administrative password for this install to succeed, as shown in Figure 8.1.

Once you've done that, it'll zip through various screens and finish up without error. There's one more step necessary: When you start up `Terminal` in OS X, make sure you add `/sw/bin` and `/sw/sbin` to your `PATH` so the commands can be found. In fact, you might also add a second environment variable while you're editing your `.cshrc` (or equivalent): `MANPATH="/sw/share/man"` to ensure that the man pages for the `fink`-
▼ installed applications can be found. *Now you're ready to get started!*

FIGURE 8.1
Administrative password prompt.

1. The `fink` application is installed in the directory `/sw/bin`, so let's start with the `list` command to see what's included in the distribution:

```
# fink list | head
Reading package info...
Information about 251 packages read.
    a2ps          4.12-4        Any to PostScript filter.
    anacron       2.3-3         A periodic command scheduler
    ant           1.4.1-2       Java based build tool.
    apache        1.3.20-2      Flexible and extensible web server
    app-defaults  20010814-1    Creates an app-defaults directory for fink
  i apt           0.5.4-1       Advanced front-end for dpkg
    audiofile     0.2.1-2       Audio File Library
    autoconf      2.13-3        System for generating configure scripts
```

One significant difference between `fink` and RPM is that `fink` has an underlying network connectivity capability that lets it list all the packages that you *could* install, with those that you *have installed* delimited with the `i` in the left edge of the listing (see the `apt` package, for example).

This means that if you want to see what packages you've installed, simply feed the output of `fink` to a `grep`:

```
# fink list | grep '^ i '
  i apt          0.5.4-1       Advanced front-end for dpkg
  i base-files   1.3-1         Directory infrastructure
  i bzip2        1.0.1-4       Block-sorting file compressor
  i debianutils  1.15-4        Misc. utilities specific to Debian (and Fink)
  i dpkg         1.9.17-2      The Debian package manager
  i fink         0.9.4-1       The Fink package manager
  i gettext      0.10.40-1     Message localization support
  i gzip         1.2.4a-5      The gzip file compressor
  i libiconv     1.7-3         Character set conversion library
  i ncurses      5.2-5         Full-screen ascii drawing library
  i tar          1.13.19-1     GNU tar - tape archiver
```

Packages that might have (i) as their status are installed, but there's a newer version available.

▼   2. Now that we have `fink` installed, we can remedy a couple of problems with the
        Darwin distribution. It's time to install `bash`, a command shell that is the first
        choice of many Unix sysadmins.

```
# fink install bash
Reading package info...
Information about 288 packages read in 1 seconds.
pkg bash   version ###
pkg bash   version 2.05-3
The following package will be installed or updated:
 bash
The following 2 additional packages will be installed:
 dlcompat readline
Do you want to continue? [Y/n] y
curl -L -O ftp://ftp.gnu.org/gnu/bash/bash-2.05.tar.gz
curl -L -O http://prdownloads.sourceforge.net/fink/dlcompat-20010831.tar.gz
curl -L -O ftp://ftp.gnu.org/gnu/readline/readline-4.2.tar.gz
mkdir -p /sw/src/dlcompat-20010831-1
tar -xvzf /sw/src/dlcompat-20010831.tar.gz
dlcompat-20010831/
dlcompat-20010831/APPLE_LICENSE
dlcompat-20010831/ChangeLog
dlcompat-20010831/dlfcn.h
dlcompat-20010831/dlopen.c
dlcompat-20010831/Makefile
dlcompat-20010831/README
make prefix=/sw
cc -Wall -O2 -DDEBUG=0 -fno-common -o dlopen.o -c dlopen.c

...lots and lots of output removed ...

mkdir -p /sw/fink/dists/stable/main/binary-darwin-powerpc/shells
dpkg-deb -b root-bash-2.05-3
/sw/fink/dists/stable/main/binary-darwin-powerpc/shells
dpkg-deb: building package `bash' in
`/sw/fink/dists/stable/main/binary-darwin-powerpc/shells/bash_2.05-3_darwin-
powerpc.deb'.
ln -sf
/sw/fink/dists/stable/main/binary-darwin-powerpc/shells/bash_2.05-3_darwin-p
owerpc.deb /sw/fink/debs/
rm -rf /sw/src/root-bash-2.05-3
dpkg -i
/sw/fink/dists/stable/main/binary-darwin-powerpc/shells/bash_2.05-3_darwin-p
owerpc.deb
Selecting previously deselected package bash.
(Reading database ... 3476 files and directories currently installed.)
Unpacking bash (from .../bash_2.05-3_darwin-powerpc.deb) ...
Setting up bash (2.05-3) ...
* Bash: (bash).            The GNU Bourne-Again SHell.
install-info: no section specified for new entry, placing at end
```
▼

▼ The output of this command was hundreds of lines of compilation and configuration information because at the time of this writing, the binary distributions of most packages were unavailable. As a result, fink automatically switched to a source code distribution, and instead of taking just a minute or two, the install took almost ten minutes to complete—two minutes to download the files, and seven minutes to compile and install.

Installing the helpful text-only Web browser lynx is a similarly easy task with fink install lynx.

3. To see what's inside a package, use fink describe *pkg*. Here's a bit more information on bash, for example:

```
# fink describe bash
Reading package info...
Information about 251 packages read.

bash-2.05-3: The GNU Bourne Again SHell
  Bash is an sh-compatible command language interpreter that executes
  commands read from the standard input or from a file.  Bash also
  incorporates useful features from the Korn and C shells (ksh and csh).
  .
  Bash is ultimately intended to be a conformant implementation of the IEEE
  Posix Shell and Tools specification (IEEE Working Group 1003.2).
  .
  Web site: http://www.gnu.org/software/bash/bash.html
  .
  Porting Notes:
  GNU Bash version 2.05 compiles (and installs correctly after
  commenting out the install-info line in doc/Makefile.in)
  .
  Maintainer: Paul Swenson <pds@mac.com>

Done.
```

4. Removing a package with fink is straightforward:

```
# fink remove lynx
Reading package info...
Information about 251 packages read.
dpkg --remove lynx
(Reading database ... 3548 files and directories currently installed.)
Removing lynx ...
Done.
```

Once you've uninstalled the package, fink is also smart enough to know that the core archive is still available, so a re-install is quite speedy:

```
# fink install lynx
Reading package info...
```
▼

▼
```
Information about 251 packages read.
dpkg -i /sw/fink/dists/stable/main/binary-darwin-powerpc/web/lynx_2.8.4-1_
➥darwin-powerpc.deb
Selecting previously deselected package lynx.
(Reading database ... 3475 files and directories currently installed.)
Unpacking lynx (from .../lynx_2.8.4-1_darwin-powerpc.deb) ...
Setting up lynx (2.8.4-1) ...
Done.
```

5. The fink man page has an extensive discussion of the command options, of course, but Table 8.2 summarizes the key options for everyday use.

TABLE 8.2   Key Options for fink

Option	Meaning
install *pkg*	Installs the specified package, and any additional packages that might be required.
remove *pkg*	Removes the specified package from the system.
list	Lists all packages—marking those installed with an i and those installed but out-of-date with (i).
describe *pkg*	Describes the specified package in detail.
selfupdate	Updates fink itself to the very latest version.

▲

The fink package is surprisingly sophisticated and quite easy to use, a boon to those Darwin users who might be relatively new to the power—and oddness—of Unix. What I most like about it is that you're shielded from having to dig around on the Web and find packages, because they're already registered in the central fink database. That's a model that the RPM team should follow.

Be aware, however, that fink is unquestionably a work-in-progress and doesn't have the benefit of years of widespread use, so don't be surprised if the version of fink you install is more than a little different from that demonstrated here.

Package Management in Solaris

Solaris uses its own package management system too, one that's more primitive than RPM in some ways, and easier to use in others. It's certainly easier to work with from the command line, one of my greatest criticisms of the RPM system.

Task 8.4: Managing Packages in Solaris

Similar to other package management systems, the Solaris pkg package management system lets you query packages, find out what's inside a package, and install new packages.

1. To see what packages you have installed, use the `pkginfo` command. Without any argument it lists everything installed:

```
# pkginfo | head -15
system       AMImega      MEGA Family SCSI Host Bus Adapter
system       CADP160      Adaptec Ultra160 SCSI Host Adapter Driver
system       CPQcnft      Compaq NetFlex Family NIC
system       CPQncr       Compaq Family SCSI HBA
system       CPQsmii      Compaq SMART-2/E Family of Array Controller
system       HPFC         Agilent Fibre Channel HBA Driver
system       MADGFmt      Madge Token Ring Family of NIC
system       MYLXflp      Buslogic FlashPoint Ultra PCI SCSI
system       NCRos86r     NCR Platform Support, OS Functionality (Root)
application  NSCPcom      Netscape Communicator
system       SK98sol      SysKonnect SK-NET Gigabit Ethernet Adapter SK-98xx
system       SKfp         SysKonnect PCI-FDDI Host Adapter
system       SUNW1251f    Russian 1251 fonts
ALE          SUNW5ttf     Traditional Chinese BIG5 True Type Fonts Package
ALE          SUNW5xmft    Chinese/Taiwan BIG5 X Windows Platform minimum
➥required Fonts Package
```

You can also feed it to `grep` to search for specific packages:

```
$ pkginfo | grep shell
system       SUNWbash     GNU Bourne-Again shell (bash)
system       SUNWtcsh     Tenex C-shell (tcsh)
system       SUNWzsh      Z shell (zsh)
```

2. The full name of a package is rather intimidating in `pkg`. A typical name is `gcc-2.8.1-sol26-sparc-local.gz`, which should be interpreted as *program-version-os-processor-installation directory*.gz.

> A good starting place to learn about Solaris packages available for download is at Steven Christensen's `http://www.sunfreeware.com/`.

To install a network application, you need to copy the file onto your Solaris system through whatever means you prefer. Typically, this will be `ftp` or through a Web browser. We'll use `ftp` for this example:

```
$ ftp ftp.sunfreeware.com
Connected to ftp.sunfreeware.com.
220 ftp.sunfreeware.com FTP server ready.
Name (ftp.sunfreeware.com:taylor): ftp
331 Guest login ok, send your complete e-mail address as password.
Password:
230 Guest login ok, access restrictions apply.
Remote system type is UNIX.
```

▼

```
Using binary mode to transfer files.
ftp> cd /pub/freeware/intel/8/
250 CWD command successful.
ftp> dir sud*
200 PORT command successful.
150 Opening ASCII mode data connection for /bin/ls.
-rw-r--r--   1 steve     staff        93934 Nov 23  1999 sudo-1.5.9p4
➥-sol8-intel-local.gz
226 Transfer complete.
ftp> lcd /tmp
Local directory now /tmp
ftp> get sudo-1.5.9p4-sol8-intel-local.gb
200 PORT command successful.
150 Opening BINARY mode data connection for 'sudo-1.5.9p4
➥-sol8-intel-local.gz' (93934 bytes).
226 Transfer complete.
local: sudo-1.5.9p4-sol8-intel-local.gz remote: sudo-1.5.9p4
➥-sol8-intel-local.gz
93934 bytes received in 1.2 seconds (76.79 Kbytes/s)
ftp> quit
221 Goodbye.
```

Now the package is copied from the Net to /tmp, so it's time to install it on the Solaris system.

3. Installation of packages is done with pkgadd, but you need to take a simple intermediate step first: unzip the file. Fortunately, that's easy, as you learned last hour, with the command gunzip sudo*gz.

```
# gunzip sudo*gz
# pkgadd -d sudo-1.5.9p4-sol8-intel-local

The following packages are available:
  1  SMCsudo      sudo
                  (i86pc) 1.5.9p4

Select package(s) you wish to process (or 'all' to process
all packages). (default: all) [?,??,q]: all

Processing package instance <SMCsudo> from </tmp/sudo-1.5.9p4-sol8-intel-local>

sudo -- (i86pc) 1.5.9p4 -- Todd Miller

The selected base directory </usr/local> must exist before
installation is attempted.

Do you want this directory created now [y,n,?,q] y
Using </usr/local> as the package base directory.
## Processing package information.
## Processing system information.
```

▼

```
## Verifying disk space requirements.
## Checking for conflicts with packages already installed.
## Checking for setuid/setgid programs.

The following files are being installed with setuid and/or setgid
permissions:
   /usr/local/bin/sudo <setuid root>

Do you want to install these as setuid/setgid files [y,n,?,q] y
Installing sudo as <SMCsudo>

## Installing part 1 of 1.
/usr/local/bin/sudo
/usr/local/doc/sudo/BUGS
/usr/local/doc/sudo/CHANGES
/usr/local/doc/sudo/COPYING
/usr/local/doc/sudo/FAQ
/usr/local/doc/sudo/HISTORY
/usr/local/doc/sudo/INSTALL
/usr/local/doc/sudo/INSTALL.configure
/usr/local/doc/sudo/PORTING
/usr/local/doc/sudo/README
/usr/local/doc/sudo/RUNSON
/usr/local/doc/sudo/TODO
/usr/local/doc/sudo/TROUBLESHOOTING
/usr/local/man/man5/sudoers.5
/usr/local/man/man8/sudo.8
/usr/local/man/man8/visudo.8
/usr/local/sbin/visudo
[ verifying class <none> ]

Installation of <SMCsudo> was successful.
```

The package is installed, and you can see that even something as simple as the
sudo command ends up including 16 different files, mostly stored in the new directory /usr/local/bin/sudo.

4. To learn more about a package, use the pkginfo command, but specify a package
   name on the command line. With the -d flag, pkginfo will also show information
   about a package before it's installed, a critical capability!

First, the already-installed bash package:

```
# pkginfo SUNWbash
system       SUNWbash          GNU Bourne-Again shell (bash)
```

Notice here that the output of the command without any arguments is minimally
informative. The real value is that it can be used to quickly ascertain if a given
package is actually installed on the system or not.

▼   The -l flag is the best way to learn about the contents of a package:

```
# pkginfo -l SUNWbash
   PKGINST:  SUNWbash
      NAME:  GNU Bourne-Again shell (bash)
  CATEGORY:  system
      ARCH:  i386
   VERSION:  11.8.0,REV=2000.01.08.18.17
   BASEDIR:  /
    VENDOR:  Sun Microsystems, Inc.
      DESC:  GNU Bourne-Again shell (bash)
    PSTAMP:  catsup20000108183519
  INSTDATE:  Jan 14 2002 21:39
   HOTLINE:  Please contact your local service provider
    STATUS:  completely installed
     FILES:      7 installed pathnames
                 5 shared pathnames
                 5 directories
                 1 executables
              1222 blocks used (approx)
```

And for the sake of completeness, the same command on the sudo package archive file:

```
# pkginfo -l -d sudo*
   PKGINST:  SMCsudo
      NAME:  sudo
  CATEGORY:  application
      ARCH:  i86pc
   VERSION:  1.5.9p4
   BASEDIR:  /usr/local
    VENDOR:  Todd Miller
    PSTAMP:  Steve Christensen
     EMAIL:  steve@smc.vnet.net
    STATUS:  spooled
     FILES:     26 spooled pathnames
                 7 directories
                 2 executables
                 1 setuid/setgid executables
                 2 package information files
               496 blocks used (approx)
```

▲

To remove a package, use pkgrm.

The Solaris package management system is less sophisticated than either Linux's RPM or Darwin's fink system, but all three of them offer system administrators the ability to control what's on the system—adding, modifying, updating, and deleting as desired.

Prior to package management systems, installing software on a Unix system was an unpleasant drudgery, but now it's easy enough that some admins are tempted to let regular non-sysadmin users run the commands!

Summary

All in all, this hour has offered a whirlwind tour of package management systems and focused on their actual use on a day-to-day basis. Although there have been distinct and even surprising differences between the package managers on the different flavors of Unix, there have also been many similarities.

Before you go wild installing every package and its brother on your system, however, ensure that you are adding important and relevant features and capabilities to the box. Keep in mind that every change to the system adds a possible instability and, worse, a possible security hole.

Q&A

Q If you could only install one package, what would it be?

A I think that bash might well be one of my crucial installs, but then again, I've spent a lot of time scripting and parsing Web pages by utilizing lynx, so that's a favorite, too. But if you really want to waste time, it's hard to beat the classic nethack!

Q Why isn't transparent access to a Web-based database of installable packages a part of RPM or pkg?

A That's a good question, actually. In the Solaris case, the pkg system was developed originally for tape and CD-ROM-based software distribution. With RPM, if you want an easier interface, it might well be time to move to one of the X Window System-based graphical RPM browsers, as mentioned in the beginning of this hour.

Workshop

Quiz

1. How do you find out how many packages you have installed on your system? (You'll need a different approach for each platform, of course.)

2. How do you find out what games you have installed, if any?

3. How do you figure out what version of Perl you have installed?

4. How do you find out what audio-related packages, if any, you have?

Answers

1. On Solaris, use `pkginfo|wc -l`; on Darwin, use `fink list|wc -l`; and on Linux, use `rpm -qa|wc -l`.

2. Use the appropriate package query command and grep the output through grep -i game. Remember to use showrpm or something similar if you want to count RPM packages!

3. You should at least have Perl 5. On Solaris, for example:

```
# pkginfo | grep -i perl
system       SUNWpl5m          Perl5 On-Line Manual Pages
system       SUNWpl5p          Perl 5.005_03 (POD Documentation)
system       SUNWpl5u          Perl 5.005_03
```

4. Linux has the greatest number of audio packages installed, most likely:

```
# showrpms.sh | grep -i audio | sort
audiofile-0.2.1-2: A library for accessing various audio file formats.
audiofile-devel-0.2.1-2: Libraries, includes and other files to develop
➥audiofile applications.
aumix-2.7-5: An ncurses-based audio mixer.
cdda2wav-1.10-4: A utility for sampling/copying .wav files from digital
➥audio CDs.
cdp-0.33-21: An interactive text-mode program for playing audio CD-ROMs.
cdparanoia-alpha9.8-2: A Compact Disc Digital Audio (CDDA) extraction tool
➥(or ripper).
esound-0.2.22-5: Allows several audio streams to play on a single audio
➥device.
gnome-audio-1.0.0-12: Sounds for GNOME events.
gnome-audio-extra-1.0.0-12: Files needed for customizing GNOME event sounds.
libao-0.8.0-1: Cross Platform Audio Output Library.
libao-devel-0.8.0-1: Cross Platform Audio Output Library Development.
libvorbis-1.0rc2-2: The Vorbis General Audio Compression Codec.
mpg321-0.1.5-1: An MPEG audio player.
vorbis-1.0rc2-1: The Vorbis General Audio Compression Codec libraries
➥and tools.
```

The next hour will be short but critically important for any Unix system administrator. It will focus on running the fsck command, the de facto program that analyzes and fixes any disk errors. As a bonus, the next hour will also demonstrate how to reboot each system into single-user mode, so that it's safe to use the fcsk command (because you sure don't want to use it on an active drive!).

PART IV

Advanced Filesystem Topics

Hour

HOUR 9

Fixing Broken Disks

Many tasks of a Unix system administrator are preventative, from managing user accounts to balancing loads on servers, to configuring and monitoring an Apache Web server. If all is going well, and the planets are not in retrograde, you should be able to manage a Unix system or two for quite a while without any problems cropping up.

There's no way to completely eliminate the dangers inherent in running a computer system, even one with an operating system as stable and mature as Unix. Many things can go wrong, but the primary failure that you're likely to see is a disk hiccup.

That's what this brief hour will focus on—how to manage when there are disk errors on your system.

In this hour, you will learn

- How to check your disks with `fsck`
- To fix problems with `fsck`

Introduction to `fsck`

The cornerstone tool for wrestling cranky disks into submission on a Unix system is `fsck`. If you're used to the Windows or Mac world, you're familiar with tools like Norton Utilities, Disk Doctor, and similar products, but in Unix, you're on your own.

Worse, the tools available are quite primitive. With a little experimentation, you'll find that the `fsck` utility isn't too horrible to work with. More importantly, don't panic, because you really shouldn't need to use the `fsck` command more than once in a blue moon, anyway.

To understand how the `fsck` (file system check) command works, it's important that we start out with a very brief explanation of how files are laid out on a typical Unix filesystem.

All hard disks are broken down into blocks, either 512-bytes or 1024-bytes in size. You can't get anything smaller than that on a disk, so even a 15-byte file really takes up a block and is either 512-bytes or 1024-bytes in size.

> That's why it's so hard to have thousands of tiny files on a file system—they end up using the disk space in an extremely inefficient manner.

Every single block has a unique number called an *inode*. An inode contains the file's owner (UID), group owner (GID), permissions, size, time of last access, and so on. Inodes can point directly to file blocks or to indirect blocks, which themselves serve as a list of data blocks or perhaps a list of pointers to other indirect blocks. In this manner, the file system can efficiently store files on the disk, whether they're very small or enormous.

If you're picturing this as a house of cards, you've probably grasped the fundamental power and limitation of this approach to laying out files on a hard disk. If you "lose" the address of the initial inode, for example, you're out of luck in a big way; it's almost impossible to traverse the disk blocks and go backward to the original inode.

As a result, there's another structure on Unix hard disks called a *superblock*, which contains various information about the disk geometry (for example, size, sectors, tracks, cylinders, block size) and *the address of the first inode on the list*.

The superblock is so critical to the correct interpretation of data on the disk that it's duplicated over and over again on the disk, and the disk subsystem keeps all the duplicate superblocks up-to-date, just in case. In fact, the superblock is duplicated every 8,192 blocks on the disk, so for a small 250MB disk, the system maintains 31 different superblocks.

This explanation has covered the `ext2` filesystem, the de facto standard of most Linux installations. Other filesystem possibilities exist, notably FFS (the Berkeley Fast File System, a de facto standard on larger Unix systems), `ext3`, FAT32, HFS, HFS+, UFS, and VFAT.

Regardless of filesystem, there's only one tool sysadmins use when things go south: `fsck`.

Task 9.1: Getting Started with `fsck`

If you need to check your main disk, or any disk that has critical system data, you'll want to shut down your system and restart in single-user mode, as explained in Hour 13, "Changing System State."

For this hour, we'll explore a new disk added to the system for just this purpose, a 250MB external `ext2` hard drive.

> In the next hour we'll hook the disk into the system, format it, create an empty Unix filesystem thereon, and hook it up. You can skip to that and come back if you *really* want.

For the purposes of this hour, the disk has been formatted properly and mounted as `/disk2`. There are some files copied onto it, but it's still pretty empty.

1. Without further ado, let's run `fsck`:

```
# cd /disk2
# fsck -c /distk2
Parallelizing fsck version 1.23 (15-Aug-2001)
e2fsck 1.23, 15-Aug-2001 for EXT2 FS 0.5b, 95/08/09
/dev/hdb is mounted.

WARNING!!!  Running e2fsck on a mounted filesystem may cause
SEVERE filesystem damage.

Do you really want to continue (y/n)?
```

This seems rather ominous. Are things really that grim?

The answer is yes. The `fsck` program tries to fix problems that it encounters, so if the file system is live and being changed simultaneously, the chances of it being corrupted are very high. Don't do this unless it's a crisis.

> Never ever run `fsck` on a mounted filesystem!!

To unmount the filesystem, use the `umount` command. If the filesystem is listed in `/etc/fstab`, the main table of filesystems and their mount points, you can specify either the mount point or the device name. Otherwise, just use the device name:

```
# umount /dev/hdb
umount: /disk2: device is busy
```

Oops! We need to move out of the `/disk2` subsystem before we can unmount the disk:

```
# umount /dev/hdb
#
```

2. Let's try that `fsck` command again!

```
# fsck /dev/hdb
Parallelizing fsck version 1.23 (15-Aug-2001)
e2fsck 1.23, 15-Aug-2001 for EXT2 FS 0.5b, 95/08/09
/dev/hdb: clean, 11/64000 files, 8094/255528 blocks
```

When `fsck` reports "clean" as a result, it means that it didn't need to run a filesystem integrity check because one had been run sufficiently recently (by default, disks only force an `fsck` when there's a reason to do so, or every few months). The information about when the next scheduled `fsck` should occur is part of what's in the superblock.

Did you catch that this is a "parallelizing" version of `fsck`? That's a good thing. It means this program can check multiple filesystems simultaneously by running parallel check processes. This means that you can boot your system quite a bit faster, even after a bad shutdown sequence.

Also, it turns out that because of the different filesystems supported on many Unix systems, `fsck` is a front-end to versions of `fsck` designed for specific filesystem formats. In this case, because the system detected that `/dev/hdb` is an `ext2` filesystem, it handed the request to check the disk off to `e2fsck` for processing.

Finally, notice that the last line reports the number of files and blocks used and available. Here there are 11 files out of 64,000 possible, and 8,094 blocks out of 255,528 possible used.

3. The `-f` flag forces `fsck` to step through a proper disk check regardless of when the next check is scheduled, and the `-c` flag causes the program to test and check for bad blocks. If you want a bit more of a clue regarding what the program is doing, use `-V` for verbose output (see Table 9.1 for a list of useful `fsck` flags).

> A *bad block* is a block on the disk that alters data. Usually it's a disk media problem, and it's a hidden lurking danger that can corrupt files. It's a good idea to check for bad blocks with `fsck` every so often for just this reason.

```
# fsck -cfV /dev/hdb
Parallelizing fsck version 1.23 (15-Aug-2001)
[/sbin/fsck.ext2 -- /dev/hdb] fsck.ext2 -c /dev/hdb
e2fsck 1.23, 15-Aug-2001 for EXT2 FS 0.5b, 95/08/09
Checking for bad blocks (read-only test): done
Pass 1: Checking inodes, blocks, and sizes
Pass 2: Checking directory structure
Pass 3: Checking directory connectivity
Pass 4: Checking reference counts
Pass 5: Checking group summary information

/dev/hdb: ***** FILE SYSTEM WAS MODIFIED *****
/dev/hdb: 11/64000 files (0.0% non-contiguous), 8094/255528 blocks
```

Here in the book the line "checking for bad blocks" whizzes by in a second or two, but when you run this command on a hard disk, even a relatively small one, it can take quite a long time. Don't be surprised if you can go out for lunch and return before it finishes this one step.

TABLE 9.1   Useful `fsck` Flags

Flag	Meaning
-s	Serialize: Don't run multiple checks in parallel, run them one after the other instead. (Use this if you're actively debugging a corrupted disk.)
-b *superblock*	Tells `fsck` to try using an alternate superblock. Recall that they're stored on the disk every 8,192 blocks, so the second superblock is 8192+1, the third is 2×8192+1, and so on.
-c	Check for bad blocks on the filesystem (actually, this invokes `bad-blocks(8)` on Linux, interestingly enough).
-f	Force `fsck` to check the disk even if it thinks it's clean.
-y	Automatically answer yes to error prompts.
-t *type*	Specifies the type of filesystem to be checked. Usually, `fsck` can autodetect the filesystem, but if you must specify the type, your most likely bet is `ext2`, or perhaps `ext3`.
-A	Check all known disks. References the list in `/etc/fstab` (as explained in the next hour).

▼

You can see now that `fsck` actually steps through the disk six times in this invocation: once to check for bad blocks; again to check for consistency of inodes, blocks, and sizes; then checking the directory structure, the directory connectivity, inode reference counts, and finally the group summary information.

▲

Even though there was no information indicating that any problems were encountered or changes made, the program ends by saying that the "filesystem was modified." Sometimes it seems that's a generic message, but it's always safest to assume it's true, which is why you do *not* want to run `fsck` while your disk is mounted!

There seem to be two classes of administrative tools available in the Unix world—those that are straightforward, and those that are tricky and offer oft-confusing output. Without a doubt, `fsck` falls into the latter category for most sysadmins. The good news is that you won't need to use it often, and when you do run the program, most of the output is sensible when you learn more about the structure of the filesystem itself.

Fixing Problems with `fsck`

In the last section, things were pretty easy because there weren't any problems on the disk. When problems do arise, it can be scary but it's not time to push the panic button yet!

Task 9.2: Fixing Disk Problems with `fsck`

To illustrate how `fsck` fixes corrupted disks, I did something dangerous: I altered the contents of `/dev/hdb` in one window while running `fsck` in a second window. Guaranteed to cause trouble, and, no surprise, it did.

1. First off, the `fsck` program was invoked with a request to check bad blocks and force a complete structure check:

```
# fsck -cfV /dev/hdb
Parallelizing fsck version 1.23 (15-Aug-2001)
[/sbin/fsck.ext2 -- /dev/hdb] fsck.ext2 -c /dev/hdb
e2fsck 1.23, 15-Aug-2001 for EXT2 FS 0.5b, 95/08/09
/dev/hdb is mounted.

WARNING!!!  Running e2fsck on a mounted filesystem may cause
SEVERE filesystem damage.

Do you really want to continue (y/n)? yes

Checking for bad blocks (read-only test): done
Pass 1: Checking inodes, blocks, and sizes
Pass 2: Checking directory structure
Pass 3: Checking directory connectivity
```

▼

▼   So far, so good. Meanwhile, in another window I copied lots of files onto the disk,
     renamed them, and ultimately deleted them, in quick succession.

     The changes underfoot caused fsck to get a bit upset on Pass 4:

```
Pass 4: Checking reference counts
WARNING: PROGRAMMING BUG IN E2FSCK!
        OR SOME BONEHEAD (YOU) IS CHECKING A MOUNTED (LIVE) FILESYSTEM.
inode_link_info[2] is 9, inode.i_links_count is 11.  They should be the same!
Inode 2 ref count is 11, should be 11.  Fix<y>?
```

2. Although the accusation that we're boneheads might be a bit harsh, the inode refer-
    ence count error is a typical fsck error message. It indicates exactly what the prob-
    lem is (inode_link_info[2] is 9, whereas inodei_links_count is 11), and then
    asks you if you want to fix it.

    Type **y** and it immediately expands it to yes and continues. There are lots of prob-
    lems introduced with my dangerous filesystem stunt:

```
Pass 5: Checking group summary information
Block bitmap differences:  +238277 +238278 +238279
Fix<y>? yes

Free blocks count wrong for group #29 (7486, counted=7483).
Fix<y>? yes

Free blocks count wrong (219063, counted=219060).
Fix<y>? yes

Inode bitmap differences:  +68 +69 +58085 +58086 +58087 +58088 +58089 +58090
Fix<y>? yes

Free inodes count wrong for group #0 (1933, counted=1931).
Fix<y>? yes

Free inodes count wrong for group #29 (1916, counted=1910).
Fix<y>? yes

Directories count wrong for group #29 (11, counted=14).
Fix<y>? yes

Free inodes count wrong (60589, counted=60581).
Fix<y>? yes

/dev/hdb: ***** FILE SYSTEM WAS MODIFIED *****
/dev/hdb: 3419/64000 files (0.5% non-contiguous), 36468/255528 blocks
```

▼   Finally, it looks like all is well. Notice that the system has changed from having 11
     files to having 3,419 files.

9

▼   3. Most system administrators will tell you that if you encounter errors with `fsck` you should run the command again and again until it finally reports no errors. It's almost a superstition, but it's also amazing how often a second pass catches new errors introduced by the fixes in the previous run. This situation is no different (I finally unmounted the disk before running these subsequent checks):

```
# fsck -V /disk2
Parallelizing fsck version 1.23 (15-Aug-2001)
[/sbin/fsck.ext2 -- /disk2] fsck.ext2 /dev/hdb
e2fsck 1.23, 15-Aug-2001 for EXT2 FS 0.5b, 95/08/09
/dev/hdb: clean, 3419/64000 files, 36468/255528 blocks
```

A classic frustration with `fsck`: It assumed that because we'd recently run the command there was no reason to run it again, so it simply reported "clean." But it's not!

The `-f` flag forces the disk integrity check to be run, and this time I'm going to add the `-y` flag, which tells `fsck` to assume I answer yes to all questions that aren't absolutely critical:

```
# fsck -fVy /disk2
Parallelizing fsck version 1.23 (15-Aug-2001)
[/sbin/fsck.ext2 -- /disk2] fsck.ext2 -f /dev/hdb
e2fsck 1.23, 15-Aug-2001 for EXT2 FS 0.5b, 95/08/09
Pass 1: Checking inodes, blocks, and sizes
Pass 2: Checking directory structure
Pass 3: Checking directory connectivity
Pass 4: Checking reference counts
Inode 2 ref count is 11, should be 10.  Fix<y>? yes

Pass 5: Checking group summary information
Block bitmap differences:  -238277 -238278
Fix<y>? yes

Free blocks count wrong for group #29 (7483, counted=7485).
Fix<y>? yes

Free blocks count wrong (219060, counted=219062).
Fix<y>? yes

Inode bitmap differences:  -58085 -58086 -58088 -58090
Fix<y>? yes

Free inodes count wrong for group #29 (1910, counted=1914).
Fix<y>? yes

Directories count wrong for group #29 (14, counted=12).
Fix<y>? yes

Free inodes count wrong (60581, counted=60585).
Fix<y>? yes
```
▼

```
/dev/hdb: ***** FILE SYSTEM WAS MODIFIED *****
/dev/hdb: 3415/64000 files (0.5% non-contiguous), 36466/255528 blocks
```

Familiar errors? Note that they're not exactly the same as the previous run (the first run reported that the inode count of 11 was incorrectly nine, whereas here it's reporting that an inode reference count is 11 and should be 10).

One more pass through for good luck:

```
# fsck -fVy /disk2
Parallelizing fsck version 1.23 (15-Aug-2001)
[/sbin/fsck.ext2 -- /disk2] fsck.ext2 -fy /dev/hdb
e2fsck 1.23, 15-Aug-2001 for EXT2 FS 0.5b, 95/08/09
Pass 1: Checking inodes, blocks, and sizes
Pass 2: Checking directory structure
Pass 3: Checking directory connectivity
Pass 4: Checking reference counts
Pass 5: Checking group summary information
/dev/hdb: 3415/64000 files (0.5% non-contiguous), 36466/255528 blocks
```

Good. All is well again in disk land.

4. We can remount the disk with `mount`:

```
# ls /disk2
#
# mount -t ext2 /dev/hdb /disk2
# ls /disk2
games/  include/  kerberos/  lost+found/
```

Although the `mount` command itself will be discussed in the next hour, it's worth pointing out that the `fsck` program created the `lost+found` directory. From the `man` page for the optional Linux command `mklost+found`, here's the exact description of what ends up there:

> `mklost+found` preallocates disk blocks to the `lost+found` directory, so when `e2fsck(8)` is being run to recover a filesystem, it does not need to allocate blocks in the filesystem to store a large number of unlinked files. This ensures that `e2fsck` will not have to allocate data blocks in the filesystem during recovery.

5. Each `ext2` filesystem has a directory called `lost+found`, and that's where orphaned or otherwise oddball directory blocks, file blocks, and file material end up. Sometimes.

In my experience, it's rare to find anything even semi-comprehensible in the `lost+found` directory. In fact, almost always it's completely empty. Here's an example from a live Web server system that's being accessed every second of every day:

▼
```
$ mount
/dev/sda5 on / type ext3 (rw)
none on /proc type proc (rw)
usbdevfs on /proc/bus/usb type usbdevfs (rw)
/dev/sda1 on /boot type ext3 (rw)
none on /dev/pts type devpts (rw,gid=5,mode=620)
/dev/sda3 on /home type ext3 (rw)
none on /dev/shm type tmpfs (rw)
/dev/sdb1 on /usr type ext3 (rw)
/dev/sdb2 on /var type ext3 (rw)
```

Without any options, mount lists the disks and devices attached to the filesystem. Each mount point (don't worry, you'll learn about these in the next hour) has its own lost+found directory, as we'd expect:

```
$ ls -a /lost+found
./   ../
$ ls -a /boot/lost+found
./   ../
$ ls -a /home/lost+found
./   ../
$ ls -a /usr/lost+found
./   ../
$ ls -a /var/lost+found
./   ../
```

▲
Nada. Which is a good thing. If you see anything in your lost+found, it means that you've had at least one file corrupted and disassembled by fsck as part of its attempt to fix the disk.

The fsck program is ugly and can be difficult to understand, but it's a lifesaver in the world of Unix system administration. Spend some time reading the man page and learning about the different filesystems your particular flavor of Unix supports.

It's much easier to learn about this when you're not panicked because the system can't boot, or a directory just vanished into thin air!

Single-User Mode

All Unix systems have the capability to reboot into so-called single-user mode, where the windowing system isn't started up, the networking connections haven't been made, and the system is generally in a pretty raw state. The purpose of this mode is to create a safe environment for manipulating and checking the otherwise busy filesystems.

To vary things a bit, I'm going to show you what it looks like to reboot a Macintosh running Mac OS X into single-user mode, and then run fsck from the command line.

Task 9.3: Single-User Mode in Darwin

Although most users of the Macintosh OS X operating system don't really think much about the power underneath the hood, we know better. Underlying the colorful and attractive graphical Aqua interface is a complete Unix environment, which means that there's a way to reboot the system and drop into single-user mode. To accomplish this, reboot the Mac and hold down Cmd-S until it begins showing boot messages (see step 1).

> To boot a Macintosh running Mac OS X into single-user mode, reboot and immediately hold down Cmd-S until you begin to see status messages from the actual boot process.

1. After lots of very Unix-y output, you'll end up at a root prompt:

    ```
    standard timeslicing quantum is 10000 us
    vm_page_bootstrap: 123986 free pages
    mig_table_max_displ = 64
    COLOR video console at 0xbc0080000 (1152x768x32)
    IOKit Component Version 1.1:
    Sun Sep  9 15:30:21 PDT 2001; root(rcbuilder):RELEASE_PPC/iokit/RELEASE
    _cppInit done
    IODeviceTreeSupport done
    Recording startup extensions.
    Copyright (c) 1982, 1986, 1989, 1991, 1993
            The Regents of the University of California. All rights reserved.

    using 1310 buffer headers and 655 cluster IO buffer headers
    USB:  25.540: [0x205E600] USB Generic Hub @ 1 (0x19)
    enableClockSpreading returned with 0
    Register ApplePMU to acknowledge power changes
    Local FireWire GUID = 0x393ff:0xfe58285c
    AppleFWOHCI:  20af000     0 AppleFWOHCI::free
    devfs enabled
    dlil_init
    IOKitSDInit
    BSD root: disk0s5, major 14, minor 5
    ADB present:8c
    devfs on /dev
    Tue Jan 29 00:11:40 PST 2002
    Singleuser boot - fsck not done
    Root device is mounted read-only
    If you want to make modifications to files,
    run '/sbin/fsck -y' first and then /sbin/mount -uw /'
    localhost#
    ```

9

▼   One nice touch here is that the single-user mode boot-up reminds you that the root filesystem is mounted read-only (which means that it's safe to run `fsck` without risk of corruption), where the `fsck` and `mount` commands are, and how to proceed.

2. Running `fsck` demonstrates the universality of this utility even across completely different Unix platforms and different filesystem layouts (this is an HFS+ system rather than an `ext2` system):

```
localhost# /sbin/fsck
** /dev/rdisk0s5
** Checking HFS Plus volume
** Checking Extents Overflow file.
** Checking Catalog file.
** Checking multi-linked files
   Orphaned indirect node temp105533
** Checking Catalog hierarchy.
** Checking volume bitmap.
** Checking volume information.
** Repairing volume.

***** FILE SYSTEM WAS MODIFIED *****

***** REBOOT NOW *****
```

The next step is to remount the filesystem read+write, and continue booting by exiting this interactive shell:

```
localhost# /sbin/mount -uw /
localhost# exit
```

Although the specifics of the output from single-user mode boot vary from platform to platform, the general concept is identical: to drop you, the system administrator, into a minimal command shell so you can run any necessary diagnostics. Exiting the shell continues the boot process and should leave the system running as normal.

One of the most common places you'll encounter the `fsck` program is when the system has a corruption problem and drops into single-user mode upon rebooting. Although you can explicitly switch into this mode, many Unix systems, upon encountering errors with the automatic `fsck` run at boot-time, will automatically switch to this mode and leave you on your own.

As you have seen, `fsck` is rather straightforward, so its occasional cryptic output isn't too intimidating, and you can easily work and fix any disk problems encoun-

▲   tered. Right?

Don't Panic!

Finally, if you do encounter any disk corruption, don't immediately panic and start breathing oddly. Instead, there are a couple of steps you can take to minimize the danger:

1. Kick off all the users and drop down into single-user mode. On most systems all this will happen automatically if you type

   init 1

   while logged in as root (see Hour 13). Beware: Users don't get any warning; they just get the boot, and quick!

2. Now that you've minimized the danger of further corruption, take a deep breath and pat yourself on the back because *you've been keeping really good backups, haven't you?*

   If you have a good backup regimen, the worst you should lose are the changes introduced that day, which isn't too bad. If you aren't backing up your system, now's a good time to start panicking.

3. Take a deep breath.

4. Make sure that the disk you need to check isn't mounted by using mount (see Hour 10, "Adding Disks to Your System").

5. Run fsck -V on the corrupt disk and see what the damage is.

6. Run fsck a second, and even a third time, until it reports no problems or corruption.

7. Reboot the machine with

   shutdown -r now

   and keep your fingers crossed.

If you have the unusual situation of the corruption not fixing itself, it might be time to try copying as much of the material as possible to a different device (you'll have varying levels of success, alas). The next step is to use fsck -c to have it check for—and identify—bad blocks. Then, run fsck again to see if that solves the problem.

In extreme cases you might need to completely reformat the disk with fdisk, but in more than 20 years of using Unix I've never encountered this particular situation. It's *very* rare to have this level of problem with a filesystem.

Summary

Compared to other operating systems, Unix is remarkably stable and reliable. It's not at all uncommon to hear of systems that have been running for months, if not years, without a single reboot.

 The main server for The Internet Mall, running Red Hat Linux, *never* crashed in almost three years of busy 24/7 operation. The only times it was rebooted was because we were working on it or needed to relocate it from one facility to another. Unix is *very reliable*!

When things do go south, however, your best friend will prove to be fsck. The fsck command really has a remarkable capability to fix almost anything that can go wrong with a Unix filesystem, and many sysadmins have spent their entire careers using the -y flag and not even paying attention to the specific error messages.

Q&A

Q Where did the ext3 filesystem come from?

A The layout of information on hard disks has a long and quite interesting history. I'll restrain myself, however, and simply note that the immediate parent of the ext3 filesystem is the ext2 filesystem, which itself came from some groundbreaking research at UC Berkeley by Kirk McKusick, Bill Joy, and Sam Leffler on something they eventually called the Berkeley Fast File System. UC Berkeley plays a very important role in the history of Unix, with BSD and many of the most popular commands in Unix spawned from the Computer Science Research Group.

Q Why don't popular PC disk maintenance utilities require you to unmount the disk?

A Actually, if you get into real trouble with your disks, you'll find that most of these utility programs require you to reboot off the included CD-ROM. The purpose of this is so that the disk-fix utility can unmount the disk before it begins to try and fix it, just like our friend fsck.

Q If you have fsck parallelizing (that is, checking multiple disks at the same time) and one of the disks turns out to have an error, how do you know what's going on?

A That's actually one of the few limitations of the parallel approach to checking disks. Fortunately, the authors of fsck thought this through and almost all parallel versions offer a "serialize" flag that forces the program to check disks one at a time rather than all at once. On Linux, for example, the `-s` flag does just that.

Workshop

Quiz

1. What's the most common Linux filesystem? Mac OS filesystem? Commercial Unix filesystem?

2. Superstition or not, most Unix sysadmins do *what* after they run `fsck` and find errors?

3. On a filesystem with 512-byte blocks, what's the minimum actual disk space used by a file that's 1025 bytes in size?

4. The Unix equivalent of the PC "File Allocation Table" (that's what "FAT" stands for on those FAT* filesystems) is called?

5. When the `fsck` program doesn't think that a check is required of the filesystem, it refers to that disk as being in what state?

6. Though it's called single-user mode, can you really use a computer in that state?

Answers

1. The most common Linux filesystem is `ext2` with `ext3` continuing to grow in popularity; on the Mac it's HFS+ (Hierarchical File System Plus), and on commercial Unix systems it's the FFS (Berkeley Fast File System).

2. Run `fsck` again.

3. If the file is 1025 bytes in size and it gets stored in 512-byte blocks, the minimum size possible is three 512-byte blocks, or 1536 bytes.

4. The superblock.

5. Disks that don't need checking are "clean."

6. No. On almost all Unix systems, networking, a windowing environment, and other necessities of modern Unix interaction, aren't started yet. It's an unfortunate name because it's really administrative mode.

In the next hour, we'll format and mount a new disk on the system, exploring partition tables, `fdisk`, `newfs` and other helpful tools.

HOUR 10

Adding Disks to Your System

The last hour explored the `fsck` command and how it can be used to diagnose and fix problems with hard disks. This hour will address the other half of the disk issue—how to add new disks, format them, and hook them up to your Unix system. It's a set of commands you won't need too often, I expect, but when you are ready, this shows the sequence needed.

With personal computer systems, the steps involved in adding and accessing a new disk tend to be hidden, but with Unix, a new disk needs to be formatted, partitioned, checked, then mounted somewhere in the filesystem.

Indeed, PC and Macintosh systems have a very primitive multiple disk configuration capability: On the PC, for example, a primary disk is C:, a CD-ROM drive is E:, and a floppy drive is A:. Add a new disk, and it's probably configured as D: or F:. On the Macintosh, all new disks appear on the desktop with mnemonic names—a small improvement, but they're still all at the topmost level of the filesystem.

The Unix approach is quite a bit more sophisticated, because you can hook new disks up wherever you'd like. If you are perverse, you could even connect your floppy drive as /tmp, or your CD-ROM drive as /home.

Disks are hooked into the system with mount, and the mount command checks the /etc/fstab file (or the equivalent) to see what should be automatically included at boot-time.

But we're getting ahead of ourselves, so let's start at the beginning with low-level disk formatting.

In this hour you learn about

- Formatting disks with fdisk
- Adding a filesystem with mke2fs
- Mounting the new disk
- Fine-tuning your /etc/fstab configuration file

Formatting Disks with fdisk

It might surprise you, but the old MS-DOS command for formatting hard disks is in fact the same one used in modern Unix systems too: fdisk. Of course, what it does behind the scenes is a bit different!

> Actually, while they seem to be the same, the Unix version of fdisk has some subtle differences, so if you want to create a disk for a Unix or Linux system, use the fdisk included with that OS.

By this point in your Unix journey, it should be no surprise that inconsistencies are rife in the Unix user interface. Although most commands have single-character command flags, some have full-word command flags. The fdisk command is a member of a third category of interface: On many systems, type **fdisk** and you'll enter a simple fdisk shell in which you can type various commands to configure your disk; then the changes actually take place as you quit. On other versions of fdisk, you'll need to specify the device name on the command line.

> If you forget to write out your changes, any configuration you make in the fdisk program will be lost.

Task 10.1: Formatting a Disk with `fdisk`

To stay focused on Unix systems administration, we're going to assume here that the hardware issues surrounding the hookup of a disk to your computer have been addressed already, and that you now have a new, raw disk sitting on the bus and ready for you to format and link into your Unix system. In reality, you'll want to check with your vendor or IT department to find out what kind of hardware and cables you need, and how to get everything neatly settled into the physical box.

1. The first step in adding a new disk to your system is to figure out its new device address. Recall that there is a logical approach to the device-naming convention in Unix, so on Red Hat Linux 7.2, for example, IDE devices are named /dev/hd*XN* where *X* is the major device number (the disk address on the bus, typically), and *N* is the partition number.

   You can see this in action with the output from the mount command:

   ```
   # mount
   /dev/hda2 on / type ext3 (rw)
   none on /proc type proc (rw)
   usbdevfs on /proc/bus/usb type usbdevfs (rw)
   /dev/hda1 on /boot type ext3 (rw)
   none on /dev/pts type devpts (rw,gid=5,mode=620)
   none on /dev/shm type tmpfs (rw)
   none on /proc/sys/fs/binfmt_misc type binfmt_misc (rw)
   ```

   Notice that the root device is /dev/hda2, which implies that it's the primary device (because a is the first letter of the alphabet) and it's partition #2. Unsurprisingly for a Unix configuration, the /boot partition is partition #1 on the same drive.

2. Having added a second IDE drive to this system, a logical guess for the device address is /dev/hdb, and a quick check with fdisk confirms it:

   ```
   # fdisk /dev/hdb
   bash: fdisk: command not found
   ```

   Oops! The fdisk command isn't in our PATH. Easy to fix:

   ```
   # echo $PATH
   /bin:/usr/bin:/usr/X11R6/bin:/usr/local/bin:/home/taylor/bin
   # PATH=${PATH}:/sbin
   ```

   And now:

   ```
   # fdisk /dev/hdb
   Command (m for help): p

   Disk /dev/hdb: 16 heads, 63 sectors, 507 cylinders
   Units = cylinders of 1008 * 512 bytes

      Device Boot    Start      End    Blocks   Id  System
   /dev/hdb1            1        507   255496+   b   FAT32

   Command (m for help): q
   ```

▼

10

You can see that fdisk has recognized the geometry of the disk: it's 507 cylinders, 63 sectors, and 16 heads (and no, I have no idea what this all means either!) Most importantly, it's identified the disk as a FAT32 system with 255,496 blocks (approximately 250MB).

If you have problems identifying the bus address of your disk (the major and minor numbers), you might need to pop open your server and check the settings on the drive (often these are called *jumpers* by disk manufacturers, and in the SCSI world this is known as the *SCSI address*).

> Each hardware platform has a completely different scheme for hooking up disks and addressing schemes for the specific device drivers. Your best bet is to check with the documentation that came with your hardware if you're managing a commercial server.

At this point in the formatting of your disk, you need to decide whether you want to partition the large disk into smaller virtual disks, or have it as a single large disk image for the system to utilize. For smaller disks, there's little value to partitioning, but if you are adding a 30GB disk (or larger), it might be very helpful to split that into two or more smaller virtual disks.

The fdisk program builds the partitions in Unix, too, and you need to figure out how big each partition should be and ensure that they add up to the entire size of the disk. What's important is that once you install a filesystem on the disk, you can't repartition it without destroying all the data on it. This, as you might expect, is a common point of frustration, because sysadmins must therefore proactively anticipate how disks need to be laid out and how to best utilize available resources.

A great example of this is with *swap space*, special areas of the disk allocated for swapping memory images (pages of memory) to disk so that other applications can utilize physical RAM. You might have enough on your system for the current configuration, but if you upgrade your RAM, will you be able to have sufficient swap space to meet the usual rule of thumb of 2x–3x RAM for swap space? If not, creating a second swap partition on a new disk prior to bringing it online can be a very easy step. Even if you don't think you need it today, you might tomorrow! Indeed, spreading the swap task across devices can improve performance, particularly on a busy system.

Our new disk is too darn small to be usefully partitioned, however—whether to anticipate additional swap space needs, or simply to allow multiple virtual disks. But let's get started:

```
# fdisk /dev/hdb

Command (m for help): m
Command action
   a   toggle a bootable flag
   b   edit bsd disklabel
   c   toggle the dos compatibility flag
   d   delete a partition
   l   list known partition types
   m   print this menu
   n   add a new partition
   o   create a new empty DOS partition table
   p   print the partition table
   q   quit without saving changes
   s   create a new empty Sun disklabel
   t   change a partition's system id
   u   change display/entry units
   v   verify the partition table
   w   write table to disk and exit
   x   extra functionality (experts only)
```

As you can see, there are many options within fdisk. The most important commands are d (delete a partition), p (print partition table), n (add a new partition), and w (write partition information and quit).

3. The process of formatting a disk without any partitions is quite straightforward, but let's start by looking at the device itself:

```
Command (m for help): p

Disk /dev/hdb: 16 heads, 63 sectors, 507 cylinders
Units = cylinders of 1008 * 512 bytes

   Device Boot    Start       End    Blocks   Id  System
/dev/hdb1             1       507    255496+   b   FAT32
```

There's a problem lurking here: We don't want the disk to be a FAT32 disk (a Windows format), but rather a Unix disk. We'll need to delete the existing partition and write a new one of the appropriate format:

```
Command (m for help): d
Partition number (1-4): 1

Command (m for help): p

Disk /dev/hdb: 16 heads, 63 sectors, 507 cylinders
Units = cylinders of 1008 * 512 bytes

   Device Boot    Start       End    Blocks   Id  System
```

Having deleted the #1 partition, the current disk is now completely unusable from a Unix perspective. Fixing it is accomplished with the n (new partition) command:

```
Command (m for help): n
Command action
   e   extended
   p   primary partition (1-4)
p
Partition number (1-4): 1
First cylinder (1-507, default 1): 1
Last cylinder or +size or +sizeM or +sizeK (1-507, default 507): 507
```

Because the partition is intended to span the entire physical disk, we can use the default cylinder specifications. Also notice that you can specify the size in bytes, kilobytes, or megabytes if you don't think in terms of cylinders.

> Wondering whether to use a primary or extended partition? If you're creating partition #1, 2, 3, or 4, you should use a primary partition, but if you need to have more than four partitions on the disk, you'll need the higher number partitions to be essentially subpartitions within an extended partition. This all stems from some poor implementation decisions in the original design of the DOS hard disk format, but that's another story…

If you need to specify a different type of partition, start by using the l command to list known partitions. It's a remarkable list:

```
Command (m for help): l
 0  Empty            1b  Hidden Win95 FA  64  Novell Netware   bb  Boot Wizard hid
 1  FAT12            1c  Hidden Win95 FA  65  Novell Netware   c1  DRDOS/sec (FAT-
 2  XENIX root       1e  Hidden Win95 FA  70  DiskSecure Mult  c4  DRDOS/sec (FAT-
 3  XENIX usr        24  NEC DOS          75  PC/IX            c6  DRDOS/sec (FAT-
 4  FAT16 <32M       39  Plan 9           80  Old Minix        c7  Syrinx
 5  Extended         3c  PartitionMagic   81  Minix / old Lin  da  Non-FS data
 6  FAT16            40  Venix 80286      82  Linux swap       db  CP/M / CTOS / .
 7  HPFS/NTFS        41  PPC PReP Boot    83  Linux            de  Dell Utility
 8  AIX              42  SFS              84  OS/2 hidden C:   df  BootIt
 9  AIX bootable     4d  QNX4.x           85  Linux extended   e1  DOS access
 a  OS/2 Boot Manag  4e  QNX4.x 2nd part  86  NTFS volume set  e3  DOS R/O
 b  Win95 FAT32      4f  QNX4.x 3rd part  87  NTFS volume set  e4  SpeedStor
 c  Win95 FAT32 (LB  50  OnTrack DM       8e  Linux LVM        eb  BeOS fs
 e  Win95 FAT16 (LB  51  OnTrack DM6 Aux  93  Amoeba           ee  EFI GPT
 f  Win95 Ext'd (LB  52  CP/M             94  Amoeba BBT       ef  EFI (FAT-12/16/
10  OPUS             53  OnTrack DM6 Aux  9f  BSD/OS           f1  SpeedStor
11  Hidden FAT12     54  OnTrackDM6       a0  IBM Thinkpad hi  f4  SpeedStor
12  Compaq diagnost  55  EZ-Drive         a5  BSD/386          f2  DOS secondary
14  Hidden FAT16 <3  56  Golden Bow       a6  OpenBSD          fd  Linux raid auto
16  Hidden FAT16     5c  Priam Edisk      a7  NeXTSTEP         fe  LANstep
17  Hidden HPFS/NTF  61  SpeedStor        b7  BSDI fs          ff  BBT
18  AST SmartSleep   63  GNU HURD or Sys  b8  BSDI swap
```

▼ 4. A quick check that everything is specified as desired:

```
Command (m for help): p

Disk /dev/hdb: 16 heads, 63 sectors, 507 cylinders
Units = cylinders of 1008 * 512 bytes

   Device Boot    Start      End    Blocks   Id  System
/dev/hdb1            1        507   255496+  83  Linux
```

and it's time to write out the new partition information for our Linux system with the w command:

```
Command (m for help): w
The partition table has been altered!

Calling ioctl() to re-read partition table.

WARNING: If you have created or modified any DOS 6.x
partitions, please see the fdisk manual page for additional
information.
Syncing disks.
```

In theory, we're done and we now have a disk that is in the appropriate Linux format. This means that we should be able to fsck it, right?

```
# fsck /dev/hdb
Parallelizing fsck version 1.23 (15-Aug-2001)
e2fsck 1.23, 15-Aug-2001 for EXT2 FS 0.5b, 95/08/09
Couldn't find ext2 superblock, trying backup blocks...
fsck.ext2: Bad magic number in super-block while trying to open /dev/hdb

The superblock could not be read or does not describe a correct ext2
filesystem.  If the device is valid and it really contains an ext2
filesystem (and not swap or ufs or something else), then the superblock
is corrupt, and you might try running e2fsck with an alternate superblock:
    e2fsck -b 8193 <device>
```

▲ Ahhh...there's no actual Unix filesystem information written to the disk yet. That's the subject of the next section.

Although fdisk has a relatively primitive interface, it's not too difficult to use, and makes slicing up a new hard disk into specific partitions straightforward. That's only the first step on the journey toward having a second drive show up as part of the Linux system.

Adding a Filesystem with mke2fs

If we can talk about computer disks as if they were paintings, then running fdisk is the equivalent to acquiring a blank canvas and putting it in the closet. There's not much you can do with it unless you can place it on your easel and pull out your paints and brush.

Task 10.2: Making a Filesystem with `mke2fs`

A filesystem is created on the hard disk with `mkfs`, and because different filesystems are so different in their underlying characteristics, most modern Unix systems have specific versions of `mkfs` for each supported filesystem.

1. Linux includes a number of applications for building a new filesystem on a disk:

```
# man -k mkfs
mkdosfs [mkfs]          (8) - create an MS-DOS file system under Linux
mkfs                    (8) - build a Linux file system
mkfs.bfs [mkfs]         (8) - make an SCO bfs filesystem
mkfs.minix [mkfs]       (8) - make a Linux MINIX filesystem
# man -k mke2fs
mke2fs                  (8) - create a Linux second extended file system
```

> Notice that `mke2fs` didn't match the `man -k mkfs`. A classic example of why you have to dig around a bit when you're searching for specific commands in Unix. Someday that'll be fixed, but for now...

By contrast, Mac OS X Darwin offers nothing that even matches `mkfs`, but if you try the variation `newfs` you find:

```
$ man -k newfs
newfs(8), mount_mfs(8)   - construct a new file system
newfs_msdos(8)           - construct a new MS-DOS (FAT) file system
```

Notice that you can create Windows-format hard disk images from within the Macintosh environment, even on the command line.

> Solaris spans the gap, offering both `newfs` and `mkfs`, and they're completely different commands. You'll want to check the `man` page and the AnswerBook material (Sun's great online documentation suite at `http://docs.sun.com`) to find out the specifics of your own version of Solaris.

2. Building a "second extended" filesystem requires the `mke2fs` command:

```
# mke2fs /dev/hdb
mke2fs 1.23, 15-Aug-2001 for EXT2 FS 0.5b, 95/08/09
/dev/hdb is entire device, not just one partition!
Proceed anyway? (y,n) y
Filesystem label=
OS type: Linux
Block size=1024 (log=0)
```

```
Fragment size=1024 (log=0)
64000 inodes, 255528 blocks
12776 blocks (5.00%) reserved for the super user
First data block=1
32 block groups
8192 blocks per group, 8192 fragments per group
2000 inodes per group
Superblock backups stored on blocks:
        8193, 24577, 40961, 57345, 73729, 204801, 221185

Writing inode tables: done
Writing superblocks and filesystem accounting information: done

This filesystem will be automatically checked every 25 mounts or
180 days, whichever comes first.  Use tune2fs -c or -i to override.
```

Notice that the program properly reminds us that we're about to install a filesystem on the overall drive, and that if there are partitions, they'll be stepped on. If we had created partitions, the mke2fs command would have to be run for each partition, perhaps as mke2fs /dev/hdb1, mke2fs /dev/hdb2, and similar.

3. The output of mke2fs is well worth a closer look. Notice, for example, that it specifies that blocks are 1024 bytes, which actually might be a bit too big for a small 250MB disk. 64,000 inodes were allocated, which means that's the upper limit on how many different files can be stored on this device, and that there are 255,528 1024-byte blocks, which translates—correctly—to 249.5MB.

Just as importantly, the superblock was written into Block 1 as expected, and duplicates were written to Blocks 8193, 24557, 40961, 57345, 73729, 204801, and 221185. Recall from fsck that if the default superblock is corrupted, you might find yourself in a situation where you have to specify a duplicate superblock. These are the addresses of those superblocks. You could write them down, but since it's a standard spacing on the disk, just jot down a note so you remember that they're 8,193 blocks.

Finally, notice that the mke2fs command has also set a flag in the core device information that specifies to fsck that the disk should be checked automatically at system boot every 25 mounts (typically boots), or 180 days. You can change this with tune2fs, but frankly the defaults are quite acceptable, and running fsck every few weeks is a very good idea anyway.

Are we done with the file formatting? Depends on what command you run, frankly:

```
# fdisk -l

Disk /dev/hda: 255 heads, 63 sectors, 1958 cylinders
Units = cylinders of 16065 * 512 bytes
```

▼

```
        Device Boot     Start       End    Blocks   Id  System
    /dev/hda1    *         1         6     48163+  83  Linux
    /dev/hda2              7      1934  15486660   83  Linux
    /dev/hda3           1935      1958    192780   82  Linux swap

    Disk /dev/hdb: 16 heads, 63 sectors, 507 cylinders
    Units = cylinders of 1008 * 512 bytes

    Disk /dev/hdb doesn't contain a valid partition table
```

Thinking about this error, though, there's nothing wrong. We didn't actually *build* a partition table on /dev/hdb because it's a small disk. We talked about it, but as it's only a 250MB drive, partitions would chop it up into chunks too small to be used. So there's no problem at all.

4. Instead, let's run an fsck and see what happens (recall that earlier fsck complained that there wasn't a superblock, which is what reminded us to run mke2fs in the first place):

```
# fsck /dev/hdb
Parallelizing fsck version 1.23 (15-Aug-2001)
e2fsck 1.23, 15-Aug-2001 for EXT2 FS 0.5b, 95/08/09
/dev/hdb: clean, 11/64000 files, 8094/255528 blocks
```

Interestingly, the newly created filesystem is marked as clean by default, so no check was done. Let's specify -cV to check for bad blocks and force a check:

```
# fsck -cV /dev/hdb
Parallelizing fsck version 1.23 (15-Aug-2001)
[/sbin/fsck.ext2 -- /dev/hdb] fsck.ext2 -c /dev/hdb
e2fsck 1.23, 15-Aug-2001 for EXT2 FS 0.5b, 95/08/09
Checking for bad blocks (read-only test): done
Pass 1: Checking inodes, blocks, and sizes
Pass 2: Checking directory structure
Pass 3: Checking directory connectivity
Pass 4: Checking reference counts
Pass 5: Checking group summary information

/dev/hdb: ***** FILE SYSTEM WAS MODIFIED *****
/dev/hdb: 11/64000 files (0.0% non-contiguous), 8094/255528 blocks
```

No bad blocks, no problems with the filesystem, and notice that from the last line summary that there are only 11 files (out of 64,000 possible—the same number that there are allocated inodes for the drive) and 8,094 blocks used (out of 255,528; again, the exact same count as mke2fs showed us).

▼

▼   5. There are a variety of different options to the mke2fs command worth exploring in
      Table 10.1.

TABLE 10.1   Useful Flags to mke2fs

Flag	Meaning
-b blocks	Specify a different block size than the default. Valid sizes are 1024, 2048, and 4096 bytes.
-c	Check the disk for bad blocks before formatting the filesystem.
-j	Enable a journaling option on an ext3 disk.
-L label	Set the volume label for the disk.
-N i	Specify that the disk should have *i* inodes rather than the default.
-v	Verbose output, showing you more of what's going on.

> To learn more about the cool new ext3 filesystem and its disk journaling
> capability, please visit http://www.redhat.com/support/wpapers/
> redhat/ext3/.

Before we leave this section, let's use the command flags to rebuild the filesystem
on the new drive to support lots more tiny files by upping the inodes available.
While we're at it, we'll also specify a volume label.

```
# mke2fs -L "Little Guy" -v -N 128000 /dev/hdb
mke2fs 1.23, 15-Aug-2001 for EXT2 FS 0.5b, 95/08/09
/dev/hdb is entire device, not just one partition!
Proceed anyway? (y,n) y
Filesystem label=Little Guy
OS type: Linux
Block size=1024 (log=0)
Fragment size=1024 (log=0)
128000 inodes, 255528 blocks
12776 blocks (5.00%) reserved for the super user
First data block=1
32 block groups
8192 blocks per group, 8192 fragments per group
4000 inodes per group
Superblock backups stored on blocks:
        8193, 24577, 40961, 57345, 73729, 204801, 221185

Writing inode tables: done
Writing superblocks and filesystem accounting information: done

This filesystem will be automatically checked every 37 mounts or
180 days, whichever comes first.  Use tune2fs -c or -i to override.
```

▼

Notice that the volume has a label now, and that the number of inodes has jumped up considerably, as desired.

A quick `fsck` demonstrates that all is as expected:

```
# fsck /dev/hdb
Parallelizing fsck version 1.23 (15-Aug-2001)
e2fsck 1.23, 15-Aug-2001 for EXT2 FS 0.5b, 95/08/09
Little Guy: clean, 11/128000 files, 16094/255528 blocks
```

Most of the work of adding a new disk to the filesystem is done by the `mke2fs` (or one of its brethren), and there are a number of different options to the command.

Mounting the New Disk

After the disk is formatted and has a filesystem skeleton added by `newfs` (or `mkfs`), it can be hooked into the filesystem. This is where Unix proves slightly different than other computer systems, because rather than add new drive images, Unix requires you to hook the new disk into the existing filesystem. That's why the `mount` output shows specific directories. Consider the following line from the `mount` output:

```
/dev/hda1 on /boot type ext3 (rw)
```

What this implies is that there's a /boot directory on the root (/) filesystem, and that its contents are hidden by the newly mounted /dev/hda1 drive.

This idea that newly mounted disks hide existing file content is critical to understand so you can best plan how to add your new disk space to your system.

Task 10.3: Adding New Drives to Your System

Imagine that we can stop the system partway through the boot sequence, after things have started running, but before any nonboot disks are mounted. At this point, there'll be a /boot directory, but nothing in it. The job of the `mount` command is to attach filesystems to a specific directory.

1. Before the new drive hdb is added to the system, let's have a look at the directory /home/taylor:

```
# cd /home/
# ls -a taylor
.                   .first_start_kde  .MCOP-random-seed
..                  .gconf            .mcoprc
.autorun.lck        .gconfd           .nautilus
.bash_history       .gnome            .sawfish
```

▼

```
.bash_logout                          .gnome-desktop        .screenrc
.bash_profile                         .gnome_private        .wmrc
.bashrc                               .gtkrc                .xauth
.DCOPserver_localhost.localdomain     .ICEauthority         .Xauthority
.DCOPserver_localhost.localdomain_:0  .kde                  .xsession-errors
Desktop                               .kderc
.emacs                                .mcop
```

Now, let's use the mount command to hook the new drive into the existing system, with /home/taylor as its initial mount point:

```
# mount /dev/hdb /home/taylor
# ls -al taylor
total 17
drwxr-xr-x   3 root      root       1024 Feb  1 14:40 .
drwxr-xr-x   3 root      root       4096 Jan 24 12:20 ..
drwxr-xr-x   2 root      root      12288 Feb  1 14:40 lost+found
```

Rather scary to see all the files gone, but they're not really gone, they're *underneath* the contents of the new disk that's been mounted.

2. To demonstrate that, umount unmounts a disk, permitting access to the previous content:

```
# umount /dev/hdb
# ls -a taylor
```

```
.                                     .first_start_kde      .MCOP-random-seed
..                                    .gconf                .mcoprc
.autorun.lck                          .gconfd               .nautilus
.bash_history                         .gnome                .sawfish
.bash_logout                          .gnome-desktop        .screenrc
.bash_profile                         .gnome_private        .wmrc
.bashrc                               .gtkrc                .xauth
.DCOPserver_localhost.localdomain     .ICEauthority         .Xauthority
.DCOPserver_localhost.localdomain_:0  .kde                  .xsession-errors
Desktop                               .kderc
.emacs                                .mcop
```

This is a very important concept that isn't clear to many Unix system administrators: Disks can only be mounted onto an existing directory, and whatever's in that directory prior to the mount will be inaccessible until the disk is unmounted again.

3. The mount command supports a variety of different methods for mounting a disk. The most important flags are summarized in Table 10.2.

▼

10

▼

TABLE 10.2 Helpful mount Flags

Flag	Meaning
-a	Ensure that all devices listed in /etc/fstab are mounted, and mount them if they are detached. This can be combined with -t to allow mount -a -t ufs, for example, which will force all UFS filesystems listed in the /etc/fstab file to be mounted if possible.
-o opts	Specify opts options to mounting. Common values are ro (read-only), rw (read/write), noatime (disable updating access times on files, speeding up disk interaction), noauto (disk can only be mounted explicitly, rather than with a mount -a), and noexec (disable execution of binaries on the disk).
-r	Mount read-only (analogous to -o ro).
-t type	Mount the disk as type type. Common values are ext2, ext3, hfs, hfs+, nfs, ufs, iso9660, and xfs, depending on which platform you're on.
-v	Verbose output. Shows more of what's happening.
-w	Mount read/write (analogous to -o rw).

As a further experiment, let's copy an executable binary onto the disk, then mount the disk read-only to demonstrate some interesting behaviors:

```
# mkdir /disk2

# cp /bin/ls /home/taylor
# umount /dev/hdb

# mount -o ro,noexec -v -t ext2 /dev/hdb /disk2
/dev/hdb on /disk2 type ext2 (ro,noexec)
# ls -alF /disk2
# ls -al /disk2
total 63
drwxr-xr-x    3 root      root         1024 Jan 28 18:14 ./
drwxr-xr-x   20 root      root         4096 Jan 28 15:38 ../
drwxr-xr-x    2 root      root        12288 Jan 28 15:34 lost+found/
-rwxr-xr-x    1 root      root        45948 Jan 28 18:10 ls*
```

As you can see, there's a copy of the executable binary for /bin/ls on the disk. But because the disk was mounted noexec, watch what happens when the executable is invoked:

```
# /disk2/ls
tcsh: /disk2/ls: Permission denied
```

▼

This can be quite puzzling if you forget that no programs can be executed from the disk, because as the ls -l shows, the file is indeed executable. How about copying to a read-only filesystem?

```
# cp /bin/cp /disk2
cp: cannot create regular file `/disk2/cp': Read-only file system
```

A considerably more helpful error message, at least!

This time mount proves a bit more helpful in reminding us what might be causing the strange behavior on this particular disk:

```
# mount
/dev/hda2 on / type ext3 (rw)
none on /proc type proc (rw)
usbdevfs on /proc/bus/usb type usbdevfs (rw)
/dev/hda1 on /boot type ext3 (rw)
none on /dev/pts type devpts (rw,gid=5,mode=620)
none on /dev/shm type tmpfs (rw)
/dev/hdb on /disk2 type ext2 (ro,noexec)
```

4. Before we leave this section, let's fix the disk so that it's a standard mount format:

```
# umount /dev/hdb
# mount -v -t ext2 /dev/hdb /disk2
/dev/hdb on /disk2 type ext2 (rw)
```

In the next section, we'll explore how to add an entry to /etc/fstab to have the disk parameters specified automatically.

5. One additional observation about the Mac OS X environment is that if you dual-boot Mac OS 9 and OS X, you'll find that old OS 9 disks are automatically mounted on the /Volumes directory:

```
# /sbin/mount
/dev/disk1s9 on / (local)
devfs on /dev (local)
fdesc on /dev (union)
<volfs> on /.vol (read-only)
/dev/disk0s8 on /Volumes/Macintosh HD (local)
automount -fstab [252] on /Network/Servers (automounted)
automount -static [252] on /automount (automounted)
```

However, you might well decide that you only want read-only access to the OS 9 disks to ensure that no corruption can occur. To do that, simply unmount the existing disk and remount it read-only:

```
# umount /dev/disk0s8
# mount -r /dev/disk0s8 /Volumes/Macintosh\ HD
# /sbin/mount
/dev/disk1s9 on / (local)
devfs on /dev (local)
```

```
fdesc on /dev (union)
<volfs> on /.vol (read-only)
/dev/disk0s8 on /Volumes/Macintosh HD (read-only)
automount -fstab [252] on /Network/Servers (automounted)
automount -static [252] on /automount (automounted)
```

When you have a disk fully configured with a filesystem and a spot on the filesystem where you can add the disk and utilize the space, it's quick work with mount to hook things up.

As you begin to work with external media, including "borrowed hard disks" and read-only devices, being able to mount disks with specific security settings (for example, noexec) can save a lot of headaches. Indeed, a good rule of thumb is that you should always mirror the logical settings of the device with the mount instructions: If you are mounting a DVD-ROM drive, use ro; if you're mounting a potentially virus-infected shareware CD-ROM, use noexec; and so on. A little bit of caution will save a lot of

hassles down the road.

If you're running Mac OS X and want to mount disks within Darwin, being aware of these security precautions can be even more beneficial. There aren't many viruses for Unix, but there are definitely Mac viruses that can

infect your system, and mounting a disk from the Darwin level might well sidestep any virus protection system you've installed.

Fine-tuning Your `/etc/fstab` Configuration File

While it's straightforward to add new disks to your system with the mount command, it's somewhat of a pain to have to remember the exact options and type everything in each time the system reboots.

Fortunately, there's a smarter solution, a configuration file that mount uses to ascertain what disks to mount where, when, and with what permissions. That file is /etc/fstab, and before we leave this hour, let's have a quick peek at what's inside.

Task 10.4: Creating the Perfect `/etc/fstab` File

It's a bit surprising, but mount is a pretty smart command for a Unix command. For example, once an entry in /etc/fstab maps a drive name to a mount point, you can manually mount disks by specifying either the mount point (/disk2), or the drive name

▼ (/dev/hdb) by itself. Even better, the default mount permissions will be read from the file too, ensuring that the DVD-ROM is *always* mounted read-only, perhaps, unless explicitly overridden.

But the most important use of /etc/fstab is to control which disks are mounted automatically at boot-time. If you wanted to include /dev/hdb as a crucial part of your filesystem, it would be unacceptable to use the mount command manually each time the system rebooted!

1. To start, let's have a look at a stock RHL7.2 filesystem list:

```
# more /etc/fstab
LABEL=/            /                  ext3     defaults         1 1
LABEL=/boot        /boot              ext3     defaults         1 2
none               /dev/pts           devpts   gid=5,mode=620   0 0
none               /proc              proc     defaults         0 0
none               /dev/shm           tmpfs    defaults         0 0
/dev/hda3          swap               swap     defaults         0 0
/dev/cdrom         /mnt/cdrom         iso9660  noauto,owner,kudzu,ro 0 0
/dev/fd0           /mnt/floppy        auto     noauto,owner,kudzu 0 0
```

There are six columns of information in this file, as detailed in Table 10.4.

TABLE 10.4 Information Contained in /etc/fstab

Column	Contains
1	Device name or label.
2	Mount point.
3	Filesystem type. Common values are ext2, ext3, hfs, hfs+, ufs, fat32, fat, proc, tmpfs, swap, and iso9660.
4	Options: ro (read-only), rw (read+write), exec (permit execution of programs on disk), noatime (prohibits update of access time; this can improve performance on disks where the atime value doesn't matter), noauto (disables automatic mounting of the device with the mount -a command at bootup), and nosuid (prohibits any SUID program running from this disk). There are probably additional options for your flavor of Unix: Check man page fstab(5) for details.
5	Indication of what dump pass this drive should be included with (see man page dump(8) and Hour 8, "Unix Package Management").
6	Indicates which pass of fsck should examine this disk on bootup. (Pass 0 = don't automatically check).

To add an entry for the new disk /dev/hdb, therefore, we'd add the following line:

```
/dev/hdb              /disk2             ext2     noauto,ro        2 0
```

▼

▼   This would define the mount point for the /dev/hdb drive as /disk2, indicate that it's a stock ext2 filesystem, should *not* be automounted at boot-time (which means that it'll have to be added by hand), should be mounted read-only, and is part of dump group 2.

2. To check that the disk won't be automatically mounted at boot-time, we can use the following sequence:

```
# umount /disk2
# mount -a
# mount
/dev/hda2 on / type ext3 (rw)
none on /proc type proc (rw)
usbdevfs on /proc/bus/usb type usbdevfs (rw)
/dev/hda1 on /boot type ext3 (rw)
none on /dev/pts type devpts (rw,gid=5,mode=620)
none on /dev/shm type tmpfs (rw)
```

As expected, the /disk2 mount point has not been listed.

To include the disk manually is now a breeze:

```
# mount /disk2
# mount
/dev/hda2 on / type ext3 (rw)
none on /proc type proc (rw)
usbdevfs on /proc/bus/usb type usbdevfs (rw)
/dev/hda1 on /boot type ext3 (rw)
none on /dev/pts type devpts (rw,gid=5,mode=620)
none on /dev/shm type tmpfs (rw)
/dev/hdb on /disk2 type ext2 (ro)
```

Notice in particular that the disk has been added at the correct mount point, and that it's read-only.

3. Changing the options in /etc/fstab will change the behavior dramatically. A switch from noauto,ro to defaults in the mount configuration file results in the following:

```
# umount /disk2
# mount -a
# mount
/dev/hda2 on / type ext3 (rw)
none on /proc type proc (rw)
usbdevfs on /proc/bus/usb type usbdevfs (rw)
/dev/hda1 on /boot type ext3 (rw)
none on /dev/pts type devpts (rw,gid=5,mode=620)
none on /dev/shm type tmpfs (rw)
/dev/hdb on /disk2 type ext2 (rw)
```

▲

Any disk that's mounted with the -a flag to mount will also be mounted at boot-time, which is exactly what we wanted.

There are many ways that disk automounting can be custom-configured for your installation, and you can also see that there are a wide variety of different file types that are supported by modern Unix systems, enabling easy disk-sharing between different operating systems, whether Macintosh, Windows, DOS, or other flavors of Unix.

To learn how to fine-tune your configuration further, you'll do well to read man page `fstab(5)` and, if you have it, man page `fs(5)`, for more information about the possible values in this configuration file. Of course, the `mount` man page offers lots of good information too!

Summary

As a system administrator, it's your job to ensure that the disk layout and configuration matches user needs. You'll also undoubtedly be expected to recognize when disk space is running low and solve the problem—probably by adding more space by including a new hard drive.

With 30GB disks priced under $250, running out of space seems hard to imagine, but your users will doubtless challenge that assumption!

Q&A

Q When I look at the contents of my `/etc/fstab`, it's not the same as you list in Table 10.2. What's up with that?

A Some flavors of Unix have different formats for the `/etc/fstab` file, confusingly enough. For example, some versions of Solaris have `device to mount`, `device to fsck`, `mount point`, `fs type`, `mount at boot` and `mount options` as the seven columns listed in the config file. No `dump` information at all.

As always, your best solution is to check with the `fstab(5)` man page to ensure that your understanding of this vital file matches the layout specified.

Q The presence of `/etc/floppy` and `/etc/cdrom` suggests that it's really easy to work with these peripheral devices in Unix. Is it *really* this easy?

A Many Unix flavors indeed make it very easy, mounting the actual device so that access to `/dev/floppy` fails or succeeds based on whether there's a floppy in the drive, or similarly with CD-ROMs.

Q My impression is that it's dangerous to experiment with `fdisk` and `newfs`?

10

A Oh yeah! Remember, when you run a disk formatting utility, you *wipe all the data on that disk,* so overwriting the superblocks on an existing drive, for example, instantly unhooks all the files and directories that were on that drive previously. Please use these commands judiciously to ensure you don't get into any trouble!

Workshop

Quiz

1. Why would you want to mount a disk read-only?

2. Why would you specify `noatime` at mount, and what does it mean?

3. If a disk is automatically mounted with `mount -a`, what does that imply about boot-time?

4. Which of the following file types is not supported by Linux: FAT12, OS/2, Plan 9, CP/M, Golden Bow, DRDOS, DOS, or BeOS.

5. If you want to have more than four partitions on a disk, will you need to use primary or extended partitions?

Answers

1. Generally, you should always match the access permissions of the peripheral itself. If you're mounting a CD-ROM, for example, you'd use read-only because your system can't write CD-ROMs. (If you have a read/write CD-ROM burner, it's a different story, of course, but even then, if you're writing a CD-ROM you'll want to unmount and remount the device to enable writing.)

2. On drives that store lots of small files and have frequent access (Usenet archive servers, for example), disabling updates to the access times for the filesystem can improve performance a bit.

3. It implies that the disk will also be automatically mounted at boot-time.

4. It's a trick question! All of these are supported by Red Hat Linux 7.2.

5. Both, actually. You'll want to have partitions 1–4 as primary partitions, and all subsequent partitions as extended.

In the next hour, we'll explore the different options for boot-time operating system selection, focused specifically on LILO and GRUB. Use of these tools enable you to boot into different operating systems as desired, a very handy capability.

Hour 11

Multiple Boot Configurations

Although it's true that after you get intimately involved with Unix you probably won't want to go back, there are times when it's helpful to boot into a variant of Microsoft Windows or another operating system. If you're on Solaris, you're out of luck—Solaris doesn't play nicely with other operating systems on the disk. If you're running Mac OS X, the best solution for you is to explore Virtual PC from Connectix.

If you are using Mac OS X, try holding down the Option key next time you reboot. You'll find that if you have Mac OS 9 on one disk and Mac OS X on the other, you can easily pick which should boot directly, rather than fussing with the Boot Disk control panel.

If you're on a PC and you have some flavor of Linux or PC Unix, this hour is for you. You can easily set up your system to boot a variety of different operating systems with a simple switcher screen displayed at boot-time. My PC systems customarily can boot into Red Hat Linux or a version of Windows (usually Windows 2000).

In this hour you will learn

- How to partition your disk for dual-booting
- Dual-boot configurations with LILO
- Dual-boot configurations with GRUB
- The theory of virtual machines

The Theory of Dual-Booting

Upon first glance, it might surprise you that your PC can have multiple operating systems installed simultaneously, without each of them stepping on and otherwise overwriting the other. Certainly, if you come from the world of Windows, you're used to being asked `Reformat disk? (all data will be lost)` during the installation process.

Understanding how dual-booting works requires a brief digression into the sequence of events that transpires when a PC is booted.

When you power-on your computer, it does not instantly start reading in the hard disk, even though it seems that way. Instead, the CPU starts by reading the BIOS, the Basic I/O System, which has a set of configuration options set in your PRAM, Programmable Random Access Memory. The PRAM settings indicate which of your multiple disks is the *boot disk*, the disk with the desired operating system image.

The secret to dual-booting is while the PC BIOS always wants to boot off of the master boot record, "sector zero" of the specified disk, the program it boots can be a *loader*, a program that simply identifies other possible operating systems on the disk and enables you to pick between them.

Both LILO and GRUB are boot loaders; simple, tiny programs that are invoked directly on power-up, they either automatically hand the CPU off to the appropriate operating system image or display a list of possible OS choices for the user to choose.

Sound simple? It is. That's the good news. The challenge of configuring a system to dual-boot is that you have to partition your disk to allow space for all your operating systems before you install *any* of them. That's the biggest hassle of the entire dual-boot process: Typically you won't decide you want to dual-boot until you already have an OS installed and decide that you want to experiment with another.

This can go in either direction, of course. Perhaps you're a PC person and have been happily living in Windows ME, but decide you want to explore the world of Linux. Or, you gave up on Microsoft and have a pure Linux system, but you suddenly realize that there are a few key applications (or games) that you can't run without a native Windows OS.

Either way, you might be forced to back up your system, repartition your hard disk, then reinstall your basic OS. Then, finally, you can install additional operating systems, each in their own partition. A caveat is that Microsoft doesn't really like this "other OS" stuff, so if you want to have a version of Windows, install that first. Otherwise, it'll stomp on whatever multi-boot information you put in the disk master boot record.

> There is a very cool alternative called VMware. Later in this hour we'll talk about how virtual machines within an OS let you sidestep a lot of this hassle.

11

Task 11.1: Partitioning Disks for Dual Boot

▼ TASK

Each combination of operating systems requires a different disk-partition structure, with Linux having the most complex. An ideal Linux configuration has three different partitions in use, whereas most other operating systems (that is, Windows) can work just fine with one big partition.

1. The first step to learning about your partition strategy is to find out the name of your boot disk device. This is most easily done with mount:

    ```
    # mount | grep boot
    /dev/sda1 on /boot type ext3 (rw)
    #
    ```

    To check your current partition strategy, use fdisk, giving it the top-level device name:

    ```
    # fdisk /dev/sda
    ```

    ```
    Command (m for help): p
    ```

```
Disk /dev/sda: 255 heads, 63 sectors, 522 cylinders
Units = cylinders of 16065 * 512 bytes

    Device Boot      Start       End      Blocks   Id  System
/dev/sda1    *           1         6      48163+   83  Linux
/dev/sda2                7       490     3887730   83  Linux
/dev/sda3              491       522      257040   82  Linux swap
```

To add an additional operating system, we would need to have a configuration that included additional partitions—they're all in use already in the above output, as you can see by comparing the disk statistics with the start and end values of the specific devices.

Given that we've consumed the entire disk with this set of partitions, the bad news is that we need to repartition the disk, destroying the /dev/sda2 partition, then reinstall Linux. Or we need to buy, format, and install a new disk.

2. The resultant partition table for a reorganized disk might look like this:

```
Disk /dev/sda: 255 heads, 63 sectors, 522 cylinders
Units = cylinders of 16065 * 512 bytes

    Device Boot      Start       End      Blocks   Id  System
/dev/sda1    *           1         6      48163+   83  Linux
/dev/sda2                7       245     1943865   83  Linux
/dev/sda3              246       490     1943865    b  Win95 FAT32
/dev/sda3              491       522      257040   82  Linux swap
```

There are other ways to partition your disk too, and many Linux experts recommend that you start with Windows, using the Windows installer to partition the disk into the four partitions needed.

If you're going to dual-boot, it's wise to read this section before you begin any installation on your disk. You could also opt for another solution that's less destructive, such as VMware, covered later in this hour.

Dual-Boot Configurations with LILO

When you have more than one operating system installed on your system, you can select your favorite at boot-time by using either LILO or GRUB. LILO is the Linux Loader, and it's surprisingly straightforward to configure.

Task 11.2: Configuring LILO

Though it has an important task in the boot sequence, LILO itself is a very simple program. The configuration file isn't too complex, but there are some nuances that are critical to understand.

1. To start, here's a `lilo.conf` file for a system that can dual-boot Red Hat Linux or Windows 2000. There are three possible boot options here: a regular RHL boot, a RHL boot into single-user mode (see Hour 13, "Changing System State"), and a boot into Windows 2000 Professional, if the user feels the need to see how the other half lives!

```
# cat /etc/lilo.conf
boot=/dev/sda
default=RHL
prompt
timeout=300
image=/boot/vmlinuz-2.4.7-10
        label=RHL
        root=/dev/sda2
        read-only
image=/boot/vmlinuz-2.4.7-10
        label="RHL-s"
        root=/dev/sda2
        append=-s
        read-only
other=/dev/sda3
        label=Windows2000
        table=/dev/sda
```

The `boot=` line specifies where the master-boot record should be written, `default` specifies the default image (OS) to boot, and `prompt` forces LILO to give you a chance to enter your preferred OS at boot-time.

The timeout setting specifies how long before the system automatically picks the boot option specified, but it's in tenths of a second, so `timeout=300` is 30 seconds, not 5 minutes. It's very important to keep this value large while you're experimenting!

> Once, a friend and I were experimenting with the settings in the `lilo.conf` file and accidentally set `timeout=10` rather than `timeout=100`. It wouldn't have been too bad except the default OS to boot into was Windows, so we couldn't get to the Linux OS to fix the configuration file. It was quite comical to watch us try and type the appropriate entry to the LILO prompt at just the right moment!

▼

For LILO-friendly operating systems (most Linux and PC-Unix systems), you can then specify the kernel file image name, the label for LILO to display at the prompt, and the root= line, indicating where the partition containing the kernel image is located.

You can see that we specify that the system should be mounted read-only, which might seem a bit weird, but we want to have the disk read-only so that fsck can check it without causing too much trouble (recall that running fsck on a mounted disk is very bad juju!). As the boot sequence proceeds, the disk is automatically unmounted and remounted as read-write.

The second boot option takes advantage of the append= option to force the kernel to boot with the -s flag, which forces single-user mode. You should rarely need something like this in day-to-day operation.

Finally, partition 3 of /dev/sda contains a separate Windows boot environment, so it's denoted by specifying the partition of the disk upon which the OS is installed, here other=/dev/sda3, and then the disk that the OS itself is found as table=/dev/sda.

There are a few other options to the lilo.conf file, and because they change from version to version (albeit subtly), your best bet is to check the LILO man page for exact details on what your version supports.

2. After you have your configuration file written, you need to install or update LILO in the master-boot record (MBR). Before you do that, however, it's critical to always test the configuration file first, by specifying -t:

```
# /sbin/lilo -t
Adding RHL *
Added RHL-s
Added Windows2000
```

After the configuration file can be read without any errors, really install it by omitting -t:

```
# /sbin/lilo
Added RHL *
Added RHL-s
Added Windows2000
```

Not very exciting output, but because it didn't generate any errors, all is well.

Note that if you forget to test the configuration and a real install fails part-way with an error, *you must fix it and reinstall before you reboot!* If you don't, your MBR will be corrupt and you will not be able to boot properly.

▼ 3. Rebooting the system now produces the standard PC bootup output messages, then clears the screen and prompts:

```
LILO boot:
```

At this point, you can just wait—and after 30 seconds the default entry in the lilo.conf file will be booted (in this case, the one with the RHL label). If you'd rather see your options, type either **?** or **TAB** and you'll see all your choices:

```
LILO boot: ?
RHL    RHL-s    Windows2000
boot:
```

You can type the operating system you desire, or, again, you can just let the system timeout.

```
boot: RHL
the long, involved Unix boot sequence begins.
```

▲

There are many fans of LILO in the Unix world, and for good reason. LILO has been reliably booting Unix and Linux systems for many years with few problems or hiccups. However, in the past few years GRUB has grown in popularity because of its flexibility and more attractive appearance. That's why Red Hat Linux installs with GRUB as the default boot loader, not LILO.

11

In any case, a good rule of thumb before you try anything discussed in this hour is to ensure that you have a boot disk available for your OS, just in case. Oftentimes that can be the install CD-ROM, but most Unixes also let you create explicit boot disks. Check the Unix install documentation if you need help.

Dual-Boot Configurations with GRUB

GRUB is the GRand Unified Boot loader, originally written by Erich Boleyn in part to sidestep the oft-confusing LILO configuration files. The most popular thing about GRUB is that it's a graphical, menu-based loader (though it does have a simple line-oriented command mode a la LILO).

Task 11.3: Configuring GRUB

▼ TASK

Working with GRUB is a little bit easier than LILO, but you still need to be careful and keep in mind the core functionality of a boot loader. You shouldn't have to change this configuration file too often, but if you do experiment, beware that you might cause lots of trouble, so always make sure you have a copy of the original GRUB configuration for your system as one of the boot-time options.

▼   All the GRUB files, including the graphic used as the background image, live in
    /boot/grub.

      1. Here's what's in /boot/grub:

```
# ls -l /boot/grub
total 239
-rw-r--r--   1 root       root            82 Jan 11 15:45 device.map
-rw-r--r--   1 root       root         10848 Jan 11 15:45 e2fs_stage1_5
-rw-r--r--   1 root       root          9744 Jan 11 15:45 fat_stage1_5
-rw-r--r--   1 root       root          8864 Jan 11 15:45 ffs_stage1_5
-rw-------   1 root       root           543 Jan 11 15:45 grub.conf
lrwxrwxrwx   1 root       root            11 Jan 11 15:45 menu.lst -> ./grub.conf
-rw-r--r--   1 root       root          9248 Jan 11 15:45 minix_stage1_5
-rw-r--r--   1 root       root         12512 Jan 11 15:45 reiserfs_stage1_5
-rw-r--r--   1 root       root         54044 Sep  5 13:10 splash.xpm.gz
-rw-r--r--   1 root       root           512 Jan 11 15:45 stage1
-rw-r--r--   1 root       root        120000 Jan 11 15:45 stage2
-rw-r--r--   1 root       root          8512 Jan 11 15:45 vstafs_stage1_5
```

        Although you should never touch most of this material without protective clothing
        (just kidding, but you really *do* want to be an expert before you fiddle with this!),
        it's worth highlighting both the GRUB configuration file, grub.conf, and the
        graphic used as the background image in menu mode, splash.xpm.gz.

> Some versions of GRUB look for the configuration in menu.lst rather than
> grub.conf. Check the man page for the preferences in your own version of
> Unix, as needed. Notice in the example that menu.lst is a symbolic link to
> grub.conf.

        If you want to have your own custom splash screen, use a program such as xfig to
        open splash.xpm.gz (after unzipping it, of course), then duplicate its size, depth
        (number of colors used) and image format. Then gzip the file and give it the same
        name, or update the splashimage value in the grub.conf file (see the following).

      2. More likely, though, you'll want to modify the configuration file, and here's how it
         looks inside:

```
# cat grub.conf
# grub.conf generated by anaconda
#
# Note that you do not have to rerun grub after making changes to this file
# NOTICE:  You have a /boot partition.  This means that
#          all kernel and initrd paths are relative to /boot/, eg.
▼         #          root (hd0,0)
```

```
#          kernel /vmlinuz-version ro root=/dev/sda2
#          initrd /initrd-version.img
#          boot=/dev/sda
default=0
timeout=10
splashimage=(hd0,0)/grub/splash.xpm.gz
title Red Hat Linux (2.4.7-10)
        root (hd0,0)
        kernel /vmlinuz-2.4.7-10 ro root=/dev/sda2
        initrd /initrd-2.4.7-10.img
title Windows 2000
   root (hd0,3)
   makeactive
   chainloader +1
```

One important note about GRUB is its disk reference notation. The root reference to (hd0,0) means that it's on hard disk 0, partition 0. If we wanted to boot off partition 3 of hard disk 1, it'd be (hd1,3).

The default parameter specifies which of the operating systems should be booted by default; zero indicates the very first of those listed (Red Hat Linux). The timeout variable specifies how long GRUB displays its menu before booting (in seconds, not the confusing tenths of a second used in LILO), and splashimage indicates the name of the background graphic to use.

Each bootable operating system is then specified with a title and a root partition indicator (again, it's disk, partition). In the case of a Unix system, you specify the kernel information on the kernel line (note the ro indicating that the disk should be mounted read-only, just as was done in LILO).

The configuration of a non-Unix operating system (for example, Windows 2000) is rather different because there isn't a kernel per se. Instead, GRUB uses a so-called chainloader, which tells GRUB to step aside and let the boot loader on the specified disk and partition take over.

2. You don't have to do anything for a new configuration to be installed, but because you don't want to run into errors in the configuration file format while you're booting, it's wise to install the new GRUB configuration explicitly, by running grub-install:

```
# /sbin/grub-install /dev/sda
Installation finished. No error reported.
This is the contents of the device map /boot/grub/device.map.
Check if this is correct or not. If any of the lines is incorrect,
fix it and re-run the script `grub-install'.

(fd0)    /dev/fd0
(hd0)    /dev/sda
```

▼   Unlike LILO, if the installer finds a problem with the configuration, it won't leave
           the system in an unusable state, so you don't have to be paranoid about running in
           test mode.

     3.   Now when you boot you'll have the choice of the two operating systems, and
           you'll have an attractive boot screen as well, shown in Figure 11.1.

FIGURE 11.1

*GRUB boot screen
with two operating
systems.*

           Considerably more information can be obtained about GRUB by exploring the GRUB
▲   info pages. Type **info grub** and you can go from there.

Other Solutions for Other Unixes

Although dual-booting and having different operating systems all living in their own partitioned worlds is appealing to many, there's another alternative if you're willing to give
up 10–30% of the performance of the secondary OS.

Both Windows and Mac OS support virtual machines, the former through some tricky
simulation of the boot loader in a protected space, and the latter through an emulation of
the Intel hardware architecture on the Apple platform.

It's beyond the scope of this book to talk too much about these, but it's worth a few
quick screenshots to show you how to create a virtual Unix OS to use for experimentation and practice, without any worries about hurting a live production system.

Task 11.4: Learning About Virtual Machines

TASK ▼

The most popular solution for running virtual machines on the Intel platform is VMware, from VMware Corporation (www.vmware.com). With this program installed, you can create *virtual* Unix-operating environments, and even have multiple Windows operating systems installed for testing. Performance is roughly 80–90% of what you'd have with a native load, so it's not quite as fast. It's worth noting that you can also install VMware on your Linux system, enabling you to run Windows within Linux.

On the Macintosh, Virtual PC from Connectix Corporation (www.connectix.com) offers a similar capability, albeit with a higher performance penalty because of the need to emulate the Intel hardware architecture (including CPU). On a very fast Mac OS X system Virtual PC runs like a slightly sluggish PC.

1. When you have VMware installed on your PC, you can install a couple of different operating systems and boot up the one of your choice by simply clicking on the appropriate icon. Figure 11.2 shows a Windows 2000 system running Red Hat Linux 7.2 within VMware.

FIGURE 11.2

VMware lets you run another OS within your OS.

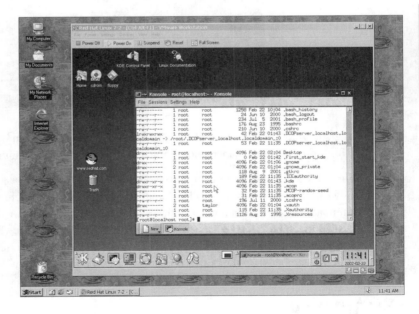

11

You can also run the virtual machine in full-screen mode, eliminating all the Windows clutter (or, if you were running VMware within Linux, you could hide all the Linux material and just appear to be running Windows directly).

▼ 2. Virtual PC on the Macintosh is quite similar in functionality. Figure 11.3 shows a Macintosh screen with Virtual PC running Red Hat Linux 7.2 again. Although too small to see, Windows 98 SE and Windows 2000 are other available operating systems on this Macintosh setup.

FIGURE 11.3
Virtual PC lets you run multiple operating systems on Mac OS X.

As with VMware, Virtual PC also lets you run a full-screen mode, which slightly ▲ improves performance and eliminates any distracting Macintosh visual clutter.

Software testers have been using products such as VMware for years to enable access to many different versions of Windows and Unix, and it's a really great way to learn Unix system administration in a manner that's considerably safer than working directly on a physical machine. Worst case, if you completely thrash things to where it won't even boot, just delete the virtual-machine image and build a new one. Better, it allows easy cut-and-paste between the native operating system and the virtual or emulated one.

Summary

This hour has focused on multiple-OS boot configurations, starting with the specifics of partitioning hard disks with Unix tools, and then examining in depth the most popular boot loaders available, LILO and GRUB. Finally, we ended by discussing the different options available for running one operating system within the environment of another.

Q&A

Q Isn't it dangerous to play with boot loader configurations?

A Oh yes. In fact, a stray character in a test `lilo.conf` file during the production of this chapter caused me no end of grief and at least eight lost hours. Again, be careful and methodical with these configuration files, and make sure you have a backup of the original set of boot parameters as one of the options. And always make sure you have boot disks, just in case....

Q Why dual-boot if VMware is so cool?

A VMware and other virtual machine systems offer a very nifty approach to running an OS within a safe environment, but it's not a native install, and you certainly wouldn't want to run a Web server from within a virtual machine. There are also some subtle nuances of network and peripheral interaction that don't matter in the macro, but might become important if you're administering a machine that people are using to develop device drivers or other low-level solutions.

Q Given that, how many operating systems do you have installed on your systems?

A I'll simply say that on my Titanium Powerbook, I have it natively booting into Mac OS X, and then with Virtual PC I can switch into full-screen mode with Linux, Solaris, Windows 2000, and Windows 98. It's sure to cause confusion when people look over my shoulder!

Workshop

Quiz

1. What does LILO stand for? GRUB?

2. The boot sequence is BIOS, PRAM, and what?

3. What is the greatest challenge facing system administrators who want to set up a system for dual-booting?

4. What do you need to watch out for with the `timeout` parameter in the `lilo.conf` file?

5. What critical design mistake in LILO did the GRUB developers fix, helping thousands of system administrators avoid a nightmare?

Answers

1. LILO is the Linux Loader, and GRUB is the GRand Unified Boot loader.

2. The BIOS gets the system started, then the PRAM is checked for the specific configuration details. One of the most important snippets of information therein is the boot disk, so the next step is switching control of the system to the code in the master boot record.

3. Having the disk properly partitioned for multiple operating systems *before installing any of them.*

4. That you've set it to a sufficiently large value: The timeout is calculated in tenths of a second, not seconds.

5. The GRUB developers fixed the program so that it won't install a bad configuration, so testing the configuration is less critical. You should still proceed with caution nonetheless.

In the next hour, you'll learn about disk quotas, both those that are built in to various Unix flavors, and those you can build yourself with some savvy shell scripts. More importantly, we'll also look at the `find` command in detail and explore how it can help with many system administration tasks.

Hour **12**

Managing Disk Quotas

There's an old joke in the system administration world that there are two different types of sysadmins: those that are happy when their users are happy, and those that are happy when they don't have any users. Without going into this too much, it's worth pointing out that happy users lead directly to an environment where you're successful and have the ability to plan and organize, rather than reactively fight fires everyday.

In that sense, we're going to look at disk quotas and managing disk usage on a per-user basis in this hour. We have already looked at disk usage in Hour 3, "Disk Usage," but that was focused on df and du, which are useful tools, but relatively primitive compared to the find power tool we'll explore this hour.

In this hour you learn

- How to implement disk quotas
- Quota nuances on other Unixes
- How to create your own quota system with find

Implementing a Disk-Quota Policy

Earlier we talked about how disk space is so cheap that it's probably easier to get an additional disk and hook it into your system, rather than complaining to users that they're consuming too much disk space. You could even charge them a disk overuse tax and let them buy their own disks.

However, that's not realistic and it's very helpful to learn about tools that are built-in to the Unix system for managing and limiting disk usage. Even better, by having it integrated into the user environment, you free yourself from having to send nastygrams, e-mail messages to users that say they're in trouble. (Rarely are they received with a positive glow!)

Disks can fill up, too, even big disks. Don't believe me? Go look at how large movie trailer files are on sites such as www.sonypictures.com. If you have a user eagerly storing them on disk, you've got a problem brewing, and it could be a problem that pops up overnight without you even realizing anything is wrong! Not good.

To address these issues, there's a disk-quota system built-in to just about every flavor of Unix. Essentially, the exact same disk-quota tools are available on Red Hat Linux, Mac OS X, and Solaris 8. This means that we'll be able to explore one in depth, and have it apply to all three of these operating systems.

 It turns out that enabling disk quotas on Mac OS X is quite a bit more tricky. We'll talk about that in a little while.

Task 12.1: Implementing Quotas

The key commands for managing a disk-quota policy are edquota to define user (or group) quotas; quotacheck to ensure everything is configured properly; quotaon to enable quotas; and finally the user-level quota command to see how much space users have left in their quota allocation.

Let's get started looking at Red Hat Linux 7.2. Our first stop is the /etc/fstab file used by mount.

1. Disk quotas need to be enabled on each physical disk or partition you want to manage. To do this you need to make a change in the /etc/fstab file and create two empty admin files at the topmost level of the disk for the system to track quota usage.

First off, to enable quotas by user, you'll need to add `usrquota` to the list of mount options in the `/etc/fstab` file. For group-based quotas (that is, a configuration where all members of a group cannot collectively exceed a specific disk allocation) use `grpquota`, and, yes, you can specify both if you would like.

I have modified the mount entry for `/disk2` because my intent is for this disk to be used for storing large media files like movies, MP3 music collections, tarballs, and so forth. Everyone will get a large quota, but I want to ensure that every user gets a fair shake at the disk space.

As a reminder, a *tarball* is a cute name for an archive of files, usually a program and its supplemental docs, stored in compressed `tar` format. See Hour 7, "Large File Management and Backups," for more about this.

```
# cat /etc/fstab
LABEL=/          /              ext3     defaults               1 1
LABEL=/boot      /boot          ext3     defaults               1 2
none             /dev/pts       devpts   gid=5,mode=620         0 0
none             /proc          proc     defaults               0 0
none             /dev/shm       tmpfs    defaults               0 0
/dev/hda3        swap           swap     defaults               0 0
/dev/cdrom       /mnt/cdrom     iso9660  noauto,owner,kudzu,ro  0 0
/dev/fd0         /mnt/floppy    auto     noauto,owner,kudzu     0 0
/dev/hdb         /disk2         ext2     defaults,usrquota      2 0
```

Note the addition of `usrquota` to the very last entry.

2. The next step is to create the two files: `aquota.user` and `aquota.group`.

Different versions of Unix differ on the name of these two files. Newer Unixes use `aquota.*`, whereas other flavors use `quota.*`. Check the man page for the final verdict on your installation.

These two files have to go at the root of the disk in question, so we'll want to create them *before* we unmount and remount the disk.

```
# cd /disk2
# touch aquota.user aquota.group
# chmod 600 aquota.user aquota.group
# ls -l aquota.*
-rw-------   1 root     root             0 Feb 22 10:10 aquota.group
-rw-------   1 root     root             0 Feb 22 10:10 aquota.user
```

12

▼ 3. Because /disk2 is already mounted to the system, I'll need to either unmount it
and mount it again, or reboot. I'll try the former first because obviously it's considerably less disruptive!

```
% umount /disk
umount: /disk2: device is busy
```

Ugh! This is one of those errors that sysadmins don't like very much. It means that
there's a process running that has a file or directory open on this disk.

If you encounter this, you can immediately step to rebooting, but there's one more
trick we can try first: wall. The wall command (think *write-all*) enables you to
send a quick message to everyone who is logged in. I'll use this to ask everyone to
pull off of /disk2 for a few minutes.

```
# wall

I'm trying to reconfigure /disk2 so if you are using this disk,
please back away and go back to your home directory for five.
Thanks. If this doesn't work, I'll need to reboot! :-)

#
```

To end my input, I used Ctrl+D. Here's what users see on their screens:

```
Broadcast message from root (pts/2) Fri Feb 22 10:14:18 2002...

I'm trying to reconfigure /disk2 so if you are using this disk,
please back away and go back to your home directory for five.
Thanks. If this doesn't work, I'll need to reboot! :-)
```

Sixty seconds later we try the umount command again and succeed! (If that hadn't
succeeded, fuser can be a real blessing—it shows what files are open by what
processes on a given file system. Check the man page for details.)

Ah, users can be nice folk sometimes!

```
# umount /disk2
# mount /disk2
#
```

4. The next step is to run quotacheck to ensure that everything is configured properly. You can specify a disk, but it's easier to just use the -a flag to have quotacheck check all the disk quotas at once:

```
# quotacheck -a
quotacheck: WARNING - Quotafile /disk2/aquota.user was probably truncated.
Can't save quota settings...
▼    #
```

▼ This isn't as dire as it seems; all it's saying is that we need to add at least one user quota. This is done with edquota, and to start, let's give user taylor a quota.

```
# edquota -u taylor
```

If you get an immediate error message that there are no disk systems with quotas, your best bet is to double-check that you modified /etc/fstab appropriately, then reboot. Once everything is settled, the system pops up a vi editor with the following information within:

```
Disk quotas for user taylor (uid 500):
  Filesystem        blocks      soft       hard      inodes      soft       hard
  /dev/hdb            1578         0          0           2         0          0
```

You can see that this user has no disk quota, though he's using 1578 blocks of disk space and consuming two inodes. You can also see that you can specify quota by disk blocks (1K each) or by the number of inodes (essentially, the number of files) the user can create. Usually, you'll specify both.

> There are two types of quotas available. Users that exceed their *soft limit* have warnings generated by the file system as they proceed, but they can continue to work. The *hard limit*, however, often stops them in their tracks, rejecting any attempts to write to the disk. Always set your soft limit significantly lower than your hard limit to avoid frustrated users.

User taylor isn't too bad a disk hog, so we'll give him relatively generous disk quotas by editing the values shown:

```
Disk quotas for user taylor (uid 500):
  Filesystem        blocks      soft       hard      inodes      soft       hard
  /dev/hdb            1578      7500       9000           2      3000       4000
```

12

Quit the editor and the quota values are saved.

If you want to copy one user's quota limits to another user, specify the -p proto-type-user flag to the edquota command. To copy taylor's quota to user sangeeth, for example, you'd use edquota -p taylor sangeeth. Or, of course, you can automate the whole shebang with a quick shell script.

5. One more step: We need to enable the quota system with quotaon. For this, I prefer to use -a, -g, -u, and -v, which are all quotas turned on, verbose output, group and user quotas checked, respectively. To do this once, we can simply type it in:

```
# quotaon -aguv
/dev/hdb [/disk2]: user quotas turned on
```
▼

▼
5. Now when user `taylor` types `quota`, he'll see

```
% quota
Disk quotas for user taylor (uid 500):
      Filesystem  blocks   quota   limit   grace   files   quota   limit   grace
        /dev/hdb    1578    7500    9000                2    3000    4000
```

On systems with quotas in place, it's often a good idea to add the quota command to the user's `.login` or `.bash_profile` files.

6. From an administrative point of view, you can use `repquota` to generate an attractive output report:

```
# repquota -a
*** Report for user quotas on device /dev/hdb
Block grace time: 7days; Inode grace time: 7days
                         Block limits            File limits
User             used   soft    hard  grace   used  soft  hard  grace
- - - - - - - - - - - - - - - - - - - - - - - - - - - - - - - - - - - - - - -
root       - -     66      0      0            5     0     0
taylor     - -   1578   7500   9000            2  3000  4000
```

7. The only issue we haven't touched on is how to automatically turn on quotas at boot-time, so you don't have to remember `quotaon` each time you restart the system.

We're jumping ahead of ourselves a little bit (the sequence of files read during bootup is covered in the next few hours) but in a nutshell, if the quota enabling code isn't already therein, you'll want to append the following lines to your `/etc/rc.local` file:

```
echo "Checking quotas. This may take a moment or two..."
/sbin/quotacheck -aguv

if [ $? -eq 0 ] ; then
  echo "Turning on disk quotas."
  /sbin/quotaon -aguv
else
  echo "*** Did not turn on disk quotas due to quotacheck errors."
fi
```

This checks the quota files for a valid format, then, if all is well (the return code, tested as $?, is equal to zero) turns on the quota-management system. Otherwise, an
▲
error is output.

Many Unix system administrators eschew disk quotas, preferring either to ignore the problem or assume that users will manage their own disk space properly. This might be true in some environments, but setting big disk quotas once and forgetting them can be a much more graceful solution. If no one ever emerges as a disk hog, you'll forget the disk quotas are even there. But, if someone starts expanding their file system usage the system will automatically flag it and help avoid bigger problems.

Quota Nuances on Other Unixes

Although the basics of turning on disk quotas are the same in just about all modern Unix operating systems, there are nuances with Solaris 8 that are worth examining briefly.

> Setting up disk quotas from the Unix level of Mac OS X is quite tricky—too tricky to explore in this book. The basic challenge is that disks other than root are mounted by autodiskmounter, so enabling quotas is quite difficult. After you do that, the standard quota commands are available, as man -k will confirm. Hopefully, as OS X matures it'll become easier to enable quotas, too. If you really want to pursue this, start by reading the quotaon man page.

Task 12.2: Quotas on Other Systems

▲ TASK

The best way to learn about the nuances of implementing quotas on your particular version of Unix is, of course, to read the man pages for the quota commands.

1.   Let's start there, on a Solaris system:

```
# man -k quota
edquota          edquota (1m)     - edit user quotas for ufs file system
quota            quota (1m)       - display a user's ufs file system disk quota
➥and usage
quotacheck       quotacheck (1m)  - ufs file system quota consistency checker
quotactl         quotactl (7i)    - manipulate disk quotas
quotaoff         quotaon (1m)     - turn ufs file system quotas on and off
quotaon          quotaon (1m)     - turn ufs file system quotas on and off
repquota         repquota (1m)    - summarize quotas for a ufs file system
rquotad          rquotad (1m)     - remote quota server
```

The commands certainly look familiar, don't they?

> Actually, one command shown here and worth knowing is rquotad, which enables you to use quotas on a shared NFS (network file system) disk.

The Solaris version of quota only reports disks where the users are *over* their soft limit, so they should probably get into the habit of using the -v flag, which reports their status on all disks with quotas enabled, over limit or not. Alternatively, you could make it a system-wide shell alias.

12

▼   2. The first change we need to make is to edit /etc/vfstab (notice that it's not fstab,
         but vfstab) to add rq to the list of mount-time options. Then, instead of creating
         quota.user and quota.group, simply create a single file quotas:

         ```
         # cd /export/home
         # touch quotas ; chmod 600 quotas
         ```

         Now, unmount the disk and remount it; then use edquota to set up a quota for a user.
         The edquota command is essentially the same, even though the actual layout of the
         information presented in the editor is slightly different.

      3. Next, ensure all is set up properly with quotacheck. The Solaris version of quo-
         tacheck differs in what flags it understands. To get the equivalent of the -aguv set in
         Linux, use -pva, which has the added benefit of checking quotas in parallel, which
         can be considerably faster!

         ```
         # quotacheck -pva
         *** Checking quotas for /dev/rdsk/c0d0s7 (/export/home)
         #
         ```

         The repquota reports the status of users on a device with quotas enabled:

         ```
         # repquota -a
         /dev/dsk/c0d0s7 (/export/home):
                             Block limits              File limits
         User      used   soft   hard   timeleft   used  soft  hard  timeleft
         taylor       0   5000   7500                  0     0     0
         ```

      4. Here's what user taylor would see on a Solaris box by using quota:

         ```
         $ /usr/sbin/quota
         $
         ```

         Remember, without the -v flag it only reports systems where the user is over quota.
         One more try:

         ```
         $ /usr/sbin/quota -v
         Disk quotas for taylor (uid 100):
         Filesystem    usage  quota  limit   timeleft  files  quota  limit   timeleft
▲        /export/home      0   5000   7500                 0      0      0
         ```

Many system administration books counsel you not to bother with disk quotas because
they're obsolete or no one really uses them. I disagree. If you have a multiuser system, it's
in everyone's best interest to set high, but meaningful, disk quotas to ensure that the
resources are shared fairly. If you set this up prior to assigning accounts, you'll never have
to argue with sore users afterward either!

Creating Your Own Quota System with `find`

Before we leave the topic of disk quotas, let's look at how you can use the powerful `find` command to build your own simple disk quota system.

The basic idea is that you want to automatically scan all disks on your system for files owned by the specified user, sum up their sizes, and then compare the total size of all files against a set limit that you've defined.

Rather than have this as a set of daemons, however, we'll just create a shell script, `fquota`, to do the work for us.

Task 12.3: Disk Quotas with `find`

There are a small number of commands that I find myself using over and over again as a system administrator, and `find` definitely makes the short list. Whether you're looking to ensure that there are no `setuid root` programs, trying to find where RPM stores its package data files, or even just helping a user find that long-lost letter to Aunt Hernia, `find` offers lots of power and capabilities. Indeed, spending 30 minutes reading the man page and trying out different `find` options is time very well spent!

> `setuid root` programs are programs that run as if they were `root`. These are very dangerous security holes, and therefore, you should always be aware of what programs on your system are `setuid root`. You can check by looking for a file permission s in an `ls -l` output, coupled with an ownership of `root`. We'll talk about this again in Hour 21, "Shell Scripting: The Administrator's Swiss Army Knife."

1. Here's a typical use of `find`, to output the equivalent `ls` string for each regular file owned by user `taylor` below the specified point on the file tree:

```
# find /disk2 -user taylor -type f -ls
    12  789 -rw-r--r-- 1 taylor    root     802068 Feb 22 10:53 /disk2/
➥vmlinuz
    15  789 -rw-r--r-- 1 taylor    root     802068 Feb 22 10:53 /disk2/
➥vmlinuz-2.4.7-10
#
```

Only two files match these criteria on `/disk2`.

12

> If you want to constrain your search to a single file system, add -xdev to the
> list of parameters.

2. I'll cast my net wider by looking across the entire file system, but because I know
   there are going to be lots of files, I'll just count lines the first time through:

```
# find / -user taylor -type f -ls | wc -l
    686
```

To sum up the sizes of all files is a good job for awk or perl: I'll opt for awk
because it's available on older Unix systems, too. The task we want is to have a
script that extracts the seventh field of each line, then sums them all up and outputs
the result. This can be done in awk with the succinct program

```
{ sum += $7} END { print sum }
```

(the END tag denotes a block of instructions that is only run *after* all the lines have
been read in).

```
# find / -user taylor -type f -ls | \
   awk '{ sum += $7 } END { print sum }'
27869349
```

Let's see; that's in bytes, so dividing by 1024×1024 will reveal that this is 26
megabytes. Not too much disk space at all, even though the number certainly looks
huge!

Of course, awk can do this math, too:

```
# find / -user taylor -type f -ls |    \
   awk '{ sum += $7 } END { print sum / (1024*1024) }'
26.5783
```

3. This suggests our simple disk-quota script—for each user account, sum up their
   disk usage and report if it's greater than MAXDISKUSAGE, a variable we'll set in the
   script. For the first version, however, let's just figure out everyone's disk usage:

```
#!/bin/sh

# FQUOTA - Disk quota analysis tool for Unix.
#          Assumes that all user accounts are >= UID 100.

MAXDISKUSAGE=20          # 20MB is our soft quota

for name in `cut -d: -f1,3 /etc/passwd | awk -F: '$2 > 99 { print $1 }'`
do
  echo -n "User $name exceeds disk quota. Disk usage is: "
```

```
find / /usr /var /home -user $name -xdev -type f -ls | \
     awk '{ sum += $7 } END { print sum / (1024*1024) " Mbytes" }'

done

exit 0
```

There are a couple of things worth mentioning about the script here. First off, the for loop is being fed a list of usernames whose UIDs are 100 or greater, to screen out system accounts. This is done with a more sophisticated expression to awk, as you can see. Then, the find we're constraining to the file systems we're interested in checking, and using -xdev to ensure that it doesn't check uninteresting systems.

The output of this version of fquota is

```
# fquota
User mthorne exceeds disk quota. Disk usage is: 0.0558786 Mbytes
User mdella exceeds disk quota. Disk usage is: 0.700355 Mbytes
User taylor exceeds disk quota. Disk usage is: 26.5783 Mbytes
User testdude exceeds disk quota. Disk usage is: 0.554475 Mbytes
```

4. Adding the final step of only listing those users whose disk usage exceeds the MAXDISKUSAGE quota is accomplished by wrapping the entire for loop in subshell parentheses, then feeding the output, again, to awk for filtering:

```
#!/bin/sh

# FQUOTA - Disk quota analysis tool for Unix.
#          Assumes that all user accounts are >= UID 100.

MAXDISKUSAGE=20

( for name in `cut -d: -f1,3 /etc/passwd | awk -F: '$2 > 99 { print $1 }'`
do
  echo -n "User $name exceeds disk quota. Disk usage is: "

  find / /usr /var /home -user $name -xdev -type f -ls | \
     awk '{ sum += $7 } END { print sum / (1024*1024) " Mbytes" }'

done ) | awk "\$9 > $MAXDISKUSAGE { print \$0 }"

exit 0
```

When this version of the program is run, it correctly reports which users are over the allocated disk quota, across the entire file system:

```
# fquota
User taylor exceeds disk quota. Disk usage is: 26.5783 Mbytes
```

A little bit more work and this could automatically e-mail the user with a gentle reminder to compress or delete some files, and free up the disk space for others to use.

12

▼   5. Now what about getting this Linux script to work on Mac OS X? Surprisingly little
       has to change. We just need to omit -xdev, which isn't understood by the Apple
       version of find. Of course, there are a few more files to consider:

```
# find / -user taylor -ls | wc -l
  87308
```

The main wrinkle is that users need to be extracted from the NetInfo database, not
/etc/passwd, so we'll need to use nireport, as discussed extensively back in
Hour 5, "Working with User Accounts."

Put all this together, and the modified script looks like this:

```
#!/bin/sh

# FQUOTA - Disk quota analysis tool for Unix.
#          Assumes that all user accounts are >= UID 100.

MAXDISKUSAGE=20

( for name in `nireport . /users name uid | awk '$2 > 99 { print $1 }'`
do
  echo -n "User $name exceeds disk quota. Disk usage is: "

  find / -user $name -xdev -type f -ls | \
      awk '{ sum += $7 } END { print sum / (1024*1024) " Mbytes" }'

done ) | awk "\$9 > $MAXDISKUSAGE { print \$0 }"

exit 0
```

The output is fun:

```
# fquota
User taylor exceeds disk quota. Disk usage is: 17162.5 Mbytes
```

▲   That taylor guy is using a *ton of disk space!!* I'll have to talk with him!

It's not particularly difficult to write a simple quota-management system in Unix. After
all, with hundreds of different utilities ready to pull into action, there's not much you
can't cobble together, frankly!

However, if your system has a built-in quota system, there are advantages to having the
file system itself enforce quota limits, particularly if you have any concern about run-
away users who might go bananas over a weekend downloading MP3s and filling up a
disk completely.

Summary

This hour has explored the concept of disk quotas and the difference between using built-in tools, and using system tools that are part of the file system. There are pluses and minuses for each of the solutions, and there are, of course, potential problems lurking if you ignore disk quotas and run out of disk space. As with many administrative issues, there are no simple answers.

Q&A

Q **Aren't quotas a bad thing? I mean, didn't the U.S. Supreme Court vote that quotas were in violation of the U.S. Constitution?**

A Um, you might well have too much time on your hands, even with this accelerated 24-hour format. The U.S. Supreme Court did overrule quotas, most notably in Regents of the University of California v. Bakke, back in 1978, but, really, is this relevant?

Q **Why are so many system admins against quotas?**

A Somewhat tied to the previous question, and certainly related to the anarchistic strain of the hacker community, many sysadmins do speak out strongly against quotas or any other artificially imposed constraints on usage. However, even with disk space a dime a megabyte, it simply cannot be that everyone can use as much space as they want. There must be some constraints, and if that's the case, quotas are a reasonably elegant, and certainly an egalitarian solution.

Q **Are disk quota systems used on Windows?**

A Yes. You can get disk quota management systems for just about any flavor of Windows available. Shareware repository `Download.com` has nine, including Northern.Net's slick Quota Server (but beware, it's $900).

Workshop

Quiz

1. What's the difference between a hard and soft quota limit?
2. What is the first step before enabling a disk quota?
3. A major limitation of quotas that are built-in to the system is....
4. What's the purpose of the `wall` command?
5. Where is a recommended location for adding a call to the `quota` command?

Answers

1. A soft limit is the maximum amount of disk space users can consume without any warnings. When they exceed their soft limit, the system complains but lets them continue. A hard limit is an inviolable constraint and the system will reject user attempts to add new files or even enlarge files.

2. The first step is to edit the /etc/fstab (or vfstab on Solaris) to enable quotas at mount time.

3. A major limitation is that the quota system doesn't span multiple file systems, so although it's possible to limit users to a specific amount of space per device, there's no built-in mechanism to limit overall disk usage.

4. The wall command lets you send an instant message to every user logged in at that moment.

5. If you enable quotas, adding a call to quota (or quota -v, as necessary) in every user's .login or .bash_profile is a very smart move.

In the next hour, we'll switch gears and start looking at process and system controls. We'll focus on starting up and shutting down Unix systems, including an extensive discussion of run levels and init states. It's required reading for any system administrator!

PART V

Process & System Controls

Hour

HOUR 13

Changing System State

Compared to a personal computer operating system, the multiuser, multiprocessing capabilities of Unix can seem a bit alien in some regards. Most notably, have you ever stopped to consider what happens when you either boot up or shut down your Unix system?

In this hour, we'll dig into the system configuration and learn exactly what processes are started and stopped (and how they're started and stopped) when you switch states, either booting, halting, rebooting, or switching between single-user and multiuser modes.

In this hour you'll learn about

- The init process and its configuration file
- Enabling specific services at different run levels
- Shutting down your system the right way

Configuring and Working with the `init` Process

The Unix operating system has a number of *run levels*, each of which define a different state of the OS, and a different set of applications and daemons that are available and running. For example, by convention, run level 0 is the shutdown state—a system that's in run level 0 is stopped.

Run levels are also called *init states* after the all-important program that defines these different run levels for your computer: `init`.

Task 13.1: The `init` Process and Configuration

To start this hour, let's delve into the internals of the `init` program and its configuration file `/etc/inittab`.

1. First off, a quick invocation of `ps` will confirm that the `init` daemon is running. This turns out to be easy because on every Unix system, the `init` program is the very first program run by the operating system. As a result, it's always process ID 1.

    On a Linux box:

    ```
    # ps -up 1
    USER        PID %CPU %MEM   VSZ  RSS TTY       STAT START    TIME COMMAND
    root          1  0.0  0.0  1412   52 ?         S     08:58   0:06 init
    ```

    On a Solaris box:

    ```
    # ps -fp 1
        UID   PID  PPID  C    STIME TTY       TIME CMD
        root    1     0  0    Jan 26 ?        0:00 /etc/init -
    ```

    And on a Mac OS X Darwin box:

    ```
    # ps -up 1
    USER    PID %CPU %MEM    VSZ   RSS  TT  STAT      TIME COMMAND
    root      1  0.0  0.1   1292   268  ??  SLs    0:00.00 /sbin/init
    ```

    If for any reason the `init` program wasn't running, your system would be stopped dead in its tracks.

    Notice that there aren't any starting options to `init`. Instead, the program figures out its configuration by reading the `/etc/inittab` file.

2. Let's focus on Linux for a while now. On Red Hat Linux, the standard `/etc/inittab` file looks like the following:

    ```
    # cat /etc/inittab
    #
    ```

```
# inittab       This file describes how the INIT process should set up
#               the system in a certain run-level.
#
# Author:       Miquel van Smoorenburg, <miquels@drinkel.nl.mugnet.org>
#               Modified for RHS Linux by Marc Ewing and Donnie Barnes
#

id:5:initdefault:

# System initialization.
si::sysinit:/etc/rc.d/rc.sysinit

l0:0:wait:/etc/rc.d/rc 0
l1:1:wait:/etc/rc.d/rc 1
l2:2:wait:/etc/rc.d/rc 2
l3:3:wait:/etc/rc.d/rc 3
l4:4:wait:/etc/rc.d/rc 4
l5:5:wait:/etc/rc.d/rc 5
l6:6:wait:/etc/rc.d/rc 6

# Things to run in every runlevel.
ud::once:/sbin/update

# Trap CTRL-ALT-DELETE
ca::ctrlaltdel:/sbin/shutdown -t3 -r now

# When our UPS tells us power has failed, assume we have a few minutes
# of power left.  Schedule a shutdown for 2 minutes from now.
# This does, of course, assume you have powerd installed and your
# UPS connected and working correctly.
pf::powerfail:/sbin/shutdown -f -h +2 "Power Failure; System Shutting Down"

# If power was restored before the shutdown kicked in, cancel it.
pr:12345:powerokwait:/sbin/shutdown -c "Power Restored; Shutdown Cancelled"

# Run gettys in standard runlevels
1:2345:respawn:/sbin/mingetty tty1
2:2345:respawn:/sbin/mingetty tty2
3:2345:respawn:/sbin/mingetty tty3
4:2345:respawn:/sbin/mingetty tty4
5:2345:respawn:/sbin/mingetty tty5
6:2345:respawn:/sbin/mingetty tty6

# Run xdm in runlevel 5
# xdm is now a separate service
x:5:respawn:/etc/X11/prefdm -nodaemon
```

This might seem overwhelming, but all lines in the /etc/inittab file have the same general format:

```
unique ID : run levels : action : process
```

13

For example, the very last line, uniquely identified as `inittab` line x, only applies to run state (`init` level) 5, and forces a respawn of the `/etc/X11/prefdm` program with the `-nodaemon` flag specified.

> The `prefdm` script manages login screens within the X Window System environment.

3. Let's define the most common `init` levels in Table 13.1 and the known `init` actions in Table 13.2.

TABLE 13.1   Common `init` Levels

Level	Meaning
0	Halt
1	Single-user mode (also called s mode on some systems)
2	Multiuser, but no remote file systems mounted; often also no networking daemons running
3	Full multiuser mode
5	Full multiuser + X11 graphics
6	Reboot

TABLE 13.2   Defined `init` Actions

Action	Meaning
boot	Process will be executed during system bootup
bootwait	Like boot, but init waits for completion
ctrlaltdel	Process will be executed when the console keyboard device driver receives a Control-Alt-Del key sequence
initdefault	Specifies the default run level to boot into on system boot
once	Like wait, but init doesn't wait for completion
respawn	Process is guaranteed to be running—the system will restarted it if it dies
sysinit	Process will be executed during boot, but before any boot or bootwait entries
wait	The process will be started once (as opposed to respawn), and init will wait for it to complete

Many versions of Unix support a number of actions that let you gracefully interact with an uninterruptible power supply (UPS), including powerwait, powerfail, powerokwait, and powerfailnow. Read the apmd man page in Linux or the powerd man page in Solaris for more details.

It's very rare for your system to not be in init level 3 (if you have a nongraphical Unix environment) or init level 5 (if you have a graphical environment; for example, Mac OS X with Aqua enabled for the fancy graphical user interface).

4. On my Web server, for example, I have the default init level set to 3—I don't need an X Window System environment running, so I save the cycles for the Web server, SSH daemon, and so on. To see what processes init runs at this run level, I simply step through the inittab looking for all lines that contain a 3 in the run levels field.

This brings up the following list:

```
l3:3:wait:/etc/rc.d/rc 3
pr:12345:powerokwait:/sbin/shutdown -c "Power Restored; Shutdown Cancelled"
1:2345:respawn:/sbin/mingetty tty1
2:2345:respawn:/sbin/mingetty tty2
3:2345:respawn:/sbin/mingetty tty3
4:2345:respawn:/sbin/mingetty tty4
5:2345:respawn:/sbin/mingetty tty5
6:2345:respawn:/sbin/mingetty tty6
```

Of these, the last six are simply processes to ensure that there's a listener program available for virtual consoles. The pr line matches power restore events. (By not specifying an init level in the powerfail action, you can imply that it applies to all states—flip back to the /etc/inittab we just listed to see what I mean.)

Finally, the very first line of output is probably the most important: When moving into init state 3, run /etc/rc.d/rc.3 and wait for it to complete. The rc directories contain a list of all the scripts that are executed (which ends up being the same statement as "list of all daemons and programs automatically started") for each specific init level. The directory /etc/rc.d/rc.3 contains scripts that control what runs (or doesn't run) at run level 3.

Similarly, init state 5 is a multiuser + graphical user interface, typically the X Window System. The entries in the /etc/inittab for run level 5 are the same as for run level 3, with the only exception being that run level 5 references /etc/rc.d/rc.5 instead.

13

▼ 5. In the next section, we'll explore those rc files more closely, but for now, let's end
this section by learning that you can switch from any run level to any other by simply typing init *n*, where *n* is the desired run level.

This means that to shut down the computer, you can type

init 0

and to reboot the computer you can type

init 6

Similarly, one way to drop into single-user mode (where no other users can log in
and there's no graphical interface), you can type

init 1

Let's do that and have a quick peek at what processes are still running in the Red
Hat Linux environment.

6. When you type **init 1**, nothing seems to happen: The shell prompts for another
command as if you'd typed **echo** or **ls**, but behind the scenes things are starting to
close down, and within a minute or so the system should log out remote terminals,
close xterms, log out of X Windows System, and end up with just a command shell
prompt on the console. Typing **ps** will reveal that there are very few processes running at this point:

```
sh-2.05# ps aux
USER       PID %CPU %MEM   VSZ   RSS TTY      STAT START   TIME COMMAND
root         1  0.0  0.6  1424   376 ?        S    08:58   0:07 init
root         2  0.0  0.0     0     0 ?        SW   08:58   0:01 [keventd]
root         3  0.0  0.0     0     0 ?        SW   08:58   0:01 [kapm-idled]
root         4  0.0  0.0     0     0 ?        SWN  08:58   0:00 [ksoftirqd_CPU0]
root         5  0.0  0.0     0     0 ?        SW   08:58   0:10 [kswapd]
root         6  0.0  0.0     0     0 ?        SW   08:58   0:00 [kreclaimd]
root         7  0.0  0.0     0     0 ?        SW   08:58   0:00 [bdflush]
root         8  0.0  0.0     0     0 ?        SW   08:58   0:01 [kupdated]
root         9  0.0  0.0     0     0 ?        SW<  08:58   0:00 [mdrecoveryd]
root        13  0.0  0.0     0     0 ?        SW   08:58   0:18 [kjournald]
root        88  0.0  0.0     0     0 ?        SW   08:58   0:01 [khubd]
root       183  0.0  0.0     0     0 ?        SW   08:59   0:00 [kjournald]
root     10412  0.1  0.7  1492   444 ?        S    14:07   0:00 minilogd
root     10636  0.0  0.6  1424   408 tty1     S    14:07   0:00 init
root     10637  0.4  1.8  2212  1136 tty1     S    14:07   0:00 /bin/sh
root     10641  0.0  1.1  2628   716 tty1     R    14:08   0:00 ps aux
sh-2.05#
```

Notice the process IDs: All the processes with PIDs less than 200 are part of the
kernel itself and stick with you regardless of run level. The higher-level processes

▼ are minilogd, init, /bin/sh, and of course, the ps command itself.

The /bin/sh is the command shell, and the init hangs around until you're done
with single-user mode. When you quit the shell (or kill the new init process), the
system boots back into the default run level (typically 5) automatically:

```
sh-2.05# exit
INIT: Entering runlevel: 5
Updating /etc/fstab                                             [  OK  ]
Checking for new hardware                                       [  OK  ]
Flushing all current rules and user defined chains:            [  OK  ]
Clearing all current rules and user defined chains:            [  OK  ]
Applying ipchains firewall rules:                              [  OK  ]
Setting network parameters:                                    [  OK  ]
Bringing up interface lo:                                      [  OK  ]
Bringing up interface eth0:                                    [  OK  ]
Starting system logger:                                        [  OK  ]
Starting kernel logger:                                        [  OK  ]
Starting portmapper:                                           [  OK  ]
Starting NFS file locking services:
Starting NFS statd:                                            [  OK  ]
Initializing random number generator:                          [  OK  ]
Mounting other filesystems:                                    [  OK  ]
Starting up APM daemon:                                        [  OK  ]
Starting automount: No Mountpoints Defined                     [  OK  ]
Starting sshd:                                                 [  OK  ]
Starting xinetd:                                               [  OK  ]
Starting lpd: No Printers Defined                              [  OK  ]
Starting sendmail:                                             [  OK  ]
Starting console mouse services:                               [  OK  ]
Starting crond:                                                [  OK  ]
Starting xfs:                                                  [  OK  ]
```

As you can see from this listing, all these services were shut down in run level 1,
so the system was impregnable from outside interference, remote users, and so on.
Once you go back into the standard multiuser graphical run environment, all the
services listed are relaunched, just as if you were booting from scratch (and indeed,
the boot from scratch steps through these init scripts in exactly the same way).

Let's end this section by rebooting the computer completely. To do this, simply
type **init 6** and then go get a cup of tea....

The init process is the traffic cop that controls all processes running on the operating
system in a Unix box, and it's configured through the inittab file. The good news is
that you don't ever have to actually edit the file (unless you want to change the default
run level or enable power management tools, for example) because all the interesting
issues of what apps are started for a given run level are pushed into the /etc/rc.d directory, and that's what we'll explore next.

13

Enabling Specific Services at Different Run Levels

While different flavors of Unix have slightly different setups for the rc files, they all have the scripts associated with a particular run level, specified either in a single file, or even better, in a specific subdirectory.

Mac OS X, for example, has three shell scripts in /etc that control this functionality: /etc/rc is the multiuser startup script (the equivalent of init 5), /etc/rc.boot is the single-user startup script (the equivalent of init 1), and /etc/rc.common holds commands and steps that are shared by both run levels. Obviously, Mac OS X Unix doesn't have the concept of six different run levels, but rather four (recall that run level 0 is shutdown and run level 6 is reboot, so they don't need any specific scripts associated with them).

Solaris 8 has a different /etc/rc*n* script for each run level (for example, rc0 and rc3), and also has a corresponding rc*n*.d directory that contains specific service startup scripts, as appropriate. For example, run level 3 is defined by the script /etc/rc3 and the contents of directory /etc/rc3.d.

Linux has a layout that's slightly easier to understand, where there's a single shared /etc/rc script and a specific directory for each of the defined run levels 0–6. Within those directories are symbolic links to scripts that define whether a particular service, daemon, or application should be started or stopped as the system transitions into the specified run level.

> Wait a second. *Stopped as you enter a run level*? Why would you do that? The answer to this puzzle is revealed by thinking about what you'd want to have happen if you, for example, switched from run level 5 to run level 3. You wouldn't want to reboot the system, and you wouldn't want to disconnect and reconnect the remote disks hooked up via NFS, but you would want to kill the X11 applications and graphical daemons. Hence the run level 3 directory might not only specify which applications to have running, but which applications should be stopped if they are currently running.

Without further ado, then, let's look into the run level 3 and run level 5 directories.

Task 13.2: Configuring Your System for Run Levels

▼ TASK

When you first log in to the system and identify the process ID of your login shell, you might be surprised to find that it will often be greater than 4,000. This means that *four thousand* different applications have been started (and most, finished) since bootup and prior to your login shell starting. This is really amazing if you think about it, because this all might happen in no more than two or three minutes.

One of the main areas where the system defines which applications are automatically launched at boot-time is within the /etc/rc directory structure.

1. To start out, let's move directly to /etc/rc.d on the Linux system to see what's inside:

```
# cd /etc/rc.d
# ls -l
total 64
drwxr-xr-x    2 root       root        4096 Jan 11 15:16 init.d
-rwxr-xr-x    1 root       root        3219 Jul 10  2001 rc
drwxr-xr-x    2 root       root        4096 Jan 11 15:45 rc0.d
drwxr-xr-x    2 root       root        4096 Jan 11 15:45 rc1.d
drwxr-xr-x    2 root       root        4096 Jan 11 15:45 rc2.d
drwxr-xr-x    2 root       root        4096 Jan 11 15:45 rc3.d
drwxr-xr-x    2 root       root        4096 Jan 11 15:45 rc4.d
drwxr-xr-x    2 root       root        4096 Jan 11 15:45 rc5.d
drwxr-xr-x    2 root       root        4096 Jan 11 15:45 rc6.d
-rwxr-xr-x    1 root       root         453 Feb 22 11:07 rc.local
-rwxr-xr-x    1 root       root       20983 Sep  9 00:00 rc.sysinit
```

As expected, each run level has its own directory, and there's a single rc script that controls the transition between states. The system keeps track of the current and previous run levels internally, and you can see for yourself, with the runlevel command:

```
# /sbin/runlevel
S 5
```

Here it's telling us that the last run level was S (a synonym for run level 1, or single-user mode), and that the current run level is, as expected, run level 5.

2. Let's look into the rc5.d directory to see what services are started and stopped for this level on this particular system:

```
# cd rc5.d
# ls
K03rhnsd        K35vncserver    S05kudzu        S17keytable     S56xinetd       S95atd
K20nfs          K46radvd        S08ipchains     S20random       S60lpd          S99local
K20rstatd       K50snmpd        S08iptables     S25netfs        S80sendmail
K20rusersd      K65identd       S10network      S26apmd         S85gpm
K20rwalld       K74ntpd         S12syslog       S28autofs       S90crond
K20rwhod        K74ypserv       S13portmap      S55sshd         S90xfs
K34yppasswdd    K74ypxfrd       S14nfslock      S56rawdevices   S95anacron
```

13

▼   Lots of stuff! Anything that begins with a ĸ is killed. Typically those are services
      that are unwanted, and probably aren't running anyway. This is just a sort of virtual
      insurance policy. Anything that begins with an s is started if it's not already running.

> More than that, this also makes it easy to re-enable a service: Simply rename
> the script with the first letter being an s instead of a ĸ and jump out of, and
> back into, the run level, and that service should be started and running!

From this list, you can see that on this system we have chosen not to run rhnsd,
nfs, rstatd, rusersd, rwalld, rwhod, yppasswdd, vncserver, radvd, and about six
other services. We do want to run 23 services, however, including syslog, netfs,
apmd, sshd, sendmail, crond, and atd.

3. Within each of these scripts—and recall they're all symbolic links to central
   scripts—the contents are fairly similar, as exemplified by the following, which ini-
   tializes the random state so that the system has more randomly chosen random
   numbers (which turns out to be important in the world of encryption):

```
# cat S20random
#!/bin/bash
#
# random        Script to snapshot random state and reload it at boot time.
#
# Author:       Theodore Ts'o <tytso@mit.edu>
#
# chkconfig: 2345 20 80
# description: Saves and restores system entropy pool for higher quality \
#              random number generation.

# Source function library.
. /etc/init.d/functions

random_seed=/var/lib/random-seed

# See how we were called.
case "$1" in
  start)
        # Carry a random seed from start-up to start-up
        # Load and then save 512 bytes, which is the size of the entropy pool
        if [ -f $random_seed ]; then
                cat $random_seed >/dev/urandom
        else
                touch $random_seed
        fi
        action $"Initializing random number generator: " /bin/true
```

▼

```
                chmod 600 $random_seed
                dd if=/dev/urandom of=$random_seed count=1 bs=512 2>/dev/null
                touch /var/lock/subsys/random

            ;;
    stop)
                # Carry a random seed from shut-down to start-up
                # Save 512 bytes, which is the size of the entropy pool
                touch $random_seed
                chmod 600 $random_seed
                action $"Saving random seed: " dd if=/dev/urandom of=$random_seed
➥count=1 bs=
512 2>/dev/null

                rm -f /var/lock/subsys/random
            ;;
    status)
                # this is way overkill, but at least we have some status output...
                if [ -c /dev/random ] ; then
                        echo $"The random data source exists"
                else
                        echo $"The random data source is missing"
                fi
            ;;
    restart|reload)
                # do not do anything; this is unreasonable
                :
            ;;
      *)
                # do not advertise unreasonable commands that there is no reason
                # to use with this device
                echo $"Usage: $0 {start|stop|status|restart|reload}"
                exit 1
esac

exit 0
```

Don't get too concerned if some of this looks like completely random input of its own! The most important thing to see here is that each script in the rc.d directory is required to accept start, stop, status, and restart as commands from the command line. This correctly implies that the main job of the /etc/rc script is to invoke *script* start for those scripts whose name start with S, and *script* stop for those whose name start with K.

This also means that you can test the status of any of these services to ensure everything is running correctly by specifying the status option:

```
# ./S20random status
The random data source exists
```

13

▼ Not too exciting in this case, but let's go see if `sendmail` is running correctly:

```
# ./S80sendmail status
sendmail (pid 11315) is running...
```

You can also use this knowledge to verify that services that aren't supposed to be running are in fact stopped:

```
# ./K20nfs status
rpc.mountd is stopped
nfsd is stopped
rpc.rquotad is stopped
```

> On my Web server, when I make changes to the Apache configuration files, I use the `restart` command to the master `httpd` script in `/etc/rc.d/init.d` to restart the server easily. I've even made it an alias to make things easy:
>
> `alias httpd="/etc/rc.d/init.d/httpd"`
>
> With this alias defined, it's easy to type `httpd status` to make sure the server is running, and `httpd restart` to restart it with a new configuration file.

5. Earlier in this hour, when we went from run level 1 to run level 5, we had a number of services list their startup messages. One stuck out:

```
Starting lpd: No Printers Defined                    [  OK  ]
```

This message is coming from within the `S60lpd` script, and it's a good guess that the daemon never started because of this. Now you know how to check:

```
# ./S60lpd status
lpd is stopped
```

Sure enough, it's not running. Because I don't have any printers hooked up, I'm going to disable this service at run level 5 so it doesn't waste time at bootup (well, to be more precise, when entering run level 5) trying to launch it. In fact, as a general rule of thumb, you should make sure that only services you explicitly want to have running are enabled at your default run level.

Doing this is remarkably easy because of the smart layout of the `/etc/rc.d` directories:

```
# mv S60lpd K60lpd
```

That's it. Easy, eh? The next time the system enters run level 5 it won't bother try-
▼ ing to start the line printer daemon `lpd`.

▼ 6. Remember in the last hour when we talked about having the quota system enabled automatically at boot-time? Now you can see the logic behind the contents of the equivalent non-Linux `rc.local` file (and why we put the lines that start up the quota system there):

```
# cat rc.local
#!/bin/sh
#
# This script will be executed *after* all the other init scripts.
# You can put your own initialization stuff in here if you don't
# want to do the full Sys V style init stuff.

touch /var/lock/subsys/local

echo "Checking quotas. This may take a moment or two..."
/sbin/quotacheck -aguv

if [ $? -eq 0 ] ; then
  echo "Turning on disk quotas."
  /sbin/quotaon -aguv
else
  echo "Did *not* turn on disk quotas due to quotacheck errors."
▲ fi
```

There's a lot to learn about the exact details of writing an `rc` script if you choose to travel down that path and enable your own service, but the simpler tasks of deciding what to turn on and turn off can be done easily. Furthermore, you can also now see that testing the status of a given service is also straightforward.

Shutting Down Your System the Right Way

Earlier in this hour, we saw that one tricky way to get your system into a different run level is to use the `init` command directly. Further, we saw that run level 0 is a full stop, and that run level 6 is a reboot state.

Does this therefore imply that `init 0` is a good way to shut your system down, and `init 6` a good way to reboot it? No. Unless you're in an emergency situation and there's no other choice, your better bet is always to use either `halt`, `shutdown`, or `reboot`.

Task 13.3: Safe Shutdowns and Reboots

The fundamental problem with just shutting down your system using a brute-force method like `init 0` is that it doesn't ensure that things shutdown gracefully. There might be specific services or daemons that need to remove temporary files as they die, and cer-

13

TASK

tainly users want at least 60 seconds of grace period to save working files and otherwise clean up behind themselves.

1. The question of warning users before the system shuts down, either to halt or reboot, is a critical one, so let's start with a vanilla shutdown and see what messages are output.

    The standard Unix way to shutdown is

    ```
    # /sbin/shutdown -h now
    ```

    This indicates that the system should be halted (-h) rather than rebooted, and that this action should occur immediately (now).

    Users then see

    ```
    Broadcast message from root (pts/2) Fri Feb 22 14:56:25 2002...

    The system is going down to maintenance mode NOW !!
    ```

    and they have no grace period before the system begins to kill processes and halt.

2. A better way to shut down a system is

    ```
    # /sbin/shutdown -h +5m &
    ```

    which queues up a shutdown event in five minutes. Note that any time you have a shutdown event in the future, you'll want to drop the program into the background with a trailing &, or it'll tie up your terminal until the specified time arrives.

One nice feature of shutdown is that while a shutdown is queued, it creates /etc/nologin, which prevents any new users from logging in.

    In this case, the message users see is

    ```
    Broadcast message from root (pts/2) Fri Feb 22 14:58:24 2002...

    The system is going DOWN for system halt in 5 minutes !!
    ```

    which is a bit less terrifying!

3. To reboot a system, rather than halting it, simply use the -r flag. You can also specify shutdown times in *hours:minutes* format, so the following will cause the system to reboot automatically at 5 a.m.:

    ```
    # /sbin/shutdown -r 05:00 &
    ```

    Note that if you have a shutdown event queued, you can always change your mind and cancel it with -c:

```
# shutdown -c
Shutdown cancelled.
[1]+  Done                    shutdown -r 05:00
```

4. This leads to the question about whether you should ever use `halt` or `reboot`. On modern Linux systems, they turn out to be links to `shutdown`, so it's not an issue, but other Unix systems allow system administrators to directly `halt` or `reboot` their system, without warning, and without any of the graceful termination of services that `shutdown` offers.

   For example, Mac OS X offers `shutdown`, which is completely flag-for-flag compatible with Linux, but the `halt` and `reboot` commands are also available. However, the `halt` man page gently reminds admins:

   > Normally, the shutdown(8) utility is used when the system needs to be halted or restarted, giving users advance warning of their impending doom.

   Solaris has a rather different version of `shutdown`, with only three flags allowed: `-y`, `-g` *graceperiod*, and `-iinitstate`. Furthermore, you specify the grace period time with the `-g` flag, rather than as a regular parameter. So a standard reboot command for Solaris, offering a five minute grace period, is

   ```
   # /usr/bin/shutdown -y -g 300 -i6
   ```

   By default, Solaris `shutdown` drops you into single-user (`init` level 1) mode. Therefore, to halt the machine, you'll want to use `-i0`, and to reboot, you'll use `-i6`.

> As a general rule of thumb, use `shutdown` regardless of your operating system, and always try to give users at least 60 seconds grace period, if possible.

5. One final note: The `-k` flag offers some interesting capabilities. On Linux, for example, you can use it to practice working with `shutdown` because it causes the program to send the shutdown warning, but doesn't actually do the shutdown requested.

   Mac OS X is even cooler: The `-k` flag kicks everybody off the system, and prevents subsequent logins from other than the console. It leaves the system in multi-user mode with all the services running, and does not halt/reboot.

There are often times when you want to reboot the system, and sporadically you'll want to halt it completely (perhaps to upgrade the hardware, or to move the server to a new physical location). Regardless, always use `shutdown` for these tasks.

13

Summary

This hour has focused on how the Unix operating system keeps track of which services to start and stop at any given run level, and how it determines the default run level for a given system. Since one rule of good system management is to only enable services that you know you need, we've also talked about how to disable specific services and change default run levels as necessary.

Q&A

Q Why are there six run levels if only four are used?

A That's an interesting historical question, actually. The theory I've heard is that early telephone switches had seven states, so when the engineers at Bell Telephone Laboratories created the first version of Unix, they naturally opted for seven run states, too: 0–6.

Q How do you figure out what all these services specified for a given run level actually do?

A Figuring out what a service like anaconda does can definitely be a challenge. Searches of the man pages, even man -k lookups, produce nothing. One solution is to search the World Wide Web. Try searching the Red Hat Linux knowledge base, for example (www.redhat.com), or even Google (www.google.com) for the program name.

Workshop

Quiz

1. Which run state reboots: init level 0 or init level 6?

2. What are the starting options to init?

3. Which of the following is not a valid *action* that might appear in an /etc/inittab line: bootwait, respawn, sysboot, or wait?

4. If you have a system running in regular multiuser mode with a graphical environment, what's its run level?

5. If you're in single-user mode, how do you get back to multiuser mode?

Answers

1. `init` level 0 halts, and `init` level 6 reboots. But use `shutdown` instead, of course.

2. There are no starting options to `init`. All the `init` configuration is stored in `/etc/inittab`.

3. The `sysboot` action is not defined.

4. A multiuser + graphical environment is run level 5.

5. To return to multiuser mode from single-user mode, simply exit the single-user command shell.

In the next hour, we'll explore how Unix manages processes, including an explanation of daemons, system processes, and user processes. Through an explanation of the `ps` command, we'll show how to ascertain what processes are running and what they're doing, and `kill` will offer the tools to remove inappropriate processes.

13

HOUR 14

Exploring Processes

We have spent a considerable amount of time talking about how to work with files, the fundamental data element of a Unix system. There's another facet of Unix that's just as important to understand, however, and that's processes. Whether it's the device driver that's listening to your keystrokes and relaying the characters to the program you're running, the X Window System window manager that's responding to mouse clicks (which are captured and sent along by the mouse device driver), or even the list of files produced by an ls invocation, Unix lives and breathes processes.

Indeed, what's interesting about Unix is that it doesn't hide system processes from you, unlike other operating systems. This means that there's a lot you can learn by poking around and seeing what programs have what performance characteristics. That's what this hour is all about—exploring processes.

In this hour you'll learn about

- Process IDs
- Using the ps command
- The artsd command
- Process prioritization
- Zapping stray processes

The Secret Life of Process IDs

Let's start at the beginning. Every process in Unix has a unique numerical identifier called a *process ID*. Typically, these are 3–4-digit numbers, and they increment one by one from the very first process started on a Unix system at boot.

Although process IDs (or PIDs, as we Unix old-timers call 'em) increment starting at PID 1 (the init process, as explored in the last hour), at a certain point process ID numbers can exceed the maximum possible integer value (usually 65536) and wrap around. In this case, you might find yourself running an application with a PID of 37 or 119. Generally, though, you'll find that any process with a one-or two-digit PID is part of the core operating system kernel.

Task 14.1: Process ID Information

TASK ▼

One thing that the incremental nature of PIDs implies is that you can check your process ID and find out how many processes have been launched between boot-time and when your login shell was launched.

1. The easiest way to identify the PID of your login shell is to use the shell variable $$, which expands to the PID of the shell automatically:

   ```
   $ echo $$
   1560
   ```

   This indicates that by the time I launch a shell in my window manager (immediately after booting), 1,559 other processes have been run by the Unix operating system. This is quite remarkable, and should make you ask "What *are* all these processes that are ahead of my shell?"

   The primary answer to that question is found within all the scripts executed as the system steps from init state to init state, starting and stopping services. There are a lot of hidden processes that run, too. For example, a shell script constantly spawns subshells for information within backticks (like `this`), information within parentheses, and anything dropped into the background.

   Just as inodes are the fundamental reference value for any files or directories on any Unix filesystem, so PIDs are the essential reference value for any process running on the system.

▲

The concept of process ID numbers is straightforward, but it's quite important that you understand how they let you reference any process running on the computer without any ambiguity. By contrast, the name of the program running is ambiguous, of course, because more than one copy of it might be running (or it might spawn copies of itself to run background tasks).

Examining Processes with the ps Command

There are a number of different commands available for examining running processes, but the most important one is ps, or process status, which first showed up in Hour 6, "Account Management." Although it's littered with lots of flags, there's a standard set of two or three flags you'll use 99% of the time to find all processes running on the system.

Give ps a specific process ID and it'll tell you about that process, identify a terminal (or virtual terminal), and it'll tell you about every process associated with that terminal. Specify a user and it'll show you everything that user is running, and lots more.

Task 14.2: Exploring ps

The ps command is somewhat akin to the ls command, in that it has dozens of different options, but most of them are safely ignored, except in unusual circumstances.

1. Enough talk, let's act! To start out, let's allow ps to tell us about our login shell:

```
# ps $$
  PID TTY     STAT   TIME COMMAND
 1636 pts/2   S      0:01 bash
```

Without any modifiers, the ps command reports the PID, the terminal associated with the process, its status, the amount of CPU time that the process has consumed so far, and the actual command itself. As you can see, I'm running the bash shell.

The most interesting column here is STAT, which is really the current status of the process. The value S indicates that it's sleeping, oddly enough, even though it's my current shell. (Don't worry, though; the shell itself sleeps while the ps command it spawned runs.)

A full list of different process states is shown in Table 14.1.

TABLE 14.1   ps Process States

State	Meaning
D	Sleep (uninterruptible, blocked for input or output)
R	Runnable (in the "run queue")
S	Sleeping
T	Traced or stopped (often with ^Z by the user)
Z	A "zombie" process (defunct or ended, but still stuck in the process queue)

14

▼   2. You can experiment a bit by omitting the $$ specification of the shell's PID. Now
        ps shows all processes associated with your terminal, real or virtual:

```
# ps
  PID TTY          TIME CMD
 1636 pts/2    00:00:01 bash
 8437 pts/2    00:00:00 ps
```

You can see that it shows we have our login shell, bash, and the ps command
itself. Notice also that it isn't showing the state of each process.

To get the state, we can add either the -l or -f flags, for long or full listings,
respectively:

```
# ps -l
  F S   UID   PID  PPID  C PRI  NI ADDR    SZ WCHAN  TTY          TIME CMD
100 S     0  9020  9018  2  69   0    -   636 wait4  pts/3    00:00:01 bash
000 R     0  9064  9020  0  77   0    -   778 -      pts/3    00:00:00 ps
# ps -f
UID        PID  PPID  C STIME TTY          TIME CMD
root      9020  9018  2 15:32 pts/3    00:00:01 bash
root      9065  9020  0 15:33 pts/3    00:00:00 ps -f
```

The output of the -f flag is more commonly used, and although it still doesn't
show us the status of the commands, it now shows the helpful PPID (parent
process ID), which clearly shows that the ps is being run by bash.

In the long output format (-l), the F column lists the process flags, S is the runtime
state (same as STAT earlier), and PID and PPID are the current and parent process
IDs. The C column indicates the percentage of CPU usage, the PRI column shows
an internal priority state and should probably be ignored, the NI column is the nice
level (relative runtime priority) of the process, and ADDR is actually a meaningless
placeholder for compatibility with earlier versions of ps. SZ is the overall memory
size (in 1K blocks), WCHAN indicates where the process is within the kernel space,
the TTY shows what terminal or virtual terminal owns the process, TIME indicates
accumulated CPU time, and finally, CMD is the actual command.

> Michael Johnson, the author of the Linux ps command, says this about the
> PRI flag: "It's a dynamic internal field from the kernel, which has semantics
> that depend on the scheduler in use."

▼   The -f output is a bit more succinct, showing the UID, PID, PPID, C, start time
    (listed as STIME), TTY, accumulated CPU time, and the command itself.

3. Is your head swimming? Mine certainly is, just trying to figure this all out! The good news is that there's a considerably more friendly output format generated by the -u (so-called "user friendly") flag:

```
# ps -u
USER        PID %CPU %MEM   VSZ  RSS TTY     STAT START    TIME COMMAND
root       9115  0.4  2.1  2544 1368 pts/2   S    16:33    0:01 bash
root       9144  0.0  1.2  2676  768 pts/2   R    16:37    0:00 ps -u
```

Helpfully, this presents information in a much more readable and understandable manner. Notice that while bash is sleeping (STATE=S), it is still using 0.4% of the CPU and 2.1% of the available memory. VSZ is the virtual memory size (in 1K blocks), and RSS is the runtime stack, the subset of needed memory that's actually in the physical RAM of the computer (again, in 1K blocks).

You can do some simple math to see your available memory based on this. If 2,544 pages (VSZ) is 2.1% of the available memory, this implies that 100% memory would be 121,142 pages, which is correct: This system has 128MB of RAM, so we're seeing 121MB available, and approximately 7MB reserved for the kernel itself.

> Realistically, the kernel will take up more than just 7MB of memory. This approach to calculating available memory should only be considered a back-of-the-envelope type of figure.

> The Linux version of ps is a bit peculiar, in that it understands both BSD-style and SYSV-style command flags. Try this: Compare the difference in output between ps -e (the System V/Posix style) and ps e (the BSD style). Other Unixes don't have this peculiar dual personality with the ps command, thankfully.

4. The most common ps flag I use is -aux. This gives you all the running processes, with enough information to get a good clue about what they're all doing.

```
# ps -aux
USER        PID %CPU %MEM   VSZ  RSS TTY     STAT START    TIME COMMAND
root          1  0.0  0.1  1412   72 ?       S    13:20    0:04 init
root          2  0.0  0.0     0    0 ?       SW   13:20    0:00 [keventd]
root          3  0.0  0.0     0    0 ?       SW   13:20    0:00 [kapm-idled]
root          4  0.0  0.0     0    0 ?       SWN  13:20    0:00 [ksoftirqd_CPU0]
root          5  0.0  0.0     0    0 ?       SW   13:20    0:01 [kswapd]
root          6  0.0  0.0     0    0 ?       SW   13:20    0:00 [kreclaimd]
```

14

```
▼   root         7  0.0  0.0      0     0 ?        SW   13:20   0:00 [bdflush]
    root         8  0.0  0.0      0     0 ?        SW   13:20   0:01 [kupdated]
    root         9  0.0  0.0      0     0 ?        SW<  13:20   0:00 [mdrecoveryd]
    root        13  0.0  0.0      0     0 ?        SW   13:20   0:04 [kjournald]
    root        88  0.0  0.0      0     0 ?        SW   13:20   0:00 [khubd]
    root       183  0.0  0.0      0     0 ?        SW   13:21   0:00 [kjournald]
    root       681  0.0  0.2   1472   160 ?        S    13:21   0:04 syslogd -m 0
    root       686  0.0  0.0   1984     4 ?        S    13:21   0:02 klogd -2
    rpc        706  0.0  0.1   1556   124 ?        S    13:21   0:00 portmap
    rpcuser    734  0.0  0.0   1596     4 ?        S    13:21   0:00 rpc.statd
    root       846  0.0  0.0   1396     4 ?        S    13:22   0:00 /usr/sbin/apmd -p
    root       902  0.0  0.0   2676     4 ?        S    13:22   0:03 /usr/sbin/sshd
    root       935  0.0  0.0   2264     4 ?        S    13:22   0:00 xinetd -stayalive
    root       962  0.0  0.5   5296   368 ?        S    13:22   0:04 sendmail: accepti
    root       981  0.0  0.0   1440    56 ?        S    13:22   0:02 gpm -t ps/2 -m /d
    root       999  0.0  0.1   1584   108 ?        S    13:22   0:00 crond
    xfs       1051  0.0  2.3   5112  1492 ?        S    13:22   0:09 xfs -droppriv -da
    daemon    1087  0.0  0.0   1444    44 ?        S    13:22   0:00 /usr/sbin/atd
    root      1095  0.0  0.0   1384     4 tty1     S    13:22   0:00 /sbin/mingetty tt
    root      1096  0.0  0.0   1384     4 tty2     S    13:22   0:00 /sbin/mingetty tt
    root      1097  0.0  0.0   1384     4 tty3     S    13:22   0:00 /sbin/mingetty tt
    root      1100  0.0  0.0   1384     4 tty4     S    13:22   0:00 /sbin/mingetty tt
    root      1101  0.0  0.0   1384     4 tty5     S    13:22   0:00 /sbin/mingetty tt
    root      1102  0.0  0.0   1384     4 tty6     S    13:22   0:00 /sbin/mingetty tt
    root      1103  0.0  0.0   2500     4 ?        S    13:22   0:00 /usr/bin/kdm -nod
    root      1110  0.3  6.0  14252  3776 ?        S    13:22   0:41 /etc/X11/X -auth
    root      1114  0.0  0.0   3340     4 ?        S    13:22   0:00 -:0
    root      1124  0.0  0.0   2236     4 ?        S    13:24   0:01 /bin/bash /usr/bi
    root      1240  0.0  1.0  16052   672 ?        S    13:24   0:02 kdeinit: dcopserv
    root      1243  0.0  3.0  17336  1916 ?        S    13:24   0:02 kdeinit: klaunche
    root      1246  0.0  7.0  17764  4412 ?        S    13:24   0:05 kdeinit: kded
    root      1247  0.0  1.3   2388   816 ?        S    13:24   0:01 fam
    root      1254  0.2  1.3   5524   852 ?        S    13:25   0:25 /usr/bin/artsd -F
    root      1268  0.0  2.2  19540  1420 ?        S    13:25   0:02 kdeinit: knotify
    root      1269  0.0  1.2  16500   772 ?        S    13:25   0:00 kdeinit: Running.
    root      1270  0.0  3.0  11632  1888 ?        S    13:25   0:06 ksmserver --resto
    root      1271  0.0  4.7  17740  2944 ?        S    13:25   0:10 kdeinit: kwin
    root      1273  0.1  7.4  18584  4632 ?        S    13:25   0:18 kdeinit: kdesktop
    root      1275  0.3  7.8  19268  4908 ?        S    13:25   0:42 kdeinit: kicker
    root      1281  2.6  5.0  17788  3148 ?        S    13:25   5:36 kdeinit: klipper
    root      1283  0.0  4.3  17360  2688 ?        S    13:26   0:01 kdeinit: kwrited
    root      1284  0.0  4.9  17024  3096 ?        S    13:26   0:06 alarmd
    root      1285  0.0  0.0   1640     4 pts/0    S    13:26   0:00 /bin/cat
    root      1559  0.0  9.3  18160  5828 ?        S    13:28   0:09 kdeinit: konsole
    root      1560  0.0  2.0   2540  1300 pts/1    S    13:29   0:01 /bin/bash
    root      9113  0.8  4.4   8148  2756 pts/1    S    16:33   0:12 xterm -fg white -
    root      9115  0.2  2.2   2544  1372 pts/2    S    16:33   0:03 bash
    root      9194  3.5  5.0   8520  3128 pts/2    S    16:52   0:11 xterm -fg white -
    root      9196  0.8  2.2   2544  1372 pts/3    S    16:52   0:02 bash
    root      9269  0.0  1.2   2680   768 pts/2    R    16:57   0:00 ps aux
```

▼   As you can see, there are a lot of processes running on this system!

5. Unsurprisingly, it's most common to feed this output to grep, to weed out the specific information you seek. Curious about what processes are *not* running as root? Try this:

```
# ps -aux | grep -vE '^root'
USER        PID %CPU %MEM    VSZ   RSS TTY    STAT START    TIME COMMAND
rpc         706  0.0  0.1   1556   124 ?      S     13:21    0:00 portmap
rpcuser     734  0.0  0.0   1596     4 ?      S     13:21    0:00 rpc.statd
xfs        1051  0.0  2.3   5112  1492 ?      S     13:22    0:09 xfs -droppriv -da
daemon     1087  0.0  0.0   1444    44 ?      S     13:22    0:00 /usr/sbin/atd
```

Note that all of these are in sleep state (STAT=S). Indeed, a quick scan of the earlier output will reveal that the ps command is the only one in run state when the process snapshot was taken by ps.

6. If you're curious about what programs are consuming the most memory, rather than dig through ps, most versions of Unix include a very helpful utility called top (or, on some systems, monitor), which shows you all running applications, but refreshes the list every few seconds. You can also get top to dump its output to the screen and quit, rather than iteratively refresh. Then you can use head to identify the half dozen processes using the most CPU time:

```
# top -b -n0 | head -20
  5:11pm  up  3:50,  4 users,  load average: 0.22, 0.09, 0.08
57 processes: 56 sleeping, 1 running, 0 zombie, 0 stopped
CPU states:  9.8% user,  5.4% system,  0.0% nice, 84.6% idle
Mem:    62264K av,   56172K used,    6092K free,       0K shrd,    1640K buff
Swap:  192772K av,   15208K used,  177564K free                  18420K cached

   PID USER      PRI  NI  SIZE  RSS SHARE STAT %CPU %MEM   TIME COMMAND
  9299 root       15   0  1032 1028   828 R    14.4  1.6   0:00 top
  1281 root        9   0  3544 3148  2372 S     1.6  5.0   5:56 kdeinit
  1254 root        9   0  1184  852   580 S     0.8  1.3   0:26 artsd
     1 root        9   0   120   72    72 S     0.0  0.1   0:04 init
     2 root        9   0     0    0     0 SW    0.0  0.0   0:00 keventd
     3 root        9   0     0    0     0 SW    0.0  0.0   0:00 kapm-idled
     4 root       19  19     0    0     0 SWN   0.0  0.0   0:00 ksoftirqd_CPU0
     5 root        9   0     0    0     0 SW    0.0  0.0   0:01 kswapd
     6 root        9   0     0    0     0 SW    0.0  0.0   0:00 kreclaimd
     7 root        9   0     0    0     0 SW    0.0  0.0   0:00 bdflush
     8 root        9   0     0    0     0 SW    0.0  0.0   0:01 kupdated
```

The first few lines of top are most interesting, as it offers a very helpful snapshot of the current state of your system. For this particular Linux server, you can see that it's 84.6% idle (lots of CPU headroom), has 561MB of memory used and 6MB free (unsurprisingly, the kernel is maximizing the amount of physical memory it's trying to use), while 152MB of swap space is used and 177MB is free.

14

What's going on? How can I be using 561MB on a system that only has 128MB of total RAM? The answer is that top is showing a cumulative total of the averages over time of usage, so the system hasn't magically found an additional 433MB. This averaging is also how CPU usage is calculated, which is why earlier we saw bash using 0.9% of the CPU even though it was in a sleep state.

Stepping into the listing itself, notice that top itself is consuming 14.4% of the CPU, kdeinit (an initialization and runtime management process for the KDE window manager) is using 1.6%, artsd is using 0.8%, and none of the other processes are making any demands on the CPU at all.

7. By contrast, top needs slightly different flags on Mac OS X to produce the same output, but the information shown is perhaps a bit more interesting:

```
# top -ul1 | head -20
Processes:  49 total, 2 running, 47 sleeping... 166 threads       11:12:50
Load Avg:  0.78, 0.78, 0.83     CPU usage: 27.9% user, 9.3% sys, 62.8% idle
SharedLibs: num =  94, resident = 23.3M code, 1.37M data, 6.04M LinkEdit
MemRegions: num = 3774, resident =  209M + 10.5M private,  125M shared
PhysMem:  45.8M wired,  165M active,  294M inactive,  505M used, 7.49M free
VM: 2.84G + 46.8M   6650(0) pageins, 591(0) pageouts

  PID COMMAND       %CPU   TIME    #TH #PRTS #MREGS RPRVT  RSHRD  RSIZE  VSIZE
  312 iTunes       13.0% 24:54.68   9   141    236  8.04M  10.5M  12.5M  74.0M
  337 Virtual PC    9.2%  7:36.81  10   139    219  79.5M  13.9M  87.5M   153M
   65 Window Man    3.0% 23:20.98   3   191    181  1.75M  54.0M  54.9M  96.2M
  359 Terminal      2.7%  0:05.54   5   116    129  2.35M+ 7.44M  5.46M+ 67.1M
  391 top           2.7%  0:00.37   1    14     15   188K   328K   428K+ 1.49M+
  336 Internet E    1.6%  1:26.15   8    99    146  8.94M  11.5M  14.8M  75.6M
  335 Microsoft     1.2%  6:02.54   5   124    335  24.6M  41.3M  37.9M   124M
  288 Microsoft     1.0% 34:40.22  13   156    338  21.1M  24.2M  35.4M   108M
    0 kernel_tas    0.9%  2:54.33  30     0      -      -      -  37.5M   336M
  294 MWBackGrou    0.3%  0:46.74   1    50     47   552K  2.15M  1.26M  30.9M
  291 Snapz Pro     0.1%  0:20.12   1    54     73  1.73M  7.39M  4.52M  61.8M
   67 update        0.1%  0:01.85   1     8     13    56K   292K   152K  1.25M
```

You can see that I'm running iTunes (a JPEG music player), Virtual PC, Internet Explorer, and various other applications, and even though I'm actively in Terminal (PID 359) running top (PID 391), there are many other applications actually using the CPU at the same time.

8. I'd like to show you the equivalent program output in Solaris 8, but Solaris doesn't include a top or monitor program, frustratingly. You're on your own to try and combine uptime and ps instead, or start with whodo -l and see what that produces:

```
# whodo -l
 12:21am  up 31 day(s), 1 hr(s), 54 min(s)  4 user(s)
```

```
        User      tty             login@  idle   JCPU   PCPU   what
        root      console         26Jan02 3days  1:25          xterm
        root      pts/2           26Jan02 6:40                 -
        root      pts/4            4:56pm 1:25                 whodo -l
        root      pts/3           10:56pm                      -
```

There's a lot in the ps output to study, and as a system administrator, one of the most important questions you'll have will be "What is this?" for some of the jobs. In particular, pay attention to jobs that are not running as root, as they'll show you how your users are consuming CPU and memory resources.

A Typical Sysadmin Task: What's `artsd`?

To give you a sense of how all the Unix tools work together, let's spend a few minutes trying to figure out what `artsd` is. I'm not sure what the `artsd` program running and eating up CPU time on my Linux box does. This is a very common situation where you'll need to use standard Unix tools to figure out what a specific task is and whether you really need it.

Task 14.3: A Little Unix Detective Work

First off, let's see if we can identify how it's been started.

1. To do this, add the w flag to the ps command, but do it a couple of times. Unlike just about any other Unix command, multiple occurrences of the w flag gives you more output:

```
# ps -auxwwwww | grep artsd
root      1254   0.1  1.3  5524  852 ?         S    13:25   0:28
➥/usr/bin/artsd -F 10 -S 4096 -s 60 -m artsmessage -l 3 -f
root      9322   0.0  0.9  1732  592 pts/2     S    17:35   0:00 grep artsd
```

The first stop is to try the man pages:

```
# man -k artsd
artsd: nothing appropriate
```

Hmmm…looks like it's going to be a bit harder to figure this one out.

2. As a next step, let's see what files have `artsd` in them by using `locate`:

```
# locate artsd
/usr/bin/artsd
/usr/bin/artsdsp
/usr/lib/libartsdsp.la
/usr/lib/libartsdsp.so
/usr/lib/libartsdsp.so.0
/usr/lib/libartsdsp.so.0.0.0
/usr/lib/libartsdsp_st.la
```

14

```
/usr/lib/libartsdsp_st.so
/usr/lib/libartsdsp_st.so.0
/usr/lib/libartsdsp_st.so.0.0.0
/usr/include/kde/arts/kartsdispatcher.h
```

Still nothing useful.

> If your locate command has no output, it might be because you haven't cre-
> ated the initial locate database. Have a look at the man page for details on
> how to accomplish this simple task.

Let's look in /usr/bin to see what's part of the arts family of applications:

```
# ls /usr/bin/arts*
/usr/bin/artsbuilder     /usr/bin/artsd        /usr/bin/artsshell
/usr/bin/artscat         /usr/bin/artsdsp      /usr/bin/artswrapper
/usr/bin/artsc-config    /usr/bin/artsmessage
/usr/bin/artscontrol     /usr/bin/artsplay
```

Quite a few applications, actually. It's surprising that there's not a single man page
for any of it.

3. Let's try one more locate before we give up and jump to a search on Google, or
   one of the Linux sites on the Web:

```
# locate artscontrol
/usr/bin/artscontrol
/usr/share/apps/artscontrol
/usr/share/apps/artscontrol/artsmidimanagerview.rc
/usr/share/apps/artscontrol/artscontrol.rc
/usr/share/icons/hicolor/16x16/apps/artscontrol.png
/usr/share/applnk/Multimedia/artscontrol.desktop
```

Ah ha! There's a directory called artscontrol in the /usr/share/apps directory.
Let's see what else is in that directory that might be relevant to our search:

```
# cd /usr/share/apps
# ls -ld arts*
drwxr-xr-x    4 root      root         4096 Jan 11 15:03 artsbuilder
drwxr-xr-x    2 root      root         4096 Jan 11 15:03 artscontrol
```

The artscontrol directory looks promising:

```
# ls /usr/share/apps/artscontrol
artscontrol.rc   artsmidimanagerview.rc
# more !$/artscontrol.rc
more /usr/share/apps/artscontrol/artscontrol.rc
```

```
<!DOCTYPE kpartgui>
<kpartgui name="artscontrol" version="3">
<MenuBar>
  <Menu name="view"><text>&amp;View</text>
    <Action name="view_fft_scope"/>
    <Action name="view_audio_manager"/>
        <Action name="view_arts_statusview"/>
    <Action name="view_midi_manager"/>
    <Action name="view_media_types"/>
    <Action name="view_freeverb"/>
        <Action name="old_volume_display"/>
  </Menu>
</MenuBar>
</kpartgui>
```

> Notice the very useful shell shortcut !$, which matches the last word of the previous command.

Well, we haven't found any documentation, but we can glean a few snippets of information from this. First off, the arts application is some sort of synthesizer player or interface system (notice arts MIDI managerview.rc: MIDI is musical interface digital instrument, and it's how synthesizers talk to each other). Secondly, notice the rc file contents indicate that it's a kpartgui, which indicates that it's part of the GUI to KDE. Most likely, then, artsd is a background daemon that helps the arts synthesizer work properly.

4. Because all the arts* applications in /usr/bin seem to be part of this program, another sneaky trick is to use the helpful strings command to search for any sort of URL that might be listed in any of the programs:

```
# cd /usr/bin
# strings arts* | grep -i http:
http://www.arts-project.org/
```

Gotcha! A quick visit to that Web site reveals that sure enough, arts is an analog real-time synthesizer. And now we know.

There are a number of different ways that you can try to isolate and identify different programs running in a ps output. It's good practice learning the various sysadmin tools, so try doing a bit of your own detective work, and see if you can identify some of the more cryptic daemons running on your own Unix system.

14

Process Priorities

One important capability that you have as sysadmin that isn't available to mere mortal users is that you can change the priority of specific tasks to meet the CPU demands of your process workload. If you have a particular program that seems to eat your processor alive, for example, you can lower its priority when you launch it, or you can even drop its priority while it's running, letting other applications have a better chance at getting a slice of CPU time. Users can change the prioritization of their own tasks, but root can change any task.

Conversely, perhaps you are running an image manipulation program or a real-time analysis tool and want to ensure that it's more important than any programs other users might launch. To do that, you would increase the priority of the process, either at launch-time, or when it's already running.

Task 14.4: Managing Process Priorities

There are two commands available for working with process priorities: nice and renice. The nice command lets you set the priority of the process before it's launched, and, you guessed it, renice lets you change the process of a running job.

Unfortunately, although you might think of a lower priority job as being less important than a higher priority job, the nice and renice commands (and Unix itself) think about this in the exact opposite way: A process with a high nice value has a lower priority than another with a lower nice value.

The nice values can range from –20 to 19. Zero is a standard priority for all login shells and applications that they spawn. Your login shell and your vi session are both priority (nice level) zero.

1. To see your current nice level, use ps -l:

```
# ps -l
  F S   UID   PID  PPID  C PRI  NI ADDR     SZ WCHAN  TTY          TIME CMD
100 S     0  9386  9384  0  69   0    -    654 wait4  pts/2    00:00:03 bash
000 R     0  9485  9386  0  76   0    -    775 -      pts/2    00:00:00 ps
```

The NI column is what we're interested in here: Notice that both jobs are, as expected, running with a nice level of zero.

Wondering if there are any jobs that are *not* at nice level zero? A fair question, easily answered with awk:

```
# ps -lx | awk '{ if ($6 != 0) print $0 }'
  F   UID   PID  PPID PRI   NI   VSZ  RSS WCHAN  STAT TTY       TIME COMMAND
040     0     4     0  19   19     0    0 ksofti SWN  ?         0:00
➥[ksoftirqd_
040     0     9     1  -1  -20     0    0 md_thr SW<  ?         0:00
➥[mdrecovery
```

There are two tasks with a nonzero nice level: mdrecovery is the most important job on the system, with a nice level of –20, and ksoftirqd is the least important with a priority of 19.

2. To launch an application with a different priority, the nice command should be used. A typical use might be to have a window watch the syslogd output file (/var/log/messages), a job that's important, but certainly less important than interactive work:

```
# nice tail -f /var/log/messages &
# ps -l
  F S  UID   PID  PPID  C PRI  NI ADDR    SZ WCHAN  TTY        TIME CMD
100 S    0  9386  9384  0  69   0    -   654 wait4  pts/2   00:00:04 bash
000 T    0  9523  9386 16  75  10    -   506 do_sig pts/2   00:00:00 tail
000 R    0  9524  9386 54  75   0    -   776 -      pts/2   00:00:00 ps
```

By default, you can see that nice adds 10 to the priority, which means that the application is run at a *lower* priority (it's less important) than all the other processes on the system.

To make it more important, specify the desired nice value:

```
# nice --5 vi importantfile &
# ps -l
  F S  UID    PID   PPID  C PRI  NI ADDR    SZ WCHAN  TTY        TIME CMD
100 S    0  14540  14539  0  73   0    -   642 wait4  pts/0   00:00:00 bash
000 S    0  14566  14540  0  74  10    -   414 nanosl pts/0   00:00:00 tail
100 T    0  14575  14540  0  69  -5    -   505 do_sig pts/0   00:00:00 vi
100 R    0  14577  14540  0  76   0    -   773 -      pts/0   00:00:00 ps
```

Did you notice that you need to use a double-dash to get a negative priority? The command nice -5 command sets it to priority 5, which is actually *less* important than the default priority of zero. Most confusing!

3. To change the priority of a running task, use renice. The renice command requires the PID, but that's easy to obtain, as you now know.

Let's bring the vi session back to the normal priority of zero to start:

```
# renice 0 14575
14575: old priority -5, new priority 0
```

Looks good. How about in the other direction? Let's make that tail process more important than regular processes by giving it a nice level of –1:

```
# renice -1 14566
14566: old priority 10, new priority -1
```

14

> As a regular user, you can `renice` your own processes, but only within the range of 0–19. It is not possible for you to make your jobs more important than the standard `nice` level of zero.

4. The `renice` command has some additional options, not the least of which is that you can change the priority of all processes owned by a specific user in a single fell swoop. For example, if user `taylor` has been whining just a bit too much about slow computers and how *Quake* just doesn't zip along like his machine at home, you might like to slow things down even further by lowering his priority for a short period of time:

```
# renice +1 -u taylor
502: old priority 0, new priority 1
537: old priority 0, new priority 1
```

More likely, you'll want to perhaps improve the throughput of your Web server by setting all the Apache processes to have a slightly higher priority. First, let's use the `-U` flag to `ps` to limit output to just the specified UID, then `renice` all the relevant jobs:

```
# ps -1U apache
  F S   UID   PID  PPID  C PRI  NI ADDR     SZ WCHAN  TTY        TIME CMD
140 S    48 13366   629  0  69   0    - 11689 semop  ?      00:00:00 httpd
140 S    48 13367   629  0  69   0    - 11696 semop  ?      00:00:00 httpd
140 S    48 13368   629  0  69   0    - 11686 semop  ?      00:00:00 httpd
140 S    48 13369   629  0  69   0    - 11695 semop  ?      00:00:00 httpd
140 S    48 13370   629  0  69   0    - 11689 semop  ?      00:00:00 httpd
140 S    48 14093   629  0  69   0    - 11689 do_sel ?      00:00:00 httpd
140 S    48 14118   629  0  69   0    - 11693 semop  ?      00:00:00 httpd
140 S    48 14322   629  0  69   0    - 11686 semop  ?      00:00:00 httpd
# renice -1 -u apache
48: old priority 0, new priority -1
```

In this case, it reports the *real group ID* of all the processes running that match. To see that this is the case, use the `-G` flag (show group IDs) to `ps` with the number given (48):

```
# ps -1G 48
  F S   UID   PID  PPID  C PRI  NI ADDR     SZ WCHAN  TTY        TIME CMD
140 S    48 13366   629  0  69  -1    - 11689 semop  ?      00:00:00 httpd
140 S    48 13367   629  0  69  -1    - 11696 semop  ?      00:00:00 httpd
140 S    48 13368   629  0  69  -1    - 11686 semop  ?      00:00:00 httpd
140 S    48 13369   629  0  69  -1    - 11695 semop  ?      00:00:00 httpd
140 S    48 13370   629  0  69  -1    - 11689 semop  ?      00:00:00 httpd
140 S    48 14093   629  0  69  -1    - 11689 do_sel ?      00:00:00 httpd
140 S    48 14118   629  0  69  -1    - 11693 semop  ?      00:00:00 httpd
140 S    48 14322   629  0  69  -1    - 11686 semop  ?      00:00:00 httpd
```

That's exactly what we wanted. Because this server is primarily a Web server, we have now prioritized all Web requests (Apache is the Web server, and its daemon is httpd) to be higher (a lower nice level) than regular login shells and other processes.

Being able to adjust and fine-tune the priority of tasks on a Unix system is a powerful—and dangerous—capability. Like any superpower, you must use it wisely and judiciously. Never change the priority of any kernel task, for example, and be cautious about lowering the priority of any regular user task.

On the other hand, being able to tweak things can be a significant benefit, too. On my Mac OS X system, for example, I have learned that using renice to set the priority of iTunes to 1 and Virtual PC to –1 significantly improves overall performance without any adverse affect on music playback.

Zapping Stray Processes

One more topic to discuss in this hour is kill. The renice command lets you lower the priority of tasks you'd like to consume fewer CPU and system resources, but what if you want to kill the process entirely?

That's what the eponymously named kill command is for. Specify a PID and you can make it vanish in a puff of greasy black smoke.

Task 14.5: The kill Command

Whether the process is wedged, running out of control, has become unresponsive to regular interaction, or is from another user who isn't authorized to run it, there are times when being able to eliminate a process is of great value.

1. From the last section, there are still a couple of jobs running that should be removed, as ps reminds us:

```
# ps -al
  F S   UID   PID  PPID  C PRI  NI ADDR    SZ WCHAN  TTY        TIME CMD
000 S     0 14539 14369  0  70   1    -   589 wait4  pts/0  00:00:00 su
100 S     0 14540 14539  0  72   0    -   642 wait4  pts/0  00:00:00 bash
000 S     0 14566 14540  0  69  -1    -   414 nanosl pts/0  00:00:00 tail
100 T     0 14575 14540  0  68   0    -   505 do_sig pts/0  00:00:00 vi
100 R     0 14701 14540  0  75   0    -   773 -      pts/0  00:00:00 ps
```

Let's kill the tail first of all, because we don't need it any more—we have instead decided to just peek at the contents of the syslog file itself once every morning:

```
# kill 14566
#
```

14

▼

The `kill` command never has any output, so traditionally sysadmins run the command a second time: If it reports nothing again, that means that the application is blocking or ignoring the signal, but if it reports `No such pid`, then the first `kill` did its job:

```
# kill 14566
bash: kill: (14566) - No such pid
[1]- Terminated                         nice tail -f /var/log/messages
```

In this case, the first `kill` terminated the `tail`, and the shell was just being polite by waiting until the end of another job to report that the job was terminated.

2. Did you notice earlier that the state of the `vi` job was `T`, not `S` or `R`? That means that it's stopped—either blocked for I/O, or stopped by the user with a `^Z` control sequence. Whether it's stopped, sleeping, or running, sending a signal to the process causes it to wake up long enough to handle the signal, either ignoring it or accepting it and performing a specific action.

There are a lot of signals that can be sent to a job, too: `kill -l` lists all the possibilities:

```
# kill -l
 1) SIGHUP        2) SIGINT       3) SIGQUIT      4) SIGILL
 5) SIGTRAP       6) SIGABRT      7) SIGBUS       8) SIGFPE
 9) SIGKILL      10) SIGUSR1     11) SIGSEGV     12) SIGUSR2
13) SIGPIPE      14) SIGALRM     15) SIGTERM     17) SIGCHLD
18) SIGCONT      19) SIGSTOP     20) SIGTSTP     21) SIGTTIN
22) SIGTTOU      23) SIGURG      24) SIGXCPU     25) SIGXFSZ
26) SIGVTALRM    27) SIGPROF     28) SIGWINCH    29) SIGIO
30) SIGPWR       31) SIGSYS      32) SIGRTMIN    33) SIGRTMIN+1
34) SIGRTMIN+2   35) SIGRTMIN+3  36) SIGRTMIN+4  37) SIGRTMIN+5
38) SIGRTMIN+6   39) SIGRTMIN+7  40) SIGRTMIN+8  41) SIGRTMIN+9
42) SIGRTMIN+10 43) SIGRTMIN+11 44) SIGRTMIN+12 45) SIGRTMIN+13
46) SIGRTMIN+14 47) SIGRTMIN+15 48) SIGRTMAX-15 49) SIGRTMAX-14
50) SIGRTMAX-13 51) SIGRTMAX-12 52) SIGRTMAX-11 53) SIGRTMAX-10
54) SIGRTMAX-9  55) SIGRTMAX-8  56) SIGRTMAX-7  57) SIGRTMAX-6
58) SIGRTMAX-5  59) SIGRTMAX-4  60) SIGRTMAX-3  61) SIGRTMAX-2
62) SIGRTMAX-1  63) SIGRTMAX
```

Almost all of these can be safely ignored, but there are three worth highlighting, as they'll be used most often: `SIGTERM` is sent if no signal is specified (as with the earlier `kill` of the `tail` process), `SIGHUP` is the "hang-up" signal and is usually a very graceful way to terminate a process that ignores `SIGTERM`, and `SIGKILL` is the "big gun" of the signal world—it's a `kill` signal that cannot be captured or ignored by a process. If you're lazy, you can also use the signal number, as in `kill -9 pid`.

As with the scary days of the Cold War, there's a sense of escalation of signals, based on the response of the process to the previous signal sent. Think of it like this: If the pistol didn't work, try the rifle. If that doesn't work either, it's time for a tactical nuke. Well, maybe that's a wee bit dramatic, but you get the idea.

▼

▼   3. To kill the vi session, I'll specify SIGTERM and see what happens:

```
# kill -TERM 14575
# kill -TERM 14575
#
```

Ahhh...vi ignores SIGTERM signals, so we'll have to try something a bit stronger: SIGHUP.

```
# kill -HUP 14575
# kill -HUP 14575
#
```

As you can see, some applications are pretty tough, able to accept and ignore many common signals. The tail command gracefully died when it received its first SIGTERM, but vi is lingering. This means it's time for a SIGKILL (aka -9):

```
# kill -9 14575
# kill -9 14575
bash: kill: (14575) - No such pid
[2]+  Killed                     nice --5 vi testme
```

That did the trick. Notice that you can specify the signal by name (for example, -KILL) or by its number. Many system administrators have the command kill -9 wired into their fingers after a bit, and don't even think about signal names.

4. If you ever find yourself in a situation where it would be useful to stop a job temporarily, then resume it later, it's worth knowing that you can send the signal equivalent of a ^Z to a process, then a resume signal to have it start up and begin running again:

```
# ps -lU taylor
  F S   UID   PID  PPID  C PRI  NI ADDR    SZ WCHAN  TTY         TIME CMD
100 S   502 14369 14368  0  70   1   -    618 wait4  pts/0   00:00:00 bash
000 S     0 14539 14369  0  70   1   -    589 wait4  pts/0   00:00:00 su
100 S   502 14717 14716  0  71   0   -    618 read_c pts/1   00:00:00 bash
000 R   502 14757 14717 27  78   0   -    445 do_sig pts/1   00:00:00 find
```

You can see that user taylor has a find running that's currently taking up 27% of the CPU. It'd be helpful to stop this find temporarily, run a few sysadmin commands, then start it up again:

```
# kill -STOP 14757
# ps -lU taylor
  F S   UID   PID  PPID  C PRI  NI ADDR    SZ WCHAN  TTY         TIME CMD
100 S   502 14369 14368  0  70   1   -    618 wait4  pts/0   00:00:00 bash
000 S     0 14539 14369  0  70   1   -    589 wait4  pts/0   00:00:00 su
100 S   502 14717 14716  0  71   0   -    618 read_c pts/1   00:00:00 bash
000 T   502 14757 14717  0  78   0   -    445 do_sig pts/1   00:00:00 find
```

now the job is stopped, we can do other stuff for a while

```
# kill -CONT 14757
# ps -lU taylor
```

14

▼
```
      F S   UID    PID  PPID  C PRI  NI ADDR    SZ WCHAN  TTY            TIME CMD
    100 S   502  14369 14368  0  70   1    -   618 wait4  pts/0      00:00:00 bash
    000 S     0  14539 14369  0  70   1    -   589 wait4  pts/0      00:00:00 su
    100 S   502  14717 14716  0  71   0    -   618 read_c pts/1      00:00:00 bash
    000 R   502  14757 14717  0  78   0    -   445 do_sig pts/1      00:00:00 find
```

▲
Some system daemons will reread their configuration files and restart themselves upon receiving a specific signal, too. If that's the case, then typically something like kill -1 *pid* does the trick easily, but double-check with the documentation before you wreak too much havoc on your system.

In a typical week of work as a system administrator, you probably won't need to kill more than one or two processes, but it's very important to realize that as sysadmin you have the tools and ability to affect the jobs running on your system. Whether it's by changing their priority with renice, or sending them specific signals like –STOP or –HUP with kill, you're in control.

And with control and power comes responsibility. You'll have your user community madder than hornets at a summer picnic if you randomly change priorities or kill processes!

Summary

This hour has popped the hood and delved into the mysterious world of Unix process management, starting by learning how to know what processes are running with the ps command, then discussing task prioritization, and finally ending by considering the different methods available for killing processes that shouldn't be running. Along the way we also explored how to solve a common system administration puzzle: identifying each of the tasks running to ascertain whether they're needed or not.

Q&A

Q Is the init program *always* PID 1?

A Certainly on every Unix system I've ever seen. The init process manages the sequence of booting up the computer, so it's the very first application started at boot-time.

Q Why is the nice value the opposite of what you'd expect, where a smaller number is more important than a bigger number?

A A very good question!

Q If there's a nice command, is there a naughty command too?

A I think we'd have to check the SCUR1 (Santa Claus Unix, Release 1, of course!) Linux man pages for that one. Alternatively, the answer might be that it depends on what you're doing with your command shell.

Workshop

Quiz

1. Could a job I run later in my session end up with a PID that's lower than the PID of my login shell?

2. What's the shortcut to identify the PID of your login shell? And how can you use that to identify what shell you're running?

3. Is it accurate to say that a process in state T is terminated, pending removal from the process queue?

4. In what situation might your login shell be listed as state S, sleeping?

5. What do you think would happen if you typed kill -9 $$?

6. One of the processes that Red Hat Linux listed in the ps output was mdrecoveryd. Do some detective work and see if you can figure out what it does. (If you don't have Linux, pick a different mysterious daemon and figure out what that does instead.)

Answers

1. It's possible to have a subsequent PID be lower, but you'd need your PIDs to cycle back to zero, which would mean that your system would have needed more than MAXINT (maximum possible integer value) processes run since boot-time. Because MAXINT is 2^{32}, that's a *lot* of processes.

2. The shortcut is $$, and you can identify your shell definitively with ps $$.

3. It is not accurate. A process in state T is either being traced, or more likely, stopped with a SIGSTOP, probably from a ^Z.

4. Any time a subprocess like ps is running, the parent shell sleeps until it completes.

5. You'd log out, lickety-split!

6. The best I can figure is that mdrecoveryd is related to RAID disk subsystems: If you don't have RAID, you probably don't need this running. But check your OS documentation to be sure!

In the next hour we'll explore the ins and outs of cron, a wonderfully helpful utility that lets you schedule jobs at any time in the future.

14

HOUR 15

Running Jobs in the Future

The gist of our study together through this point in the book has been learning how to accomplish tasks, and then how to automate them with aliases and shell scripts (though the latter will be covered in greater detail later in the book). What's been missing has been any sort of scheduler, a way whereby you can instruct the Unix system to run a specified command or set of commands in the future.

That's what this hour focuses on, and it's one of my favorite parts of Unix: crontab. Through the cron mechanism, as crontab is called generally, you can specify Unix commands or shell scripts to run at a specific minute, hour, day, or date. Just as importantly, you can also specify how frequently it should be run, so if you want to perpetually sidestep the problem of forgetting your anniversary by scheduling an annual e-mail greeting to your spouse, it's a breeze with cron.

If you want to run administrative tasks every 15 minutes, at midnight, or on Sunday of each week, they're also quickly and easily accomplished with cron.

Here's what you'll learn in this hour:

- Enabling crontab for users
- Building crontab files
- System cron jobs in /etc
- Scheduling future jobs with at

Allowing User Access to crontab

Before you can start using cron, you need to ensure that the system is enabled and that you've created a list of users that you, as sysadmin, explicitly allow or prevent from using crontab.

This leads to an important point: The crontab facility is not only helpful for system administration, it's a generally useful Unix utility even on those systems where you do not have administrative access. On most systems on which I have an account, I eventually have some scripts running from within cron.

Task 15.1: Turning on crontab

The very first step required in working with cron is to ensure that the crond daemon is launched and running when you boot up your system.

1. To ascertain whether it's running, use ps:

```
# ps -aux | grep crond
root       820  0.0  0.1  1584   660 ?        S    Mar09   0:00 crond
taylor   21117  0.0  0.1  1728   584 pts/0    S    13:59   0:00 grep crond
```

Looks good. If crond wasn't running, you would look in /etc/rc.d/rc3.d (if you are at run level 3) or /etc/rc.d/rc5.d (if you are at run level 5) to ensure that the cron facility was enabled:

```
# /sbin/runlevel
N 3
# ls /etc/rc.d/rc3.d/*cron*
/etc/rc.d/rc3.d/S90crond  /etc/rc.d/rc3.d/S95anacron
```

You can see that on this Linux box, we can use runlevel to confirm that we're at run level 3 (the first argument is the previous run level, and N means it was booting). A quick peek at the appropriate rc.d directory reveals that both crond and anacron are launched (their file names start with S).

▼   If for any reason you find that cron should be running but isn't, you can start it by
       typing

       /etc/rc.d/init.d/crond start

       The anacron system is a new replacement for cron, its big difference being
       that anacron doesn't assume that you're running your server 24/7. See the
       man page for more information about this alternative to cron, though my
       recommendation is that you stick with cron on your systems.

2. By default, cron allows all users to create their own crontab files (a text file
    owned by each user that details what jobs to run and with what frequency), but if
    you want to limit it to specific users and prevent others, you can either do this
    inclusively or exclusively.

    That is, if you create a file called /etc/cron.allow, then only those users listed in
    that file can use the cron facility. Alternatively, if you create a file called
    /etc/cron.deny, then users that are *not* listed in the file can use cron. The format
    for these files is a simple list of account names, one per line.

3. While we're looking at the underbelly of cron, let's have a peek at the spool direc-
    tory that the program uses to store user crontab files:

    ```
    # ls -l /var/spool/cron
    total 2
    -rw-------   1 root     coders         357 Dec 17 23:01 root
    -rw-------   1 root     root           273 Mar 14 14:13 taylor
    ```

    You can see that root and taylor both have crontabs. Notice also that all
    crontab files are owned by root. As you'll see momentarily, this is *not* a security
▲   problem.

Because the cron facility is such an important part of standard Unix, just about every
flavor of Unix has it enabled and ready to run by default. Each user has a specific file of
instructions called a crontab, and they are all stored in the /var/spool/cron directory.

Building crontab Files

Now that you've confirmed that the cron facility is up and running, let's jump in and
build a new crontab file. The crontab file is a series of lines that take the form "when
what." The first five fields on each line specify when the job should run, and the remaining fields are the command given to the shell for execution.

The time specification is a bit tricky. Each of the first five fields can accept an asterisk, a numeric value, list, range of values, or a mnemonic name. The fields are as specified in Table 15.1.

TABLE 15.1   crontab Field Values

Field	Acceptable Values
minute	0–59
hour	0–23
day of month	1–31
month	1–12 (or mnemonic names Jan, Feb)
day of week	0–7 (or mnemonic names Sun, Mon)

> If you're doing your math, you realize that a day-of-the-week specifier than can range from 0–7 has *eight* days. We're not referencing a Beatles song here, the cron mechanism lets you use either 0 or 7 as Sunday, depending on how you prefer to count.

Ranges can be specified by having a begin, end, and a dash between them, and a list is separated by commas, so 2-5 and 2,3,4,5 both match value = 2, value = 3, value = 4, or value = 5. You can also specify a skip-factor on lists, so if you wanted to only run a command on odd numbered days, for example, you could use 1-31/2 as the day-of-month specifier (which is the same as 1,3,5,7,9,11,13,15,17,19,21,23,25,27,29,31, but quite a bit easier to type.

Task 15.2: Building a crontab File

Understanding the time specification format is 90% of the work of building and reading crontab files, so the best way to proceed is with some examples. Let's explore the basic language of crontab files, then we'll talk about how to build the files and submit them to the cron scheduler.

1. To have a process run every single minute of every hour of every day, you'd simply have asterisks for every field. In this unusual case, your crontab entry would look like

   ```
   *  *  *  *  *      /home/taylor/scripts/everyminute
   ```

This is unlikely, so let's instead have the script run every hour at 15 minutes after the hour. To specify this, all that has to happen is that the `minute` field needs to be specified:

```
15  *  *  *  *    /home/taylor/scripts/hourly
```

2. More common uses of `cron` are to have scripts run every day at a specified time, or weekly on a specified day. The former should be a straightforward step from the last example:

```
15  3  *  *  *    /home/taylor/scripts/daily
```

In this case, it's going to run `/home/taylor/scripts/daily` every day at 3:15 a.m. (remember, it's minute-hour, not hour-minute).

```
15  3  *  *  Mon  /home/taylor/scripts/weekly
```

This runs the `weekly` script every Monday at 3:15 a.m.

3. Now let's turn our attention to the `crontab` program, which is how you create, remove, edit, and even list `crontab` files.

> Yes, it's quite confusing to have the command `crontab` have the same name as the data file `crontab`. There are even two different `man` pages for the command: `man 1 crontab` is for the command, and `man 5 crontab` contains information about the data file.

The `crontab` program is straightforward, and has four meaningful flags: `-e` lets you edit (or create, if you don't yet have) your `crontab` file, `-l` lists the `crontab` file, `-r` removes it, and `–u` *user* lets you, as `root`, work with a specified user's `crontab` file.

We can start working with `crontab` by using `crontab -e`, which drops us into `vi` with a blank `crontab` data file. This isn't very friendly in my opinion, so I invariably type in the following as the first few lines of any `crontab` file I work on:

```
# CRONTAB for root
#
#   min  hour  day-of-month  month  day-of-week   command
```

With that at the top of the file, you have an easy mnemonic reminder of how to create individual `crontab` entries.

4. I'd like to capture the first few lines of the `top` command, which offers a nice snapshot of how my system is doing at any given moment, and e-mail it to myself every day at 5 p.m.

▼   The first step is to figure out the exact command required. This can be done at the
command line, of course:

```
# top -b -n1 | head -9
```

```
 9:53am  up 6 days,  9:30,  1 user,  load average: 0.00, 0.00, 0.00
44 processes: 43 sleeping, 1 running, 0 zombie, 0 stopped
CPU0 states:  0.0% user,  0.0% system,  0.0% nice, 100.0% idle
CPU1 states:  0.0% user,  0.1% system,  0.0% nice, 99.0% idle
Mem:   512872K av, 232612K used, 280260K free,     72K shrd,   65808K buff
Swap: 1048568K av,      0K used, 1048568K free                  80808K
➥cached
```

That's what we want. Now it's just a matter of feeding that directly to the `mail`
program, and we have a command ready to go into a `crontab` file:

```
top -b -n1 | head -9 | mail -s "top status" taylor
```

All that's left is to specify the exact time constraints that will match "every day at
5 p.m." Here's how that would look:

```
0  17  *  *  *  top -b -n1 | head -9 | mail -s "top status" taylor
```

We need to use 17 rather than 5 because otherwise `cron` can't differentiate between
a.m. and p.m. times.

Now that this line has been added to the `crontab` file, the job can be loaded and
installed into the scheduler by writing the temp file out and quitting the editor (use
`:wq` if you're using `vi`). The `crontab` program confirms `crontab: installing
new crontab` and we're done.

5. To list the `crontab` file for the current user, use the `-l` flag:

```
# crontab -l
# DO NOT EDIT THIS FILE - edit the master and reinstall.
# (/tmp/crontab.23687 installed on Fri Mar 15 09:59:01 2002)
# (Cron version -- $Id: crontab.c,v 2.13 1994/01/17 03:20:37 vixie Exp $)
# CRONTAB for root

# Format is:
#   min  hour  day-of-month  month  day-of-week    command

0  17  *  *  *  top -b -n1 | head -9 | mail -s "top status" taylor
```

Notice that the `crontab` program has prefaced our material with a warning not to
edit the raw file (which is, incidentally, sitting in `/var/spool/cron`). That's good
advice: If you want to change the contents of a `crontab` file, use the `crontab` com-
▼   mand, rather than swooping directly into the `/var/spool/cron` directory!

6. One of the trickier characteristics of cron is that it runs commands and scripts with a very limited PATH, so it's quite common for it to be unable to find commands that aren't located in /bin. It's a good idea, therefore, for us to make one slight change to the existing cron job and specify the full path to the top command. This can be done by requesting the opportunity to edit the crontab file with the -e flag, but before we do, let's double-check the location of top:

```
# which top
/usr/bin/top
```

Armed with that information, crontab -e drops us into vi with the crontab file displayed, albeit without the warning lines that showed up in the -l output. Here's how things would look once I've added the appropriate path for the top command:

```
# CRONTAB for root

# Format is:
#   min  hour  day-of-month  month  day-of-week   command

0  17  *  *  *  /usr/bin/top -b -n1 | /bin/head -9 | /bin/mail -s "top" taylor
```

Quitting the editor again installs the crontab file in the correct place and we're good to go!

7. For reference, here are some additional crontab entries. See if you can figure out what they do (the answers are later in this hour).

```
# crontab -l
# DO NOT EDIT THIS FILE - edit the master and reinstall.
# (/tmp/crontab.23687 installed on Fri Mar 15 09:59:01 2002)
# (Cron version -- $Id: crontab.c,v 2.13 1994/01/17 03:20:37 vixie Exp $)
# CRONTAB for root

# Format is:
#   min  hour  day-of-month  month  day-of-week   command

0  17  *  *  *  top -b -n1 | head -9 | mail -s "top status" taylor
0  5   *  *  *  cd /web/chatter/comics; ./build-comics-page.sh > ./index.html

0  12  1  *  *  /home/taylor/scripts/doitall
0  0   3  8  *  mail -s "happy birthday Dave" taylor@intuitive.com < birthday.note
5  5   *  *  Mon-Fri    uptime | mail -s uptime root
23 0-23/2 * * *         echo "when does this run?" | mail root
30 4  1,15 * 5          /home/taylor/scripts/when_is_it
0  9,16 *  *  *          /home/taylor/scripts/rotatefiles
```

▼ The `crontab` system is remarkably helpful, whether you're working on the system as a system administrator or just a regular user, but there are some nuances to creating and specifying times. One classic example is if you want to have a job run on, say, just August 3 every year, your temptation might be to specify that as

```
*  *  3  Aug  *     daves.birthday.script
```

but that would be wrong. Can you figure out what's wrong with it?

The problem is that we haven't constrained it to a specific hour and minute. This would run the script *every minute* of the matching day, 1,440 times. Instead, simply pick a time
▲ and specify the minute and hour, too.

System cron Jobs in /etc

Earlier in this hour, you saw the `root` `crontab` file and might have been surprised how little was actually listed therein. On older Unix systems, the `root` `crontab` was typically 20–30 lines long, with all the nightly, weekly, and monthly administrative jobs listed. Clearly they aren't there any more. So where did they go?

The answer is that the rewrite of the `cron` system for Linux extended the service by adding support for special directories that contain `root` administrative `cron` jobs that should be run on an hourly, daily, weekly, or monthly basis.

Task 15.3: Exploring the Administrative cron Jobs

The directories in question are all in `/etc` and are logically named `cron.hourly`, `cron.daily`, `cron.weekly`, and `cron.monthly`. What's interesting about this approach is that you no longer have to worry about the time specifier—if it's in the `cron.daily` directory, it'll be run once each day by `crond`.

1. Let's have a look at what's in these directories:

```
# ls -R /etc/cron.*
/etc/cron.d:
sysstat

/etc/cron.daily:
00-logwatch    0anacron     makewhatis.cron    slocate.cron    tmpwatch
00webalizer    logrotate    rpm                sysstat

/etc/cron.hourly:

/etc/cron.monthly:
0anacron

/etc/cron.weekly:
0anacron    makewhatis.cron
```

The entries in /etc/cron.d are formatted as regular crontab lines; they just let you avoid having a very large crontab file. Otherwise, all the other files are simple shell scripts.

2. It should be easy for you to now understand what the /etc/cron.d/sysstat file specifies, and when it should be run by the cron system:

```
# more /etc/cron.d/sysstat
# run system activity accounting tool every 10 minutes
*/10 * * * * root /usr/lib/sa/sa1 1 1
```

This specifies to run sal every 10 minutes.

> Notice how the use of comments helps you understand what's happening. As a general rule, you should always try to have a comment explaining your desired frequency before each line in your crontab file.

3. The weekly cron jobs are a good place for us to start, so let's have a peek at the default files included with Red Hat Linux:

```
# cd /etc/cron.weekly
# more *
::::::::::::::
0anacron
::::::::::::::
#!/bin/sh
#
# anacron's cron script
#
# This script updates anacron time stamps. It is called through run-parts
# either by anacron itself or by cron.
#
# The script is called "0anacron" to assure that it will be executed
# _before_ all other scripts.

anacron -u cron.weekly

::::::::::::::
makewhatis.cron
::::::::::::::
#!/bin/bash

LOCKFILE=/var/lock/makewhatis.lock

# the lockfile is not meant to be perfect, it's just in case the
# two makewhatis cron scripts get run close to each other to keep
# them from stepping on each other's toes.  The worst that will
```

```
# happen is that they will temporarily corrupt the database...
[ -f $LOCKFILE ] && exit 0
trap "rm -f $LOCKFILE" EXIT
touch $LOCKFILE
makewhatis -w
exit 0
```

As is typical with these administrative scripts, both of these examples are essentially a single line long each. The first, 0anacron, calls anacron -u cron.weekly, and the second makewhatis.cron rebuilds the whatis database (used by man -k) every week with makewhatis -w.

4. The daily scripts are more interesting, and there are more of 'em, so let's see if there's anything unusual or otherwise exemplary:

```
# wc -l *
    691 00-logwatch
      8 00webalizer
     12 0anacron
      3 logrotate
     13 makewhatis.cron
      4 rpm
      3 slocate.cron
      5 sysstat
      7 tmpwatch
    746 total
```

The logwatch script is remarkably long at 691 lines. Otherwise, you can see that the scripts are all quite short. A few offer interesting techniques:

```
# cat 00webalizer
#! /bin/bash
# update access statistics for the web site

if [ -s /var/log/httpd/access_log ] ; then
    /usr/bin/webalizer
fi
```

This is a common construct for an admin script—if a specific data file exists, run the program that analyzes it. In this case, it's checking to see if the Web server (httpd) received any hits. If it did, webalizer will produce some rudimentary log file analysis.

```
# cat slocate.cron
#!/bin/sh
renice +19 -p $$ >/dev/null 2>&1
/usr/bin/updatedb -f "nfs,smbfs,ncpfs,proc,devpts" -e "/tmp,/var/tmp,/
➥usr/tmp,/afs,/net"
```

15

▼ This is a terrific example of a succinct script that is written by someone who really understands the nuances of shell scripts. The renice command lowers the priority of its own shell (recall $$ is the PID of the shell) as much as possible by setting it to +19. Every other task on the system is now more important than this shell script. The very next line does the real work by launching updatedb, which rebuilds the locate filename database.

5. One more example, a rather sophisticated use of shell scripting and file name expansion through patterns.

```
# cat tmpwatch
/usr/sbin/tmpwatch 240 /tmp
/usr/sbin/tmpwatch 720 /var/tmp
for d in /var/{cache/man,catman}/{cat?,X11R6/cat?,local/cat?}; do
    if [ -d "$d" ]; then
        /usr/sbin/tmpwatch -f 720 $d
    fi
done
```

The tmpwatch program removes files that haven't been accessed in more than a specified number of hours, and here you can see that it helps keep the uncompressed man page directories clear of old man pages (the /cat directories). Here, it's expiring files more than 720 hours (30 days) old.

You can have administrative jobs run with the cron system through a number of different ways. You can create an explicit crontab file for root, drop a new script with a time specifier in /etc/cron.d, or write a script and place it in cron.hourly, cron.daily, cron.weekly, or cron.monthly and let the cron system schedule it automatically.

For regular users, the only option available is crontab files, but as has been demonstrated, they're reasonably straightforward to create, so it's not too onerous.

Explanation of crontab Entries Presented Earlier

Every day at 5 p.m.:

```
0  17  *  *  *  top -b -n1 | head -9 | mail -s "top status" taylor
```

Every day at 5 a.m.:

```
0  5   *  *  *  cd /web/chatter/comics; ./build-comics-page.sh > ./index.html
```

At noon on the first day of each month:

```
0  12  1  *  *          /home/taylor/scripts/doitall
```

At midnight on the 3rd day of August each year:

```
0  0  3  8  *    mail -s "happy birthday Dave" taylor@intuitive.com < birthday.note
```

```
Monday through Friday at 5:05 a.m.:

5   5  *  *  Mon-Fri     uptime | mail -s uptime root
```

Every other hour at 45 minutes after the hour:

```
45  0-23/2 * * *         echo "when does this run?" | mail root
```

This one's tricky: cron matches either the day of week or the day of month if both are specified, so this says at 4:30 a.m. on the first of the month, 15th of the month, and every Friday (day = 5):

```
30  4 1,15 * 5           /home/taylor/scripts/when_is_it
```

Twice daily at 9 a.m. and 4 p.m.:

```
0   9,16  * * *          /home/taylor/scripts/rotatefiles
```

Once in the Future with at

There's another utility worth mentioning for scheduling jobs in the future if you only want to do them once, rather than repeatedly—the at command. Don't be surprised if it's not actually running on your system, however, especially if you have a laptop installation. As the Mac OS X default distribution states in /etc/crontab:

```
# Disabled by default, since it causes disk access every 10 minutes,
# which is useless unless you use at(1).  Enable as needed.
#*/10   *       *       *       *       root    /usr/libexec/atrun
```

Notice here that it's also only being run every 10 minutes (*/10), so if you want to have a job run three minutes in the future, it's not going to be quite that precise.

Task 15.4: Working with at

The stock Red Hat Linux distribution has at enabled, so we can experiment with it briefly before wrapping up this hour.

1. You can confirm that at is running with ps, as usual:

```
# ps -aux | grep atd
rpcuser    605  0.0  0.1  1688  836 ?        S     Mar09   0:00 rpc.statd
daemon     861  0.0  0.1  1444  568 ?        S     Mar09   0:00 /usr/sbin/atd
root     23814  0.0  0.1  1728  584 pts/0    S     11:11   0:00 grep atd
```

2. To schedule a job in the future, you can specify the time in one of several ways. Generally, you either type in the command immediately following the at specification, or you pipe a shell script into the at command.

In all these cases, let's kick off `fquota`, as discussed earlier in the book in Hour 12, "Managing Disk Quotas":

```
# at midnight < ~/bin/fquota
Job a01027320.000 will be executed using /bin/sh
# at teatime < ~/bin/fquota
Job a01027140.000 will be executed using /bin/sh
# at 5:18pm < ~/bin/fquota
Job a0102718e.000 will be executed using /bin/sh
# at noon Aug 3 < ~/bin/fquota
Job a01058934.000 will be executed using /bin/sh
# at noon tomorrow < ~/bin/fquota
Job a010275f0.000 will be executed using /bin/sh
```

> Yes, `teatime` is a valid time! It's 4 p.m., for those of you that don't already know. Ain't Unix fun?

3. With all these injected into the system, the `atq` command shows what's queued to run:

```
# atq
Date                Owner   Queue   Job#
16:00:00 03/15/02   root    a       a01027140.000
17:18:00 03/15/02   root    a       a0102718e.000
00:00:00 03/16/02   root    a       a01027320.000
12:00:00 03/16/02   root    a       a010275f0.000
12:00:00 08/03/02   root    a       a01058934.000
```

Notice that the last job isn't scheduled for quite a while. In fact, it's five months away.

4. If you decide to give up on that job, you can remove an at job with `atrm`:

```
# atrm a01058934.000
#
```

As with `kill` and so many other Unix commands, `atrm` doesn't confirm success, it only flags failure.

```
# atq
Date                Owner   Queue   Job#
16:00:00 03/15/02   root    a       a01027140.000
17:18:00 03/15/02   root    a       a0102718e.000
00:00:00 03/16/02   root    a       a01027320.000
12:00:00 03/16/02   root    a       a010275f0.000
```

In the interest of fair disclosure, I have been using Unix systems since my first login in 1980. In all those years, when I've administered a variety of large and small systems, I have never once used the at command. It's simple and elegant, but I have always found that I either want to do jobs once, now, or with some frequency in the future through cron. Your mileage will undoubtedly vary, but you may well never use at in your Unix work.

Summary

Though not as exciting as H.G. Wells' *The Time Machine*, this hour has focused on Unix tools that allow you to execute commands either once in the future (with at), or on a repeating basis (with cron). There are hidden depths to cron, so this hour also explored the configuration along with hourly, daily, weekly, and monthly scheduled system jobs.

Q&A

Q Why can't crontab accept time formats like 5:00pm Sundays?

A Date parsing is quite a challenge on computer systems, actually. Some applications have lots and lots of code trying to offer a highly flexible date input format. The cron system isn't one of those, alas. It'd be nice to either have a smarter cron, or a front end that would let you specify things in English and translate them to the five-field crontab format, but as far as I have encountered, they don't exist.

Q Earlier you commented that having all crontab files owned by root isn't a security risk. Can you expand upon that comment?

A One of the important things to realize about cron is that it runs all jobs with an effective UID of the owner of the crontab, *not* the crontab file owner (which is root). Some Unix users don't really get this and think that because the crond program is running as root, therefore all cron jobs will run as root, too. It's not true.

Workshop

Quiz

1. Does crontab expect hour minute or minute hour format?
2. How do you delete a crontab file if you no longer need it?
3. Will this work as an hour specifier: 0,3,6-9,11-19/2? If so, what does it mean?
4. There's a common problem in many first time crontab entries. What is it, and how do you fix it?
5. When is teatime according to at?

Answers

1. The crontab file specifies minute hour as the first two fields of a time specifier.

2. The command crontab -r removes a crontab file forever.

3. It sure will, complex as it is. It matches the following enumerated list: 0,3,6,7,8,9,11,13,15,17,19.

4. The problem is that the PATH used by the cron program is almost certainly different from your login shell. To sidestep this problem, always specify full pathnames for commands referenced within the crontab line, and within any shell scripts invoked by cron on your behalf.

5. As my Mum and Dad would most certainly confirm, teatime in all civilized countries is 4 p.m. Precisely.

In the next hour, we'll see some practical uses for cron by analyzing and managing the growth of the many log files in Unix. We'll also learn about a nifty new utility called logrotate in Linux, and how to simulate it in other Unixes.

15

HOUR 16

Managing Your Log Files

One of the most important tasks for a system administrator is to keep an eye on system and disk space. Earlier we spent some time exploring df, du, and find, and learned how they can be used to better understand the allocation of disk space on your system.

In this hour, we'll delve into the specific log files used by the different Unix services, learn how to analyze them to flag any potential problems, and how to keep them from overrunning your disk.

In this hour you learn about

- Exploring the contents of log files
- Tracking hackers through log events
- Cracking open the httpd log file
- Trimming log files with logrotate
- Building your own log rotation tool

Understanding Log Files

Whether it's the boot process itself, the FTP server, the mail server, or any other service running on your computer, if it does something or someone interacts with it, the event is logged. Some services have their own log files, but many use a shared central log mechanism called syslog. syslog writes all messages to a log file typically called either messages or syslog.

Unix flavors vary on where they put log files, but generally you'll find them all in /var/log by default.

Task 16.1: Rummaging Around in Log Files

Different systems have a different number of log files, based both on how many services are running and how the logging for each service is configured.

1. First, a peek at the /var/log directory:

```
# ls -s
total 1836
    0 boot.log        63 ksyms.2         0 pgsql           0 spooler.3
    0 boot.log.1      63 ksyms.3        18 rpmpkgs          0 spooler.4
    5 boot.log.2      63 ksyms.4        18 rpmpkgs.1        1 squid
    0 boot.log.3      63 ksyms.5        18 rpmpkgs.2        1 vbox
    0 boot.log.4      63 ksyms.6        18 rpmpkgs.3       42 wtmp
   51 cron            20 lastlog        18 rpmpkgs.4       40 wtmp.1
  257 cron.1           2 maillog         1 sa              0 xferlog
  253 cron.2           5 maillog.1       1 samba           0 xferlog.1
  254 cron.3           4 maillog.2       1 secure          0 xferlog.2
  252 cron.4           3 maillog.3       5 secure.1         0 xferlog.3
   11 dmesg            3 maillog.4       4 secure.2         0 xferlog.4
    1 fax              1 messages        2 secure.3        23 XFree86.0.log
    1 gdm              6 messages.1      1 secure.4        24 XFree86.9.log
    1 httpd           26 messages.2      0 spooler
   63 ksyms.0          2 messages.3      0 spooler.1
   63 ksyms.1          1 messages.4      0 spooler.2
```

Notice that files have version number suffixes. As you'll learn later in this hour, this indicates that they're being rotated—the higher the number, the older the file. The version that has no version identification is the current log file.

2. The most basic log file is syslog's file, and on a Linux box, it's called /var/log/messages.

```
# grep "^Mar 11" messages
Mar 11 00:13:23 staging su(pam_unix)[12835]: session closed for user root
Mar 11 00:14:14 staging sshd(pam_unix)[12796]: session closed for user taylor
Mar 11 04:02:18 staging syslogd 1.4.1: restart.
Mar 11 11:19:32 staging sshd(pam_unix)[14368]: session opened for user taylor
➥ by (uid=0)
Mar 11 14:09:06 staging su(pam_unix)[14539]: session opened for user root by
➥taylor(uid=502)
```

```
Mar 11 16:02:05 staging sshd(pam_unix)[14716]: session opened for user taylor
➥by (uid=0)
Mar 11 16:28:10 staging sshd(pam_unix)[14716]: session closed for user taylor
Mar 11 16:28:19 staging su(pam_unix)[14539]: session closed for user root
Mar 11 16:28:21 staging sshd(pam_unix)[14368]: session closed for user taylor
```

This is a list of all logged messages for March 11, 2002. Not too exciting, but you can see that su logs events and that the sshd (ssh daemon) logs when users connect and disconnect.

Looking at the contents of this file, we can ascertain that user taylor was logged in until 00:14 when the sshd session ended, and that there was also an su session alive (as root) when the clock rolled over to the March 11. At 4:02 a.m., syslogd restarted, and user taylor logged in twice that day, once at 11:19 a.m. and a second time at 4:02 p.m. (16:02). During that time, taylor switched to root and left a root shell running from 11:19 a.m. to 4:28 p.m. (16:28).

A quick look in earlier log files by searching for Mar 10 will identify the initial su, to see if that was also from taylor:

```
# grep "^Mar 10" messages.1 | grep 'su'
Mar 10 23:39:49 staging su(pam_unix)[12835]: session opened for user root by
➥taylor(uid=502)
```

Sure enough, at 11:39 p.m., taylor used the su command to become root.

3. Perhaps more important than unthreading the logins for a given day is to scan for any potential security problems. One obvious one: Did anyone try to use the su facility and fail to log in?

```
# grep "su(" message* | grep -vE '(session opened|session closed)'
messages:Mar 18 12:52:14 staging su(pam_unix)[5330]: authentication failure;
➥logname=taylor uid=502 euid=0 tty= ruser= rhost=  user=root
messages.1:Mar 12 20:56:09 staging su(pam_unix)[17297]: authentication failure;
➥logname=taylor uid=502 euid=0 tty= ruser= rhost=  user=root
messages.3:Feb 23 21:09:16 staging su(pam_unix)[15552]: authentication failure;
➥logname=taylor uid=502 euid=0 tty= ruser= rhost=  user=taylorsu
```

You can see that in the time window that includes all the logged events, there were three failed su attempts, on February 23, March 12, and March 18, all by user taylor. Two were attempts to become root, and one to become taylorsu.

You can also verify that all the sus that succeeded were from known users by building a quick summary and using the helpful uniq utility to see what differences there were:

```
# grep 'session opened' message* | awk '{print $12 " became " $10 }' | \
  sort | uniq -c
      2 taylor(uid=0) became taylor
     15 taylor(uid=502) became root
      2 taylor(uid=502) became taylorsu
      4 (uid=0) became judi
     35 (uid=0) became taylor
```

It's a bit complex, but we extract all the "session opened" messages, strip out the From and To account information, and output a simple three-word value. Then `sort` ensures they're in order, and `uniq -c` counts unique occurrences of each string and outputs a single line for each unique string, prefaced with a repeat count. The second line, for example, shows that `taylor` used the `su` utility to become `root` 15 times.

4. On a Mac OS X system, by contrast, the `syslog` file is known as `system.log`, and it contains all sorts of interesting information. For example, wonder what happens when your system goes to sleep and wakes up again?

```
Mar 18 11:35:02 dsl-132 mach_kernel: UniNEnet:  0  0 UniNEnet::
    putToSleep - turning off cell clock!!!
Mar 18 11:35:02 dsl-132 mach_kernel: System Sleep
Mar 18 11:35:02 dsl-132 mach_kernel: System Wake
Mar 18 11:35:02 dsl-132 mach_kernel: Wake event 0020
```

More usefully, both `su` and `sudo` are logged here:

```
# grep "su:" system.log
Mar 15 09:42:38 dsl-132 su: taylor to root on /dev/ttyp1
# grep "sudo:" system.log
Mar 11 22:02:45 dsl-132 sudo:   taylor : TTY=ttyp1 ; PWD=/Users/taylor/bin ;
  USER=root ; COMMAND=./docron weekly
Mar 11 22:05:14 dsl-132 sudo:   taylor : TTY=ttyp2 ; PWD=/Users/taylor ;
  USER=root ; COMMAND=/bin/ls /
```

There's no evidence of any users other than `taylor` running `su` or `sudo` in this log file.

You can easily figure out what period of time is recorded in a log file by looking at the first and last lines:

```
# head -1 system.log ; tail -1 system.log
Mar 11 22:02:28 dsl-132 syslogd: restart
Mar 18 12:20:58 dsl-132 WindowServer[65]: CGXGetWindowLevel:
Invalid window 623
```

Here you can see that this represents approximately one week: 10:02 p.m. on March 11 through 12:20 p.m. on March 18.

5. The next log file to examine is `boot.log`, which shows you all the messages output to the screen during boot-time. Because most Unix systems aren't booted every day (hopefully!), this will often be empty, as you can see in the `ls` listing in step 1.

```
# head -20 boot.log.2
Feb 25 22:44:42 staging atd: atd shutdown succeeded
Feb 25 22:44:44 staging httpd: httpd shutdown succeeded
Feb 25 22:44:44 staging sshd: sshd -TERM succeeded
```

```
Feb 25 22:44:44 staging sendmail: sendmail shutdown succeeded
Feb 25 22:44:44 staging xinetd: xinetd shutdown succeeded
Feb 25 22:44:44 staging crond: crond shutdown succeeded
Feb 25 22:44:45 staging dd: 1+0 records in
Feb 25 22:44:45 staging dd: 1+0 records out
Feb 25 22:44:45 staging random: Saving random seed:  succeeded
Feb 25 22:44:45 staging nfslock: rpc.statd shutdown succeeded
Feb 25 22:44:45 staging portmap: portmap shutdown succeeded
Feb 25 22:44:46 staging syslog: klogd shutdown succeeded
Feb 25 22:47:37 staging syslog: syslogd startup succeeded
Feb 25 22:47:37 staging syslog: klogd startup succeeded
Feb 25 22:47:37 staging portmap: portmap startup succeeded
Feb 25 22:47:37 staging nfslock: rpc.statd startup succeeded
Feb 25 22:47:11 staging rc.sysinit: Mounting proc filesystem:  succeeded
Feb 25 22:47:11 staging rc.sysinit: Unmounting initrd:  succeeded
Feb 25 22:47:11 staging sysctl: net.ipv4.ip_forward = 0
Feb 25 22:47:11 staging sysctl: net.ipv4.conf.default.rp_filter = 1
```

These messages document a system shutdown (or change in init state that required a set of shutdown events prior to starting up new services) on February 25. Probably most important things to look for are errors, warnings, and similar:

```
# grep -E '(warning|error|crit|fail)' boot.log*
#
```

Nothing's wrong. Terrific!

6. By contrast, checking the syslog file on Solaris 8 (Solaris doesn't have a separate boot log file; all information about booting goes into syslog) with the same regular expression reveals:

```
# egrep '(warning|error|crit|fail)' syslog
Jan 14 22:36:35 solaris sendmail[347]: [ID 702911 mail.crit] My unqualified
➥host
  name (solaris) unknown; sleeping for retry
Jan 15 00:06:08 solaris sendmail[223]: [ID 702911 mail.crit] My unqualified
➥host
  name (solaris) unknown; sleeping for retry
Jan 15 00:34:43 solaris sendmail[224]: [ID 702911 mail.crit] My unqualified
➥host
  name (solaris) unknown; sleeping for retry
```

Clearly there's a problem with sendmail resolving its own name at boot-time. This is something well worth exploring further, and ultimately fixing.

Any theory on what might be wrong based on the sendmail error shown in the Solaris log file? My guess is that somewhere we need to set the hostname properly and aren't. Clearly solaris isn't a good unqualified hostname, and isn't going to reverse DNS lookup properly.

7. Let's quickly look through some of the other log files to understand what's going on:

```
# head -5 cron
Mar 17 04:05:00 staging CROND[27157]: (root) CMD
  (/usr/bin/mrtg /etc/mrtg/mrtg.cfg)
Mar 17 04:10:00 staging CROND[27160]: (root) CMD
  (/usr/bin/mrtg /etc/mrtg/mrtg.cfg)
Mar 17 04:10:00 staging CROND[27161]: (root) CMD
  (/usr/lib/sa/sa1 1 1)
Mar 17 04:15:00 staging CROND[27164]: (root) CMD
  (/usr/bin/mrtg /etc/mrtg/mrtg.cfg)
Mar 17 04:20:00 staging CROND[27167]: (root) CMD
  (/usr/bin/mrtg /etc/mrtg/mrtg.cfg)
```

As expected, the cron log file shows commands and actions taken by the crond daemon. In parenthesis it shows the user account, and also shows the command. If you think someone is using a cron-based program to try and break security, it'll be logged here.

8. If you're ready to become paranoid about people trying to get to your computer, have a look at xferlog or ftp.log, depending on your OS. On my Mac OS X server, for example, the log file shows

```
# cat ftp.log | grep -v taylor
Jan 21 12:24:36 dsl-132 ftpd[369]: connection from dsl-155.dsldesigns.com
Jan 21 12:24:40 dsl-132 ftpd[369]: FTP LOGIN REFUSED
  FROM dsl-155.dsldesigns.com, root
Jan 21 12:28:06 dsl-132 ftpd[390]: connection from 63.101.93.250
Jan 21 12:35:40 dsl-132 ftpd[412]: connection from dsl-155.dsldesigns.com
Jan 21 19:44:24 dsl-132 ftpd[491]: connection from 63.101.93.250
Jan 21 19:45:28 dsl-132 ftpd[492]: connection from dsl-155.dsldesigns.com
Jan 21 20:00:39 dsl-132 ftpd[516]: connection from 63.101.93.250
Jan 22 09:45:04 dsl-132 ftpd[332]: connection from webpac.clemson.edu
Jan 22 12:27:23 dsl-132 ftpd[460]: connection from 63.101.93.250
Jan 22 12:34:18 dsl-132 ftpd[461]: connection from 63.101.93.250
Jan 24 18:00:40 dsl-132 ftpd[369]: connection from dsl-151.dsldesigns.com
Jan 26 22:44:59 dsl-132 ftpd[927]: connection from dsl-155.dsldesigns.com
Jan 29 18:27:33 dsl-132 ftpd[359]: connection from 157.161.112.208
Jan 29 21:48:12 dsl-132 ftpd[378]: connection from
  port-212-202-160-251.reverse.qdsl-home.de
Jan 29 21:48:13 dsl-132 ftpd[378]: ANONYMOUS FTP LOGIN REFUSED
  FROM port-212-202-160-251.reverse.qdsl-home.de
Feb  6 12:10:23 dsl-132 ftpd[525]: connection from 199.88.128.27
Feb  6 15:54:41 dsl-132 ftpd[554]: connection from pd955f64e.dip.t-dialin.net
Feb  6 21:52:56 dsl-132 ftpd[605]: connection from pd955f64e.dip.t-dialin.net
Feb  6 21:52:58 dsl-132 ftpd[605]: ANONYMOUS FTP LOGIN REFUSED
  FROM pd955f64e.dip.t-dialin.net
Feb  7 00:01:09 dsl-132 ftpd[612]: connection from maptech-inc.com
Feb  7 00:01:12 dsl-132 ftpd[613]: connection from maptech-inc.com
Feb  7 00:01:21 dsl-132 ftpd[614]: connection from maptech-inc.com
```

There are no files available to the general public, and the IP address of our system is not advertised anywhere. How these sites are finding our system is a mystery, but what's not a mystery is that they're trying to connect and log in.

This is an obvious attempt to break the security on our system, so it's a good time to turn the ftpd program *off* until I'm ready to re-enable it. In Mac OS X, the fastest way to do this is to go into the System Preferences, Sharing control panel and uncheck Enable FTP Access. That not only turns it off from future activity, but kills the currently running ftpd as well.

9. Another log file worth keeping an eye on is maillog, which records all electronic mail transactions as they occur. If I send a quick e-mail message to myself, for example, the following two lines are written out to the file:

```
# tail -2 maillog
Mar 18 14:24:35 staging sendmail[5459]: g2IMOZb05459: from=root, size=58,
class=0, nrcpts=1, msgid=<200203182224.g2IMOZb05459@staging.intuitive.com>,
relay=root@localhost

Mar 18 14:24:52 staging sendmail[5462]: g2IMOZb05459: to=taylor@intuitive.com,
ctladdr=root (0/0), delay=00:00:17, xdelay=00:00:17, mailer=esmtp, pri=30058,
relay=mail-fwd.verio-web.com. [161.58.148.40], dsn=2.0.0,
stat=Sent (036711929 Message accepted for delivery)
```

Lots of stuff, but most importantly notice that the two lines can be matched with the jobID (g2IMOZb05459), and that the first entry indicates from= and the second indicates to=. Without any fancy footwork, we can sort by field value, then extract the from= and to= values to see what's going on:

```
# sort -k6 maillog* | awk '{print $7 }' | grep -v root | grep '@'
to=taylor@intuitive.com,
```

It's a bit complex, but this pipe extracts all the from= and to= values from the log file, strips out mail sent to or from root, then reports all off-system addresses. As expected on this server, only one message has been sent.

There are a lot of log files to keep track of, no question, and there are important snippets of information in each. It's well worth your time to explore each file and keep returning to each as your system runs to begin to understand what's contained within them.

Tracking a Hacker

One common thing you'll find in your log files is that there are weird and surprising entries. Let's try to track one backward and see if we can ascertain what's going on.

Task 16.2: Tracking Backward

Although some Unix systems have all their log entries dropped into the syslog file, Linux offers a different, and helpful, log file called secure that contains all security-related log events.

1. On Linux, there's a very important log file called secure, and it's well worth looking at its contents:

```
# head secure
Mar 10 10:22:14 staging sshd[12114]: Did not receive identification
    string from 208.37.77.153.
Mar 10 22:27:39 staging sshd[12659]: Could not reverse map address
    198.76.82.132.
Mar 10 22:27:42 staging sshd[12659]: Accepted password for taylor
    from 198.76.82.132 port 49154 ssh2
Mar 10 23:39:43 staging sshd[12796]: Accepted password for taylor
    from 198.76.82.132 port 49156 ssh2
Mar 11 11:19:29 staging sshd[14368]: Could not reverse map address
    198.76.82.132.
Mar 11 11:19:32 staging sshd[14368]: Accepted password for taylor
    from 198.76.82.132 port 49152 ssh2
Mar 11 16:02:00 staging sshd[14716]: Could not reverse map address
    198.76.82.132.
Mar 11 16:02:05 staging sshd[14716]: Accepted password for taylor
    from 198.76.82.132 port 49153 ssh2
Mar 11 17:15:38 staging sshd[14891]: Did not receive identification
    string from 129.132.250.236.
Mar 12 15:01:13 staging sshd[16846]: Could not reverse map address
    198.76.82.132.
```

This logs all security-related events, including sshd connections. As you can see, taylor logged in from 198.76.82.132 (a known IP address), but there was also a connection from 208.27.77.153.

The host command can do reverse IP mapping, so given an IP address, we can ascertain its domain:

```
# host -dv 208.37.77.153
;; res_nmkquery(QUERY, 153.77.37.208.IN-ADDR.ARPA., IN, PTR)
;; res_send()
;; ->>HEADER<<- opcode: QUERY, status: NOERROR, id: 65086
;; flags: rd; QUERY: 1, ANSWER: 0, AUTHORITY: 0, ADDITIONAL: 0
;;      153.77.37.208.IN-ADDR.ARPA, type = PTR, class = IN
;; Querying server (# 1) address = 192.216.138.10
;; new DG socket
;; got answer:
;; ->>HEADER<<- opcode: QUERY, status: NOERROR, id: 65086
;; flags: qr rd ra; QUERY: 1, ANSWER: 1, AUTHORITY: 4, ADDITIONAL: 0
```

```
;;       153.77.37.208.IN-ADDR.ARPA, type = PTR, class = IN
153.77.37.208.IN-ADDR.ARPA.  2H IN PTR  w153.z208037077.nyc-ny.dsl.cnc.net.
77.37.208.IN-ADDR.ARPA.  2H IN NS  nameserver3.concentric.net.
77.37.208.IN-ADDR.ARPA.  2H IN NS  nameserver.concentric.net.
77.37.208.IN-ADDR.ARPA.  2H IN NS  nameserver1.concentric.net.
77.37.208.IN-ADDR.ARPA.  2H IN NS  nameserver2.concentric.net.
rcode = 0 (Success), ancount=1
The following answer is not authoritative:
The following answer is not verified as authentic by the server:
153.77.37.208.IN-ADDR.ARPA  7200 IN PTR  w153.z208037077.nyc-ny.dsl.cnc.net
For authoritative answers, see:
77.37.208.IN-ADDR.ARPA  7200 IN NS     nameserver3.concentric.net
77.37.208.IN-ADDR.ARPA  7200 IN NS     nameserver.concentric.net
77.37.208.IN-ADDR.ARPA  7200 IN NS     nameserver1.concentric.net
77.37.208.IN-ADDR.ARPA  7200 IN NS     nameserver2.concentric.net
```

The resolved name is buried in the middle of this information:

```
w153.z208037077.nyc-ny.dsl.cnc.net.
```

2. The next step is to look up the complete domain registration record:

```
# whois -r cnc.net
[whois.crsnic.net]

Whois Server Version 1.3

Domain names in the .com, .net, and .org domains can now be registered
with many different competing registrars. Go to http://www.internic.net
for detailed information.

    Domain Name: CNC.NET
    Registrar: NETWORK SOLUTIONS, INC.
    Whois Server: whois.networksolutions.com
    Referral URL: http://www.networksolutions.com
    Name Server: NAMESERVER.CONCENTRIC.NET
    Name Server: NAMESERVER3.CONCENTRIC.NET
    Updated Date: 05-nov-2001

>>> Last update of whois database: Tue, 19 Mar 2002 05:21:50 EST <<<


[whois.networksolutions.com]

Registrant:
Concentric Network Corporation (CNC6-DOM)
    1400 Parkmoor Avenue
    San Jose, CA 95126-3429

    Domain Name: CNC.NET
```

16

▼

```
Administrative Contact:
   Schairer, David R  (DRS9)  njal@CONCENTRIC.NET
   Concentric Network Corp.
   1400 Parkmoor Ave
   Cupertino, CA 95014
   (408) 817-2800 (800) 745-2747 ext. 2800 (FAX) (408) 817-2630
Technical Contact:
   DNS & IP ADMIN  (DIA-ORG)  hostmaster@CONCENTRIC.NET
   Concentric Network Corporation
   1400 Parkmoor Avenue
   San Jose, CA 95126-3429
   (408) 817-2800
   Fax- (408) 817-2630
Billing Contact:
   XO Communications, Hostmaster  (CNCXCH-ORG)  hostmaster@XOHOST.COM
   XO Communications
   1400 Parkmoor Ave
   San Jose, CA 95126
   408-817-2800
   Fax- 408-817-2810

Record last updated on 02-Mar-2001.
Record expires on 06-Mar-2004.
Record created on 05-Mar-1997.
Database last updated on 18-Mar-2002 22:31:00 EST.

Domain servers in listed order:

NAMESERVER3.CONCENTRIC.NET    206.173.119.72
NAMESERVER2.CONCENTRIC.NET    207.155.184.72
```

Concentric Networks is a large ISP based in Northern California.

3. We'll send them an e-mail message, but, alas, I don't expect any sort of meaningful response:

```
# mail -s "One of your customers was trying to hack into my system"
abuse@cnc.net
Hello. I have tracked backward and found that one of the computers in
your domain (w153.z208037077.nyc-ny.dsl.cnc.net) was trying to hack into my
Linux server. In the "/var/log/secure" log file, I find the following message
from 'sshd':

Mar 10 10:22:14 staging sshd[12114]: Did not receive identification string
from 208.37.77.153.

A reverse lookup of that IP address returns:

153.77.37.208.in-addr.arpa. domain name pointer w153.z208037077.nyc-ny.dsl.
➥cnc.net.
```

▼

▼
```
Can you please work backward in your usage logs to ascertain what computer has
the specified IP address of 208.37.77.153, and identify the culprit?
Needless to say, I don't want people port-scanning my server!

Thanks for your assistance on this matter.

Dave Taylor
taylor@intuitive.com
     .
```

4. About 15 minutes later, we receive the following:
```
The original message was received at Tue, 19 Mar 2002 13:46:52 -0500 (EST)

    ----- The following addresses had permanent fatal errors -----
abuse@cncx.net
    (expanded from: <abuse@cnc.net>)

    ----- Transcript of session follows -----
550 abuse@cncx.net... Host unknown (Name server: cncx.net: host not found)
```

Oh well, at least we can see how to work backward in our log files, and at least we ▲ tried....

It's not uncommon to find people trying to probe your ports: Indeed, it's a matter of five minutes of shell programming to write a "port scanner" that will pick an IP address, then see what Internet services, if any, are listening. Once that's ascertained, there are tools available to try and break in using a specific service "exploit."

If it sounds a bit depressing, it should. The best thing you can do for security is to ensure that your system is properly configured, that you keep an eye on your log files, that you have a properly configured firewall, and that you have reliable backups just in case.

There are also some very good books about Unix security, three of which I'll highlight here:

Hacking Linux Exposed by Brian Hatch et al. (McGraw-Hill) has a good explanation of what hackers do to try and gain entry into your system, though at the expense of less coverage of how to avoid the problem in the first place.

Practical Unix and Internet Security by Simson Garfinkel and Gene Spafford (O'Reilly) is more academic, but a definitive reference on this topic.

Maximum Linux Security by Anonymous (Sams) is another option. A quick search on Amazon or Barnes & Noble will reveal quite a few other choices if none of these jump out at you.

We'll return to the topic of security again in the last hour.

The `httpd` Log File

There's another log file that is well worth exploring in some detail, as it's often the main purpose for a Unix server in the first place: the Web server log.

There are different Web servers available, but by far the most popular is Apache, a freely distributed HTTP daemon that offers remarkable flexibility, power, and configurability. It is included on just about every modern Unix distribution, and you can download the Apache distribution at www.apache.org.

Task 16.3: Exploring the `httpd` Log File

The last log file we'll examine in this hour is the Apache Web server log file, actually a set of files all stored in /var/log/httpd.

1. Here's what's typically in that directory:

```
# cd /var/log/httpd
# ls -s
total 984
   35 access_log         3 error_log       1 ssl_engine_log     0 ssl_request_log
  252 access_log.1      32 error_log.1      0 ssl_mutex.19348    0 ssl_scache.sem
  217 access_log.2      44 error_log.2      0 ssl_mutex.4700
  141 access_log.3      27 error_log.3      0 ssl_mutex.627
  188 access_log.4      44 error_log.4      0 ssl_mutex.641
```

To make things more interesting, however, we'll analyze the log files from a busier Web server with larger log files:

```
# ls -s
total 4200
2594 access_log   654 agent_log    33 error_log   919 referer_log
```

2. The first snippet of information you would like to extract from your log files is a count of hits, which proves remarkably easy to do:

```
# wc -l access_log
  12384 access_log
```

12,384 hits, but in what period of time? Again, just look at the first and last lines of the log file to find out:

```
# head -1 access_log ; tail -1 access_log
centaurus.4web.cz - - [18/Mar/2002:00:09:53 -0500] "GET / HTTP/1.0" 200
➥229 "-" "Woko robot 3.0"
node-c-c10f.a2000.nl - - [18/Mar/2002:18:05:05 -0500] "GET
[ic:cc]/taylor/Graphics/biohazard.gif HTTP/1.1" 200 5330
"http://forum.fok.nl/showtopic.php/119057/1/50" "Mozilla/4.0 (compatible;
➥MSIE 6.0; Windows 98)"
```

▼   This represents all usage between midnight and 6:05 p.m., a total of 18 hours. This
         means that this server is seeing a respectable, but not overwhelming, 688 (12384÷18)
         hits per hour, or 11.4 (688÷60) hits per minute.

3. To extract more information from this log file, a quick summary of the log file for-
    mat is required. I won't explain everything in this hour (we'll look at Apache in
    more detail later in the book), but here's the essential field layout:

```
visitor-domain - - date&time timezone operation URL - return-code
➥bytes-sent ...
```

With this information, we can quickly extract interesting information, like what
domains account for the greatest number of hits:

```
# awk '{print $1}' access_log  | sort | uniq -c | sort -rn | head -10
    305 193.190.216.249
    208 pc03.wimbp.zgora.pl
    175 164.156.231.55
    145 204.185.56.252
    117 216.35.169.126
    110 slb-proxy-03.boeing.com
     84 194.131.98.235
     78 216-203-142-177.customer.algx.net
     75 61.11.78.180
     70 209.248.92.29
```

Again, the hosts command can do a reverse lookup for the topmost domain:

```
# host -dv 193.190.216.249 | grep "IN SOA"
216.190.193.IN-ADDR.ARPA.  2h59m40s IN SOA  www.senate.be. sysadmin.senate.be.
```

A computer in the Belgian Senate accounts for more traffic than any other system
visiting the Web site in this 18 hour window. Surprised?

```
# host -dv 164.156.231.55 | grep "IN SOA"
156.164.IN-ADDR.ARPA. 3H IN SOA  jasper.cmic.state.pa.us. security.
➥state.pa.us
```

IP address number three is the Pennsylvanian office of Social Security!

4. Another common query to the Apache log file is about what URLs are most com-
    monly requested. This is easy to calculate when you notice that field seven is the
    requested URL:

```
# awk '{print $7}' access_log | sort | uniq -c | sort -rn | head
   1334 /cgi-local/etymologic.cgi
    699 /cgi-local/trivial.cgi
    508 /
    437 /taylor/Graphics/biohazard.gif
    219 /sites/trivial/Graphics/kudos.gif
    217 /sites/trivial/Graphics/intsys.gif
    213 /sites/etymologic/Graphics/bottom-bar.gif
    212 /sites/etymologic/Graphics/top-bar.gif
    204 /sites/etymologic/Graphics/bonus-com.gif
    203 /sites/etymologic/Graphics/linkbw2.gif
```

16

5. Many users like to keep track of the entire number of bytes sent from their server to calculate the approximate percentage of bandwidth utilized per day. This is field ten, and the analysis is easier than the earlier examples:

```
# awk '{ sum += $10} END { print "total = " sum/1024 " Kb" }' access_log
total = 41583.9 Kb
```

This equates to a reasonable transfer rate of 2.25MB/hour (41583÷18)÷1024.

6. The other log files are also worth a quick peek. The agent_log is just the Web browser identification string from each visitor:

```
# head agent_log
Woko robot 3.0
Mozilla/4.0 (compatible; MSIE 5.5; Windows 98)
Mozilla/4.0 (compatible; MSIE 5.5; Windows 98)
Mozilla/4.0 (compatible; MSIE 5.5; Windows 98)
Mozilla/4.0 (compatible; MSIE 5.5; Windows 98)
Mozilla/4.0 (compatible; MSIE 5.5; Windows 98)
Mozilla/4.0 (compatible; MSIE 5.5; Windows 98)
Woko robot 3.0
Mozilla/4.0 (compatible; MSIE 5.0; AOL 7.0; Windows 98; DigExt)
Mozilla/4.0 (compatible; MSIE 5.0; AOL 7.0; Windows 98; DigExt)
```

Fair warning: Some Apache Web server configurations don't record this information, and others only include it in the access_log.

Again, the powerful combination of sort|uniq -c|sort -rn|head will reveal the most commonly used browsers:

```
# sort agent_log | uniq -c | sort -rn | head
   1049 Mozilla/4.0 (compatible; MSIE 5.0; Windows 98; DigExt)
    816 Mozilla/4.0 (compatible; MSIE 6.0; Windows 98)
    732 Mozilla/4.0 (compatible; MSIE 5.01; Windows NT 5.0)
    619 Mozilla/4.0 (compatible; MSIE 5.5; Windows 98; Win 9x 4.90)
    604 Mozilla/4.0 (compatible; MSIE 5.5; Windows 98)
    438 Mozilla/4.0 (compatible; MSIE 5.5; Windows NT 5.0)
    434 Mozilla/4.0 (compatible; MSIE 5.01; Windows 98)
    333 Mozilla/4.0 (compatible; MSIE 5.5; Windows NT 4.0)
    326 Mozilla/5.0 (Windows; U; WinNT4.0; en-US; rv:0.9.4)
➥Gecko/3 Netscape6/6.2
    287 Mozilla/4.0 (compatible; MSIE 6.0; Windows NT 5.0)
```

Given that any agent with MSIE in its string is Microsoft Internet Explorer, this shows quite graphically that Internet Explorer certainly does lead the Web browser pack by quite a margin (of the 5,638 browser agents listed in this top ten list, all but 326 (5.7%) are MSIE).

7. The `referrer_log` is somewhat interesting, but it takes a bit of data massaging to see what's really inside. The file contains a list of the last URL someone was at before visiting a Web site on this server:

```
# head -5 referer_log
http://search.yahoo.com/search/msie?o=1&m=i&a=fd&p=trivia+games&b=121&h=s -> /
http://www.intuitive.com/sites/trivial/index.html ->
➥/sites/trivial/Graphics/intsys.gif
http://www.intuitive.com/sites/trivial/index.html ->
➥/sites/trivial/Graphics/play-the-game.gif
http://www.intuitive.com/sites/trivial/index.html ->
➥/sites/trivial/Graphics/kudos.gif
http://www.intuitive.com/sites/trivial/index.html ->
➥/sites/trivial/Graphics/animated-banner.gif
```

The problem is that many of these URLs prove to be quite long, thus preventing us from doing any meaningful analysis because the URL includes a timestamp, session ID, and so on.

Instead, cut lets us chop out just the base domain name and see what we find:

```
# cut -d/ -f3 referer_log | sort | uniq -c | sort -rn | head
   9589 www.intuitive.com
    164 www.google.com
    116 pub43.ezboard.com
    115 pub44.ezboard.com
    107 forum.fok.nl
     48 search.msn.com
     47 search.yahoo.com
     39 www.dancing.baby.net
     34 www.yellow.baby.net
     34 images.google.com
```

Some very interesting results!

8. The final log file is `error_log`, and here again, we're going to see security problems as people try to break into our server:

```
# head -4 error_log
[Mon Mar 18 00:14:54 2002] [error] [client 66.77.73.219] File does
➥not exist: /w/web/intui2/robots.txt
[Mon Mar 18 00:30:47 2002] [error] [client 198.107.235.65] File does
➥not exist: /u/web/intui2/custer
[Mon Mar 18 00:34:45 2002] [error] [client 12.233.27.11] File does
➥not exist: /u/web/intui2/robots.txt
[Mon Mar 18 01:11:07 2002] [error] [client 64.128.250.173] File does
➥not exist: /u/web/intui2/OLD/Images/social-guide-title.gif
```

Again, you can see that the format is very uniform, so you can easily search for `does not exist`, extract the actual requested file, `sort|uniq` it, and have a list of the most common incorrect references:

```
# grep "does not exist" error_log | awk '{print $13}' | sort | \
  uniq -c | sort -rn | head
```

```
  34 /u/web/intui2/custer
  26 /u/web/intui2/robots.txt
  17 /u/web/intui2/origins/
  15 /u/web/intui2/favicon.ico
  13 /u/web/intui2/origins/Graphics/nav/newswire-off.gif
  13 /u/web/intui2/apps/Graphics/nav/newswire-off.gif
  11 /u/web/intui2/OLD/Images/social-guide-title.gif
  11 /u/web/intui2/OLD/Images/coolweb-ad.gif
   8 /u/web/intui2/coolweb/apps/relayto.cgi
   8 /u/web/intui2/apps/search-everything.cgi
```

More importantly, you can exclude those errors and see what other problems might have arisen:

```
# grep -v "does not exist" error_log  | head
[Mon Mar 18 04:48:51 2002] [error] [client 213.106.38.231] Premature
end of script headers: /u/web/intui2/cgi-local/etymologic.cgi
[Mon Mar 18 05:24:40 2002] [error] [client 210.183.67.209] Client sent
malformed Host header
[Mon Mar 18 07:51:48 2002] [error] [client 206.114.36.6] script not found or
unable to stat: /u/httpd/cgi-bin/PDG_Cart
[Mon Mar 18 08:16:16 2002] [error] [client 213.77.101.163] script not found or
 unable to stat: /u/web/intui2/cgi-local/apps/querty.cgi
[Mon Mar 18 08:16:44 2002] [error] [client 213.77.101.163] script not found or
unable to stat: /u/web/intui2/cgi-local/apps/querty.cgi
[Mon Mar 18 11:45:20 2002] [error] [client 193.63.5.67] attempt to invoke
directory as script: /u/web/intui2/cgi-local/apps
[Mon Mar 18 11:46:31 2002] [error] [client 193.63.5.67] attempt to invoke
 directory as script: /u/web/intui2/cgi-local/apps
[Mon Mar 18 12:38:40 2002] [error] [client 164.156.231.55] attempt to invoke
 directory as script: /u/web/intui2/cgi-local
[Mon Mar 18 13:53:23 2002] [error] [client 213.97.216.50] (11)Resource
temporarily unavailable: couldn't spawn
child process: /u/web/intui2/cgi-local/switcher.pl
[Mon Mar 18 13:53:24 2002] [error] [client 213.98.97.138] (11)Resource
temporarily unavailable: couldn't spawn
child process: /u/web/intui2/cgi-local/switcher.pl
```

Definitely some things to explore. Why, for example, is there a call to apps/querty.cgi? What's resource temporarily unavailable mean?

We'll re-address Apache issues in the last two hours of the book.

Of all the log files that can be analyzed and explored, few are more interesting than the Web server itself. Armed with basic Unix tools, it proves easy to extract meaningful information and produce rudimentary statistics in just a moment or two.

Analyzing an access_log file is a clear task for a cron-launched script that can produce a report and e-mail it to the Web administrators. This will be left as an exercise to the reader.

Trimming Log Files with `logrotate`

Let's put the question of detecting security problems aside for the rest of this hour and look at the issue of managing the log files themselves.

On a busy server, it's not unusual to see log files that are enormous, and adding lines every few seconds. On a busy Web server, for example, a `tail -f` `/var/log/httpd/access_log` might well spit out 50–100 lines each minute as the sites are visited.

The challenge is to simultaneously minimize the size of the log files, while still making sure that they're accessible and available as needed.

Task 16.4: The `logrotate` Program

▼ TASK

Historically, system administrators have written their own scripts to manage and trim log files, but with the latest generation of Linux, there's a very helpful utility included called `logrotate`, and it does a very sophisticated job of rotating all the log files in `/var/log` automatically.

1. By convention, the `logrotate` command is called from `cron` on a daily basis. Based on the discussion in the last hour, it should be no surprise that it's located in `/etc/cron.daily`:

```
# cd /etc/cron.daily
# ls
00-logwatch   0anacron    makewhatis.cron   slocate.cron   tmpwatch
00webalizer   logrotate   rpm               sysstat
# more logrotate
#!/bin/sh

/usr/sbin/logrotate /etc/logrotate.conf
```

Before we look at the command, then, let's have a peek at the configuration file.

2. If you think about the task that's being accomplished, you'll start to see the elegance of the `logrotate` solution. We have a log file that we want to have automatically renamed *file*.1, and we want `file.1` to be renamed `file.2`, and so on. After a certain count, we want the oldest files to be deleted, so we have a running window of "rotate–frequency" days of events in the past.

The first few lines of the configuration file specify those two key settings:

```
# cat /etc/logrotate.conf
# see "man logrotate" for details
# rotate log files weekly
weekly

# keep 4 weeks worth of backlogs
rotate 4
```

▼

16

In this case, the frequency is `weekly` and the rotation is 4, so we have a running window of the last month of activity on the server.

```
# create new (empty) log files after rotating old ones
create

# uncomment this if you want your log files compressed
# compress
```

Some daemons are very picky about log files, and will refuse to create a log file if it doesn't already exist. If that's the case, the `create` command is very useful, and it's the default setting for `logrotate`. Also notice how easy it is to decide that the historic log file archives should be stored in a compressed (`gzip`) format by default!

```
# Keep a longer archive of the "secure" logs, and compress them
/var/log/secure {
  rotate 8
  compress
}
```

In this example, the `secure` log files are kept for eight weeks rather than the default of four, and they're compressed to save space.

```
# Rotate the Apache log files when they get over 25K in size
# Keep an archive of six weeks, compressed, and mail the new
# rotated log to a special email address too:
/var/log/httpd/access_log {
  rotate 6
  size 25k
  mail web-log-archive@intuitive.com
  compress
  postrotate
    /etc/rc.d/rc3.d/S15httpd restart
  endscript
}
```

This is a fancy use of `logrotate` that really demonstrates its capabilities. Rather than having the rotation tied to a specific calendar day, the program will rotate the log file whenever it grows larger than 25K. It'll keep a six-week archive compressed, and the oldest log file (which will be deleted once the rotation is complete) will be sent via e-mail to the special address web-log-archive@intuitive.com as part of the processing. Once the rotational sequence is completed, `logrotate` will call the specified shell script (the `httpd` control script that `init` uses) to force a restart, so each log file starts out with a Web server boot event.

This level of sophistication is far more than we'll create in our own script later in this hour, and it's a strong testimony to why the `logrotate` command can be such a powerful utility to the smart system administrator.

▼   One last example:

```
# no packages own lastlog or wtmp -- we'll rotate them here
/var/log/wtmp {
  monthly
  create 0664 root utmp
  rotate 1
}
```

The `wtmp` file is a log of who logged in (logins are recorded in `utmp` while the user is still logged in, and then moved to `wtmp` after she's logged out), and it's of value, but it usually doesn't grow very quickly. In this case, we'll rotate it monthly and only keep a two month window. Notice that the new empty `utmp` file has very specific creation parameters that must be specified—the permission is `0644` and the owner of the file is `root`.

3. Using the `logrotate` command is quite simple: Log out and let `cron` do the work. Every night, `cron` will call `logrotate`, which reads the configuration file and does the actions specified.

   To test out your configuration, use the –d (debug) flag:

```
# logrotate -d /etc/logrotate.conf
reading config file /etc/logrotate.conf
reading config info for /var/log/secure
reading config info for /var/log/httpd/access_log
reading config info for /var/log/wtmp
Handling 3 logs
rotating pattern: /var/log/secure  weekly (8 rotations)
empty log files are rotated old logs are removed
rotating file /var/log/secure
log does not need rotating
rotating pattern: /var/log/httpd/access_log  25600 bytes (6 rotations)
empty log files are rotated old logs mailed to web-log-archive@intuitive.com
rotating file /var/log/httpd/access_log
log needs rotating
renaming /var/log/httpd/access_log.6.gz to /var/log/httpd/access_log.7.gz
renaming /var/log/httpd/access_log.5.gz to /var/log/httpd/access_log.6.gz
renaming /var/log/httpd/access_log.4.gz to /var/log/httpd/access_log.5.gz
renaming /var/log/httpd/access_log.3.gz to /var/log/httpd/access_log.4.gz
renaming /var/log/httpd/access_log.2.gz to /var/log/httpd/access_log.3.gz
renaming /var/log/httpd/access_log.1.gz to /var/log/httpd/access_log.2.gz
renaming /var/log/httpd/access_log to /var/log/httpd/access_log.1
creating new log mode = 0644 uid = 0 gid = 0
running postrotate script
running script with arg /var/log/httpd/access_log: "
    /etc/rc.d/rc3.d/S15httpd restart
"
compressing new log with: /bin/gzip -9 '/var/log/httpd/access_log.1'
executing: "/bin/mail -s '/var/log/httpd/access_log.7.gz'
  web-log-archive@intuitive.com < /var/log/httpd/access_log.7.gz"
```

16

▼
```
removing old log /var/log/httpd/access_log.7.gz
rotating pattern: /var/log/wtmp  monthly (1 rotations)
empty log files are rotated old logs are removed
rotating file /var/log/wtmp
log does not need rotating
```

Rather a lot of output, but if you step through it, you'll see that `logrotate` is indicating exactly what it'll do. Notice the invocation of the necessary commands for restarting the `httpd` service and sending the oldest compressed archive file via email to a longer-term archive.

▲

Unfortunately, `logrotate` is only available in certain Linux and Unix distros as of this writing (Caldera, Red Hat, Solaris), though there's no doubt it'll eventually be widely available to the general Unix community.

Not to fear, however, because the last section of this hour will explore a shell script that can do simple rotation, albeit in a less sophisticated manner.

Building Your Own Log Rotation Tool

Now that you've seen how `logrotate` works, you should be inspired to write a flexible, general purpose log rotator that can be easily distributed to all the different Unix systems you maintain. Fortunately, that's not too difficult to accomplish.

Task 16.5: Rotating Your Own Logs

▼ TASK

The basic algorithm for rotating log files is to recursively select all the files in the `/var/log` directory that are "plain files" (for example, not directories, not pipes, not sockets, not device drivers) and don't have a digit as the last letter of their name. With that list, create a set of new filenames that have the appropriate sequential suffixes, and rotate all the files.

1. Selecting just the files desired is perhaps the hardest part of this script, and it can be done with `find`. The required addition is the `-not` logical flag, which reverses the logic of the given test:

```
# find /var/log -type f -not -name '*[0-9]' -print
./messages
./lastlog
./secure
./maillog
./spooler
./wtmp
./gdm/:0.log
./xferlog
./pgsql
```

▼

```
./httpd/error_log
./httpd/access_log
./httpd/ssl_engine_log
./httpd/ssl_request_log
./httpd/ssl_scache.sem
./dmesg
./cron
./boot.log
./XFree86.0.log
./XFree86.9.log
./rpmpkgs
```

16

As you can see, this correctly listed all the log files that we'd like to rotate (and a few extra: the ssl_scache.sem file and the Xfree86 logs).

2. To refine this search further, we'll add a few more tweaks to the find loop, including a test to only match files greater than 1KB, and skipping the Xfree86 logs completely:

```
# cat rotatelogs.sh
#!/bin/sh

for name in `find /var/log -type f -size +1k -not -name '*[0-9]'
    -not -name 'XFree*' -not -name ':0*' -print`
do
   echo Log file $name is ready to rotate
done
```

This intermediate loop offers what we want:

```
# rotatelogs.sh
Log file /var/log/lastlog is ready to rotate
Log file /var/log/maillog is ready to rotate
Log file /var/log/wtmp is ready to rotate
Log file /var/log/gdm/:0.log is ready to rotate
Log file /var/log/httpd/error_log is ready to rotate
Log file /var/log/httpd/access_log is ready to rotate
Log file /var/log/dmesg is ready to rotate
Log file /var/log/cron is ready to rotate
Log file /var/log/rpmpkgs is ready to rotate
```

3. Now let's just jump into the entire script, so you can see how to accomplish the increments:

```
#!/bin/sh

cd /var/log

for name in `find . -type f -size +1k -not -name '*[0-9]' -not -name 'XFree*' -n
ot -name ":0*" -print`
do
   back1="${name}.1"; back2="${name}.2";
   back3="${name}.3"; back4="${name}.4";
```

```
      # rotate, starting with the oldest log
      if [ -f $back3 ] ; then
        mv -fv $back3 $back4
      fi
      if [ -f $back2 ] ; then
        mv -fv $back2 $back3
      fi
      if [ -f $back1 ] ; then
        mv -fv $back1 $back2
      fi
      if [ -f $name ] ; then
        mv -fv $name $back1
      fi
      touch $name; echo chmod 0600 $name
    done

    exit 0
```

4. That'll do what we want. Let's see what happens when we run this:

```
# rotatelogs.sh
`lastlog' -> `lastlog.1'
chmod 0600 lastlog
`maillog.3' -> `maillog.4'
`maillog.2' -> `maillog.3'
`maillog.1' -> `maillog.2'
`maillog' -> `maillog.1'
chmod 0600 maillog
`wtmp.1' -> `wtmp.2'
`wtmp' -> `wtmp.1'
chmod 0600 wtmp
chmod 0600 error_log
chmod 0600 access_log
`dmesg' -> `dmesg.1'
chmod 0600 dmesg
`cron.3' -> `cron.4'
`cron.2' -> `cron.3'
`cron.1' -> `cron.2'
`cron' -> `cron.1'
chmod 0600 cron
`rpmpkgs.3' -> `rpmpkgs.4'
`rpmpkgs.2' -> `rpmpkgs.3'
`rpmpkgs.1' -> `rpmpkgs.2'
`rpmpkgs' -> `rpmpkgs.1'
chmod 0600 rpmpkgs
`./httpd/error_log.3' -> `./httpd/error_log.4'
`./httpd/error_log.2' -> `./httpd/error_log.3'
`./httpd/error_log.1' -> `./httpd/error_log.2'
`./httpd/error_log' -> `./httpd/error_log.1'
chmod 0600 ./httpd/error_log
`./httpd/access_log.3' -> `./httpd/access_log.4'
`./httpd/access_log.2' -> `./httpd/access_log.3'
```

```
`./httpd/access_log.1' -> `./httpd/access_log.2'
`./httpd/access_log' -> `./httpd/access_log.1'
chmod 0600 ./httpd/access_log
```

Voila! The final step is to drop this into the appropriate `cron` file or directory, set it to run weekly, and we're done.

There are some refinements you could make to this script, most notably having the log files compressed with `gzip`, but in general, this will do a nice job of rotating all the log files on a given Unix system. Note that not all Unixes support the `-v` flag to `mv`, however, so you might have to chop that out before your script runs correctly.

16

Q&A

Q As it's impossible to document all possible Unix log files in this book, how do I figure out what program creates a given log file on *my* Unix system?

A Usually, the log file corresponds to the name of the program, which makes it easy (for example, `syslogd.log` for `syslog`, `ftpd.log` for `ftp`). If not, `man -k` is a smart way to look. You can also strip a trailing `d` if there is one.

Q Tracking hackers seems quite interesting. How often does it produce positive results?

A Well...the reality is that it's very unlikely that you'll accomplish anything meaningful. On the other hand, if we don't try to notify administrators of malicious users, it certainly won't improve things.

Workshop

Quiz

1. What are the two primary reasons to pay attention to your log files?

2. What's in the `messages` log file, and what is it commonly called on other Unix systems?

3. Using the tips suggested in this hour, what's in `ksyms` on a Linux system?

4. What's the basic technique for the reverse lookup of an IP address to ascertain its domain?

5. Earlier in the hour, we analyzed the `access_log` file to figure out what domains were hitting our Web server. How would you modify that command to identify just the most popular top-level domains?

Answers

1. Always pay attention to your log files so you are aware of attempted break-ins, and so you can keep track of disk space on your server.

2. The `messages` log file is used by `syslogd`, and on some systems it's called `/var/log/syslog`.

3. On a Linux box:

```
# man -k ksyms
genksyms                  (8)  - generate symbol version information
ksyms                     (8)  - display exported kernel symbols
```

4. Use the `host` command and make sure you specify the `-dv` flags for maximal output (see the man page).

5. There are a couple of ways to accomplish this, but I really like using the `rev` command to reverse the domain name, cut the first field out, reverse it again, and do "the usual" sequence after that:

```
# awk '{print $1}' access_log  | rev | cut -d. -f1 | rev | sort | \
  uniq -c | sort -rn | head -10
   2256 net
   2198 com
    570 es
    348 us
    339 pl
    317 edu
    311 249
    228 ca
    205 uk
    198 55
```

In the next hour we'll move to a new topic—network configuration. We'll start with an exploration of IP addresses and netmasks, and then we'll look at the steps necessary to configure a Unix box to work on an Ethernet or PPP network.

PART VI

Network Topics

Hour

Hour **17**

Basic Network Configuration

It's hard to imagine a computer, Unix or otherwise, that isn't directly connected to the Internet. Whether via a direct LAN connection in an office, a high-speed home connection through a digital subscriber line (DSL) or cable modem, or, perhaps a modem/router combination to power your network, if you're administering a Unix system, you need to know how to get it on—and keep it on—the Internet. Even if you're still stuck with a modem.

That's what the next few hours are all about. Starting with this first hour that explores how to hook a Unix system into an existing hard-coded IP or DHCP network, we'll extend coverage in subsequent hours to include network services, domain name servers, and the complex but critical `sendmail` program.

In this hour, we'll cover

- Connecting to the Internet using Linux
- Configuring your network with other Unixes
- Testing and evaluating connectivity

Hooking Up a Linux Box to the Internet

Whether you're adding a Unix box to your existing network, or whether you're adding a Windows or Macintosh, there are two basic types of connections: hard-coded IP addresses and DHCP. Older facilities and those sites that have had complex networks for years often still run with fixed IP addresses for each system. In this scenario, you'll assign a unique, unused address within the available *address range* for each workstation or network device on the LAN.

This implies that your facility has either installed a proxy server that enables you to use IP addresses independent of the rest of the Internet[1], or your facility has either a Class B IP block or one or more Class C blocks. Each Class C block has 254 addresses, and each Class B block has more than 65,000 addresses.

> It's worth noting that an IP address block is .0 to .255, but that by convention .0 and .255 are reserved for loopback (a shorthand for your own system) and broadcast (a shorthand for all systems on the local network), and aren't assigned individual workstations or devices.

Much more common than fixed IP addresses is a dynamic IP assignment protocol. That's what the Point-to-Point Protocol (PPP) is, as used by America Online, Earthlink, and other ISPs. Within a LAN, however, PPP proves less efficient than the alternative, the Dynamic Host Configuration Protocol (DHCP).

Task 17.1: Hooking Up a Linux System

If you are running DHCP, the job of hooking a new system up to the network is a breeze: The only task required is to specify DHCP as the connection choice during the initial installation of the operating system.

Hard-coded IP systems are a bit more tricky to configure. There are six essential numbers you'll need: the new system IP address, the netmask, the gateway (or router) address for the new system (which will vary depending on which subnet the system is connected into), a network and broadcast address, and at least one domain name system (DNS) server address.

1. If you're unsure whether your Linux box is trying to connect to the Internet via DHCP or a fixed IP, the place to look on a Red Hat system is in /etc/sysconfig.

---

[1]*This works because the proxy server automatically maps internal IP addresses to an IP address known by the rest of the Internet for all external queries. It also helps keep your internal network private, a great side effect.*

First off, make sure you've enabled networking in the first place by looking in
`network`:

```
# cat /etc/sysconfig/network
NETWORKING=yes
HOSTNAME=sombrero.dsldesigns.net
```

This is also where the hostname is set. Make sure you specify a full domain path
here, rather than just the basic hostname. Or not…(see the Caution).

> The contents of the `network` file is a fine example of the divergence of stan-
> dardization even within the Linux world: Red Hat encourages sysadmins to
> use the hostname and not the domain name; SuSE Linux uses the hostname,
> and has a separate variable (in `/etc/rc.local`, just like Mac OS X) called
> `FQHOSTNAME` for the hostname and domain together; and Mandrake has two
> variables in its configuration file, `HOSTNAME` and `DOMAINNAME`. Pay attention to
> the configuration material included with your Linux system to ensure that
> you set yours correctly if you're changing things post-installation!

17

The details of how the system talks with the rest of the network is contained within the
interface configuration file for the specific interface. Most likely, the system uses `eth0` as
the default Ethernet configuration, so the configuration file in question is `/etc/syscon-
fig/network-scripts/ifcfg-eth0`:

```
# cat ifcfg-eth0
DEVICE=eth0
BOOTPROTO=dhcp
ONBOOT=yes
TYPE=Ethernet
USERCTL=no
PEERDNS=no
NETWORK=0.0.0.0
BROADCAST=255.255.255.255
```

> Remember the filename mnemonic here: `if` = interface, and `cfg` = config,
> so `ifcfg-eth0` is the interface configuration file for the `eth0` Ethernet
> connection.

Most of the fields in this file are unnecessary on a system that's using DHCP, but
the critical one to eyeball is `BOOTPROTO`. If that's DHCP, as we see here, the system
kicks off a program called the DHCP client daemon (`dhcpcd`) that manages the
client-side DHCP interaction.

2. The default setup for dhcpcd is fine for 99% of the situations that you're likely to encounter as a Unix system administrator. The program has a variety of options that can be specified in the ifcfg file. These are alluded to in the following fragment of the important /sbin/ifup script, which brings up a specified interface:

```
if [ -n "${DYNCONFIG}" ]; then
    PUMPARGS=$PUMPARGS
    DHCPCDARGS="$DHCPCDARGS -n"
    if [ -n "${DHCP_HOSTNAME}" ]; then
        PUMPARGS="-h ${DHCP_HOSTNAME}"
        DHCPCDARGS="-h ${DHCP_HOSTNAME}"
    fi
    if [ -n "${NEEDHOSTNAME}" ]; then
        PUMPARGS="${PUMPARGS} --lookup-hostname"
        DHCPCDARGS="${DHCPCDARGS} -H"
    fi
    if [ "${PEERDNS}" = "no" ]; then
        PUMPARGS="${PUMPARGS} -d"
        DHCPCDARGS="${DHCPCDARGS} -R"
    fi
```

If you ignore the pump options (pump is an older alternative to dhcpcd in Linux, and most sites ignore it except for historical reasons), you can see that the arguments given to dhcpcd are the initial value of DHCPCDARGS plus -n, -h *dhcp hostname* if specified as DHCP_HOSTNAME, -H if the system hostname should be set by the DHCP server (controlled by the presence of NEEDHOSTNAME in the config file), and -R if the existing /etc/resolv.conf DNS server list file should *not* be replaced by the information given by the DHCP server.

That's a bit confusing, so let's look again at the stock DHCP configuration. The variables that can affect how dhcpcd is invoked are DHCP_HOSTNAME, NEEDHOSTNAME, and PEERDNS. You'll notice that in /etc/sysconfig/network-scripts/ifcfg-eth0 the variable PEERDNS is set to "no," but the others are not referenced. This means that dhcpcd is invoked as

```
dhcpcd -n -R
```

which, as expected, prevents dhcpcd from overwriting the /etc/resolv.conf file, but otherwise assumes that the system is properly set up with its correct hostname.

That's the -R flag explained. What about the -n that's used regardless of configuration? Well, recall that DHCP is the Dynamic Host Configuration Protocol. One subtle ramification of the "dynamic" part of this is that while a DHCP server will assign an IP address to a specific workstation on request, it doesn't guarantee that IP address will stick with that workstation forever. Instead, systems are given a *lease* on their DHCP information, and have to renew the lease (for example, confirm that they're still up and online) with the DHCP server every so often.

▼ It's a lease renewal that is trigged by the -n flag to dhcpcd; though if the system is just starting up from scratch a renewal will have the effect of requesting a new IP address.

The internals of the DHCP protocol are quite interesting, but a bit beyond the focus of this particular book. If you'd like to learn more, a great place to start is at the Internet Software Consortium, where they also have a good alternative DHCP client protocol implementation that's freely available: http://www.isc.org/products/DHCP/.

3. To see what information the DHCP server has handed the client program, peek at the information file in /etc/dhcpcd:

```
# cd /etc/dhcpcd
# ls
dhcpcd-eth0.cache  dhcpcd-eth0.info
# cat *info
IPADDR=192.168.131.67
NETMASK=255.255.255.0
NETWORK=192.168.131.0
BROADCAST=192.168.131.255
GATEWAY=192.168.131.254
DNS=192.216.138.10
DHCPSID=192.168.131.254
DHCPGIADDR=0.0.0.0
DHCPSIADDR=0.0.0.0
DHCPCHADDR=00:03:FF:FF:FF:FC
DHCPSHADDR=00:03:FF:FF:FF:FF
DHCPSNAME=
LEASETIME=4294967295
RENEWALTIME=536870911
REBINDTIME=536870911
```

The time values are in seconds since January 1, 1970, and you can see by the significant difference between LEASETIME and RENEWALTIME that this particular DHCP server hands out (virtual) IP addresses until a point far, far into the future, without any renewal of lease required. Many DHCP configurations will differ in this regard, and it's a policy setting accessible within the DHCP server itself.

The time value of seconds-since January 1, 1970 is a typical Unix-ism, but *not* one you can count on definitively. Each Unix flavor has the option of defining its own "epoch" for the seconds-since date format. Check your ctime(3) man page for a likely spot where it's defined for your OS.

▼

17

4. By contrast with the DHCP client, consider the same two configuration files on a Linux system with fixed IP addresses, on a completely different network:

```
# cd /etc/sysconfig
# cat network
NETWORKING=yes
HOSTNAME=staging.intuitive.com
# cat network-scripts/ifcfg-eth0
DEVICE=eth0
BOOTPROTO=static
ONBOOT=yes
IPADDR=10.10.2.200
GATEWAY=10.10.2.1
TYPE=Ethernet
USERCTL=no
NETMASK=255.255.255.0
NETWORK=10.10.2.0
BROADCAST=10.10.2.255
PEERDNS=no
```

Clearly, having a fixed IP address requires that other information be included, so let's spend a few minutes talking about the different values required and how to calculate them.

The first value is the IP address itself, of course, and that should be easy to ascertain based on your network. If you're using fixed IPs, you have a block of them and should have a master allocation table (perhaps just a sheet of paper in your desk drawer—a not-uncommon solution) that has IP address and host pairs for each of the IP addresses in the block. Those that haven't yet been assigned are blank and available.

In our office, we have a nonadjacent block of five IP addresses, one of which is used by the gateway itself, so our IP allocation table looks like Table 17.1.

TABLE 17.1 Typical Fixed IP Allocation Table

IP Address	Assigned To
198.76.82.129	Gateway
198.76.82.131	Laptop
198.76.82.132	G4 Mac
198.76.82.150	Win2K and iMac (shared, ugh!)
198.76.82.151	HP LAN printer

▼ As you can see, we have fewer IP addresses than we need, which is why the PC and iMac system are sharing one IP. This is *not* a good configuration[2]. The solution is for us to set up one of the systems as a DHCP server, but we'll get to that a bit later in this hour.

In total, our ISP gave us the following information when we first gained network connectivity, as shown in Table 17.2.

TABLE 17.2   Information from our ISP

Field Name	Value
IP Range	198.76.82.131, 132, 150, 151
Gateway	198.76.82.129
Subnet Mask	255.255.255.128
DNS Servers	192.216.138.10 and .11

> By convention, if you see two IP addresses and the latter only has a single value prefaced by a dot, it means that the first three "octets" are the same, so the two DNS servers are 192.216.138.10 and 192.216.138.11.

These values can be directly dropped into the `/etc/sysconfig/network-scripts/ifcfg-eth0` file as `IPADDR`, `GATEWAY`, and `NETMASK`. In the earlier example, the values differed because that particular Linux server is on a different network (just in case you're trying to puzzle out why they're different values).

So where do `NETWORK` and `BROADCAST` come from? Unless you've been given specific values by your connectivity provider, most often those values are simply the first three octets of the IP address with a trailing `0` or `255`. In the case of the configuration details given by our ISP, we'd specify a `NETWORK=198.76.82.0` and a `BROADCAST=198.76.82.255`.

The only other file to create is `/etc/resolv.conf`, a list of the DNS servers available to the system. The format is quite straightforward:

```
# cat /etc/resolv.conf
dns1.dsldesigns.net 192.216.138.10
dns2.dsldesigns.net 192.216.138.11
```

▼ You can add as many name servers as you'd like to this file, and if you opt to have a DNS cache server (a topic we'll discuss in depth in Hour 18, "Running Your Own Name Server"), you'd add the IP address of the cache server here as well.

---

[2]*Among other things, this means that they can't both be on the Internet at the same time, a situation that often causes frustration in our office!*

5. Whether your network uses DHCP or fixed IP, this should be sufficient information to get things properly configured and on the network. To actually bring the system online, you can reboot (usually the preferred strategy), or you can use the ifup or init.d/network scripts.

I prefer using the init.d/network script because it allows status queries, too:

```
# ./network status
Configured devices:
lo eth0
Currently active devices:
eth0 lo
```

More importantly, you can easily restart all the networking services on a Red Hat Linux system with a single command:

```
# ./network restart
Shutting down interface eth0:         [ OK ]
Setting network parameters:           [ OK ]
Bringing up interface lo:             [ OK ]
Bringing up interface eth0:           [ OK ]
```

If you'd prefer working with just the Ethernet interface and not touching the loopback mechanism (lo), you can use the ifup and ifdown commands in /sbin:

```
# /sbin/ifdown eth0
# /sbin/ifup eth0
Determining IP information for eth0... done.
#
```

Typically, bringing down the interface has no output, and bringing up the interface offers only minimal feedback on success.

6. Another common task in the DHCP world is to set up a DHCP server. Although there are many nuances to this task, the basics are easy to explain. The DHCP server daemon is called dhcpd, probably most confusing part of configuring the service.

The configuration for dhcpd is stored in /etc/dhcpd.conf:

```
# cat /etc/dhcpd.conf
subnet 198.76.82.0 netmask 255.255.255.128 {
    option routers        198.76.82.129;
    option subnet-mask    255.255.255.128;
    option domain-name    "intuitive.com";
    option domain-name-servers   dns1.dsldesigns.net, dns2.dsldesigns.net;

    option time-offset    -8;      # Pacific Standard Time

    host imac {
      option host-name "imac.intuitive.com";
```

```
       hardware Ethernet 00:A0:DD:8E:C3:F9;
       fixed-address     198.76.82.151
    }

range 198.76.82.131 198.76.82.132
}
```

As you can see, most of the information is identical to that specified for a single client on the network. The host imac is the iMac system, and it's always assigned the same fixed IP address. Finally, the range of available IP addresses here is quite small: .131 to .132. Normally we'd have quite a few more IP addresses than that for the DHCP pool.

You'll want to create the empty dhcpd.leases file so that the server can create timestamp and lease information, which can easily be done with

touch /var/lib/dhcpd.leases

> The dhcpd server automatically rotates the dhcpd.leases file as needed, renaming the old lease file dhcpd.leases~. On very rare occasions the system could crash in the midst of this lease rotation, in which case you'll want to rename the ~ file back to the original name (for example, mv dhcpd.leases~ dhcpd.leases) to ensure that any DHCP leases currently assigned are still valid and known.

To start or stop the server, create the appropriate link (in Red Hat Linux, at least) to the /etc/rc.d/init.d/dhcp from within the /etc/rc.d/rc*n*.d directory for run state *n*.

Although configuring a Linux system to be a good network citizen isn't quite as simple and straightforward as a Mac or Windows box, it's not too far off. If you opt to use some of the graphical interfaces to Linux (notably linuxconf), you can set up almost everything shown here in just a few minutes.

Also, if you find that you don't have dhcpd on your Red Hat Linux distro, it might be because you didn't install the optional packages on the additional CD-ROMs, or because you didn't specify the server configuration upon installation. Verify this by using RPM (rpm -qa | grep -i dhcp will do the trick). You can remedy this omission most easily by flipping back to Hour 8, "Unix Package Management," and searching Pbone or a similar archival site for the dhcp package, and installing it with rpm.

Network Configuration on Other Unixes

Before we go too far into the topic of other Unixes, please make sure that you didn't skip the last section because you aren't running Linux. There's lots of information that we won't repeat in this later section that you'll want to know.

The good news is that the basic concepts of DHCP client configuration and fixed IP configuration are the same regardless of which flavor of Unix the system you're configuring is running. The location of the specific configuration files—well, that's going to vary a bit as you might expect, but if you can identify all the critical values to feed into the configuration, it's not too bad.

Task 17.2: Configuring Solaris and Mac OS X

▼ TASK

Considering that Sun Microsystems widely touts its vision of the world as "The Network is the Computer," it would be reasonable to expect that configuring a Solaris system to be a full member of the Internet would be a breeze. Similarly, Apple has always had a significant advantage in how easily Mac OS lets you add systems to your network, an advantage that you would expect to translate into a straightforward configuration in the Mac OS X world.

And you'd be wrong in both cases.

1. To start out, the network configuration for a Solaris 8 system resides in a sprawl of different files, including /etc/resolv.conf, /etc/hostname.*ifname*, /etc/dhcp.*ifname*, /etc/nodename, /etc/inet/hosts, and more. Let's step through them, one by one, to see what's what:

   ```
   # cat /etc/resolv.conf
   search dsldesigns.net
   nameserver 192.216.138.10
   nameserver 192.216.138.11
   ```

   No big surprises—this file is fairly typical of DNS name server lists. The first line is worth mentioning because it's the primary spot where Solaris is told the domain name of the current system for DNS lookup purposes.

   Trying to figure out where to drop the proper hostname for this system is a bit more confusing, as it's located in *two* configuration files:

   ```
   # ls /etc/hostname.*
   /etc/hostname.pcn0
   # cat /etc/hostname.pcn0
   solaris.dsldesigns.net
   # cat /etc/nodename
   solaris.dsldesigns.net
   ```

▼   You will need to change both of these files to update the name of your host, and if
     you've guessed that pcn0 is the Ethernet interface on a Solaris 8 system, you'd be
     correct.

2. Digging deeper than this rudimentary configuration causes us to hit a bit of a stum-
    bling block: Solaris is in the midst of transitioning from a pure IPv4 to a mixed
    IPv4/IPv6 environment, and some of the configuration files in Solaris 8 (and ear-
    lier) will be deprecated in Solaris 9. Chief among these is /etc/hosts, which also
    lists your current host name, among others. From Solaris 7 to Solaris 8 they dupli-
    cated /etc/hosts as /etc/inet/hosts (which we'll examine in a second), but by
    Solaris 9, all of these should be replaced by the file /etc/inet/ipnodes to ensure
    maximum confusion (well, that's not why Sun did it, that's just the likely effect).

    Anyway, because the sample system is still running Solaris 8, we have just about
    every possible configuration file still on the disk, even if some of them might be
    secretly marked for obsolescence....

    The router (gateway) IP address is in a file called defaultrouter:

    ```
    # cat /etc/defaultrouter
    198.76.82.129
    ```

    The subnet mask is stored in /etc/netmasks, which turns out to be a symbolic link
    to one of the inet directory files, /etc/inet/netmasks:

    ```
    # cat /etc/inet/netmasks
    #
    # The netmasks file associates Internet Protocol (IP) address
    # masks with IP network numbers.
    #
    #       network-number  netmask
    #
    # The term network-number refers to a number obtained from the Internet
    Network
    # Information Center.  Currently this number is restricted to being a class
    # A, B, or C network number.  In the future we should be able to support
    # arbitrary network numbers per the Classless Internet Domain Routing
    # guidelines.
    #
    # Both the network-number and the netmasks are specified in
    # "decimal dot" notation, e.g:
    #
    #               128.32.0.0 255.255.255.0
    #
    198.76.82.128   255.255.255.128
    ```

▼   Lots of helpful explanatory information in this directory, as you can see.

It's worth noting that, as stated in the comment, Solaris up through version 8, at least, does not support classless domain routing. This means that if you have a nonadjacent subset of a Class C IP range, Solaris can only consider it as a complete Class C for networking purposes. This could prove a significant limitation, depending on your network topology.

The mirror of `/etc/hosts` is `/etc/inet/hosts`:

```
# cat /etc/hosts
#
# Internet host table
#
127.0.0.1        localhost
198.76.82.131    laptop
198.76.82.132    mac
198.76.82.150    win2k
198.76.82.155    solaris loghost solaris.dsldesigns.net
# cat /etc/inet/hosts
#
# Internet host table
#
127.0.0.1        localhost
198.76.82.131    laptop
198.76.82.132    mac
198.76.82.150    win2k
198.76.82.155    solaris loghost solaris.dsldesigns.net
```

It turns out that `/etc/hosts` is a symbolic link to `/etc/inet/hosts`, so there's a quite logical reason that they're always in sync! There's a third `hosts` file to check too, however—the new `ipnodes`:

```
# cat ipnodes
#
# Internet host table
#
::1              localhost
127.0.0.1        localhost
198.76.82.131    laptop
198.76.82.132    mac
198.76.82.150    win2k
198.76.82.155    solaris solaris.dsldesigns.net
```

Again, the system tries to keep them all in sync (though notice the first noncommented line in `ipnodes` is new: `::1`).

3. If you're keeping track, we've figured out where to place just about every snippet of information, *except our IP address*. Where does that get stored? It turns out that it's dropped into the `/etc/hosts` file, so let's go back and get a better understanding of

the relationship between the files where the fully-qualified hostname is specified (officially the nodename file), and the matching value appears, in the hosts file:

```
# cat /etc/nodename
solaris.dsldesigns.net
# grep `cat /etc/nodename` /etc/inet/hosts
198.76.82.155   solaris loghost solaris.dsldesigns.net
```

To change the IP address of this particular system, therefore, we need only change its address in the hosts file and ensure that any host renaming therein also matches exactly the name specified in the nodename file, too.

We can check the IP address by invoking the ifconfig program (which we'll talk about a bit later in this hour):

```
# /sbin/ifconfig pcn0
pcn0: flags=1000843<UP,BROADCAST,RUNNING,MULTICAST,IPv4> mtu 1500 index 2
        inet 198.76.82.155 netmask ffffff80 broadcast 198.76.82.255
        ether 0:50:56:54:a5:9d
```

Notice in particular the inet value in the second line to confirm the IP address of this host.

4. To switch from a fixed IP scheme to a DHCP connectivity solution, we need to delve into the world of dhcpagent, the default DHCP client software for Solaris. Pleasantly, Solaris includes a bunch of DHCP-related commands:

```
# man -k dhcp | grep 1
dhcpagent       dhcpagent (1m)  - Dynamic Host Configuration Protocol (DHCP)
➥client daemon
dhcpconfig      dhcpconfig (1m) - DHCP service configuration utility
dhcpinfo        dhcpinfo (1)    - display values of parameters received
➥through DHCP
dhcpmgr         dhcpmgr (1m)    - graphical interface for managing DHCP
service
dhtadm          dhtadm (1m)     - DHCP configuration table management utility
in.dhcpd        in.dhcpd (1m)   - Dynamic Host Configuration Protocol server
pntadm          pntadm (1m)     - DHCP network table management utility
```

The specific configuration file is named after the interface that requires a DHCP connection—in this case, /etc/dhcp.pcn0. But wait, there's great news! Delete the contents of a couple of fixed IP files and create a bunch of empty DHCP-related files, and the system will automatically create the configuration file and any other DHCP file needed at the next system boot. Very helpful.

Here's exactly what we'd need to do to switch from a fixed IP to a DHCP configuration upon the next boot:

```
# alias zero="cat /dev/null > "
# zero /etc/hostname.pcn0
# zero /etc/dhcp.pcn0
# zero /etc/notrouter
```

17

```
# zero /etc/defaultrouter
# zero /etc/default/dhcp
# zero /etc/resolv.conf
```

That's just about it. The files that existed and were zeroed had their contents erased, and the files that didn't exist now exist (notably /etc/dhcp.pcn0).

The only other step is to chop just about everything out of the /etc/inet/hosts file so that it has a line for the localhost and nothing else. It should look like this:

```
# cat /etc/inet/hosts
127.0.0.1            localhost
```

The other lines associated with this host will be filled in upon boot and IP assignment by the DHCP client.

> If you want to learn how to set up a Solaris system as a DHCP server, your best bet is to download the Solaris-compatible dhcpd from the Internet Software Consortium Web site (www.isc.org) and follow their clear, coherent directions.

5. Let's turn our attention to Mac OS X before we leave the question of configuring Unix systems for network connectivity. The Mac is, well, quite a different creature when it comes to command-line based network configuration.

   Frankly, if you're rational, your best bet is to simply use the Mac OS X System Preference Network panel, as shown in Figure 17.1.

FIGURE 17.1

The Network panel in System Preferences.

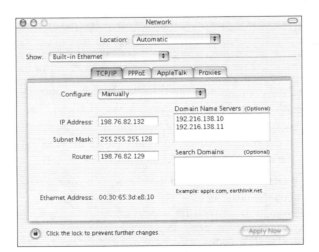

But how dull life would be if we stuck to being rational and the simple, smart way to solve problems.

Instead, let's dig into Mac OS X a little bit to find out where the information from this control panel is saved: If we can identify the specific archival file, we can then modify it by hand, right? Kinda yes, kinda no.

6. The file that stores these configuration values is part of the Mac OS X System Configuration area, and can be found in /var/db:

```
# head -20 /var/db/SystemConfiguration/preferences.xml
<?xml version="1.0" encoding="UTF-8"?>
<!DOCTYPE plist SYSTEM
"file://localhost/System/Library/DTDs/PropertyList.dtd">
<plist version="0.9">
<dict>
    <key>CurrentSet</key>
    <string>/Sets/0</string>
    <key>NetworkServices</key>
    <dict>
        <key>0</key>
        <dict>
            <key>AppleTalk</key>
            <dict>
                <key>ConfigMethod</key>
                <string>Node</string>
            </dict>
            <key>DNS</key>
            <dict>
                <key>ServerAddresses</key>
                <array>
                    <string>192.216.138.10</string>
                    <string>192.216.138.11</string>
```

This is just the top of what turns out to be a 461-line XML[3] file. No neat and easy `variable: value` sequences, but rather a complex and confusing XML-formatted file. Nonetheless, once you recognize that the `variable: value` sequence is more likely to look like

```
<key>variable</key>
    <string>value</string>
```

Then you can start to see a little bit of what's going on within the `preferences.xml` file shown in the preceding code. For example, AppleTalk has a `ConfigMethod` of `Node`, and the DNS service is using the `ServerAddresses` of `192.216.138.10` and `192.216.138.11`.

---

[3]*XML is the eXtensible Markup Language, a variant of HTML that was designed specifically to enable easily parsed data in a universal format. It's simultaneously brilliant that Apple uses it for preference files, and darn frustrating as it's very hard to work with on the command line.*

17

▼

Armed with this, let's work backward and see if we can identify the network configuration values in this file, starting with IP address:

```
# grep -5 198.76.82 preferences.xml
            </dict>
            <key>IPv4</key>
            <dict>
                <key>Addresses</key>
                <array>
                    <string>198.76.82.132</string>
                </array>
                <key>ConfigMethod</key>
                <string>Manual</string>
                <key>Router</key>
                <string>198.76.82.129</string>
                <key>SubnetMasks</key>
                <array>
                        <string>255.255.255.128</string>
                </array>
            </dict>
```

That was a good call looking for five lines of context (the -5 flag) around the matches for the Class C (the first three numbers in the IP address) here. You can see all the relevant variables from the Network panel: Addresses, Router, SubnetMasks, and from earlier in this section, DNS ServerAddresses.

Therefore, if you really want to, are comfortable editing XML files, and are ready to live life on the very edge of danger, you could directly edit this file. Make a backup copy first, however, just in case.

7. This would be an interesting time to try using sed, the stream editor, which is perfect for in-place editing tasks of this nature.

To copy this configuration to a second computer, you could transfer the preferences.xml file across via scp (secure cp, which allows for easy copying of files across a network in a safe, encrypted fashion), perhaps, and change just the IP address:

```
scp referencehost:/var/db/SystemConfiguration/preferences.xml - | \
  sed 's/198.76.82.132/198.76.82.133/' > \
  /var/db/SystemConfiguration/preferences.xml
```

This would copy the file from the master referencehost, change the old .132 IP address to the new .133 IP address, then save the newly changed file in the correct place. We'd still need to ensure that the file ownership and permissions are correct:

```
# cd /var/db/SystemConfiguration
# ls -l preferences.xml
-rw-r--r--  1 root  wheel  11151 Apr  6 22:46 preferences.xml
```

▼

▼ But otherwise that would work, and it would also enable us to quickly duplicate DHCP configurations from a single DHCP client reference system.

There are other issues regarding Mac OS X network configuration that we're going to skip here, because as you can see, command-line based network configuration is not a trivial task in Mac OS X. In fact, it's really the first area where you can see that the *Mac* part of Mac OS X has become more important than the Unix under-

▲ neath it (Darwin).

> Don't be fooled into thinking that because Mac OS X has Darwin under-
> neath, it's completely compatible with Darwin or FreeBSD, its ancestor. It's
> not. Those use `/etc/iftab` and `/etc/hostconfig` to specify network parame-
> ters, but Mac OS X ignores those files for network configuration issues *if the
> file SystemConfiguration/preferences.xml is present.* If you wanted to
> really hack around, you could remove that and see what happens, but
> you're way outta warranty, and few people will be able to help you resusci-
> tate the client at that point. Oh, and the user might not appreciate it either!

There is an amazing amount of variety between the different flavors of Unix when it comes to networking code. It's odd, because network connectivity is the "killer capabil-ity" of Unix, and the reason why it's still in widespread use over 25 years after first ship-ping to customers. Can you imagine running Windows 95 in the year 2020? Or Mac OS 9 in 2024?

However, critical or not, it's one area where you'll need to study the manuals and docu-mentation included with your particular flavor or flavors of Unix, to ensure that your beliefs and understanding of the boot process and network configuration sequence matches that of the OS you're administering.

Testing and Evaluating Connectivity

One last topic worth discussion in this hour before we wrap up is a group of the network diagnostic utilities included with Unix. Different Unixes have different programs for the most part, but there are a few core applications and system utilities that can be quite informative, notably `ifconfig`, `netstat`, and `ping`.

Each of these commands deserves more space than we'll be able to offer in this book, so you're encouraged to read the `man` page for each one and experiment to learn more about its capabilities.

17

Task 17.3: Evaluating Connectivity

The first task for evaluating connectivity is to see how the current system is configured, then to step out onto the Internet and use ping and traceroute to see how things are traveling about....

1. To evaluate your network configuration, the first and only important stop is ifconfig. Use the -a flag to ask for all interfaces on this machine, or to specify the name of the Ethernet interface itself:

```
# /sbin/ifconfig -a
eth0      Link encap:Ethernet  HWaddr 00:A0:C9:AD:20:E2
          inet addr:10.10.2.200  Bcast:10.10.2.255  Mask:255.255.255.0
          UP BROADCAST RUNNING MULTICAST  MTU:1500  Metric:1
          RX packets:37310 errors:0 dropped:0 overruns:0 frame:0
          TX packets:36045 errors:0 dropped:0 overruns:0 carrier:0
          collisions:0 txqueuelen:100
          RX bytes:4134689 (3.9 Mb)  TX bytes:15175268 (14.4 Mb)
          Interrupt:5 Base address:0xa000

lo        Link encap:Local Loopback
          inet addr:127.0.0.1  Mask:255.0.0.0
          UP LOOPBACK RUNNING  MTU:16436  Metric:1
          RX packets:98 errors:0 dropped:0 overruns:0 frame:0
          TX packets:98 errors:0 dropped:0 overruns:0 carrier:0
          collisions:0 txqueuelen:0
          RX bytes:7176 (7.0 Kb)  TX bytes:7176 (7.0 Kb)
```

Red Hat is notable in that its ifconfig offers quite a bit of information (most are more succinct than this). The eth0 is the Ethernet interface, and you can see that it has an Internet address of 10.10.2.200 on this particular server, with a broadcast address of 10.10.2.255 and a network mask of 255.255.255.0.

One important tuning value is the maximum transfer unit (MTU) value, which is 1500 here. For Ethernet, 1,500 bytes is the maximum MTU according to the protocol, but if you have FDDI token ring, you could kick this up to 4,500 for better network throughput. If you are on Ethernet and your MTU is less than 1500, use ifconfig to restore it to its proper value (for example, ifconfig eth0 mtu 1500).

The UP starting the third line of output is important too—it shows that the system thinks that the Ethernet connection is up and alive. Always good. Note also that the eth0 interface has received (RX) 37,310 packets of information with no errors, no dropped packets, and no overruns. This is also very good to see, and it's also transmitted (TX) 36,045 packets with no glitches.

> If your client systems have RX and TX errors, or drops/overruns that account for more than about 10% of the overall packets, you might have overly busy subnets. The solution is to break up your subnets further. If you have zero (as seen here), the logical conclusion is that there's plenty of room for more servers on the wire.

The summary line showing RX bytes is a nice addition that saves some hand calculations: This server has received packets totaling 3.9MB and transmitted 14.4MB of packets.

2. In contrast to the loquacious output from Red Hat Linux, consider the same `ifconfig` output from Mac OS X:

```
# ifconfig -a
lo0: flags=8049<UP,LOOPBACK,RUNNING,MULTICAST> mtu 16384
        inet 127.0.0.1 netmask 0xff000000
en0: flags=8863<UP,BROADCAST,b6,RUNNING,SIMPLEX,MULTICAST> mtu 1500
        inet 198.76.82.132 netmask 0xffffff80 broadcast 198.76.82.255
        ether 00:30:65:3d:e8:10
        media: autoselect (10baseT/UTP <half-duplex>) status: active
        supported media: none autoselect 10baseT/UTP <half-duplex> 10baseT/UTP
        <full-duplex> 100baseTX <half-duplex> 100baseTX <full-duplex>
```

Quite different, and no RX/TX statistics here at all. Same proper 1500-byte MTU, though.

Solaris offers an even more concise result:

```
# /sbin/ifconfig -a
lo0: flags=1000849<UP,LOOPBACK,RUNNING,MULTICAST,IPv4> mtu 8232 index 1
        inet 127.0.0.1 netmask ff000000
pcn0: flags=1000843<UP,BROADCAST,RUNNING,MULTICAST,IPv4> mtu 1500 index 2
        inet 198.76.82.155 netmask ffffff80 broadcast 198.76.82.255
        ether 0:50:56:54:a5:9d
```

Even more minimal, but it still offers the core information necessary for verifying the setup of the Ethernet interface, with the IP address, netmask (albeit in a more difficult-to-interpret format), broadcast address, and MTU.

3. It's useful to have a good picture of the network traffic on a given system, and that's what the multipurpose `netstat` network status command offers.

```
# netstat
Active Internet connections (w/o servers)
Proto Recv-Q Send-Q Local Address        Foreign Address        State
tcp      0     208 10.10.2.200:ssh        dsl-132.dsldesign:49172 ESTABLISHED
```

17

▼
```
Active UNIX domain sockets (w/o servers)
Proto RefCnt Flags       Type       State        I-Node Path
unix  7      [ ]         DGRAM                   905    /dev/log
unix  2      [ ]         DGRAM                   1226
unix  2      [ ]         DGRAM                   1207
unix  2      [ ]         DGRAM                   1162
unix  2      [ ]         DGRAM                   961
unix  2      [ ]         DGRAM                   914
unix  2      [ ]         STREAM     CONNECTED    628
```

By default, the first section shows the active established network connections (here it's showing an ssh connection to 10.10.2.200 from dsl-132.dsldesign, with a connection ID of 49172). The second section is a list of all open sockets, some associated with daemons, some tied to specific files (such as /dev/log), and most fairly cryptic.

Similar output is produced by netstat on other Unixes, though the exact format often varies. Solaris has a particularly helpful output format:

```
# netstat

TCP: IPv4
    Local Address         Remote Address       Swind Send-Q Rwind Recv-Q  State
------------------- -------------------- ----- ------- ----- ------ -------
solaris.32804         mac.6000             33304       0 66608      0 ESTABLISHED

Active UNIX domain sockets
Address  Type        Vnode       Conn  Local Addr      Remote Addr
e106dd88 stream-ord  00000000       00000000
e106dea8 stream-ord  e0e79920 00000000   /tmp/.X11-unix/X0
```

Clearly denoting that there's a remote X11 event occurring.

Various flags to netstat produce different output. Most useful is -a, which offers a different format that includes what protocols are listening, as well as established:

```
# netstat -a
Active Internet connections (servers and established)
Proto Recv-Q Send-Q Local Address           Foreign Address         State
tcp        0      0 *:32768                 *:*                     LISTEN
tcp        0      0 localhost.localdo:32769 *:*                     LISTEN
tcp        0      0 *:sunrpc                *:*                     LISTEN
tcp        0      0 *:http                  *:*                     LISTEN
tcp        0      0 *:ssh                   *:*                     LISTEN
tcp        0      0 localhost.localdom:smtp *:*                     LISTEN
tcp        0      0 *:https                 *:*                     LISTEN
tcp        0    224 10.10.2.200:ssh         dsl-132.dsldesign:49172
➥ESTABLISHED
udp        0      0 *:32768                 *:*
udp        0      0 *:793                   *:*
▼ udp      0      0 *:sunrpc                *:*
```

```
Active UNIX domain sockets (servers and established)
Proto RefCnt Flags       Type      State       I-Node Path
unix  7      [ ]         DGRAM                 905    /dev/log
unix  2      [ ]         DGRAM                 1226
unix  2      [ ]         DGRAM                 1207
unix  2      [ ]         DGRAM                 1162
unix  2      [ ]         DGRAM                 961
unix  2      [ ]         DGRAM                 914
unix  2      [ ]         STREAM    CONNECTED   628
```

We can see that this system is supporting SunRPC (remote procedure call), http (for the Apache Web server), ssh (secure shell), smtp (for e-mail), https (secure Apache connections) and that there's an established ssh connection. There are also a few UDP listeners.

The output of netstat -a is one way you can verify that the services you think you've disabled really aren't running. (See Hour 19, "Running Internet Services," for more information about disabling services.)

4. The netstat command also offers transmit/receive statistics in a quite concise manner if the -i flag is used:

```
# netstat -i
Kernel Interface table
Iface   MTU Met   RX-OK RX-ERR RX-DRP RX-OVR   TX-OK TX-ERR TX-DRP TX-OVR Flg
eth0    1500  0   37507      0      0      0   36220      0      0      0 BMRU
lo     16436  0      98      0      0      0      98      0      0      0 LRU
```

This is consistent with what ifconfig reported: lots of in and out packets with nary a single hiccup or glitch.

Solaris reports I and O (in and out) packets, rather than RX and TX packets, but otherwise the data is quite similarly presented:

```
# netstat -i
Name Mtu  Net/Dest       Address     Ipkts  Ierrs Opkts  Oerrs Collis Queue
lo0  8232 loopback       localhost   125    0     125    0     0      0
pcn0 1500 198.76.82.128  solaris     6780   0     4728   0     0      0
```

Finally, Mac OS X is a bit more odd, but the same basic information *is* included in this longer output:

```
# netstat -i
Name Mtu   Network   Address          Ipkts Ierrs   Opkts Oerrs Coll
lo0  16384 <Link>                     1662  0       1662  0     0
lo0  16384 127       localhost        1662  0       1662  0     0
en0  1500  <Link>    00.30.65.3d.e8.10 6565 0       11226 0     0
en0  1500  198.76.82.128 dsl-132.dsldesi 6565 0     11226 0     0
```

Ipkts are input packets (RXs), and Opkts are output packets (TXs).

5. Let's turn from analyzing the system to exploring the network connectivity itself. There are two basic tools to accomplish this task: ping and traceroute.

The ping command, which takes its name from the sound a submarine sonar makes when trying to identify a remote object, sends an ECHO_REQUEST packet to a specified remote system, times the duration of the send plus the echo back, and reports that to you.

By convention, the first step with ping is to always try and check the connection to the router. If that's up and working, we've confirmed that the network card is working, the Ethernet wire is okay, and that this computer can talk to its Ethernet card.

```
# ping -c 10 198.76.82.129
PING 198.76.82.129 (198.76.82.129): 56 data bytes
64 bytes from 198.76.82.129: icmp_seq=0 ttl=255 time=59.642 ms
64 bytes from 198.76.82.129: icmp_seq=1 ttl=255 time=33.371 ms
64 bytes from 198.76.82.129: icmp_seq=2 ttl=255 time=33.787 ms
64 bytes from 198.76.82.129: icmp_seq=3 ttl=255 time=33.842 ms
64 bytes from 198.76.82.129: icmp_seq=4 ttl=255 time=55.218 ms
64 bytes from 198.76.82.129: icmp_seq=5 ttl=255 time=33.934 ms
64 bytes from 198.76.82.129: icmp_seq=6 ttl=255 time=60.519 ms
64 bytes from 198.76.82.129: icmp_seq=7 ttl=255 time=69.425 ms
64 bytes from 198.76.82.129: icmp_seq=8 ttl=255 time=34.3 ms
64 bytes from 198.76.82.129: icmp_seq=9 ttl=255 time=34.241 ms

--- 198.76.82.129 ping statistics ---
10 packets transmitted, 10 packets received, 0% packet loss
round-trip min/avg/max = 33.371/44.827/69.425 ms
```

The -c 10 specifies that ping should send 10 ECHO_REQUEST packets, spaced one second apart by default. Each ping displays its own statistics, where you can see that system vagaries cause the echo time to vary from 33.3 milliseconds to 69.4 milliseconds. The last two lines are the most important: percentage of loss (0%) and average speed (44.8ms).

If you'd rather not see the individual lines of output, the -q flag hides them, limiting ping to the first and last lines of output only, as shown in this next example, where ping shows connection speed to the "other end of the wire," a DNS server at our ISP:

```
# ping -q -c10 dns1.dsldesigns.com
PING dns1.dsldesigns.com (192.216.138.10): 56 data bytes

--- dns1.dsldesigns.com ping statistics ---
10 packets transmitted, 10 packets received, 0% packet loss
round-trip min/avg/max = 33.851/58.407/113.713 ms
```

Remarkably similar performance to the local router, so the connection between them is clearly not a significant slowdown.

6. Finally, a few `ping`s to popular systems around the world can demonstrate overall connection speed:

```
# ping -q -c5 www.yahoo.com
PING www.yahoo.akadns.net (66.218.71.89): 56 data bytes

--- www.yahoo.akadns.net ping statistics ---
5 packets transmitted, 5 packets received, 0% packet loss
round-trip min/avg/max = 37.965/61.338/88.798 ms
```

An average of 61 milliseconds to Yahoo! and back—very fast.

```
# ping -q -c5 news.bbc.co.uk
PING newswww.bbc.net.uk (212.58.240.34): 56 data bytes

--- newswww.bbc.net.uk ping statistics ---
5 packets transmitted, 5 packets received, 0% packet loss
round-trip min/avg/max = 111.539/121.965/149.242 ms
```

A round trip of 121 milliseconds from California to London, where the BBC World Service hosts its Web server.

```
# ping -q -c5 www.koreaherald.co.kr
PING www.koreaherald.co.kr (211.200.28.40): 56 data bytes

--- www.koreaherald.co.kr ping statistics ---
5 packets transmitted, 0 packets received, 100% packet loss
```

This is an interesting situation because a Web browser will demonstrate that there's a site at this URL, so there must at least be a box answering queries from the Web. But it's not answering `ping`. How can that be?

It turns out that there are some forms of so-called *denial-of-service* attacks that essentially look like a vast flood of `ping` ECHO_REQUEST packets. As a result, many sites that are likely to see dissension/hackers will block all ECHO_REQUEST packets, leading to curious results, like a 100% packet loss on a `ping`.

```
# ping -qc5 www.news.co.kr
PING www.news.co.kr (203.248.249.170): 56 data bytes

--- www.news.co.kr ping statistics ---
5 packets transmitted, 5 packets received, 0% packet loss
round-trip min/avg/max = 160.874/172.319/201.883 ms
```

Another Korean site, but this one echoes back ECHO_REQUEST packets and produces an average `ping` time of 172 milliseconds. Not lightning fast, but if you consider that the little Ethernet packet traveled at least 5,600 miles in each direction, that's not a bad speed[4].

There's lots more that can be discussed about network connectivity and analysis, and much of the remainder of the book will focus on this critical and quite interesting topic.

---

[4]*If we assume 5,600 miles each way, that's 11,200 miles in 0.172 seconds, or a whopping 234.4 million miles per hour!*

Summary

This hour has covered the essentials of Unix network configuration, focusing on Red Hat Linux as a prototypical distro, and then exploring how things change on Solaris and Mac OS X. And change they do! Finally, we covered some testing and validation tools, and talked briefly about copying network configurations to multiple systems.

Q&A

Q I'm overwhelmed! Surely there are non-command-line ways to configure Unix systems other than Mac OS X? If so, why don't you talk about them here instead?

A The good news is that yes, there are GUI utilities for configuring networking in just about every Unix you'll find—if you can run a GUI interface. That's part of the problem; if you have a Unix system running as a server in a big collocation facility, or if you have a rack-mounted system in the MIS department, or if you are servicing 150 workstations, you might not be able to kick off an X application, let alone a full X Window System environment. Nonetheless, rational system administrators seek the fastest and easiest solutions, and a tool like linuxconf can be a lifesaver. Just beware of heterogeneous environments where you have lots of OSes that you are responsible for; how many different tools do you want to learn just to bring new clients up on the network? It's a conundrum.

Q What do you recommend, DHCP or fixed IP?

A Finally, an easy Q in the Q&A of this book! If you can, run DHCP, even for a small home network. It simplifies everything.

Workshop

Quiz

1. Which has more IP addresses, a Class B or a Class C address block?
2. What's a handy trick for figuring out the broadcast address and network address if you know the IP address?
3. What's the importance of the DHCP lease?
4. What's stored in /etc/resolv.conf?
5. In Solaris 9, /etc/hosts (which is really /etc/inet/hosts anyway) is going to be replaced by what configuration file?
6. Complete the sentence: If you're a smart Mac OS X system administrator and are very comfortable with Unix, your best bet to configure new clients so that they're on the network is _____.

Answers

1. A Class B block has 256 Class C blocks within it, and a Class C block has 254 usable IP addresses.

2. Drop the last of the octets in the IP address and replace it with 255 for the broadcast, and 0 for the network address. So, 192.37.18.33 would have the corresponding broadcast address of 192.37.18.255 and a network address of 192.37.18.0.

3. The DHCP server hands out IP addresses to DHCP clients for a specified amount of time, the duration or which is the lease. At the end of the lease, a client is required to renew its lease on the information or request a new IP address.

4. The names and IP addresses of the DNS servers for the system are in /etc/resolv.conf.

5. /etc/hosts will become /etc/inet/ipnodes.

6. If you're a smart Mac OS X system administrator and are very comfortable with Unix, your best bet to configure new clients so that they're on the network is to use the graphical Network control panel.

A common task among Unix admins is to set up a DNS or name server. This involves working with BIND, named, and setting up the /etc/resolv.conf file properly, as well as configuring and testing a DNS server, all of which we'll cover in the next hour. We'll also discuss traceroute, dig, and host, all important Unix system administrator commands.

17

Hour **18**

Running Your Own Name Server

A common task among Unix system administrators is setting up and running a domain name system (DNS) server. Though we're used to thinking of Web sites, e-mail recipient systems, and other network information as specific names, the Internet actually uses unique numbers. The DNS server system maps names to numbers.

When you type a URL into your Web browser, for example, it first contacts your local DNS server asking for the IP address of the Web host you are requesting. If your local DNS server does not know the IP address, it will then forward the request to another DNS server, often one of the root DNS servers[1]. The root server typically won't answer the query, but will instead forward you along, reporting the IP address of the authoritative DNS server for the domain you are requesting. Your local DNS server then contacts this DNS server, and finally receives the correct IP address.

---

[1]*There are 13 root servers scattered around the world. They all contain the IP addresses of the name servers that are registered with a particular domain.*

In this hour, we'll have a tour of the DNS system, with specific emphasis on how to maintain a DNS server on your Unix systems.

In this hour, you'll learn about

- Working with BIND and zone files
- Configuring `named`, the name server daemon
- Working with `rndc`, the best DNS admin tool
- Testing DNS installations

The Berkeley Internet Name Domain Package

To manage a DNS database, systems running as DNS servers often run the Berkeley Internet Name Domain (BIND) system, a powerful and flexible DNS server. RedHat Linux 7.2 ships with BIND version 9. Indeed, it turns out that early versions of BIND are notorious for having security problems, so if you're going to start running a DNS server, it's a smart idea to upgrade to the latest release. Of course, as with any software that interacts with the outside network, it's always a good idea to keep BIND up-to-date with the latest security patches and bug repairs.

> The official distribution of BIND is from the Internet Software Consortium (`www.isc.org`) and includes the DNS server `named`, the resolver library, and some very useful tools for analysis.

Task 18.1: Exploring BIND and Zone Files

It is important to note that `named` only needs to be run if you are going to be providing authoritative name services for one or more domains. What's an *authoritative name?* It's the official host on the Internet that's authorized by the domain name record to answer DNS queries.

1. To see what DNS servers are the authoritative name servers for a given domain, use the `whois` command:

   ```
   $ whois intuitive.com

   Whois Server Version 1.3

   Domain names in the .com, .net, and .org domains can now be registered
   with many different competing registrars. Go to http://www.internic.net
   for detailed information.
   ```

▼
```
Domain Name: INTUITIVE.COM
Registrar: NETWORK SOLUTIONS, INC.
Whois Server: whois.networksolutions.com
Referral URL: http://www.networksolutions.com
Name Server: NS11A.VERIO-WEB.COM
Name Server: NS11B.VERIO-WEB.COM
Updated Date: 05-nov-2001

>>> Last update of whois database: Fri, 19 Apr 2002 05:03:06 EDT <<<

The Registry database contains ONLY .COM, .NET, .ORG, .EDU domains and
Registrars.
```

You can see in this record that the authoritative name servers are NS11A.VERIO-WEB.COM and NS11B.VERIO-WEB.COM. But where does the information that these are the authoritative name servers for this specific domain come from? A DNS server...

2. To be an authoritative name server, the most important part of the configuration is to have a zone file for each domain.

Zone files describe the domain you are providing name services for, and the individual hosts that have been given names. Each domain will usually contain two zone files, one for normal lookups and one for reverse lookups (converting an IP address to its fully qualified domain name).

Zone files typically contain one or more lines of directives, followed by multiple lines listing individual resource types and their hostname and IP address pairs. Here's a typical entry, the one that serves as the statement or zone of authority (SOA) for intuitive.com:

> By convention, these zone files are stored in /var/named/ and have filenames that match the domain name, so this is called /var/named/intuitive.com.zone on our server.

```
# cat /var/named/intuitive.com.zone
$ORIGIN intuitive.com.
$TTL 86400

@       IN      SOA     feed11.verio-web.com. hostmaster.verio-web.com. (
                            2002041100 ; serial
                            7200       ; refresh
                            3600       ; retry
                            604800     ; expiry
                            86400 )    ; minimum
```
▼

```
                                    86400   IN    NS      ns11a.verio-web.com.
                                    86400   IN    NS      ns11b.verio-web.com.
                                    86400   IN    MX      50 mail-fwd.verio-web.com.
            www.intuitive.com.      86400   IN    MX      50 mail-fwd.verio-web.com.

            intuitive.com.          86400   IN    A       161.58.20.91
            ftp                     86400   IN    A       161.58.20.91
            smtp                    86400   IN    A       161.58.20.91
            www                     86400   IN    A       161.58.20.91
            urlwire                 86400   IN    A       63.101.93.250
            staging                 86400   IN    CNAME   urlwire
```

There's a lot in this zone file, so let's take it one step at a time. First off, notice that the very first line has a trailing dot after the domain name (for example, `intuitive.com.`). It turns out that this trailing dot is very important, and omitting it is a common mistake for DNS administrators: If you forget, then the hostname is automatically prepended, which is usually wrong.

The second line has the Time-To-Live (TTL) directive, and it's in units of seconds: 86,400 = 24 hours. Think of this as the expiration date: Once the TTL has expired, any DNS cache is required to request a fresh copy of the data.

3. The remainder of the zone file is comprised of resource records. The first resource record is a Statement Of Authority (SOA), and it has its own TTL, administrative address associated with the domain record (albeit with the usual @ replaced with a dot), and a number of configuration parameters, as detailed in Table 18.1.

TABLE 18.1   Statement of Authority Fields in a Zone File

Name	Exemplary Value	Explanation
Serial	2002041100	A unique serial number for this version of this domain record. This should change each time the zone file is edited. By convention, most sysadmins use YYYYMMDD and tack on a two-digit revision value, so this serial number represents a zone file last modified on April 11, 2002.
Refresh	7200	Number of seconds that secondary servers can use this record without it expiring and needing to be refreshed.
Retry	3600	How frequently a secondary server should try to contact the primary server to refresh the DNS data in the cache.
Expiry	604800	The length of the time after which the secondary server should stop responding as an authoritative on the domain when no response has been received from the master.
Minimum	86400	The length of time other name servers should cache this information, in seconds.

▼ Notice that the zone file inherently includes the concept of having a secondary, as well as a primary, domain server. This is a smart fail-safe architecture: By having multiple servers able to act authoritatively, users are less likely to have a DNS query fail if the primary server is offline. However, having multiple primary servers leads to a puzzle that this also solves—which of the multiple servers "owns" the domain name record? That's what all the refresh, expiry, and other values specify—they tell authoritative, but nonprimary, name servers how to interact with the primary for this specific domain name.

4. All the subsequent lines in the zone file specify explicit types of domain information. Notice the column that has NS, MX, A, and CNAME values—those indicate whether the specified record is a *name server*, *mail exchange*, *address queries*, or *alternate (canonical) name*, respectively.

For example, we can see explicitly that ns11a.verio-web.com and ns11b.verio-web.com are the name servers (NS) for this domain, and that e-mail receipt queries resolve to mail-fwd.verio-web.com. The second MX record, explicitly listing www.intuitive.com, allows mail sent to a user @www.intuitive.com to resolve properly and drop into the correct mailbox.

> This is an important nuance: The same domain name can return different IP addresses, based on the type of query specified. This zone file specifies that all general queries for intuitive.com resolve to 161.58.20.91, except mail exchange queries, which are answered by mail-fwd.verio-web.com.

Finally, there is a set of resource records that actually map domain and subdomain names to explicit IP addresses. Here we can see that intuitive.com and the host ftp, smtp, and www are assigned the same IP address as the main domain record, but urlwire is a completely different IP address. This correctly implies that Web and mail queries to urlwire.intuitive.com are handled by a different server.

The very last record demonstrates a helpful shorthand available in zone files: A CNAME record is essentially an alias, so the line

```
staging        86400 IN    CNAME    urlwire
```

indicates that queries for staging.intuitive.com should be answered exactly the same as queries for urlwire.intuitive.com.

Commonly, www subdomains are aliases to the main Web server through a CNAME in just this fashion. Indeed, the zone file would be just as valid if the last few lines were written as

```
intuitive.com.          86400   IN      A       161.58.20.91
www                     86400   IN      A       161.58.20.91
smtp                    86400   IN      CNAME   www
```
▼

```
ftp              86400   IN   CNAME  www
urlwire          86400   IN   A      63.101.93.250
staging          86400   IN   CNAME  urlwire
```

The eagle-eyed among you will have noticed that fully qualified domain names (FQDNs in DNS parlance: a domain that includes all elements—intuitive.com—versus the unqualified domain name www) always have that trailing dot, whereas subdomains do not. It's important to keep this straight, so as not to corrupt your DNS system.

5. Before we leave the discussion about zone files, let's have a peek at a different type, a reverse lookup zone file:

```
# cat /var/named/20.58.161.in-addr.arpa
$TTL 86400

@       IN     SOA     feed11.verio-web.com. hostmaster.verio-web.com. (
                               2002041200 ; serial
                               7200       ; refresh
                               3600       ; retry
                               604800     ; expiry
                               86400 )    ; minimum

        86400   IN     NS      ns11a.verio-web.com.
        86400   IN     NS      ns11b.verio-web.com.

91                      IN     PTR     www.intuitive.com.
```

Much of this is the same as the earlier zone file, including the TTL, NS, and SOA records. The difference lies in the very last line, which lists the fourth octet of the domain IP address (for example, 91).

We only need the fourth octet here rather than the entire IP address because we're working with a Class C subnet. If your network has a Class B or Class A subnet, you will need to specify more of the IP address in the reverse lookup zone file. The name should also change to reflect the subnet for the zone. For management purposes, it is better to split your Class A or Class B subnets into Class C zones.

Notice that an inherent limitation of zone files is that we can only list one subnet per file, so a separate reverse lookup zone file is required to permit a reverse lookup for the staging.intuitive.com domain name (for example, the 63.101.93.x subnet).

Writing zone files from scratch is quite confusing, and there are few tools available to help. One that might offer some respite from the potential headache that this represents is available at www.dnstools.com, and it's well worth exploring. Unfortunately, it's only available for Linux as of this writing. Mac OS X users might find DNSetup a useful, albeit less powerful, alternative tool (homepage.mac.com/dnsetup/).

Configuring named

The zone files that we've explored up to this point are the data files that are fed to the actual DNS name server, named. The named program runs by reading a named.conf file, which is typically found in /etc/. The next step in our journey is to dig into this configuration file and see how it ties in with the individual zone files.

Task 18.2: Configuring the Name Server named

The named daemon reads the /etc/named.conf file to identify which zone files it needs to load. All options and statements within the configuration file are terminated with a semicolon.

1. To start, let's check out the named.conf file:

```
# cat /etc/named.conf
options {
        directory "/var/named";
        /*
         * If there is a firewall between you and nameservers you want
         * to talk to, you might need to uncomment the query-source
         * directive below.  Previous versions of BIND always asked
         * questions using port 53, but BIND 8.1 uses an unprivileged
         * port by default.
         */
        // query-source address * port 53;
};

controls {
        inet 127.0.0.1 allow { localhost; } keys { rndckey; };
};
zone "." IN {
        type hint;
        file "named.ca";
};

zone "localhost" IN {
        type master;
        file "localhost.zone";
        allow-update { none; };
};

zone "0.0.127.in-addr.arpa" IN {
        type master;
        file "named.local";
        allow-update { none; };
};

zone "intuitive.com" IN {
        type master;
        file "intuitive.com.zone";
```

18

```
                allow-update { none; };
};

zone "20.58.161.in-addr.arpa" IN {
        type master;
        file "20.58.161.in-addr.arpa.zone";
        allow-update { none; };
};

include "/etc/rndc.key";
```

There's quite a bit in this file, but a quick glance reveals that there are a few control statements at the top, then a recurring zone block, and a final include at the bottom. Don't be too intimidated!

> Notice that there are two different styles of comments here: the C style that begins with /*, ends with */, and can range over many lines, and the Java style //, which denotes that the rest of that line is a comment.

The first statement we have is options, which is used to control the assorted options available to named. In this configuration, the only option set is directory, which informs named where to look for the zone files.

There's a very helpful administrative utility called rndc, and the next statement in the configuration file specifies who can make changes to named while it's running. The controls statement indicates that named is only monitoring the local loopback address for localhost, and that connections must be verified using the secret key rndckey (defined in the included file at the end).

> For inexplicable reasons, the default /etc/named.conf file included with some versions of Red Hat Linux has a keys value of key, which is invalid. For you to be able to use rndc, you will have to edit named.conf so that it reads rndckey.

2. The remainder of the configuration file contains blocks of zone file inclusion statements (except the last line, which we'll talk about shortly).

   The first zone specifies the root of the DNS tree with .. These are the root servers for the entire Internet. When named receives a request for a host it doesn't know about, it will contact one of the root servers asking for the DNS server registered with the domain name.

   After the name of the zone, the class is required. The class is always IN for Internet.

The different options for each zone are specified within its block, delimited by open and closed curly brackets. Our first option is the type of zone being specified. Just about all of them will be master, but the root domain shows up as hint. No other zone block should specify hint if things are configured properly.

The next option is the name of the zone file, and you can see why a standard naming scheme is quite helpful at this point. Oddly, the root domain has a zone file with the default name of named.ca. It is located in /var/named, as expected, so you can easily peek inside this 83-line default zone file if you'd like.

The next four zones work together as pairs, a forward-looking (name-to-IP number) and reverse looking (IP number-to-name) zone for each domain.

3. Let's look at the next two zones together, as they describe the loopback interface:

```
zone "localhost" IN {
        type master;
        file "localhost.zone";
        allow-update { none; };
};

zone "0.0.127.in-addr.arpa" IN {
        type master;
        file "named.local";
        allow-update { none; };
};
```

The named zone goes first by convention, and it's important to have the name specified match the $ORIGIN value in the zone file itself:

```
# grep ORIGIN /var/named/localhost.zone
$ORIGIN localhost.
```

Again, notice where there's a trailing dot and where there isn't. It is just as important to omit the trailing dots in the named.conf file as it is to ensure that they're properly specified in the individual zone files.

There are various types of zones that can be specified in the configuration file, but as we are hoping to be the authoritative name server for the specified domains, we want to be the master. The other possibility is slave, in which case we act as a backup authoritative name server, but get the master data from another more authoritative server.

Finally, the block specifies the name of the zone file, followed by an optional list of hosts that have the authority to update this zone, if any.

> It is dangerous to enable other hosts to update your zone configuration files. Best practices dictate that one person be in charge of maintaining the configuration files and restarting named when changes are made.

▼

The last entry in the `named.conf` file is an `include` statement, which causes `named` to include the contents of the specified file as if it were part of the `named.conf` file itself. Why do this? To enable the system administrator to hide sensitive data in a separate file with permissions that prevent unauthorized access.

In our example, `named` loads a file containing the secret key for the `named` administrative utility `rndc` (explained later this hour).

4. Because you need to have at least two name servers online for any given domain name, being able to have `slave` zone definition blocks is a boon. Without it, you'd have to manually distribute all the zone files to multiple systems and/or edit two or more files for each change required.

A sample `slave` entry in the `named.conf` file on a secondary, or backup DNS server, would look like this:

```
zone "intuitive.com" IN {
        type slave;
        file "intuitive.com.zone";
        masters { 161.58.20.91; };
};
```

▲

This zone block tells `named` to contact host `161.58.20.91` for the zone configuration information, and to store it in a file named `intuitive.com.zone`.

The `named.conf` file and the individual zone files stored in `/var/named` combine to let a system administrator create a fully functional domain name server for anywhere from two or three to thousands of domain names.

Working with `rndc`

The `named` daemon only reads its configuration files on startup, which implies that each time you modify a zone file or the `named.conf` file you should restart the server. Rather than starting and stopping each time a change is made, however, you should use the remote name daemon control (`rndc`) program.

Task 18.3: Learning `rndc`

There are a variety of useful administrative tasks that can be accomplished with `rndc`, but let's just consider a couple of the most basic—you can read the `rndc` man page for more information if you're curious or need additional capabilities.

1. The most common operation is to force a reload of the configuration files. This is accomplished using the reload command:

```
# rndc reload
#
```

▼ If you have a lot of zone files and want to save time on the reload, explicitly specify reconfig instead and named will only scan the named.conf file and any new zone files it finds. Again, there's no output unless an error is encountered:

```
# rndc reconfig
#
```

2. Other common rndc options that you might find useful are listed in Table 18.2.

TABLE 18.2 Useful rndc Commands

Command	Meaning
reconfig	Reload the named.conf file and any new zone files found.
reload	Reload all zone files.
reload *zone*	Reload the given zone only.
stop	Stop the server, saving any changes to the master files of the updated zones.
halt	Stop the server immediately. No changes are saved, but they will be rolled forward from the journal files when the server is restarted, so they won't be lost.

rndc is only used with BIND version 9, and carries most of the same commands that were available in ndc, the named daemon control program from previous versions of BIND.

3. The rndc command has its own configuration file, /etc/rndc.conf. The default is probably quite sufficient, particularly because the controls statement in named.conf enables you to state who is allowed to send commands to named using rndc.

```
# cat /etc/rndc.conf
options {
        default-server  localhost;
        default-key     "key";
};

server localhost {
        key     "rndckey";
};

key "rndckey" {
        algorithm       hmac-md5;
        secret
"k0sYAWycZNcPVfLojkdnKWkgqYJsbNCtR0GyXYkldQehDcurizoHtQbFhqNp";
};
```

4. Before you're done with rndc, it's quite helpful to run the utility named-checkzone to verify the syntax of each zone file. To use this utility, specify a zone name and zone file:

▼ `# /etc/named-checkzone intuitive.com /var/named/intuitive.com.zone`

18

▼

You could also drop this into a loop, as in the following:

```
cd /var/named
for name in *
do
  domain="`echo $name | sed 's/\.zone//'`"
  echo "Domain $domain:"
  /etc/named-checkzone $domain /var/named/$name
```
▲
```
done
```

A simple utility, the `rndc` command is critical to effective management of `named` and your local name server.

Testing DNS Setups

Now that you have your configuration and zone files straight, it's time to test it and make sure everything is copacetic.

In the old days, there was a great utility called `nslookup` that offered a simple way to interact with name servers. In the last few years, `nslookup` has been put out to the proverbial pasture and replaced with two new tools, `dig` and `host`.

Task 18.4: Testing with `dig` and `host`

TASK

Of the two tools, you'll doubtless find `dig` (the Domain Information Groper) the most useful, but let's look at both of them and see what they can offer.

▼

1. In its basic form, `dig` just needs a domain name to retrieve information:

```
# dig intuitive.com
; <<>> DiG 9.1.3 <<>> intuitive.com
;; global options:  printcmd
;; Got answer:
;; ->>HEADER<<- opcode: QUERY, status: NOERROR, id: 51083
;; flags: qr rd ra; QUERY: 1, ANSWER: 1, AUTHORITY: 2, ADDITIONAL: 1

;; QUESTION SECTION:
;intuitive.com.                    IN      A

;; ANSWER SECTION:
intuitive.com.          28067   IN      A       161.58.20.91

;; AUTHORITY SECTION:
intuitive.com.          79973   IN      NS      ns11a.verio-web.com.
intuitive.com.          79973   IN      NS      ns11b.verio-web.com.

;; ADDITIONAL SECTION:
ns11b.verio-web.com.    149498  IN      A       161.58.148.98
```
▼

```
;; Query time: 5 msec
;; SERVER: 192.168.1.250#53(192.168.1.250)
;; WHEN: Fri Apr 12 01:23:58 2002
;; MSG SIZE  rcvd: 113
```

If you get back something that looks similar to this, everything is working fine with your configuration. If not, go back and double-check your settings.

> If you find that `dig` can't report information on domains on which you have set up `master` records, check the `syslog` log file for detailed problems encountered by `named` upon startup. Most likely, the `syslog` output will be called `/var/log/messages`.

2. The fourth line of the output gives us a status code `status: NOERROR` telling us that our query was completed successfully. Line five gives us some stats: how many queries, answers, authorities, and additional information was found for the specified domain.

   The next lines are broken up into sections detailing the question asked, the answer found, the authority providing the answer, and any additional information.

   We asked the simple question, "Who is `intuitive.com`?" The answer is IP address `161.58.20.91`. The authority answering the question is the two name servers `ns11a.verio-web.com` and `ns11b.verio-web.com`. And finally, the additional section gives us the IP address of `ns11b.verio-web.com`.

3. This was a simple example to ensure `named` responds to requests, but clearly it didn't return all the information in our zone file.

   How can we see it all? By asking for a zone transfer. The wrinkle is that you can only request a zone transfer from the authoritative server, whether it's an NS or SOA. The solution is to ask `dig` for it explicitly:

```
# dig intuitive.com soa
; <<>> DiG 9.1.3 <<>> intuitive.com soa
;; global options:  printcmd
;; Got answer:
;; ->>HEADER<<- opcode: QUERY, status: NOERROR, id: 19035
;; flags: qr rd ra; QUERY: 1, ANSWER: 1, AUTHORITY: 2, ADDITIONAL: 1

;; QUESTION SECTION:
;intuitive.com.                    IN      SOA
```

18

▼
```
;; ANSWER SECTION:
intuitive.com.          27849   IN      SOA     feed11.verio-web.com. hostmaster
.verio-web.com. 2001121419 7200 3600 604800 86400

;; AUTHORITY SECTION:
intuitive.com.          79548   IN      NS      ns11b.verio-web.com.
intuitive.com.          79548   IN      NS      ns11a.verio-web.com.

;; ADDITIONAL SECTION:
ns11b.verio-web.com.    149073  IN      A       161.58.148.98

;; Query time: 5 msec
;; SERVER: 192.168.1.250#53(192.168.1.250)
;; WHEN: Fri Apr 12 01:31:03 2002
;; MSG SIZE  rcvd: 151
```

Now we can ask ns11b.verio-web.com to give us all records for intuitive.com.
There are quite a few different queries you can perform, but a zone transfer is specified with axfr:

 # dig @ns11a.verio-web.com intuitive.com axfr

```
; <<>> DiG 9.1.3 <<>> @ns11a.verio-web.com intuitive.com axfr
;; global options:  printcmd
intuitive.com.          86400   IN      SOA     feed11.verio-web.com. hostmaster
.verio-web.com. 2001121419 7200 3600 604800 86400
intuitive.com.          86400   IN      NS      ns11a.verio-web.com.
intuitive.com.          86400   IN      NS      ns11b.verio-web.com.
intuitive.com.          86400   IN      MX      50 mail-fwd.verio-web.com.
intuitive.com.          86400   IN      A       161.58.20.91
ftp.intuitive.com.      86400   IN      A       161.58.20.91
smtp.intuitive.com.     86400   IN      A       161.58.20.91
www.intuitive.com.      86400   IN      MX      50 mail-fwd.verio-web.com.
www.intuitive.com.      86400   IN      A       161.58.20.91
urlwire.intuitive.com.  86400   IN      A       63.101.93.250
staging.intuitive.com.  86400   IN      A       63.101.93.250
intuitive.com.          86400   IN      SOA     feed11.verio-web.com. hostmaster
.verio-web.com. 2001121419 7200 3600 604800 86400
;; Query time: 169 msec
;; SERVER: 161.58.148.62#53(feed11.verio-web.com)
;; WHEN: Fri Apr 12 01:38:34 2002
;; XFR size: 13 records
```

4. To ask for a specific type of query, specify any one of a (network address), any (all
   information about the domain), mx (mail exchange), ns (name servers), soa (the
   zone of authority record), hinfo (host info), axfr (zone transfer), or txt (arbitrary
▼ strings of text).

Knowing this, it's interesting to query a busy, well-known server to see how it's set up. For example, AOL's mail exchange records should prove interesting:

```
$ dig aol.com mx

; <<>> DiG 9.1.3 <<>> aol.com mx
;; global options:  printcmd
;; Got answer:
;; ->>HEADER<<- opcode: QUERY, status: NOERROR, id: 19186
;; flags: qr rd ra; QUERY: 1, ANSWER: 4, AUTHORITY: 4, ADDITIONAL: 18

;; QUESTION SECTION:
;aol.com.                        IN      MX

;; ANSWER SECTION:
aol.com.                530     IN      MX      15 mailin-04.mx.aol.com.
aol.com.                530     IN      MX      15 mailin-01.mx.aol.com.
aol.com.                530     IN      MX      15 mailin-02.mx.aol.com.
aol.com.                530     IN      MX      15 mailin-03.mx.aol.com.

;; AUTHORITY SECTION:
aol.com.                136764  IN      NS      DNS-01.NS.aol.com.
aol.com.                136764  IN      NS      DNS-02.NS.aol.com.
aol.com.                136764  IN      NS      DNS-06.NS.aol.com.
aol.com.                136764  IN      NS      DNS-07.NS.aol.com.

;; ADDITIONAL SECTION:
mailin-04.mx.aol.com.   13      IN      A       64.12.137.121
mailin-04.mx.aol.com.   13      IN      A       64.12.137.152
mailin-04.mx.aol.com.   13      IN      A       152.163.224.122
mailin-04.mx.aol.com.   13      IN      A       64.12.136.153
mailin-01.mx.aol.com.   9       IN      A       64.12.137.184
mailin-01.mx.aol.com.   9       IN      A       152.163.224.26
mailin-01.mx.aol.com.   9       IN      A       64.12.136.57
mailin-01.mx.aol.com.   9       IN      A       205.188.156.122
mailin-01.mx.aol.com.   9       IN      A       64.12.137.89
mailin-02.mx.aol.com.   183     IN      A       64.12.136.121
mailin-02.mx.aol.com.   183     IN      A       64.12.137.89
mailin-02.mx.aol.com.   183     IN      A       64.12.137.184
mailin-02.mx.aol.com.   183     IN      A       64.12.136.89
mailin-02.mx.aol.com.   183     IN      A       205.188.156.154
DNS-01.NS.aol.com.      136764  IN      A       152.163.159.232
DNS-02.NS.aol.com.      136764  IN      A       205.188.157.232
DNS-06.NS.aol.com.      136764  IN      A       149.174.211.8
DNS-07.NS.aol.com.      136764  IN      A       64.12.51.132

;; Query time: 34 msec
;; SERVER: 207.182.224.5#53(207.182.224.5)
;; WHEN: Fri Apr 19 13:59:26 2002
;; MSG SIZE  rcvd: 507
```

18

5. Another utility used to check DNS records is host. In its simplest form, host converts back and forth between a domain name and its IP address:

```
# host intuitive.com
intuitive.com. has address 161.58.20.91
# host 161.58.20.91
91.20.58.161.in-addr.arpa. domain name pointer www.intuitive.com.
```

If we add the -v (verbose) flag to the command, the output is very similar to dig:

```
$ host -v intuitive.com
Trying "intuitive.com."
;; ->>HEADER<<- opcode: QUERY, status: NOERROR, id: 22099
;; flags: qr rd ra; QUERY: 1, ANSWER: 1, AUTHORITY: 2, ADDITIONAL: 1

;; QUESTION SECTION:
;intuitive.com.                 IN      A

;; ANSWER SECTION:
intuitive.com.          26740   IN      A       161.58.20.91

;; AUTHORITY SECTION:
intuitive.com.          78646   IN      NS      ns11a.verio-web.com.
intuitive.com.          78646   IN      NS      ns11b.verio-web.com.

;; ADDITIONAL SECTION:
ns11b.verio-web.com.    148171  IN      A       161.58.148.98

Received 113 bytes from 192.168.1.250#53 in 5 ms
```

Using the -l (list) command is the same as asking for zone (axfr) information using dig, but host presents the information in a friendlier format. You still need to specify an authoritative server for this to work:

```
# host -l intuitive.com ns11a.verio-web.com
Using domain server:
Name: feed11.verio-web.com
Address: 161.58.148.62#53
Aliases:

intuitive.com. SOA feed11.verio-web.com. hostmaster.verio-web.com.
   2001121419 7200 3600 604800 86400
Using domain server:
Name: feed11.verio-web.com
Address: 161.58.148.62#53
Aliases:

intuitive.com. name server ns11a.verio-web.com.
Using domain server:
Name: feed11.verio-web.com
Address: 161.58.148.62#53
Aliases:
```

▼   intuitive.com. name server ns11b.verio-web.com.
        Using domain server:
        Name: feed11.verio-web.com
        Address: 161.58.148.62#53
        Aliases:

        intuitive.com. mail is handled by 50 mail-fwd.verio-web.com.
        Using domain server:
        Name: feed11.verio-web.com
        Address: 161.58.148.62#53
        Aliases:

        intuitive.com. has address 161.58.20.91
        Using domain server:
        Name: feed11.verio-web.com
        Address: 161.58.148.62#53
        Aliases:

        ftp.intuitive.com. has address 161.58.20.91
        Using domain server:
        Name: feed11.verio-web.com
        Address: 161.58.148.62#53
        Aliases:

        smtp.intuitive.com. has address 161.58.20.91
        Using domain server:
        Using domain server:
        Name: feed11.verio-web.com
        Address: 161.58.148.62#53
        Aliases:

        www.intuitive.com. mail is handled by 50 mail-fwd.verio-web.com.
        Using domain server:
        Name: feed11.verio-web.com
        Address: 161.58.148.62#53
        Aliases:

        www.intuitive.com. has address 161.58.20.91
        Using domain server:
        Name: feed11.verio-web.com
        Address: 161.58.148.62#53
        Aliases:

        urlwire.intuitive.com. has address 63.101.93.250
        Using domain server:
        Name: feed11.verio-web.com
        Address: 161.58.148.62#53
        Aliases:

        staging.intuitive.com. has address 63.101.93.250
▼   Using domain server:

▼
```
Name: feed11.verio-web.com
Address: 161.58.148.62#53
Aliases:
intuitive.com. SOA feed11.verio-web.com. hostmaster.verio-web.com.
➥2001121419 7200 3600 604800 86400
```
▲

The two utilities dig and host are similar to each other, and both provide the same information. Because of the breadth of options that are available with dig, it can be more powerful than host, but host is a good tool to use because of its simplicity.

Summary

This hour has focused on the basic concepts and configuration of a domain name server using the popular Berkeley BIND package. We've explored zone files, the named.conf file, and discussed master and slave servers. In addition, we explored various useful utilities that are quite useful whether you're running a name server or not. In particular, host offers a helpful reverse-IP lookup utility that can make reading through log files much more informative.

Q&A

Q I want to control my domain name record, but not run a BIND server. Am I out of luck?

A A year or two ago the answer would have been "yes, you're outta luck," but there are a number of different Web-accessible domain name servers that enable you to easily manage your own DNS records without the hassle of BIND, zone files, and so on. I use one myself: http://www.mydomain.com/.

Q What are the numbers just before the domain names in MX records? A search for the MX records for AOL, for example, prefaced each MX server with 15. What does it mean?

A The number is the priority value associated with each of the MX servers for that domain. The lower the number, the higher the priority. If there are multiple servers with the same priority, the system load-balances by randomly picking one as the recipient system.

Workshop

Quiz

1. What's the main reason for updating your version of BIND?

2. What happens if you omit the trailing dots on domain names in the ORIGIN section of a zone file?

3. What would happen if a TTL for a master record was set to 60? Would that be good or bad?

4. What should you always remember to do when you edit a zone file?

5. Why is it dangerous to let other hosts update your zone configuration files through rndc?

6. What very important thing happens if you use the command rndc stop that doesn't occur with rndc halt?

Answers

1. In a word: security.

2. ORIGIN names that lack a trailing dot have the hostname automatically prefaced, changing the intent of the statement in the zone file in most cases.

3. Setting the TTL too low will cause the network to saturate, as DNS caches keep asking for new authoritative records again and again. It'd definitely be bad.

4. Update or increment the serial number in the zone file.

5. See Answer #1.

6. The stop command saves any changes to the zone information by rewriting the master files. The halt command does not change the master files.

A name server is a single Internet service, as is a Web server (covered in the last two hours of this book). The next hour will focus on a variety of different Internet services, including a discussion of how to enable or disable ftp access, and an exploration of the useful telnet utility.

18

HOUR 19

Running Internet Services

Although there are specific network services that your Unix system runs as separate programs, notably the Apache Web server, there's an entire class of daemons that are launched from a program that monitors incoming network connections and hands specific queries off to the right software.

That program is called inetd, and it's simultaneously your best friend as the system administrator of a network-based computer and your worst enemy—it's a well-known open door for hackers.

This hour will focus on this important service and its more sophisticated Linux cousin xinetd. Along the way, we'll talk about TCP Wrapper, a helpful quasi-firewall specifically for services launched from inetd.

In this hour, you'll learn about

- Configuring and managing inetd
- How to configure TCP Wrapper for security
- Working with xinetd and why it's a mixed blessing
- Configuring anonymous FTP

The `inetd` Super-Daemon

If daemons had T-shirts hiding under their normal clothes, Apache might have a big thumbs-up on its shirt, but without question, `inetd` would be the service with the big blue "S" for super-daemon!

> Some people have incorrectly assumed some sort of satanic meaning behind the use of *daemon* to describe network and background services, assuming it's a misspelling of demon. It's not. It's a word first used by Socrates, and it means "indwelling spirit." No good or bad connotation, just a hidden capability within your Unix box.

The motivation behind creating `inetd` was that as more and more network services began popping up on Unix systems, they started to consume system resources far beyond their utility. It's certainly useful to have an occasional user connect via `ftp` to download a file, for example, but does that require having a daemon running all the time?

Hence the birth of `inetd`, a program that listens to multiple incoming ports and can launch and relay incoming requests to the appropriate daemon as needed.

Task 19.1: Understanding and Working with `inetd`

Before we go further, a brief word on *ports*, or *sockets*, as they're also known. Although your server probably only has a single Ethernet wire or network connection, there are a variety of different services that it can offer through that wire. These are differentiated by having unique port addresses, akin to unique frequencies on a TV tuner. (Indeed, your cable connection has a single wire transmitting dozens of different channels, and it's the job of your TV tuner to ignore everything but the specific channel you want to watch.)

1. All of these ports are defined in a file called `/etc/services`, and it's quite long as it defines the port for hundreds of different services, some available cross-platform, and others available only on one specific OS or flavor of Unix. On Red Hat Linux, for example, it defines almost 500 different services!

   Here are a few representative lines:

   ```
   ftp           21/tcp
   ftp           21/udp
   ssh           22/tcp                    # SSH Remote Login Protocol
   ssh           22/udp                    # SSH Remote Login Protocol
   telnet        23/tcp
   telnet        23/udp
   smtp          25/tcp        mail
   smtp          25/udp        mail
   time          37/tcp        timserver
   time          37/udp        timserver
   ```

The general format is to list the service name followed by the port and protocol, any aliases, and then (sometimes) a comment prefaced with the usual # character. You'll notice that all these services shown have both a TCP and UDP port defined: TCP (the Transmission Control Protocol) maintains *state* in its communications, and is therefore ideal for back-and-forth dialogs between server and client apps. UDP (the User Datagram Protocol) is *stateless*, and is used for broadcast services and other services where it doesn't matter if packets are received. An example of this is a service that might broadcast the current time every 120 seconds—it's not an error if no one is listening.

> You'll probably never need to change anything in the /etc/services file
> unless you're writing your own system daemon. In more than 20 years of
> working with Unix systems, I've never edited /etc/services.

2. The main program that we're interested in learning more about, of course, is inetd, and the inetd program is usually launched as part of the standard run level 3 service set:

```
# ls */*inetd*
init.d/inetd*    rc1.d/K37inetd@  rc3.d/S37inetd@  rc5.d/S56inetd@
rc0.d/K37inetd@  rc2.d/K37inetd@  rc4.d/S37inetd@  rc6.d/K37inetd@
```

Unwrapping this just a wee bit (and remembering that the K prefix means "kill" and the S prefix means "start"), we can see that on this system, inetd is only supposed to be running at run levels 3, 4, and 5.

On a Mac OS X system, things are different. For example, in addition to a 2066-line /etc/services file, there's also a set of services defined in the NetInfo database:

```
# nidump services . | wc -l
   1013
```

On the Mac, inetd is launched from the hard-to-find IPServices file, as shown here:

```
# head -12 /System/Library/StartupItems/IPServices/IPServices
#!/bin/sh

##
# Run the Internet super-server.
##

. /etc/rc.common

ConsoleMessage "Starting TCP/IP services"

inetd
```

▼ Regardless of where it is, once `inetd` is started on a Unix system, it has control over quite a few network services, as defined in the `/etc/inetd.conf` file.

To check that `inetd` is running, of course, we can easily use the `ps` command:

```
# ps aux | grep inet
root     231   0.0  0.0      1288    184 ??  Ss     0:00.01 inetd
root     778   0.0  0.0      1112    220 std R+     0:00.00 grep inet
```

A more sophisticated way would be to look for the file `/var/run/inetd.pid` and use its contents to see if the program is still running:

```
# ps `cat /var/run/inetd.pid`
  PID TT  STAT       TIME COMMAND
  231 ??  Ss      0:00.01 inetd
```

If it isn't running (as is the case in Red Hat Linux, where it's been replaced with `xinetd`), this generates an error message instead.

3. Now that we can figure out whether `inetd` is running or not, let's have a look at the all-important configuration file and see what's inside.

The most important check is to see what lines are *not* commented out: Any service that's commented out is disabled:

```
# grep -v '^#' /etc/inetd.conf
telnet  stream  tcp     nowait  root    /usr/libexec/tcpd               telnetd
```

This shows that the only service enabled through `inetd` on this system is `telnet`. Shortly, we'll enable `ftp`, but for now, this is sufficient for our exploration.

The format for lines in the `inetd.conf` file is

service socket proto flags user path args

where *service* is the name of the specific service (it must correspond to a matching entry in `/etc/services`, which is why that file is important), *socket* defines how the server and client should communicate, and the most common values are `stream` (for TCP) and `dgram` (for UDP). *proto* specifies the communication protocol, though it's implied in the *socket* type as well, of course. Values can be `TCP`, `UDP`, or `RPC`, the last for remote-procedure calls.

The *flags* setting is a bit tricky: It lets the sysadmin specify whether an individual instantiation of the daemon can handle multiple connection requests or not. Most cannot (if they could, they'd probably be running all the time like Apache). To specify that the daemon requires one application per connection—the most common— use `nowait`, whereas `wait` indicates that the service can handle lots of connections.

A very important parameter is *user,* because it informs `inetd` what user should own the process when launched. Most standard system daemons run as `root`, but if you add something that isn't vetted by your vendor, you'd be wise to use a different
▼ *user* to minimize security risks.

Finally, the *path* to the executable is specified, and the *command args* are specified, always starting with the name of the program itself. In this example, you can see that `telnet` uses the `/usr/libexec/tcpd` TCP Wrapper program, and that the program name itself is `telnetd`.

4. For the most part, removing the leading # in the `inetd.conf` file will automatically enable that service on your system. The only additional step required is to send a SIGHUP signal to the `inetd` daemon to force a reread of the configuration file.

> Well, the software required for some daemons might not be preinstalled. If it isn't, check an RPM or other package repository (see Hour 8, "Unix Package Management," for more information on Unix package managers).

Demonstrating this is easy: The `telnet` command allows easy access to any service on the local system, and we can even specify the service by name (`telnet` maps the name to a service port by referencing `/etc/services`). For example:

```
# telnet localhost ftp
Trying 127.0.0.1...
telnet: Unable to connect to remote host: Connection refused
```

We're trying to access `ftp`, but as is obvious, the service isn't enabled.

To enable it, just strip out the # before `ftp` in `/etc/inetd.conf`, and have `inetd` reread its configuration file:

```
# grep -v '^#' /etc/inetd.conf
ftp     stream  tcp    nowait  root    /usr/libexec/tcpd
ftpd -l
telnet  stream  tcp    nowait  root    /usr/libexec/tcpd
telnetd
# kill -HUP `cat /var/run/inetd.pid`
```

and...

```
# telnet localhost ftp
Trying 127.0.0.1...
Connected to localhost.
Escape character is '^]'.
220 dsl-132.dsldesigns.net FTP server (Version 6.00LS) ready.
```

Ready to go. Type QUIT to drop the `ftp` connection.

5. Before we leave this discussion, let's have a look at the different log files, and where information about what we've just done is recorded. First off, the `ftp` program itself has a log file (in Mac OS X it's called `/var/log/ftp.log`, but on other Unix systems it's more likely to be called `/var/log/xferlog` or similar):

```
# tail -1 ftp.log
Apr 22 20:32:08 dsl-132 ftpd[807]: connection from localhost
```

19

▼ Many systems also log `inetd` events themselves (particularly restarts), and they'd be in the `syslog` file. However, most modern Unix systems only log errors here (depending on how you've configured `syslogd`, actually. See the `man` page for more details!).

The other log file of interest is the TCP Wrapper (remember, `inetd` launches `/usr/libexec/tcpd`, not `ftpd` directly). We'll examine this more closely in the next section, however.

6. Perhaps the most important consideration with `inetd` is that it's very easy to enable services that you don't really need, and that *every service you enable offers more ways for a bad guy to get in.* As a result, a standard rule of thumb for smart system administrators is to *disable everything.* Sounds harsh, but it's a good policy—only enable those services that are "must have" services, and for which there aren't smarter, more secure alternatives.

For example, instead of `telnet` and `ftp`, run `sshd` (SSH is the Secure Shell), which supports both logging in directly and transferring files back and forth, only with encrypted communication that's considerably more secure.

> Interestingly, `sshd` isn't something that's run from `inetd` or `xinetd`. Instead, it's almost always an always-running daemon launched from `/etc/rc.local`, or one of the `/etc/rc.d/n.d` directories.

Here's a handy shell script that will check to see what's going on with `inetd`: You might even invoke this automatically from your `.login` script:

```
# cat enabled
#!/bin/sh

# enabled - show what services are enabled with inetd

iconf="/etc/inetd.conf"

if [ -r $iconf ] ; then
  echo "Services enabled in $iconf are:"
  grep -v '^#' $iconf | awk '{print "  " $1}'
  echo ""
  if [ "`ps -aux | grep inetd | egrep -vE '(xinet|grep)'`" == "" ] ; then
    echo "** warning: inetd does not appear to be running"
  fi
fi
exit 0
```
▼

▼

Before we finish up this section, let's disable *all* the services in `inetd.conf` (use `vi` and add # before each enabled service). We can double-check the results with the `enabled` script:

```
# enabled
Services enabled in /etc/inetd.conf are:
#
```

▲

The `inetd` super-daemon is a great help for the harried sysadmin trying to keep track of what services are enabled, and what binaries the daemons actually use for each service. It's easy to not pay attention and have unnecessary services enabled, which is a definite problem, so you should always double-check the state of the `inetd.conf` file on your servers. In particular, make sure that the default configuration from the vendor doesn't enable a bunch of unnecessary services. And check again each time you upgrade your OS, just in case things change.

Managing `inetd` Security with TCP Wrapper

Although some systems run a stock `inetd` service and have the program launch daemons directly, this isn't the best security policy in the world. Among other problems, this doesn't enable any sort of control over which remote systems can or cannot access a given service. For example, perhaps your server should allow FTP access from anywhere else in the company, but reject connections from elsewhere on the Internet; or there are competitors who would love to break in through `telnet`, and you'd like to disable their access.

TCP Wrapper enables just this level of control over access to individual services, and it lets you specify access through allow lists or deny lists.

Task 19.2: Working with TCP Wrapper

▼ TASK

Originally written by Wietse Venema of Eindhoven University of Technology in the Netherlands, TCP Wrapper is actually a rather simple service, but quite helpful nonetheless. It's also installed by default on many flavors of Unix.

1. Services monitored with TCP Wrapper are logged in the `syslogd` log file, usually `/var/log/messages` or `/var/log/system.log`, depending on the OS. On Mac OS X, for example, an earlier `telnet` connection and the `ftp` test from a remote system are logged as

```
# tail -4 /var/log/system.log
Apr 22 21:39:38 dsl-132 telnetd[922]: connect from 63.101.93.250
Apr 22 21:41:17 dsl-132 ftpd[943]: connect from 63.101.93.250
Apr 22 21:41:18 dsl-132 ftpd[943]: connection from 63.101.93.250
Apr 22 21:41:21 dsl-132 ftpd[943]: ANONYMOUS FTP LOGIN REFUSED FROM
➥63.101.93.250
```

▼

19

▼

The connect from messages are from TCP Wrapper (though it identifies the requested service rather than itself), while the connection and LOGIN REFUSED messages are from ftpd itself.

2. Configuring TCP Wrapper is fairly easy, particularly if used in conjunction with the inetd service: Simply create either an /etc/hosts.allow or /etc/hosts.deny file; then list specific services, hosts, and optionally, a command that should be run upon queries to that service.

For example:

```
# cat /etc/hosts.allow
# /etc/hosts.allow
#
# Allow telnet from anywhere
telnetd: ALL
# ftp can only be from within my own subnet:
ftpd: LOCAL, .dsldesigns.com, 137.44.
```

This specifies that ALL hosts can use the telnetd service, whereas only LOCAL hosts (those hostnames that don't contain a dot), hosts within the .dsldesigns.com domain (note the leading dot in this domain name; without that, it would be an exact match only), and hosts whose names have 137.44. as their first two octets in their IP address can use the ftpd service.

Contrast that with a deny file:

```
# cat /etc/hosts.deny
# /etc/hosts.deny
#
# Reject all hosts with suspect hostnames
ALL: PARANOID
```

This nifty TCP Wrapper trick lets us automatically reject all connections from systems where the name either doesn't match the IP address (from a reverse IP lookup; see the discussion in the last hour for more details), or where there isn't a name associated with the IP address.

In fact, the recommended configuration is to have ALL:ALL in the hosts.deny file, then to explicitly allow certain hosts to use specific services in the hosts.allow file.

3. There's not much more to say about TCP Wrapper, other than that if you are finding that there aren't any entries in the appropriate log file, it might well be that you've configured syslog to be overly minimal in what information is logged. To experiment, add the following to the file /etc/syslog.conf:

```
*.*     /dev/console
```

which, once you send a SIGHUP (a hang-up signal) to the syslogd program, will cause all messages handed to syslog to also appear on the system console. Very

▲   interesting output results.

It's very worthwhile to study how `syslog` works. Start by reading the `syslog` man page; then also read the `syslog.conf(5)` man page and look at your own `/etc/syslog.conf` file.

Though simple in concept, the TCP Wrapper program is a great boon for sysadmins because it lets you add access control to any network service. Without it, you'd have to either develop a firewall solution, or rewrite the service itself to allow access control.

As you'll see in a moment, one advantage of `xinetd` is that it includes a built-in TCP Wrapper-like facility.

Super-inetd: `xinetd`

Initially released on Red Hat Linux, the more sophisticated big brother of `inetd` is `xinetd`, and it's about as different as two programs can be while sharing the same conceptual basis. Although it isn't in widespread use yet, it's also included in Mandrake Linux. Expect it to migrate onto other platforms over time, because it's a smart alternative to `inetd`.

In `inetd`, as you saw, there's a single configuration file that controls which services are enabled and the parameters that define their operation on the system.

By contrast, `xinetd` has a directory of individual configuration files, one per service, and a central master configuration file that defines all the default settings for services. For the most part, your system will have one or the other—I'd stick with the default either way.

Task 19.3: Working with `xinetd`

TASK ▼

Actually, if you imagine that each line in the `inetd.conf` file is dropped into its own file, and that each field of each line is then written in a *fieldname = value* format, you'd be pretty close to the `xinetd` format.

1. The master configuration file is `/etc/xinetd.conf`:

```
# cat /etc/xinetd.conf
#
# Simple configuration file for xinetd
#
# Some defaults, and include /etc/xinetd.d/

defaults
{
        instances               = 60
        log_type                = SYSLOG authpriv
```

▼

19

▼
```
            log_on_success              = HOST PID
            log_on_failure              = HOST
            cps                         = 25 30
    }

includedir /etc/xinetd.d
```

This demonstrates the basic structure of xinetd configuration. A service is listed, then a set of parameters within curly brackets are set with *name = value* pairs. In this instance, the special service defaults enables certain parameters to be set for all enabled services.

The specific settings here are instances (the maximum number of concurrent connections a service is permitted), log_type (it's using syslog, with the authpriv facility—see the syslog discussion a bit earlier in this hour), and on successful connections, it logs HOST and PID, while on failures it logs HOST only. Finally, there's a fail-safe connections-per-second parameter that specifies that services can accept a maximum of 25 connections per second, and if the rate exceeds this value, the service will be shut down completely for 30 seconds.

The last line is the most important: It indicates that the remainder of the configuration information is located in individual files in the /etc/xinetd.d directory.

> There are quite a few different parameters that can be specified in the xinetd.conf files. Rather than list them all here, we'll focus on the most important. For a complete list, see the xinetd.conf(5) man page.

2. To continue this exploration, we'll switch our attention to the includedir directory:
```
# cd /etc/xinetd.d
# ls -s
total 18
    1 chargen        1 echo          1 rexec         1 sgi_fam       1 time-udp
    1 chargen-udp    1 echo-udp      1 rlogin        1 talk          1 wu-ftpd
    1 daytime        1 finger        1 rsh           1 telnet
    1 daytime-udp    1 ntalk         1 rsync         1 time
```

There are seemingly quite a few services enabled with xinetd, but further examination of a specific configuration file—in this case telnet—shows that it's not quite as bad as it seems:
```
# cat telnet
# default: on
# description: The telnet server serves telnet sessions; it uses
#       unencrypted username/password pairs for authentication.
## CHANGED TO DISABLE TELNET 12/2001
```
▼

```
service telnet
{
        flags          = REUSE
        socket_type    = stream
        wait           = no
        user           = root
        server         = /usr/sbin/in.telnetd
        log_on_failure += USERID
        disable        = yes
}
```

Most of the specific flags should be familiar from the format of the inetd.conf file, including socket_type, wait, user, and server. flags lets you specify one of a wide variety of different low-level network options. In this case, REUSE means that this service has a specific *reuse-address* flag set (see the xinetd.conf(5) man page for more details. Beware, it's very low-level!).

There's a wonderful feature demonstrated in the log_on_failure parameter in this service definition. Notice that it's using +=, which means that in addition to the default values logged on failure, the telnet service will additionally log USERID. Table 19.1 lists the parameters that can be logged upon the success or failure of a given connection.

TABLE 19.1 Information Logged from xinetd

Value	Used When	Explanation
ATTEMPT	Failure	Logs the fact that a failed attempt was made
DURATION	Success	Logs the duration of a service session
EXIT	Success	Logs when the server quits
HOST	Success or Failure	The remote host address
PID	Success	The process ID of the server application
RECORD	Failure	Records as much information as possible from the remote end
USERID	Success or Failure	The userid of the remote host, if available

19

Finally, the last line in the telnet configuration listing is perhaps the most important. The disable parameter can be yes or no. If it's yes, the service cannot be started by xinetd and connection attempts will fail. If it's set to no, the service is enabled.

3. The use of the disable parameter leads to the greatest problem with xinetd—it's rather difficult to figure out what services are enabled and which are disabled.

Fortunately, it's a great place for a shell script, and to accomplish this, we'll simply extend the `enabled` script earlier to check either `inetd` or `xinetd`, depending on the system configuration:

```
# cat enabled
#!/bin/sh

# enabled - show what services are enabled with inetd and xinetd,
# if they're available on the system.

iconf="/etc/inetd.conf"
xconf="/etc/xinetd.conf"
xdir="/etc/xinetd.d"

if [ -r $iconf ] ; then
  echo "Services enabled in $iconf are:"
  grep -v '^#' $iconf | awk '{print "  " $1}'
  echo ""
  if [ "`ps -aux | grep inetd | egrep -vE '(xinet|grep)'`" == "" ] ; then
    echo "** warning: inetd does not appear to be running"
  fi
fi

if [ -r $xconf ] ; then
  # don't need to look in xinietd.conf, just know it exists
  echo "Services enabled in $xdir are:"

  for service in $xdir/*
  do
    if [ "`grep disable $service | grep 'yes'`" == "" ]; then
      echo -n "  "
      basename $service
    fi
  done

  if [ "`ps -aux | grep xinetd | grep -v 'grep'`" == "" ] ; then
    echo "** warning: xinetd does not appear to be running"
  fi
fi

exit 0
```

This script now makes it clear what services are enabled and which are disabled with `xinetd`:

```
# enabled
Services enabled in /etc/xinetd.d are:
  sgi_fam
```

A bit of poking around, and the identify of `sgi_fam` is ascertained:

```
# grep server /etc/xinetd.d/sgi_fam
        server       = /usr/bin/fam
```

▼
```
# man -k fam
fam                     (1m)  - file alteration monitor
fam                     (3x)  - File Alteration Monitor (FAM) library routines
grolj4                  (1)   - groff driver for HP Laserjet 4 family
```

Apparently it's a file alteration monitor. We may or may not want to keep this
enabled, but otherwise it's reassuring to ascertain that no other stray services are
▲ running on this server.

There's more to xinetd and its configuration files, particularly in terms of the many
parameters that can be specified. If your system is running xinetd, you would be well
advised to put 30 minutes aside and read through the xinetd and xinetd.conf files to
learn exactly how to control this important function on your system.

An Example: Enabling ftp

One of the most helpful commands in the Unix pantheon has always been ftp. Though
not pretty by any means—the running joke is that it's always been stuck in debug
mode—it's a straightforward way of transferring files between computer systems.

With the addition of attractive FTP client interfaces for the X Window System along with
Mac and Windows computers, using this mechanism has been considerably simplified.

So how do you enable ftp on a server?

Task 19.4: Enabling ftp (and Why You Might Not Want To)

19

Admit it, your interest is piqued with that curious section title. Before I explain why you
might not want to enable ftp, let's look at the steps required to enable basic access.

TASK
▼

1. To enable valid account access only (for example, access for those users who have
   accounts on the system and know the appropriate account password), simply enable
   ftpd, either within the /etc/inetd.conf file, or the ftp (or, perhaps, wu-ftp) file
   within /etc/xinetd.d.

   A quick test before enabling ftp shows that it's off:

   ```
   # ftp localhost
   ftp: connect: Connection refused
   ftp> quit
   ```

   Once the line is un-commented out in the inetd.conf file (or the enable option is
   set to yes with xinetd, which will also change the first line below to the statement
   needed to restart xinetd, of course), do a quick reread of the configuration file.

   ```
   # kill -HUP `cat /var/run/inetd.pid`
   # ftp localhost
   ```
▼

```
Connected to localhost.
220 dsl-132.dsldesigns.net FTP server (Version 6.00LS) ready.
Name (localhost:taylor): ftp
530 User ftp unknown.
ftp: Login failed.
ftp> quit
221 Goodbye.
#
```

If you're running a Mac OS X system, note that you can most easily enable FTP by clicking on the Enable FTP Access check box in the Sharing control panel, accessible from Apple, System Preferences. You'll still have to configure anonymous FTP by hand, however.

2. Notice that although the ftp program now listens for connections and presents a regular ftpd dialog, anonymous FTP access is still disabled. (The standard way to connect to an anonymous FTP server is to log in as ftp with your e-mail address as the password.)

> The anonymous FTP service lets users on the Internet connect to your server and rummage around, downloading files, and if permissions are really set up wrong, upload files of their own. It's a classic mixed bag from a security perspective. On the one hand, it's friendly and convenient to offer anonymous access to the system, but on the other hand, it's very risky, as lots of crackers poke around looking for FTP servers to exploit.

To enable the anonymous FTP service, you need to create some special directories and drop specific files and copies of executable Unix binaries in them. The idea is to create a closed subset of the file system that contains critical files (ls and a pruned-down /etc/passwd), then trap the anonymous FTP user in that area.

> If you're running Red Hat Linux or another Unix system that's RPM-compatible (see Hour 8 for more details on using RPM), your best bet is to just install the anonftp package rather than go through these individual steps).

The first necessary step is to create the ftp user account. Set the home directory of this account to /bin/false or another program that will prevent anyone using it for telnet or other sessions. You can set the password to just about anything, because it's never checked by the ftp program itself (remember, anonymous ftp users specify their e-mail address as the password, by convention).

Once that account is created, move into its home directory and type the following commands:

```
# cd ~ftp
# mkdir bin etc lib pub
# chown root.root bin etc lib
# chown root.ftp pub
# chmod 111 bin etc
# chmod 755 lib
# chmod 2755 pub
```

This creates a directory structure in the ftp home directory that mirrors some of the core parts of the standard Unix file system.

The next step is to copy specific files into the lib and bin directories. This varies by flavor of Unix, however: Red Hat Linux requires libraries in lib because of its dynamic loader architecture, while other Unixes might not require anything in lib. Because this is such a critical configuration issue, check with your vendor for specific guidelines for your version of your operating system.

Let's continue with the Red Hat Linux configuration:

```
# cp /lib/{ld-2.1.1,libc-2.1.1,libnsl-2.1.1,libnss_files-2.1.1}.so ~ftp/lib
# chmod 755 ~ftp/lib/*
# cp /usr/bin/compress ~ftp/bin
# cp /bin/{cpio,gzip,ls,sh,tar} ~ftp/bin
# chmod 111 ~ftp/bin/*
```

A few symbolic links are also required:

```
# cd ~ftp/lib
# ln -s ld-2* ld-linux.so.2
# ln -s libc* libc.so.6
# ln -s libnsl* libnsl.so.1
# ln -s libnss* libnss_files.so.2
# cd ../bin
# ln -s gzip zcat
```

Now everything should be set up for a Red Hat Linux configuration.

> Notice the slick shell pattern-matching notation of {a,b,c}, which produces three filenames, a, b, and c. A nice shortcut.

If you have a different Unix, your install might look more like this:

```
# cp /bin/ls ~ftp/bin
# chmod 111 ~ftp/bin/ls
```

Quite a bit easier, eh?

▼ 3. The final step required is to create a dummy `passwd` and `group` file in `~ftp/etc`.
We can copy our existing files, but it's better to create a very minimal new file
instead, as shown:

```
# cat ~ftp/etc/passwd
root:*:0:0:::
bin:*:1:1:::
operator:*:11:0:::
ftp:*:14:50:::
nobody:*:99:99:::
# cat ~ftp/etc/group
root::0:
bin::1:
daemon::2:
sys::3:
adm::4:
ftp::50:
```

With all of these changes in place, users can now anonymously log in to the `ftp`
server:

```
# ftp localhost
Connected to localhost (127.0.0.1).
220 staging.intuitive.com FTP server (Version wu-2.6.1-18) ready.
Name (localhost:taylor): ftp
331 Guest login ok, send your complete e-mail address as password.
Password:
230 Guest login ok, access restrictions apply.
Remote system type is UNIX.
Using binary mode to transfer files.
ftp>
```

4. Now it's time to talk about security, and why you might not want to run FTP at all,
let alone anonymous FTP.

First off, imagine what would happen if you accidentally left the `pub` directory
writable by everyone. In a short time, some cracker would stumble across it and
create a subdirectory, and you would find your system being used as a repository
for illegal software (called "warez" in the lingo), or even pornography.

Worse, the `ftpd` daemon is a popular application to try and exploit to break into a
system (the infamous Internet Worm of many years ago pried the lid off remote
systems through `ftpd`, for example), so even running it at all opens you up to dangerous activity.

Perhaps the most damning aspect of `ftp`—and this is a characteristic shared by
`telnet`, too—is that it doesn't encrypt any of the information it shares with the
client computer. Account names, passwords, data—it's all in clear-text. This means
that bad guys can rather easily grab account and password pairs from the network
▼ data stream with a packet analyzer, or a similar tool.

Fortunately, there's a very good alternative available on just about every popular Unix system today: ssh. The secure shell not only encrypts data between the client and server, it also offers a simple and effective ftp-like capability accessible on the Unix command line with sftp. The interaction is almost the same (though anonymous sftp is not supported).

If you would like to offer file transfer capabilities to your user community, there's no question in my mind—use ssh and teach them how to use it, too. Then permanently disable telnetd and ftpd. Oh, and you'll have to accept that there's no anonymous ssh option.

 If you decide to run anonymous ftp, please, at least study ftpaccess (see the man page) and set that up to help offer the maximum possible security.

One of the most enjoyable aspects of running a Unix server is the breadth of services available to your users. Although some are glorious examples of the power and flexibility of Unix (like Apache, which is discussed in detail in the last two hours of this book), and some are pretty nifty (the ntp network time protocol that automatically ensures your system clock is always accurate is cool), there are a couple that are quite dangerous and should be avoided if at all possible. At the top of that list is ftpd, with telnetd a close runner-up.

Summary

This hour explored the important inetd and xinetd configuration files, with detours into TCP Wrapper and syslogd. In addition, you've learned how to configure an anonymous FTP server for a variety of different Unix platforms, and perhaps just as importantly, learned some compelling reasons why it's not a good idea.

Q&A

Q Wow. Strong words about FTP! Are you sure about this?

A It's quite rare to find anonymous FTP on systems nowadays, particularly with the advent of the Web and the ease at which users can download files directly through a Web server (which, of course, has security problems of its own, but that's another story).

Q Which do you prefer, `inetd` or `xinetd`, and why?

A It might be old-dog-new-tricks syndrome, but I still prefer the simplicity of `inetd`. There's great value in being able to eyeball a single file and know instantly what services are enabled and what are not.

Workshop

Quiz

1. What was the primary motivation for the creation of `inetd`?

2. What simple pattern should you use to ascertain which services listed in `/etc/inetd.conf` are actually enabled?

3. When it comes to socket values in the `inetd.conf` file, `stream` implies ____, while `dgram` implies _____?

4. What common Unix program enables the easy testing of any network service?

5. Being vaguely paranoid, the best rule of thumb with `inetd` or `xinetd` is what?

6. Using TCP Wrapper, you can allow or deny connections by specifying the appropriate information where?

7. Anonymous FTP accessibility isn't necessary because you can easily make files accessible to anonymous users through what popular mechanism?

Answers

1. To combat the growing number of daemons consuming system resources as they hung around waiting for a connection.

2. Search for the # as the first character. To find all enabled services, use `grep -v '^#'`.

3. The `stream` socket implies TCP, while `dgram` implies UDP.

4. `telnet`, a great utility for any system administrator.

5. The best rule of thumb is *disable everything*.

6. To allow connections, specify rules in `/etc/hosts.allow`, while deny rules should go in `/etc/hosts.deny`.

7. Use the Web server: Apache can delivery any type of file or information, not just HTML and JPEG graphics.

The next hour explores another network service in great detail. If you've been trying to understand low-level electronic mail, you'll find Hour 20's exploration of `sendmail` a boon.

HOUR **20**

Working with E-mail

System administration involves managing a wide variety of services on one or more Unix system, but the one service that's guaranteed to get you into hot water if it breaks is electronic mail. Regardless of the level of sophistication of your user base, if they can't send and receive e-mail, you'll hear about it.

This hour focuses on how to work with sendmail, the standard *mail transfer agent* (MTA) on Unix systems. There are other MTAs available, including the popular postfix, exim, qmail, and smail programs, but just about every Unix I've seen ships with sendmail as the default.

It's also important to differentiate a mail transfer agent from other e-mail-related software. The program that lets you read, organize, and compose messages is know as a *mail user agent*, and examples of that range from Elm and Pine to Entourage and Outlook. There are X Window System-based applications, graphical applications like Apple Mail, and a wide variety of command line or shell-based mailers, but in Unix they all work by handing off outgoing messages to an MTA. The MTA—sendmail—is the program that either delivers mail locally, or connects to a remote system and feeds the message along the wire to the destination system (which is quite possibly also running sendmail).

Having said that, it's important to state that we are *not* going to dig into the famously complicated `sendmail.cf` configuration file. An arcane language unto itself, typical `sendmail.cf` files can be huge. The default size of this file in Red Hat Linux is 1,490 lines, in Mac OS X it's 1,214 lines, and on Solaris 8 it's 1,191 lines. If you must learn more, I suggest you check out the book *sendmail* (O'Reilly), by Brian Costales and original `sendmail` programmer Eric Allman.

Alright, so what are we going to cover? How to work with and use `sendmail` and its powerful alias facility to ensure that your users have a pleasant and painless e-mail experience, day in and day out.

Here's what you'll learn this hour:

- Using `sendmail` to test mail connectivity
- Mail logs and mail queues
- Creating `sendmail` aliases
- `sendmail` aliases within Mac OS X

Testing Mail Connectivity with `sendmail`

A logical place to start exploring the complexities of `sendmail`, where you're essentially in a maze of twisty passages, is to learn how to use the `sendmail` flags to test mail connectivity for your server.

The twisty passage bit is a reference to the great 70s Adventure program, written in Fortran for Unix. The first interactive fiction game that I ever played, it has been an inspiration for generations of cool D&D-style games since.

Task 20.1: Using `sendmail` to Verify Connectivity

TASK

The `sendmail` program has a wide variety of flags, most of which start with b or o if they're to be used when the program runs as a daemon. Commonly, you'll see options like –bd to run in daemon mode, -bp to print the mail queue, and –bi to initialize the alias database.

1. Before we go too far, let's figure out what version of `sendmail` you're running. This'll give you a good sense of how to work with this program:

```
# sendmail -bg -d0.1 < /dev/null
Version 8.11.6
```

```
Compiled with: LDAPMAP MAP_REGEX LOG MATCHGECOS MIME7TO8 MIME8TO7
               NAMED_BIND NETINET NETINET6 NETUNIX NEWDB NIS QUEUE SASL SCANF
               SMTP TCPWRAPPERS USERDB
Invalid operation mode g

============ SYSTEM IDENTITY (after readcf) ============
      (short domain name) $w = staging
  (canonical domain name) $j = staging.intuitive.com
         (subdomain name) $m = intuitive.com
              (node name) $k = staging.intuitive.com
```

Pleasantly, this Red Hat installation is running a recent version of sendmail (it's identified in the first line: 8.11.6).

The very same command run on Mac OS X reveals the following:

```
# sendmail -bt -d0.1 < /dev/null
Version 8.10.2
 Compiled with: MAP_REGEX LOG MATCHGECOS MIME7TO8 MIME8TO7 NAMED_BIND
                NETINET NETINFO NETISO NETUNIX NEWDB NIS QUEUE SCANF SMTP
                USERDB XDEBUG
/etc/mail/sendmail.cf: line 81: fileclass: cannot open
➡/etc/mail/local-host-names: Group writable directory

============ SYSTEM IDENTITY (after readcf) ============
      (short domain name) $w = dsl-132
  (canonical domain name) $j = dsl-132.dsldesigns.net
         (subdomain name) $m = dsldesigns.net
              (node name) $k = dsl-132.dsldesigns.net
========================================================

ADDRESS TEST MODE (ruleset 3 NOT automatically invoked)
Enter <ruleset> <address>
```

And on Solaris 8:

```
# /usr/lib/sendmail -bt  -d0.1 < /dev/null
Version 8.10.2+Sun
 Compiled with: LDAPMAP MAP_REGEX LOG MATCHGECOS MIME7TO8 MIME8TO7
                NAMED_BIND NDBM NETINET NETINET6 NETUNIX NEWDB NIS NISPLUS
                QUEUE SCANF SMTP USERDB XDEBUG

============ SYSTEM IDENTITY (after readcf) ============
      (short domain name) $w = solaris
  (canonical domain name) $j = solaris.dsldesigns.net
         (subdomain name) $m = dsldesigns.net
              (node name) $k = solaris.dsldesigns.net
========================================================

ADDRESS TEST MODE (ruleset 3 NOT automatically invoked)
Enter <ruleset> <address>
```

20

▼   Notice that both the Mac OS X and Solaris versions of `sendmail` are a version behind Red Hat Linux. The official repository of `sendmail` is the open source Sendmail Consortium at `http://www.sendmail.org/`.

2. As is suggested by the flags and output format of the resultant information, `sendmail` is a program that only its mother could love. The output tends to be cryptic, but the capabilities of the system are remarkable.

By default, `sendmail` wants to run as a daemon, which is easily done by launching it as `sendmail -bd`. Typically, you also specify how often it should process the queue with `-qn`, where *n* is a frequency indicator, such as `10m` for 10-minute intervals, or `2h` for a two-hour interval.

We'll talk more about mail queues in the next section, however, but you might be wondering where this configuration information comes from for your default boot sequence.

On a Red Hat system, it's—unsurprisingly—in `/etc/sysconfig`:

```
# cat /etc/sysconfig/sendmail
DAEMON=yes
QUEUE=1h
```

If you wanted to prevent `sendmail` from automatically starting up and listening for incoming mail, for example, you could change the first line to `DAEMON=no`, and if you'd rather it process the outbound mail queue more frequently, you could specify `QUEUE=15m` or similar.

Solaris 8 has a similar mechanism, if configured. Look in `/etc/default` for a file called `sendmail`, where it could contain `QUEUEINTERVAL=value` and the more generic `OPTIONS=value`, which are both directly fed to `sendmail` as if they were command-line options.

Mac OS X is quite different, partially because by default `sendmail` isn't started at boot-time, and partially because the default `sendmail.cf` file (at least up through 10.1.5) is missing a setting that will make it better understand the Mac OS X environment.

To get it to work, first edit `/etc/mail/sendmail.cf` and replace the line that reads

```
#O DontBlameSendmail=safe
```

with

```
O DontBlameSendmail=GroupWritableDirPathSafe
```

Now you can start the daemon up by hand with `sendmail -bd -q10m`. To have it automatically start with the options of your choice, there are two possible solu-
▼   tions.

The first, more OS X-like solution is to change the line `MAILSERVER=-NO-` in the `/etc/hostconfig` file to `MAILSERVER=-YES-`. Alternatively, the more typical Unix solution is to add a line or two to the `/etc/rc` file. For example:

```
# start up the sendmail program as needed:

if [ -f /usr/sbin/sendmail -a -f /etc/mail/sendmail.cf ] ; then
 /usr/sbin/sendmail -bd -q30m &
   echo "sendmail started."
fi
```

The next time you boot up the Macintosh system, it'll be a mail server in addition to a mail client.

> The name `DontBlameSendmail` should give you a hint that we're circumventing a security problem on the stock Mac OS X configuration. The `sendmail` program is very picky about file and directory permissions, and we're overriding its complaint that by default the `/` directory shouldn't have group write permission. You can change that and fix the problem, but anecdotal evidence suggests that other Mac OS X applications will hiccup later.
>
> Be aware of what's going on by checking the online information at `http://www.sendmail.org/tips/DontBlameSendmail.html`.

3. To check the status of your `sendmail` program (as opposed to identifying its version number), you can most easily use the startup script that the system uses at boot-time. To make this easier, let's create an alias:

```
alias sm=/etc/rc.d/init.d/sendmail
```

Now, to check the status:

```
$ sm status
sendmail (pid 801) is running...
```

Solaris doesn't support the `status` argument, so we'll have to do some quick fiddling to identify if it's running. One way would be to `grep` the output of `ps` to see whether the `sendmail` process is there, but let's use the more elegant solution of checking to see whether there's a `sendmail.pid` file, then checking to see whether the specified process is running. Here's a simple shell script that adds the useful new `sm` command to the system:

```
# cat /users/root/bin/sm
#!/bin/sh

# smstat - check sendmail status by checking for pid file, then
#       checking to see if it's running.
```

20

```
pidf=/var/run/sendmail.pid

if [ -f $pidf ] ; then
  pid=`head -1 $pidf`
  if [ "`ps -p $pid | wc -l `" -lt 2 ] ; then
    echo "Sendmail appears to NOT be running (pid = $pid)"
  else
    echo "Sendmail appears to be running (pid = $pid)"
    echo "Command was: `tail -1 $pidf`"  # note the digit '1'
  fi
else
  echo "Sendmail is not running (no pid file)"
fi

exit 0
```

If run when `sendmail` isn't running, `sm` will report the status as appropriate. If it is running, however, `sm` is smart enough to show the second line of the `.pid` file, a line that duplicates the calling sequence:

```
# sm
Sendmail appears to be running (pid = 334)
Command was: /usr/lib/sendmail -bd -q30m
```

4. Now that we've got a handle on the basics of the `sendmail` program, let's look at what might well be the most useful feature of the program, the –v flag. With this verbose output flag, you can watch how the system delivers messages to any e-mail address, including alias expansions, remote connections, and so on. Note that it doesn't start the `sendmail` daemon; it just runs the app to deliver this specific message and quits:

```
# sendmail -v taylor@intuitive.com
Subject: test message from Mac OS X

just testing. Please ignore.
.
taylor@intuitive.com... Connecting to mail-fwd.verio-web.com. via esmtp...
220 mail11b.verio-web.com SMTP RS ver 1.0.60s
>>> EHLO dsl-132.dsldesigns.net
500 Command unrecognized
>>> HELO dsl-132.dsldesigns.net
250 mail11b.verio-web.com Hello dsl-132.dsldesigns.com [198.76.82.132],
➥I'm listening
>>> MAIL From:<taylor@dsl-132.dsldesigns.net>
250 taylor@dsl-132.dsldesigns.net... Sender ok
>>> RCPT To:<taylor@intuitive.com>
250 taylor@intuitive.com... Recipient ok
>>> DATA
354 enter mail, end with '.' on a line by itself
>>> .
```

▼
```
250 041745238 Message accepted for delivery
taylor@intuitive.com... Sent (041745238 Message accepted for delivery)
Closing connection to mail-fwd.verio-web.com.
>>> QUIT
221 mail11b.verio-web.com closing connection
```

Notice that though we specified intuitive.com as a domain name, the system knew to open a connection to mail-fwd.verio-web.com, the system that is the MX (mail exchange) record holder for the intuitive.com domain. This is set as part of the DNS record for the domain, as detailed in the previous hour.

This message went through fine, and was delivered without incident. The Command unrecognized on the fourth line of output showed up because sendmail tried to use the extended SMTP protocol (called ESMTP, it's characterized by EHLO, rather than the regular SMTP HELO command), and the remote server didn't know ESMTP and rejected it. The client then simply sent a more normal SMTP HELO and proceeded.

An attempt to deliver a message to a bogus address is informative:

```
# sendmail -v junk@this-is-not-likely-to-work.org < /dev/null
taylor... Connecting to local...
taylor... Sent
```

"Informative?" you ask—it's informative in that it *didn't connect to a remote site*. This implies that sendmail couldn't resolve the domain name specified, and bounced it locally. To understand what happened, we'll need to look in the mail log, which we'll do in the next section.

▲

There's a lot more we could explore with the basic uses of sendmail, but if you want to get that deep into the muck, your best bet is to check out some of the great online reference works at www.sendmail.org, or possibly grab a book on Unix e-mail management.

For now, let's spend a bit more time looking at mail logs and mail queues, then explore some of the capabilities of sendmail that can make it a great help to you as a system administrator.

Mail Logs and Mail Queues

By default, sendmail tries to deliver all mail the moment it arrives. This means that the majority of mail is delivered within seconds of its receipt, and it also means that the outbound mail queue should be quite small. What happens, however, when there are messages to systems where the remote SMTP server isn't running, or is rejecting connections?

20

In those instances, mail is queued for later delivery. Depending on your configuration settings, mail in the queue can have delivery attempted every ten minutes, two hours, or even once daily for as many days as you have specified as the delivery attempt period in the `sendmail.cf` file. Once that time expires, if the message hasn't been delivered, it's bounced back to the sender with a `Bounced: network is unreachable` error or similar.

For the most part, `sendmail` does its own thing and you don't have to intervene too much, but sometimes it's very helpful to be able to know what's in the queue (if anything) and why.

Task 20.2: Mail Logs and Mail Queues

To see what's in the mail queue, many systems include a command called `mailq`, which turns out to be a link to the `sendmail` program itself. An alias such as

```
alias mailq='/usr/sbin/sendmail -bp'
```

will let you accomplish the exact same thing.

Before we look at the mail queue, however, let's peek into the `maillog` file (where all e-mail-related events are logged) to see the fate of the two messages sent in the earlier section of this hour.

1. To learn the fate of e-mail messages, look in `/var/log/maillog` (Linux), `/private/var/log/mail.log` (Mac OS X), or `/var/log/messages` (Solaris 8). Either way, they all have essentially the same format, as demonstrated in this entry from a Mac OS X server:

```
# tail -6 /private/var/log/mail.log
Mar 22 18:11:39 dsl-132 sendmail[486]: g2N2BQ000486: from=taylor, size=66,
class=0, nrcpts=1, msgid=<200203230211.g2N2BQ000486@dsl-
132.dsldesigns.net>,
relay=root@localhost
Mar 22 18:11:45 dsl-132 sendmail[486]: g2N2BQ000486:
to=taylor@intuitive.com,
ctladdr=taylor (501/20), delay=00:00:19, xdelay=00:00:06, mailer=esmtp,
pri=30066, relay=mail-fwd.verio-web.com. [161.58.148.30], dsn=2.0.0,
stat=Sent (041745238 Message accepted for delivery)
Mar 22 18:16:25 dsl-132 sendmail[488]: g2N2GPj00488:
from=taylor, size=0, class=0, nrcpts=1,
msgid=<200203230216.g2N2GPj00488@dsl-132.dsldesigns.net>,
relay=root@localhost
Mar 22 18:16:26 dsl-132 sendmail[488]: g2N2GPj00488:
to=junk@this-is-not-likely-to-work.org, ctladdr=taylor (501/20),
delay=00:00:01, xdelay=00:00:01, mailer=esmtp, pri=30000,
relay=this-is-not-likely-to-work.org, dsn=5.1.2, stat=Host unknown
(Name server: this-is-not-likely-to-work.org: host not found)
Mar 22 18:16:26 dsl-132 sendmail[488]: g2N2GPj00488:
g2N2GPk00488: DSN: Host unknown
```

```
(Name server: this-is-not-likely-to-work.org: host not found)
Mar 22 18:16:26 dsl-132 sendmail[488]: g2N2GPk00488: to=taylor,
delay=00:00:00, xdelay=00:00:00, mailer=local, pri=30100, dsn=2.0.0,
stat=Sent
```

To understand what happened here, notice that the sixth field is the unique message ID: All lines in the log file with the same ID are associated with the same `send-mail` event. Therefore, the first message had the ID of q2N2BQ000486, and the second had an ID of q2N2BQ000488.

The second entry of this log file shows that a message of 66 bytes was sent from user `taylor`. The fifth line indicates the result of the attempt to send the message to the specified address (`taylor@intuitive.com`) using ESMTP (`mailer=esmtp` on the sixth line) relayed through `mail-fwd.verio-web.com` (the MX record server for `intuitive.com`), and that it ended with a `stat=Sent Message accepted for delivery` message.

By contrast, the last lines show a failure: The new message from `taylor` to `junk@this-is-not-likely-to-work.org` failed with `stat=Host unknown`. On the subsequent line is a more explicit error condition: `Host unknown (Name server: this-is-not-likely-to-work.org: host not found)`. The final two lines show that the bounced message was then sent to user `taylor` (for example, bounced to the sender), and that it was `stat=Sent`-delivered without incident.

On a busy system, you could use awk or Perl to extract the `stat=` field, then scan for those that don't equal `Sent` to get a quick idea of what problems you might have on the server.

2. Jumping onto a busy FreeBSD system, a quick invocation of sendmail's queue display feature reveals the following:

```
# sendmail -bp | head -15
                Mail Queue (147 requests)
--Q-ID-- --Size-- -----Q-Time----- ----------Sender/Recipient-----------
SAA14346     290 Tue Mar 26 18:45 xaith
                 (office@iandistudio.com... reply: read error from
mail.iandis)
                                  office@iandistudio.com
SAA16063*   2283 Tue Mar 26 18:54 <lincoln@dlair.net>
                                  <RSwarts@SAS.Samsung.com>
                                  <rswarts@austin.rr.com>
                                  <gotoray@texas.net>
                                  <ATANZI@SPRD1.MDACC.TMC.EDU>
                                  <PRINCESSANDFROG@HOTMAIL.COM>
SAA10097    7031 Tue Mar 26 18:25 MAILER-DAEMON
                     (Deferred: Connection refused by fmailh8.real-net.net.)
                                  <send@fmailh5.real-net.net>
QAA21483*   4651 Tue Mar 26 16:46 <lori@salesinminutes.net>
                     (Deferred: Connection timed out with delphi.mail.eds.com.)
                                  <miirish@delphi.com>
```

20

▼

```
QAA18380    4651 Tue Mar 26 16:39 <lori@salesinminutes.net>
              (Deferred: Connection timed out with delphi.mail.eds.com.)
                                   <miirish@delphi.com>
```

The first line shows the total number of requests in the outbound mail queue—147—and then each request is listed with its queue-ID, size (in bytes), when it entered the queue, a sender/recipient list, and a status, if known.

The first message in the queue, for example, has been queued for about three hours (use `date` to get the current date and time, then compare it to the timestamp shown), which, given that the system is trying to send mail every 10 minutes, means that it's already tried approximately 18 times to deliver this message and failed.

The message is being sent by `xaith` to `office@iandistudio.com`, and the specific error is `reply: read error from mail.iandis`. This particular error usually indicates that the remote system is out of disk space or otherwise unable to receive mail, though its SMTP daemon is listening and answering queries that come in.

Notice on the second entry that the queue-ID value has a trailing asterisk. This means that there's an active `sendmail` trying to deliver it right now. If it's delivered successfully, this entry will vanish from the queue. Notice that there's no queue error message, suggesting that this is the first time that the system has tried to deliver this e-mail.

Compare that to the fourth entry, which also has an asterisk indicating that `send-mail` is actively trying to deliver it, but because there's an error message (`Deferred: Connection refused by fmailh8.real-net.net`), you can see that it's been in the queue for at least one delivery cycle.

Actually, the fourth entry is the most interesting because it's from MAILER-DAEMON. This tells us that a message came into our system for a specific user from `send@fmailh5.real-net.net`, and it then bounced locally. The bounced message (which automatically has MAILER-DAEMON as the sender) is queued to go back to the sender, but the MX record for `real-net.net` is `fmailh8`, which isn't accepting connections.

> A cockeyed setup like the fourth entry strongly suggests a spam message to me: It's coming from one mail server, from a generic address (user `send`?), and the responding MX record for the sender domain is rejecting connections. Hmmm....

▼

3. There are three main reasons that messages end up in a queue: local system failures, lookup and name resolution problems, and remote connection failures.

A `connection refused` message is a remote connection failure. Although sometimes this is caused by the system being down for a backup, relocation, or having crashed, many times it indicates systems that don't have an SMTP daemon running and don't want to get e-mail. Searching for this in the queue shows the following:

```
# mailq | grep refused | sort | uniq -c | sort -rn
      16                    (Deferred: Connection refused by mail.zwallet.com.)
       4                    (Deferred: Connection refused by 66.106.197.165.)
       3   8BITMIME         (Deferred: Connection refused by fgit.maillist.com.tw.)
       3                    (Deferred: Connection refused by postoffice.randbad.com.)
       2                    (Deferred: Connection refused by cors.estsale.ac.ma.)
       1   8BITMIME         (Deferred: Connection refused by www.mundomail.net.)
       1                    (Deferred: Connection refused by william.monsterjoke.com.)
       1                    (Deferred: Connection refused by webchi.com.)
       1                    (Deferred: Connection refused by smtp.apsoffers.com.)
       1                    (Deferred: Connection refused by mta1.mail.hotbot.com.)
       1                    (Deferred: Connection refused by lamx01.mgw.rr.com.)
       1                    (Deferred: Connection refused by billingproblemmail.
➡doteasy.c)
```

I've sorted and "uniq'd" them to shrink the output a bit. There are 16 messages queued for `mail.zwallet.com`, which suggests that either it's a very popular site, or someone is dumping messages to it.

4. Another message you might see is a name lookup error:

```
# mailq | grep lookup | sort | uniq -c | sort -rn
       7                    (host map: lookup (Liberty4Success.com): deferred)
       5                    (host map: lookup (poorrichardsenterprises.com): deferred)
       3                    (host map: lookup (NewSouthConstruction.net): deferred)
       2                    (host map: lookup (sdd.com): deferred)
       2                    (host map: lookup (gaystufftodo.net): deferred)
       2                    (Deferred: Name server: zero.nochill.com.: host name
➡lookup f)
       1   8BITMIME         (host map: lookup (virtueltv.com): deferred)
       1                    (host map: lookup (webmastermindsonline.com): deferred)
       1                    (host map: lookup (spinstudios.com): deferred)
       1                    (host map: lookup (pretaluz.com): deferred)
       1                    (host map: lookup (palesedesign.com): deferred)
       1                    (host map: lookup (maos.org): deferred)
       1                    (host map: lookup (libertywebdevelopment.com): deferred)
       1                    (host map: lookup (grundvig.com): deferred)
       1                    (host map: lookup (chequemail.com): deferred)
```

20

▼   Many of these look suspiciously like spam to my jaded eye, particularly
liberty4success.com, poorrichardsenterprises.com, and chequemail.com.
Because you, as system administrator, are responsible for your user community and
for ensuring that people stick to the Acceptable Use Policy (AUP), you'd do well to
investigate these.

One way to investigate is to simply find the recipient and sender associated with
these messages. This can be done with grep, particularly with the –B*n* flag, which
indicates that you'd like *n* lines of context prior to each match. Because deferred
lookups are always for the recipient, it's a safe bet that this will reveal what we
want:

```
# mailq | grep -B1 -i liberty4
QAA17284      4657 Tue Mar 26 16:36 <lori@salesinminutes.net>
                   (host map: lookup (Liberty4Success.com): deferred)
                                     <Karen@Liberty4Success.com>
--
QAA15045      4657 Tue Mar 26 16:30 <lori@salesinminutes.net>
                   (host map: lookup (Liberty4Success.com): deferred)
                                     <Karen@Liberty4Success.com>
--
AAA18116       269 Tue Mar 26 00:06 ximinute
                   (host map: lookup (Liberty4Success.com): deferred)
                                     Karen@Liberty4Success.com
--
AAA27255       269 Mon Mar 25 00:04 ximinute
                   (host map: lookup (Liberty4Success.com): deferred)
                                     Karen@Liberty4Success.com
--
AAA27203       269 Sun Mar 24 00:04 ximinute
                   (host map: lookup (Liberty4Success.com): deferred)
                                     Karen@Liberty4Success.com
--
AAA00798       269 Sat Mar 23 00:05 ximinute
                   (host map: lookup (Liberty4Success.com): deferred)
                                     Karen@Liberty4Success.com
--
AAA20693       269 Fri Mar 22 00:04 ximinute
                   (host map: lookup (Liberty4Success.com): deferred)
                                     Karen@Liberty4Success.com
```

As suspected, almost every one of these messages is from ximinute to Karen@lib-
erty4success.com. Notice the times of these messages: all approximately at midnight, on March 22, March 23, March 24, March 25, and March 26. I suspect a
cron job or similar automated mail system, and I suspect some sort of spam. I'd
talk with this user to ask what's going on if I were the main sysadmin for this box.

5. Another strategy you can use is to go into the actual mail queueing area, typically
/var/spool/mqueue. It'll have lots of files, including a bunch of config and data
▼   files for each queued message, as detailed in Table 20.1.

TABLE 20.1 Files Commonly Found in the `mqueue` Directory

Prefix	Contents
df	The body of the message
Qf	Created if the message bounced and could not be returned
qf	The header of the message (the control file)
tf	A temporary version of the qf file while delivery is being attempted
Tf	Created if 32 or more locking attempts have failed
xf	Transcript of a specific error message from a remote server

Let's create a simple message and dig into the different possible files:

```
# sendmail -O DeliveryMode=d -t
From: ximinute
To: Karen@Liberty4Success.com
Subject: fabulous offer

You are authorized to receive a fabulous offer...
.
#
```

This immediately queues the message (that's what `DeliveryMode=d` does), so we can then see what it looks like in the queue with `mqueue`, which among its waves of output, shows:

```
g2R8OWC14928       50 Wed Mar 27 00:24 ximinute
                              Karen@Liberty4Success.com
```

The two files created by default are the `df*` and `qf*` files:

```
# cat df*
You are authorized to receive a fabulous offer...
# cat qf*
V4
T1017217472
K0
N0
P120
I8/18/26706
Fb
$_ximinute@localhost
Sximinute
Aximinute@staging.intuitive.com
RPFD:Karen@Liberty4Success.com
H?P?Return-Path: <?g>
H?D?Date: Wed, 27 Mar 2002 00:24:32 -0800
H?M?Message-Id: <200203270824.g2R8OWC14928@staging.intuitive.com>
```

20

```
H??From: ximinute
H??To: Karen@Liberty4Success.com
H??Subject: fabulous offer
       .
```

Without going into exhaustive detail about each line in the `qf*` file, suffice to say that it has all the headers, and considerable queuing information. While a delivery is being attempted, an empty file `xfg2R8OWC14928` is created.

The actual files in the mail queue directory `/var/spool/mqueue` can reveal some interesting information and can help you identify which users might be spamming, whether you have an open relay or other possible problems. It's worth keeping an eye on its contents.

> However, again, be conscious of privacy issues: It would be easy to read the contents of every e-mail message leaving your system. Your users might not be thrilled if they find out, however.

Creating `sendmail` Aliases

I expect that your head is fairly swimming from delving into some of the internals of the `sendmail` program, so let's tackle an easier topic for a break: mail aliases.

The concept is quite straightforward—instead of only accepting mail for specific login names on your system, mail aliases let you accept e-mail and forward it to an individual on another system, a group of individuals, a file listing a number of mailing addresses, or even a specific program or file.

> Mac OS X has a completely different way of managing mail aliases, through the `NetInfo` mechanism. It'll be covered in the last section of this hour.

Task 20.3: Mail Aliases

The original `sendmail` program enabled you to have aliases pointing to a wide variety of different destinations, including files, programs, remote addresses, and even lists of e-mail addresses. In the last few years, more effort has been put into security in the e-mail world, and it's affected `sendmail` most directly in the more limited aliases available on a standard system configuration.

▼   We'll have a quick look at some of the more advanced aliases in this last section, but don't be surprised if your Unix OS blocks them by default, often with a cryptic error message.

1. The most basic alias is to have a different name point to an existing mailbox. This seems silly, but can prove quite useful to ensure that users get e-mail sent to them, regardless of whether senders know their specific login names.

    For example, on my server, my account is `taylor`, but what happens if you send mail to `dave` instead? It would bounce by default. This can be easily fixed, however, by adding the following to `/etc/aliases`:

    ```
    dave:    taylor
    ```

    That's all we need to do, and once the aliases file is rebuilt—with the `newaliases` command—then mail sent to `dave` will be properly delivered in the `taylor` mailbox.

    As a result, many sites will automatically add common alternatives for a given name as aliases, to ensure that there are minimal bounces. If a new user Susan McGill joined the firm, here's the set of aliases that might be created:

    ```
    mcgill:        susan
    macgill:          susan
    smcgill:       susan
    susanm:        susan
    susan_mcgill:     susan
    susan.mcgill: susan
    ```

    Notice the second alias in particular: Because we expect that some people will misspell Susan's last name, it's easy to add an alias to ensure mail sent to `macgill@`*ourserver* works.

2. The second type of alias is a redirect off-system:

    ```
    john:        john@aol.com
    ```

    In this case, any mail sent to `john` on the local system, whether or not he has an account set up, will automatically be redirected to his AOL mailbox.

    You can combine both types of alias in a simple list, too:

    ```
    split:       mary, mary@Delphi.net
    ```

    In this instance, mail sent to `split@`*ourserver* is duplicated and sent to `mary` locally (assuming that there isn't a separate alias set up), and `mary@Delphi.net`.

    You can also use this list feature to create rudimentary mailing lists:

    ```
    writers:       dave,dee-ann,gideon,rima,smithers@some.host.com
    ```

    In this case, mail sent to `writers` would automatically be expanded to `dave`, `dee-ann`, `gideon`, `rima`, and, off-system, `smithers@some.host.com`.

20

3. There's a better way to manage lists of addresses, however, and that's to use a file inclusion alias. These look a bit peculiar, but prove tremendously helpful:

```
writers:     :include:/home/taylor/writers.list
```

In this situation, any mail sent to `writers` will be sent to every e-mail address in the specified file. The file contents will be read on demand each time a message is sent, so if it changes between `newaliases` runs, the changes are seen at once.

The real advantage of the `:include:` notation is that your users can manage their own mailing lists without you having to touch (or let them touch!) the actual `/etc/aliases` file. This can significantly simplify your day-to-day system administration tasks!

4. To redirect to a file, an alias can be written as

```
archive:     /private/mail/archive
```

However, most `sendmail` configurations now disable saving directly to files because of security issues (though what security issues are associated with writing directly to a file escapes me, unless you had something wacky like `/etc/passwd` as the archive file—in which case you could e-mail a line like `root::0:0::::` and have an instant superuser login).

5. Another mechanism that used to be widespread in `sendmail` installations, but is now quite limited, is the capability to have an alias point directly to a program on the server. To address the security problems, modern `sendmail` installations now include a special program `smrsh`, the `sendmail` restricted shell, which is used explicitly as a safe "sandbox" for running programs that are part of an alias. The alias looks like this:

```
ps:      "|/bin/ps"
```

If your installation has good error messages, an attempt to send to the `ps` alias will result in the following information as part of the bounced test message:

```
    ----- The following addresses had permanent fatal errors -----
"|/bin/ps"
   (reason: service unavailable)
   (expanded from: toprog)

    ----- Transcript of session follows -----
smrsh: ps not available for sendmail programs
554 5.0.0 "|/bin/ps"... Service unavailable
```

Notice the reference to `smrsh` in the second-to-last line: We thought we were specifying `/bin/ps`, but `smrsh` automatically stripped the path specification and looked in its own list of known programs for `ps`.

To learn more about how to configure `smrsh` to enable access to the popular `vacation` program, `filter`, `procmail`, and other sophisticated e-mail filtering programs, read the `smrsh` man page.

The specifics of creating a flexible and functional set of mail aliases for your user community are going to vary, but being able to have a centralized alias system, compensate for common spelling mistakes, normalize e-mail addresses within an organization while simultaneously letting users pick their own login names, and the `:include:` mechanism all demonstrate the many facets of `sendmail`'s tremendous power and flexibility.

It is worth mentioning that many Unix configurations will let users have their own `.forward` file in their home directory that, if permissions are set properly, will let them have simple redirects, comma-separated lists, and other mechanisms without any changes required in the `aliases` file itself.

Also, there are some very powerful mailing list managers available that hook up as `|prog` mechanisms, but then offer a complete list management service. You've probably seen some of them, they're called `majordomo`, `listserv`, and so on. If your user community has a need for flexible mailing lists, Table 20.2 offers some good starting places to learn more.

TABLE 20.2   Common Unix-based Mailing List Managers

Name	Home URL
ListProc	www.cren.net
Mailman	www.list.org
Majordomo	www.greatcircle.com
SmartList	www.procmail.org

Of these choices, by the way, I'd recommend you start by looking at Mailman—it's a nice package that includes a straightforward Web-based interface, and it's a big hit with users and mailing list managers.

`sendmail` Aliases Within Mac OS X

20

As you learned earlier when exploring how to add new users to a Darwin/Mac OS X system, even though Apple has Unix as the foundation of its new operating system, it still has some twists and quirks that make working with it not quite as straightforward as other Unix flavors.

In particular, Apple has centralized all the databases that were spread across `/etc/passwd`, `/etc/groups`, `/etc/aliases`, and so on, and dropped them all into a centralized database called `NetInfo`. It's cropped up before in this book, and this time we'll need to work with the `NetInfo` system to create and test e-mail aliases, rather than edit the more common file `/etc/aliases` (or, on some systems, `/etc/mail/aliases`).

Task 20.4: Mac OS X and `sendmail` Aliases

Fortunately, the two tools that we used earlier to work with the `/etc/passwd` file will let us also easily manipulate the e-mail aliases section of the `NetInfo` database: `nidump` and `niutil`.

1. A simple one-line script starts us out:

```
# cat showaliases
#!/bin/sh

# showaliases - list all current email aliases from NetInfo

nidump aliases .
```

Running this requires changing it to executable mode, then ensuring that its in your current PATH. Once that's accomplished, here's a typical output:

```
# showaliases
administrator: root
postmaster: root
MAILER-DAEMON: postmaster
MAILER-AGENT: postmaster
nobody: root
dumper: root
manager: root
operator: root
```

Nothing too exciting, as you can see!

2. Adding an alias requires a little bit more fancy footwork in the script, because we have to ensure that the new alias doesn't step on the toes of an existing alias (that is, it doesn't use a name that's already in use). Here's the `addalias` script:

```
# cat addalias
#!/bin/sh

# addalias - add a new alias to the email alias database...

showaliases=/Users/taylor/bin/showaliases

echo -n "Alias to create: "
read alias

# now let's check to see if that alias already exists...

existing=`$showaliases | grep "^${alias}:"`

if [ "$existing" != "" ] ; then
  echo "mail alias $alias already exists:"
  echo "      $existing"
  exit 0
fi
```

```
# looks good. let's get the RHS and inject it into NetInfo

echo -n "pointing to: "
read rhs

niutil -create . /aliases/$alias
niutil -createprop . /aliases/$alias name $alias
niutil -createprop . /aliases/$alias members $rhs

echo "Alias $alias created without incident."

exit 0
```

In a manner common to most system administrators who write lots of shell scripts, you can see that my second script here calls the first. Also note the use of the -n flag to echo, which prevents a trailing carriage return. As will become obvious in a moment, this means that you have nice prompts for input requests.

Here's addalias in action:

```
# addalias
Alias to create: operator
mail alias operator already exists:
      operator: root
```

Oops! That's already in use. Score one for addalias.

```
# addalias
Alias to create: author
pointing to: taylor
Alias author created without incident.
# showaliases | tail -1
author: taylor
```

That worked just fine, as is demonstrated by the addition of the new alias in the showaliases output.

3. The aliases explained in the previous section can also be quickly added to the Mac OS X system with the addalias script:

```
# addalias
Alias to create: writers
pointing to: dave,dee-ann,gideon,rima,smithers@some.host.com
Alias writers created without incident.
# addalias
Alias to create: writer-list
pointing to: :include:/Users/taylor/writers.list
Alias writer-list created without incident.
# addalias
Alias to create: ps
pointing to: "|ps"
Alias ps created without incident.
```

20

▼

And verified with `showaliases`:

```
# showaliases
administrator: root
postmaster: root
MAILER-DAEMON: postmaster
MAILER-AGENT: postmaster
nobody: root
dumper: root
manager: root
operator: root
author: taylor
writers: dave,dee-ann,gideon,rima,smithers@some.host.com
writer-list: :include:/Users/taylor/writers.list
ps: "|ps"
```

4. It's worth pointing out again that having these aliases set up doesn't mean that they'll work! A few quick examples with `sendmail -v` on Mac OS X:

```
# sendmail -v writer-list < /dev/null
writer-list... aliased to :include:/Users/taylor/writers.list
:include:/Users/taylor/writers.list... including file
/Users/taylor/writers.list
:include:/Users/taylor/writers.list... Cannot open /Users/taylor/writers.list:
➥No such file or directory
taylor... Connecting to local...
taylor... Sent
```

We've set up the alias, but the included file `writers.list` doesn't exist, and the message bounced.

```
# sendmail -v ps < /dev/null
ps... aliased to "|ps"
"|ps"... Connecting to prog...
taylor... Connecting to local...
taylor... Sent
```

That appears to have worked. Let's double-check the `/private/var/log/mail.log` file to see:

```
# tail -6 mail.log
Mar 28 00:13:12 dsl-132 sendmail[433]: gethostbyaddr(198.76.82.132) failed: 1
Mar 28 00:13:12 dsl-132 sendmail[433]: g2S8DCL00433: from=taylor, size=0,
➥class=0, nrcpts=1, msgid=<200203280813.g2S8DCL00433@dsl-132.
➥dsldesigns.net>, relay=root@localhost
Mar 28 00:13:12 dsl-132 smrsh: uid 1: attempt to use ps
Mar 28 00:13:12 dsl-132 sendmail[433]: g2S8DCL00433: to="|ps",
➥ctladdr=ps (1/0), delay=00:00:00, xdelay=00:00:00, mailer=prog,
➥pri=30000, dsn=5.0.0, stat=Service unavailable
Mar 28 00:13:12 dsl-132 sendmail[433]: g2S8DCL00433: g2S8DCM00433: DSN:
➥Service unavailable
Mar 28 00:13:12 dsl-132 sendmail[433]: g2S8DCM00433: to=taylor,
➥delay=00:00:00, xdelay=00:00:00, mailer=local,
pri=30100, dsn=2.0.0, stat=Sent
```

▼

As you can see, the message in fact failed: `smrsh: uid 1: attempt to use ps`, followed by a `Stat=Service unavailable` and a bounce.

> To enable `ps`, or any other command you'd like to have at the end of an e-mail pipe, read the discussion and details on the `smrsh man` page.

Summary

Pleasantly, once you create a few tools to help you work with the `NetInfo` system directly from the command line, it's quite easy to create Mac OS X e-mail aliases that conform to the standard `sendmail` aliases as found within `/etc/aliases` on most other Unix systems.

Q&A

Q **If I don't want to run `sendmail`, what would you recommend as a replacement MTA?**

A There are two MTA replacements that have good reputations in the Unix industry: `exim` and `postfix`. In the last six months or so, lots of people have been talking about how `postfix` installed easily on their OS X systems and simplified the configuration and management of their e-mail servers. You can learn about these two alternatives at `www.exim.org` and `www.postfix.org`, respectively.

Q **I ran `sendmail -v` on a message and it failed. Now what?**

A The first step in debugging a `sendmail` problem—as with any Unix system problem—is to check the information in the log files. In this case, you'll want to check `maillog` (or `mail.log`, depending on your flavor of Unix). If that doesn't reveal the problem, check the permissions and briefly skim through the `sendmail.cf` file to see whether there's anything obviously wrong. If those don't solve the problem, go back a few hours in this book to read a bit about using `ping` and `dig`.

Q **I've heard a lot about the dangers of "open relays." What are they, and how do I know if I have one?**

A An open relay is a system that will forward e-mail from someone offsite to another person also offsite, effectively relaying the mail. Spammers love this, and as a result, open relay systems can end up blocked by many spam-unfriendly sites. You can check to see whether you're an open relay, and learn how to fix it, online at `http://www.mail-abuse.org/tsi/`.

20

Workshop

Quiz

1. How do you ascertain the most recent version of `sendmail`?

2. What would be wrong with setting the QUEUE value of the `/etc/sysconfig/sendmail` file to 1m?

3. Try sending a message to an AOL account from the command line with `sendmail -v`. Do you get the error message 550 REQUESTED ACTION NOT TAKEN: DNS FAILURE? What do you think it means?

4. What's tricky about analyzing the contents of the mail queue?

5. What do each of the following mail aliases accomplish?

   ```
   curly: moe,larry
   moe: :include:/home/lists/stooges
   larry: "|vacation"
   ```

Answers

1. You can figure out your own version of `sendmail` with the odd-looking command `sendmail -bg -d0.1 < /dev/null`, and you can ascertain the latest version of the program itself at www.sendmail.org.

2. If your queue value is too small, your system will be constantly spinning, trying to deliver messages in the queue. It won't get them delivered any faster, but it could significantly affect your overall performance.

3. DNS FAILURE means that AOL tried to do a reverse lookup on your IP address and failed to get a hostname that matched what you are announcing when you connect. It's a spam filter trick in their mail daemon.

4. The challenge is that the mail queue is constantly in flux: Any snapshot of the information (such as the output of the `mailq` command) is sliding into obsolescence while you're reading through it....

5. The `curly` alias points to two addresses, `moe` and `larry`. `moe` then points to a list of e-mail addresses called `/home/lists/stooges`, and `larry` hands off all his e-mail to the `vacation` program through a *toprog* pipe notation (`"|vacation"`).

In the next hour, we'll tackle a topic that has pervaded this entire book, but we'll finally focus on it exclusively: shell scripting. As has been demonstrated over and over, being able to write simple and effective shell scripts is perhaps the single biggest time saver for any savvy Unix system administrator, so you'll want to warm up your brain cells to really get the most possible out of Hour 21.

PART VII

Web Server Management & Shell Programming

Hour

HOUR 21

Shell Scripting: The Administrator's Swiss Army Knife

If I had to pick one core skill that differentiated good system administrators from mediocre ones, it would be shell scripting. It's useful to know the tools in the operating system (or systems) you use, of course, but being able to put those tools together and build something that addresses the specific needs and requirements of your user community is a critical capability.

Throughout this book, you've had a chance to see many shell scripts, ranging from simple one-liners to rather sophisticated scripts with loops, conditional execution, return code analysis, and much more.

In this hour, we'll focus specifically on the language and capabilities of shell scripts, re-examine some of the earlier scripts to see exactly what they accomplish, and introduce some new scripts to expand your programming horizons.

There are tasks that cannot be accomplished in the shell, of course, and for those you'll want to move to awk, Perl, or C, depending on the task, and of course, your level of familiarity with the development environment.

In this hour, you will learn:

- The basics of shell scripting
- How to control a script's flow

The Basics of Shell Scripting

The first and most important question for anyone developing shell scripts is: *what shell*?

The answer to that varies somewhat in the Unix system administrator community, but most sysadmins, myself included, believe that the best scripting environment is the Bourne Shell (sh). Whether you use csh, tcsh, zsh, or whatever, just about every shell script you'll find uses the Bourne Shell as its interpreter.

> Of course, on many systems /bin/sh is actually a hard link to /bin/bash, meaning that sh is really an instance of bash. That's fine: bash has the exact same syntax and semantics as the older Bourne Shell, and offers some great capabilities in addition, and a solid, constantly improving code base.

Task 21.1: Basic Shell Scripts

▼ TASK

Like any procedural programming language, shell scripts are executed from the first line to the last, and errors in the script are only encountered when the *interpreter* (the shell) reads the line just prior to execution.

1. By default, all shell scripts are executed by your login shell or the shell specified by the SHELL environment variable, unless you specify otherwise. As a result, all well-written shell scripts *do* specify otherwise—the first line of all shell scripts should specify the desired shell and any starting arguments desired. A typical first line looks like this:

   ```
   #!/bin/sh
   ```

   The #! notation has special meaning in Unix, and the shell that's reading the script initially uses the information in that first line to ascertain what program should actually execute (run) the script. For example, Perl scripts have

   ```
   #!/usr/bin/perl
   ```

▼

▼

and Python programs might well have

```
#!/usr/local/bin/python
```

as their first line.

2. The Bourne Shell[1] has a variety of starting flags that can be specified on this first line of the script, with interesting and often valuable results. Foremost among these is the -x flag, which turns on debugging mode. We'll see an example of this a bit later in the hour.

Another useful flag that's popular with script writers is -f, which disables reading any sort of rc or other configuration file. You won't have any of your aliases available, but you will have your scripts start out and run quite a bit faster.

To add a starting flag, simply append it to the first line:

```
#!/bin/sh -f
```

A third starting flag, one that might not be available in all versions of the Bourne Shell, is -n, which will scan through a script ensuring that the syntax is acceptable, but won't actually execute the script or any of the commands therein. This probably wouldn't appear within the script, but rather would be something you invoke on the command line as a special test:

```
$ sh -n mytestscript
```

just as you can also turn on debugging conditionally by invoking the shell script as

```
$ sh -x mytestscript
```

3. Enough discussion—let's see a very simple shell script in its entirety to see how they're organized.

```
$ cat showaliases
#!/bin/sh

# showaliases - list all current email aliases from NetInfo

nidump aliases .
```

This very simple shell script has three lines: an indication of what shell should be used, a comment that describes briefly the purpose of the script, and the actual Unix command to run.

A slightly longer example might be more interesting:

```
$ cat diskhogs
#!/bin/sh

# diskhogs - report which users are taking up the most disk space
```

▼

---

[1]*Or whatever shell you have that's emulating the Bourne Shell (for example, bash).*

21

```
echo "Disk Hogs Report for System `hostname`"

bigdir2="`du -s /Library/* | sed 's/ /_/g' | sort -rn | cut -f2- | head -5`"

echo "The Five biggest library directories are:"
echo $bigdir2

for dirname in $bigdir2 ; do
  echo ""
  echo Big directory: $dirname
  echo Four largest files in that directory are:
  find "`echo $dirname | sed 's/_/ /g'`" -type f -ls | \
    awk '{ print $7" "$11 }' | sort -rn | head -4
done

exit 0
```

Hopefully, you're starting to see a pattern emerge. The first line is the same, the second line is a brief comment, and the rest of the script is the actual executable section.

Like other programming environments, shell scripts let you define script *constants*—mnemonic names that represent common directories, programs, commands, or values. In this script, it's the `bigdir2` line near the top. One of the best programming techniques you can practice with shell scripts is to define your constant values at the top of the script. This not only makes it easier to move to a new Unix environment, but it also makes it a *lot* more readable, too!

Most of the work in this shell script is done in the `for` loop, which we'll discuss shortly. The only point that's important to note here is that structurally, you can see that you can have more than one command on the same line by separating them with a semicolon (notice the `;  do` at the end of the `for` line), and that if you have a long, complex pipe or command line, you can split it across multiple lines by simply ending a line with a backslash (\).

If you use backslashes to split long lines, make sure you don't have *any characters after the slash*. Even a trailing space or tab character will cause odd and confusing error messages when the script is run.

4. As the previous shell script demonstrates, shell scripts can have variables that are either assigned an initial value that's constant throughout execution, or have their value change as the script runs.

An example of the latter is the following:

```
$ cat countfiles
#!/bin/sh

# countfiles - return a count of the files matching the specified pattern

pattern="${1:-dave}"
locate=/usr/bin/locate

for name in `$locate $pattern`
do
  count="`expr ${count:-0} + 1`"
done

echo "I counted $count files that matched pattern $pattern"

exit 0
```

This is an interesting script, because it has variables performing three different functions: locate is a constant that makes it easy to reconfigure the script for different Unixes that have the locate command in odd places (or not at all, perhaps replacing it with a find). The count variable is a numeric counter that increments by one each time it's referenced in the line:

```
count="`expr ${count:-0} + 1`"
```

The pattern variable holds the filename pattern that's being counted, or, if no value is initially specified on the command line, dave as the default pattern.

The unusual notation of ${variable:-default} should be read as a very convenient shorthand for the following logic: if $variable is defined, then $variable; otherwise the default value $default. In the initial assignment to pattern, you can now see that the line

```
pattern="${1:-dave}"
```

really means "let pattern equal $1 if the user specified a pattern on the command line, otherwise use the default pattern of dave."

5. This shell script also demonstrates that you can use the helpful expr command for simple math functions, particularly within shell scripts.

For example, here's a variation on the preceding shell script that calculates the total number of lines, and the average number of lines per file as well:

```
$ cat countfiles
#!/bin/sh

# countfiles - return a count of the files matching the specified pattern,
# and average line counts too.
```

21

```
pattern="${1:-dave}"
locate=/usr/bin/locate

for name in `$locate $pattern`
do
  count="`expr ${count:-0} + 1`"
  lines="`wc -l < $name`"
  totalines="`expr ${totalines:-0} + ${lines:-0}`"
done

echo "$count files, with $totalines lines, match pattern $pattern"
echo "for an average of `expr $totalines / $count` lines per file."

exit 0
```

When run, this script reports the following:

```
$ ./countfiles
5 files, with 68 lines, match pattern dave
for an average of 13 lines per file.
```

Nice and neat.

6. Let's have a closer look at the various special notations you can use with variables, as that's quite helpful for shell programming. First, let's look at positional parameters in Table 21.1.

TABLE 21.1 Shell Positional Parameters

Notation	Explanation
$1..$9	The first through ninth argument on the command line.
${10}...	The tenth through the nth parameter on the command line (even 10 parameters are quite a few, though, so you'll most likely never need to use this notation).
$#	The number of parameters given to the command.
$*	A list of all the parameters (commonly used by *wrapper* scripts that might log the use of a command, then hand all its starting arguments and flags to the real binary).
$@	The same as $*, but all arguments are quoted. Probably safer to use in almost all cases.

A very common test in shell scripts is one that ensures that the positional parameters are specified as desired. If countfiles insisted on a pattern being specified, an easy test at the top of the script would be

```
if [ $# -ne 2 ]
then
  echo "Usage: countfiles PATTERN"
  exit 0
fi
```

Nicely, this conditional statement (if *condition*) will also catch when the user specifies *too many* positional parameters as well.

> If you're stepping through positional parameters, a very useful shell function called shift is worth knowing. When invoked, all positional parameters move down one value, so $2 becomes $1, $3 becomes $2, and so on.

Generally, all variables should be referenced with the notation ${*name*}, but in practice, it's only necessary when there would be confusion over the exact variable name. Examples: Is $11 really $1 and a 1, or referencing the eleventh variable? Is echo "$joe:" referring to $joe, and if so, how does the shell interpret :" as a special notation? Does $1ish reference $1 and append ish to it, or is it a variable called 1ish?

In all of the preceding cases, the curly brackets resolve the ambiguity: ${1}1, echo "${joe}:", and ${1}ish.

7. There are also some important substitution notations that are well worth knowing for shell scripting, as summarized in Table 21.2.

TABLE 21.2   Shell Variable Reference Notation

Notation	Explanation
${variable:-*default*}	$variable if defined, *default* otherwise.
${variable:=*default*}	$variable if defined, otherwise set variable to the specified *default* value and return that value as well. This acts similarly to "if not defined, then $variable = *default*."
${variable:?*message*}	$variable if defined, or an error message is printed consisting of the variable name followed by the specific message. For example: ${SHELL:?You must have a shell defined for this script}.
${variable:+*value*}	If $variable is defined, return *value*, otherwise return null. For example: ${name:+1} would return 1 if the variable name was assigned a value.
${variable:*offset*}	Return the value of $variable starting at character *offset*. For example: ${name:3} would return the third through last characters of $name.
${variable:*offset*:*length*}	A variation on ${variable:*offset*}, this returns a substring of the specified *length*, starting at *offset* of the variable specified. For example: ${name:3:1} would return the third letter of the value assigned to $name.

21

▼   When working with mathematical notation, it's particularly important to use substitution notation to ensure that you don't generate out-of-range or undefined result errors. A common technique to avoid dividing by an undefined value, for example, might be:

```
result="`expr $num / ${denom:?Can't be undefined}`"
```

To avoid dividing by zero requires a more elaborate conditional statement:

```
if [ ${denom:-0} -eq 0 ] ; then
  echo "Can't divide by zero. Error."
  exit 0
fi
```

This also demonstrates the value of the `: -` notation: In this case, even if the variable `$denom` is undefined, this conditional statement will catch it and avoid the potential problem.

8. It's worth spending a few minutes looking at the `expr` statement itself before we move on to conditional statements and loops.

The `expr` command is one of the hidden gems of Unix. Although it might not be a particularly friendly interactive command, it does let you calculate a wide variety of mathematical and other results, as shown in Table 21.3.

TABLE 21.3   Common expr Functions

Function	Meaning
+	Addition.
-	Subtraction.
/	Division.
*	Multiplication (be careful not to have this expand as a shell wild card in use! Use `\*` if it's not in a quoted string).
%	Division, returning the remainder.
length *string*	Length of *string*.
substr *string pos length*	Returns the substring of *string* starting at *pos* for *length* characters. This is, of course, identical to `${string:pos:length}`.

In addition to the helpful mathematical functions, `length` solves an otherwise tough puzzle: How do you figure out how long a string is within a shell script?

Knowing this function, it's a straightforward process to find out which login accounts have a login name that exceeds the standard eight-character limit of Unix:

```
$ cat longname
#!/bin/sh
```

```
# longname - scan all login names in /etc/passwd, output any that
#            are longer than 8 chars

maxlength=8

for login in `cut -d: -f1 /etc/passwd`
do
  if [ `expr length $login` -gt $maxlength ]
  then
    echo Warning: login $login exceeds $maxlength character max.
  fi
done

exit 0
```

On a system that's well organized, there shouldn't be any problems reported at all. However, one of the systems I use, a FreeBSD box, reports the following:

```
$ ./longname
Warning: login postmaster exceeds 8 character max.
```

Something worth fixing.[2] Notice also that the use of maxlength to define the value 8 in one place really clarifies the logic of the script, and also makes it easier if in fact only seven characters were recognized.

> Another way to ascertain the number of characters in a string variable within the shell is to reference ${#variable}; for example, the preceding test could be done with if [${#login} -gt $maxlength] instead.

We can spend quite a bit of time on shell script programming, as you are starting to suspect. Not only is it helpful, it's just very interesting, and one of my favorite parts of writing this book is creating these nifty little example shell scripts. You could, for example, check out Sriranga Veeraraghavan's *Sams Teach Yourself Shell Programming in 24 Hours*, but we'll go faster than that here and see how it goes!

Flow Control

It's just about impossible to demonstrate one feature of shell script programming without delving into others along the way, so you have already seen a number of examples of both conditional statements (if-then) and looping mechanisms.

21

---

[2] *Or not—all this means is that postmast, postmaste, and postmaster are all synonymous, because only the first eight characters of the login are checked. Not a huge crisis, unless you forgot and tried to create postmaster2 and postmaster3 as separate accounts.*

Because there are so many different ways to build complex conditional statements, and because loops are so essential to smart shell script programming, it's quite helpful to examine them in closer detail. Finally, this section will also briefly introduce shell functions.

Task 21.2: Conditionals, Looping, and Functions

It is certainly possible to have useful shell scripts that move in a linear fashion through a set of steps without any conditional tests or loops needed, but it's unlikely. Almost every helpful script at least checks to ensure the starting parameters are valid. Let's see how it's done.

1. To start, let's back up a bit and realize that there's a problem with the version of `countfiles` shown earlier. To wit: What happens if we specify a pattern that doesn't have any matches?

```
$ ./countfiles linda
 files, with  lines, match pattern linda
for an average of / lines per file.
```

Ugh. Not too good. What's happened is, because there were no matches, all the conditional variables were blank (undefined), and the final `expr` ended up seeing the command

```
expr /
```

so it (logically) returned the `/` as its result.

To fix this, we'll want to add a conditional test prior to emitting the summary information. This can be done by changing the output lines to wrap them in a test:

```
if [ $count -eq 0 ] ; then
  echo "No files found that match pattern $pattern"
else
  echo "$count files, with $totalines lines, match pattern $pattern"
  echo "for an average of `expr $totalines / $count` lines per file."
fi
```

Seem correct? Let's test it:

```
$ ./countfiles linda
./countfiles: [: -eq: unary operator expected
 files, with  lines, match pattern linda
for an average of / lines per file.
$
```

A classic shell scripting error! The `count` variable isn't defined, so the test `$count -eq 0` ends up being `-eq 0`, and the conditional test function thinks it's an error.

To fix this properly, either a substitution operator is needed (if [${count:-0}
-eq 0]), or the variable should be quoted and the logic of the test should change to
a string test, rather than a numeric test:

```
if [ "$count" = "" ] ; then
    echo "No files found that match pattern $pattern"
else
    echo "$count files, with $totalines lines, match pattern $pattern"
    echo "for an average of `expr $totalines / $count` lines per file."
fi
```

One more check to see how many files contain the pattern linda:

```
$ ./countfiles linda
No files found that match pattern linda
```

Much better!

> Many shell programmers would approach this a slightly different way, writ-
> ing if [X$count = X] ; then to sidestep the odd quote notation. If
> $count has any value, the value won't be just X, but if it's undefined,
> X$count will be exactly equal to the value X.

2. The Bourne Shell actually invokes a command called test (or has a copy of the
code for test compiled directly into the shell for improved performance), which
supports a remarkable range of tests, both on files and variables. Table 21.4 summarizes some of the most helpful.

TABLE 21.4   Conditional Tests

Condition	Explanation
File Comparisons	
-d file	True if file exists and is a directory
-e file	True if file exists
-f file	True if file exists and is a file (for example, not a directory)
-r file	True if file exists and allows read access
-s file	True if file exists and is not empty
-w file	True if file exists and allows write access
-x file	True if file exists and allows execute access
-O file	True if file exists and is owned by the current user
-G file	True if file exists and is in the same group as the current user
file1 -nt file2	True if file1 is newer than file2
file1 -ot file2	True if file1 is older than file2

21

▼

TABLE 21.4 Continued

Condition	Explanation
String Comparisons	
str1 = *str2*	True if *str1* equals *str2* (note that it's not ==)
str1 != *str2*	True if *str1* is not equal to *str2*
str1 < *str2*	True if *str1* is less than *str2*
str1 > *str2*	True if *str1* is greater than *str2*
-n *str*	True if *str* is a nonzero length
-z *str*	True if *str* is zero-length
Numeric Comparisons	
x -eq *y*	True if *x* is numerically equal to *y*
x -ge *y*	True if *x* is numerically greater than or equal to *y*
x -gt *y*	True if *x* is numerically greater than *y*
x -le *y*	True if *x* is numerically less than or equal to *y*
x -lt *y*	True if *x* is numerically less than *y*
x -ne *y*	True if *x* is numerically not equal to *y*

That's a lot of possible tests listed in Table 21.4, so don't be too surprised if you find it overwhelming. Let's explore by writing a script that exercises many of these tests to identify characteristics of a specified file or directory:

```
$ cat finfo
#!/bin/sh

# finfo - list some information about a specified file or directory

if [ $# -ne 1 ] ; then
  echo "Usage: finfo file-or-directory-name"
  exit 0
fi

file=$1

if test -e $file
then
  echo -n "$file exists,"
else
  echo "$file does not exist."
```

▼

```
     exit 0
fi

if test -s $file; then
  echo -n " is not empty, "
fi

if test -r $file ; then
 perm="and is read"
else
  perm="and is "
fi
if test -w $file ; then
  perm="$perm+write"
fi
if test -x $file ; then
  perm="$perm+execute"
 fi
if test -O $file ; then
  info="$file is owned by $LOGNAME"
else
  info="$file is not owned by $LOGNAME"
 fi
if test -G $file ; then
  info="$info, same group as $LOGNAME"
else
  info="$info, and is not in any group that $LOGNAME is in"
fi

echo $perm
echo $info

exit 0
```

There are other ways to accomplish the tasks that finfo does here, but it's a terrific example of how all these tests work. Also note that instead of using the [shortcut, we can call test directly instead. In this latter case, we don't need a trailing].

```
$ finfo $HOME
/home/taylor exists, is not empty, and is read+write+execute
/home/taylor is owned by taylor, same group as taylor
$ finfo baddir
baddir does not exist.
$ finfo countfiles
countfiles exists, is not empty, and is read+write+execute
countfiles is owned by taylor, same group as taylor
$ finfo /etc/passwd
/etc/passwd exists, is not empty, and is read
/etc/passwd is not owned by taylor, and is not in any group that taylor is in
```

21

3. There are three basic types of conditional statements: if-then-fi, if-then-else-fi, and if-then-elsif-then-fi, (as is common in the bash shell, the statement reversed is the end-of-statement delimiter, so fi ends an if statement) as exemplified here:

```
if test -x $file ; then # executable
  perm="$perm+execute"
 fi
if test -O $file ; then # owned by user
  info="$file is owned by $LOGNAME"
else
  info="$file is not owned by $LOGNAME"
 fi
if test -d $file ; then # is a directory
  echo "$file is a directory"
elsif test -f $file ; then # is a file
  echo "$file is a file"
else
  echo "$file doesn't exist"
fi
```

The first is a straightforward conditional; if the condition (test -x $file) is true, the statement following, assigning $perm+execute to variable perm, will be executed. If it's not true, the shell will skip to the subsequent instruction.

The second is a bit more complicated, but still easy to understand: If test -O $file is true, the second line is executed. If not, the else statement causes the fourth line (for example, not owned by $LOGNAME) to be executed.

Finally, the third example (elsif) is a shorthand way of writing the following loop:

```
if test -d $file ; then
  echo "$file is a directory"
else
  if test -f $file ; then
    echo "$file is a file"
  else
    echo "$file doesn't exist"
  fi
fi
```

The advantage of the elsif is that it helps avoid overly deep nesting on complex statements. You can imagine if we had a script that had four or five else-if conditionals that having the last dozen lines as fi-fi-fi-fi would look odd and be potentially confusing.

4. Of course, one way to address a sequence of elsif statements is to turn the sequence into a case statement, where you can test against a number of different values in a more elegant fashion. This works in some situations, but not others.

Indeed, where each condition is against a different test option, it wouldn't work, but in many situations, where you're testing the same variable or value against a number of possible values, a case statement is ideal.

Here's a considerably longer and more complex shell script to demonstrate the use of a case statement and conditional statements. Pay attention to how the indentation helps clarify the control flow:

```
$ cat docron
#!/bin/sh

# DOCRON - simple script to run the daily, weekly and monthly
#          system cron jobs on a system where it's likely that
#          it'll be shut down at the usual time of day when
#          this would occur        For Mac OS X Unix only.
#
# By Dave Taylor <taylor@intuitive.com>

# Note: most of this is copied from /etc/crontab

SHELL=/bin/sh
PATH=/bin:/sbin:/usr/bin:/usr/sbin
HOME=/var/log

if [ $# -ne 1 ] ; then
  echo "Usage: `basename $0` [daily|weekly|monthly]"
  exit 0
fi

if [ "`id -u`" -ne 0 ] ; then
  echo "Please enter your 'sudo' password for authorization"
  sudo $0 $1
  if [ $? -ne 0 ] ; then
    echo "(didn't run `basename $0` because sudo auth failed)"
  fi
  exit 0
fi

case $1 in
  daily )

    sh /etc/daily   2>&1 | tee /var/log/daily.out | \
        mail -s "`hostname` daily output"  root
    ;;

  weekly )

    sh /etc/weekly 2>&1 | tee /var/log/weekly.out  | \
        mail -s "`hostname` weekly output"  root
    ;;
```

21

▼

```
     monthly )

        sh /etc/monthly 2>&1 | tee /var/log/monthly.out | \
          mail -s "`hostname` monthly output" root
        ;;

     * ) echo "Usage: `basename $0` [daily|weekly|monthly]"
esac

exit 0
```

This is a longer shell script, but if we look at it in sections, it's really no more complex than the earlier examples. In particular, notice that the case statement structure is

```
case $1 in
  daily ) statements
    ;;
  weekly ) statements
    ;;
  monthly ) statements
    ;;
    *     ) statements
esac
```

This is more or less equivalent to

```
if [ $1 = daily ] ; then
   statements
elsif [ $1 = weekly ] ; then
   statements
elsif [ $1 = monthly ] ; then
   statements
else
   statements
fi
```

The only difference is that case statement clauses can do wildcard pattern matching, so whereas a conditional test with an `if` statement that matched `dail*` would be difficult to write, it's a breeze as part of a case statement: `dail* )`

Indeed, you'll often see complex regular expressions as part of case statements, and a set of choices to allow for, say, both single-character and longer flags is very common, and might look like this:

`-a | --append ) statements`

Also note that in the case statement that each block is ended with the all important double semicolon (`;;`), without which the script will drop through into the statements associated with the next condition. On the last case, of course, there is no "next" condition, so it can be omitted.

▼

5. The other looping mechanisms in shell scripts are `for`, `while`, and `until` loops. We've already seen many examples of the `for` loop at work, but it's a real workhorse in scripting, so let's have another look.

   The following simple script searches all the directories in your PATH for a given filename, using a simple `for` construct. There is one fancy trick here: the IFS variable is the shell's *input field separator*, and by changing it to a colon, it lets us very easily chop up the $PATH into its component directories. This neatly also allows us to match directories with spaces in their names without any sort of hiccup:

```
$ cat search.sh
#!/bin/sh

# search - look for the specified file name in the PATH directories

IFS=:

for directory in $PATH
do
  if [ -e $directory/$1 ] ; then
    echo Found $1 in directory $directory
  fi
done

exit 0
```

   When this is run, the output is succinct:

```
$ search xterm
Found xterm in directory /usr/X11R6/bin
$ search vi
Found vi in directory /bin
$ search search
Found search in directory /home/taylor/bin
$ search not-found
$
```

   It would be useful to have an error condition so that instead of returning nothing upon failure (as you can see in the last example of the preceding code fragment), it would say `not found`. That task will resurface as an exercise later in this (rather long!) hour.

   An interesting shortcut with the `for` loop is that if you don't specify an `in` clause, it automatically steps through the starting arguments, as demonstrated in the following:

```
$ cat args
#!/bin/sh

# args - step through starting args

for arg
do
```

21

```
    echo got argument $arg
done
```

```
$ args this is a test
got argument this
got argument is
got argument a
got argument test
$
```

> This for loop trick can simplify parsing starting arguments on a more sophis-
> ticated shell script, though if you want to have a number of startup options,
> getopts is a smarter way to go. See man 1 getopts for details.

6. The remaining loop structures are fundamentally the same, the only difference
   being if they're testing for a condition that will eventually go false or become true.
   Consider this example:

```
$ cat args2
#!/bin/sh

# args2 - step through starting args, stop at '--' if seen

while [ "$1" != "--" -a X$1 != X ]
do
  echo ... processing flag $1
  shift
done

if [ "$1" = "--" ] ; then
  shift          # to get past the '--'
fi

echo Ended loop with post-flag arguments $*
exit 0
```

This script demonstrates that conditional expressions can actually be quite complex: The test that's part of the while loop actually is checking to see if $1 is "--",
which indicates the end of starting flags by Unix convention, or if it simply ran out
of starting arguments. The -a is an AND notation, so you could read this as while
$1 isn't '--' AND X$1 isn't X do.

Also note the use of the shift instruction to move all the numeric arguments down
one value. That is, $2 becomes $1, $3 becomes $2, and so on.

```
$ ./args2 a b -- c d
... processing flag a
... processing flag b
```

```
Ended loop with post-flag arguments c d
$ ./args2 a b c d
... processing flag a
... processing flag b
... processing flag c
... processing flag d
Ended loop with post-flag arguments
```

7. The last type of flow control isn't really a loop, per se, but an approach to taking a block of code and making it a completely different entity—a shell *function*. Generically, shell functions can be written either as

```
function functionname
{
    shell commands
}
functionname()
{
    shell commands
}
```

What makes this interesting is that you can pass parameters to functions, though they can only return numeric return code values to the calling script. For example:

```
function listit()
{
    if [ -f $1 -a -r $1 ] ; then
        cat $1
    else
        echo "Error: $1 is not a file, or is not readable"
    fi;
}
```

This simple function will list the contents of a file if it is in fact a file (not a directory) and is readable; otherwise it'll output a succinct error message.

One point of confusion when working with functions is that you need to ensure that the function is defined prior to its first use in the script, so a typical shell script that uses functions has all the function definitions presented first in the file, then the actual script itself at the end.

A common place to see shell functions is in the /etc/rc.d/init.d files, or in the /etc/rc.d/init.d/functions shared library. Two interesting examples from Red Hat Linux are worth showing:

```
# Check if $pid (could be plural) are running
checkpid() {
        while [ "$1" ]; do
           [ -d /proc/$1 ] && return 0 # '&&' is AND
           shift
        done
        return 1
}
```

21

```
confirm() {
   local YES=$"yY"
   local NO=$"nN"
   local CONT=$"cC"

   while : ; do
       echo -n $"Start service $1 (Y)es/(N)o/(C)ontinue? [Y] "
       read answer
       if strstr "$YES" "$answer" || [ "$answer" = "" ] ; then
          return 0 # '||' is an OR condition above
       elif strstr "$CONT" "$answer" ; then
          return 2
       elif strstr "$NO" "$answer" ; then
          return 1
       fi
   done
}
```

Mac OS X has startup scripts in the /etc/rc.local file (a typical BSD location for
them), and within that file there are some interesting additional shell functions:

```
##
# Print a message to the console and display it in the startup screen
##
ConsoleMessage()
{
    local Message="$*"

    echo "${Message}"
}
##
# Determine if the network is up by looking for any non-loopback
# internet network interfaces. - uses "sed", the stream-editor, to
# make simple modifications to information in a pipe. See sed(1)
##
CheckForNetwork()
{
    local test

    if [ -z "${NETWORKUP:=}" ]; then
       test=$(ifconfig -a | sed -e '/127.0.0.1/d' | sed -e '/0.0.0.0/d' | \sed -
⮕n '/inet/p' | wc -l)
       if [ "${test}" -gt 0 ]; then
             NETWORKUP="-YES-"
       else
             NETWORKUP="-NO-"
       fi
    fi
}
```

Two more examples of shell functions, then we'll move into exploring some interesting scripts, okay? The following implement the `start` and `stop` functionality for the anacron daemon with Red Hat Linux:

```
start() {
    echo -n $"Starting $prog: "
    daemon anacron
    RETVAL=$?
    [ $RETVAL -eq 0 ] && touch /var/lock/subsys/anacron
    echo
    return $RETVAL
}

stop() {
    if test "x`pidof anacron`" != x; then
        echo -n $"Stopping $prog: "
        killproc anacron
        echo
    fi
    RETVAL=$?
    [ $RETVAL -eq 0 ] && rm -f /var/lock/subsys/anacron
    return $RETVAL
}
```

Notice how they conform to the standard function syntax, and that, like most of the other examples shown, they return zero upon success, and nonzero return codes on failure.

We don't have the space to dig deeply into the specific functionality of these diverse shell functions, but I hope that they make sense to you based on the information presented here.

It's well worth learning more about shell script programming if you're motivated, and there's no better place to do so than by starting with the shell scripts that are all over your own Unix system.

If you're starting to suspect that there's quite a bit to shell script programming, you're correct. The good news is that once you master the peculiar syntax of the `test` command and the general structure of `if`, `case`, and `while`/`until` loops, you'll be able to read and understand at least 75% of the system shell scripts included with your Unix OS.

Add functions to that list, and you're ready to read and understand just about every shell script on your system, and, more importantly, create your own. Remember, just like the answer to the immortal question "How do you get to Carnegie Hall?" you need to practice writing your own shell scripts before you can really begin to master this critical system administrator skill!

Some Cool Examples

Before we wrap this hour up, it's valuable to look at a few fully functional shell scripts that offer useful sysadmin features.

Task 21.3: Some Example Scripts

These scripts are all generic and will run on just about any Unix, though they're each written for the OS specified in the description.

1. One of the programs that I miss the most when I work in the Solaris environment is `locate`. The `locate` command itself is simple to create: It's `grep`, but the file it searches is slightly more tricky to create. That's what `mklocatedb` does:

```sh
#!/bin/sh

# mklocate - build the locate database. This is a simple job for the 'find'
#     command. Note that we want to ignore everything in the /proc directory on
# this build, so there's a little bit of trickery needed to ensure we get all
# the top level directories EXCEPT /proc and /xfn

# This should be run by cron every night, or thereabouts

locatedb=/tmp/locatedb

checkall="`ls -a / | egrep -v '(^\.$|^\.\.$|^proc$|^xfn$)' | sed 's/^/\//g'`"

nice find $checkall -print > $locatedb

echo done. Listed `wc -l < $locatedb` entries in the db.

exit 0
```

If this is run every night (probably from `cron`), a simple alias gives you complete functionality:

```
alias locate='cat /tmp/locatedb | grep -i'
```

If you specify an argument to an alias, it's automatically appended to the end; so a search for, say, `locate config` is exactly the same as typing `cat /tmp/locatedb | grep -i config`.

```
$ mklocatedb
Done. Listed 45426 entries in the db.
$ locate terminal
/.dt/wsmenu/Tools/Terminal
/kernel/misc/terminal-emulator
/usr/openwin/share/include/X11/bitmaps/terminal
/usr/openwin/share/include/images/terminal.icon
/usr/openwin/share/include/images/terminal_mask.icon
/usr/dt/appconfig/help/C/Terminal.sdl
/usr/dt/config/en_US.UTF-8/wsmenu/Tools/Terminal
/usr/dt/config/C/wsmenu/Tools/Terminal
```

You'd want to run `mklocatedb` as `root` so you can access all the directories on the system, but once it's built, all users can easily be given the `locate` alias and informed of the new functionality.

2. A longer example that demonstrates many of the control structures discussed in this hour is `domaincheck`:

```sh
#!/bin/sh

# Usage: domaincheck [flags] domain list
#    -a          show all information
#    -d          show DNS records
#    -e          expiration date of domain record
#    -r          show registrar

case $1 in

  -a ) shift

        for name
        do
          whois $name
        done
        ;;

  -d ) shift

        for name
        do
          echo ${name}:
          whois -n $name | grep -E '^    Name Server:'
        done
        ;;

  -e ) shift

        for name
        do
          echo -n "${name} "
          whois $name | grep -i 'Record expires on' | \
              sed 's/Record expires on//'
        done
        ;;

  -r ) shift

        for name
        do
          echo -n ${name}:
          whois -n $name | grep 'Registrar:'
        done
        ;;
```

21

```
        * )
            echo "Usage: domaincheck [flags] domain list"
            echo "   -a              all information"
            echo "   -d              DNS name servers"
            echo "   -e              expiration date"
            echo "   -r              registrar"
            ;;
esac

exit 0
```

This script lets you easily interact with the domain name registration database through the Linux `whois` command, extracting interesting and relevant information as desired:

```
$ domaincheck
Usage: domaincheck [flags] domain list
   -a              all information
   -d              DNS name servers
   -e              expiration date
   -r              registrar
$ domaincheck -r abctv.com
abctv.com:    Registrar: NETWORK SOLUTIONS, INC.
$ domaincheck -e nbc.com
nbc.com     16-Jun-2011.
$ domaincheck -d espn.com amctv.com
espn.com:
   Name Server: AUTH50.NS.UU.NET
   Name Server: AUTH03.NS.UU.NET
amctv.com:
   Name Server: STANTZ.CABLEVISION.COM
   Name Server: TULLY.CABLEVISION.COM
```

Notice in the last of the three examples that by using the `for` loop without any `in` clause, it automatically lets you step through any number of domain names specified on the command line.

The big result, of course, is the `-a` flag. Rather than show you all the output, here's a concise summary of some of the information you can glean about any domain on the Internet:

```
$ domaincheck -a disney.com
(roughly 50 uninteresting lines removed)
Disney Enterprises, Inc. (DISNEY-DOM)
   500 S. Buena Vista Street
   Burbank, CA 91521
   US

   Domain Name: DISNEY.COM
```

▼

```
Administrative Contact, Technical Contact, Billing Contact:
    idNames, Accounting  (IA90-ORG)  accounting@IDNAMES.COM
    idNames from Network Solutions, Inc
    440 Benmar
    Suite #3325
    Houston, TX 77060
    US
    703-742-4777
    Fax- - 281-447-1160

Record last updated on 28-Mar-2002.
Record expires on 22-Mar-2008.
Record created on 21-Mar-1990.
Database last updated on 2-Apr-2002 15:46:00 EST.

Domain servers in listed order:

HUEY.DISNEY.COM               204.128.192.10
NS2-AUTH.SPRINTLINK.NET       144.228.254.10
NS3-AUTH.SPRINTLINK.NET       144.228.255.10
NOC.UNT.EDU                   129.120.110.1
```

3. One more quickie: `findsuid` finds all the `setuid` scripts, then checks to see whether the files are also owned by `root` and marked as executable. If all conditions are true, it lists the questionable file in a meaningful and helpful manner:

```
# cat findsuid
#!/bin/sh

# findsuid - find all SUID files or programs on the system other
#     than those that live in /bin and /usr/bin, and
#     output the matches in a friendly and useful format.

screen="egrep -vE '(^/usr/bin|^/bin)'"

echo "Executable SUID programs found on the system:"

for match in `find / -type f -perm +5000 -print | $screen`
do
  if [ -x $match ] ; then
    owner="`ls -ld $match | awk '{print $3}'`"
    lastmod="`ls -ld $match | awk '{print $6\" \"$7\" \"$8}'`"
    echo "  " $match " (owner is \"$owner\" and lastmod is $lastmod)"
  fi
done

exit 0
```

▼

21

▼

When run (as `root`, of course, so you can see every file on the system), the output looks like this:

```
# findsuid
Executable SUID programs found on the system:
    /usr/bin/suidperl  (owner is "root" and lastmod is Aug 9 2001)
    /usr/bin/sperl5.6.0  (owner is "root" and lastmod is Aug 9 2001)
    /usr/bin/chage  (owner is "root" and lastmod is Aug 27 2001)
    /usr/bin/gpasswd  (owner is "root" and lastmod is Aug 27 2001)
    /usr/bin/at  (owner is "root" and lastmod is Aug 2 2001)
    /usr/bin/passwd  (owner is "root" and lastmod is Aug 6 2001)
    /usr/bin/chfn  (owner is "root" and lastmod is Aug 26 2001)
    /usr/bin/chsh  (owner is "root" and lastmod is Aug 26 2001)
    /usr/bin/newgrp  (owner is "root" and lastmod is Aug 26 2001)
    /usr/bin/crontab  (owner is "root" and lastmod is Jun 24 2001)
    /usr/bin/kcheckpass  (owner is "root" and lastmod is Sep 8 2001)
    /usr/bin/ssh  (owner is "root" and lastmod is Sep 6 2001)
    /usr/bin/rcp  (owner is "root" and lastmod is Jul 24 2001)
    /usr/bin/rlogin  (owner is "root" and lastmod is Jul 24 2001)
    /usr/bin/rsh  (owner is "root" and lastmod is Jul 24 2001)
    /usr/bin/sudo  (owner is "root" and lastmod is Jul 23 2001)
    /usr/sbin/ping6  (owner is "root" and lastmod is Aug 27 2001)
    /usr/sbin/traceroute6  (owner is "root" and lastmod is Aug 27 2001)
    /usr/sbin/sendmail  (owner is "root" and lastmod is Aug 31 2001)
    /usr/sbin/usernetctl  (owner is "root" and lastmod is Sep 9 2001)
    /usr/sbin/userhelper  (owner is "root" and lastmod is Aug 27 2001)
    /usr/sbin/traceroute  (owner is "root" and lastmod is Jun 25 2001)
    /usr/sbin/suexec.old  (owner is "root" and lastmod is Sep 5 2001)
    /usr/X11R6/bin/Xwrapper  (owner is "root" and lastmod is Sep 5 2001)
    /bin/ping  (owner is "root" and lastmod is Aug 27 2001)
    /bin/mount  (owner is "root" and lastmod is Jul 24 2001)
    /bin/umount  (owner is "root" and lastmod is Jul 24 2001)
    /bin/su  (owner is "root" and lastmod is Jul 23 2001)
    /sbin/pwdb_chkpwd  (owner is "root" and lastmod is Sep 24 2001)
    /sbin/unix_chkpwd  (owner is "root" and lastmod is Sep 24 2001)
```

Very interesting output, and if you used the helpful `diff` command and archived earlier output so you could automatically compare, you'll have a very helpful utility that will help quickly identify possible trojan horses.

4. There are hundreds of different shell scripts on your system, and you can find them with a script:

```
# cat findscripts
#!/bin/sh

for match in `find / -type f -perm +0111 -print`
do
  if [ "`file $match | grep -i 'shell script'`" != "" ] ; then
    echo $match is a shell script
  fi
done
```

▼

▼
▲

Red Hat Linux reports 651 scripts present (`findscripts | wc -l`). Plenty of material for you to study!

Summary

Writing shell scripts is easy—you can start by taking whatever command you'd type on the command line and drop it into a file. Creating truly cool shell scripts, however, is more of an art, and the best system administrators can produce some amazing scripts. Keep your eye out for them, and spend time reading through the many shell scripts on your own system. There's always lots to learn!

Q&A

Q   When do shell scripts get so complex that it makes more sense to switch to a more powerful programming language like Perl?

A   This is a question that will garner different answers depending on how comfortable the sysadmin questioned feels about writing shell scripts. There's no standard rule of thumb, that's for sure. I'll switch to a different programming language if I'm doing more data manipulation and relatively little system interaction. Your mileage may vary, of course!

Q   What's the most common error in shell script programming?

A   The most common error I make is forgetting either that a conditional test of strings should be a = b rather than a == b, or that it should be a = b rather than a -eq b. Unnecessary spaces after a backslash continuation at the end of a line is another common hiccup.

Workshop

Quiz

1. Does it matter what login shell you have when writing shell scripts?
2. What's a handy trick for debugging shell scripts?
3. The `test` command can also be referenced as what common punctuation character? What needs to also be included if you use this shortcut?
4. List both ways that you can ascertain the number of characters stored in a string variable.
5. How do you increment a numeric variable by 3?
6. What does the notation $# indicate?

21

Answers

1. Your login shell doesn't matter, as long as you remember to always specify `#!/bin/sh` as the first line of your scripts.

2. Running a shell script as `sh -x` *script* offers lots of useful output for debugging any problems.

3. The `test` command is also known as `[`, but if you use the square bracket, you need to include a trailing `]` as well, or it'll be an error.

4. You can invoke `` `expr length $variable` ``, or you could use the `${#variable}` notation to ascertain the number of characters in `$variable`.

5. Typically, you'd use `var="`expr $var + 3`"`.

6. The notation `$#` indicates the number of arguments given to the script when invoked.

In the next hour we'll use a combination of `awk` and Perl to further explore ways to customize the administrative environment and simplify repetitive tasks.

HOUR 22

Power Scripting with awk and Perl

The evolutionary path of a good system administrator usually goes from commands to pipes to aliases to shell scripts to something bigger. The something bigger step is usually C, C++, or Perl, but many system administrators opt to take the intermediate step of learning how to use the powerful awk language along the way.

Throughout this book, we've explored sophisticated Unix interaction, and the last hour (or perhaps hour and a half!) was focused on learning how to get the most out of shell scripts, including a number of programming-like structures and examples.

At some point in your long journey as a sysadmin, you'll reach the point where shell scripts are too confining. Maybe you'll be doing complex math, and all the calls to expr make your head swim. Maybe you'll be working with a data file with many columns, and repeated calls to cut no longer, ahem, cut it. At this point, you've outgrown shell scripts, and you're ready to move to awk or Perl.

In this hour we'll have a brief overview of awk, the original pattern-matching programming language in the Unix environment, then spend some time looking at how the popular Perl language can help with many common system administration tasks. Needless to say, it's impossible to convey the depth and sophistication of either language in this brief space, so we'll also have some pointers to other works, online and off, to continue the journey.

In this hour, you will learn about

- The oft-forgotten awk language
- How to write basic Perl programs
- Advanced Perl programming tips and tricks

The Elegant awk Language

Named after its inventors Aho, Weinberg, and Kernighan, awk has been a part of the Unix environment since the beginning, and is a part of every current shipping distro today.

> awk is also available for pre-OS X Mac and Windows systems through the GNU project's reimplementation of the language. See www.gnu.org/software/gawk/gawk.html.

awk is ideally suited to the analysis of text and log files, using its "match and act" method of processing. An awk program is basically a series of conditions, with a set of actions to perform if those conditions are met or a string is found. Think of the -exec clause in the find command, combined with the searching capabilities of grep. That's the power of awk.

Task 22.1: An Overview of awk

Conditions in awk are defined using regular expressions, similar to those available with the grep command. The statements to perform upon matching the condition are delimited with open and closing curly brackets.

1. Let's say we want to scan through /etc/passwd to find user accounts that don't have a login shell defined. To do this, we look for lines that end with a colon. In awk, for all lines that end with a colon, print that line:

```
$ awk '/:$/ {print $0}' /etc/passwd
bin:x:1:1:bin:/bin:
daemon:x:2:2:daemon:/sbin:
```

```
adm:x:3:4:adm:/var/adm:
lp:x:4:7:lp:/var/spool/lpd:
mail:x:8:12:mail:/var/spool/mail:
```

The pattern to match is a regular expression, surrounded by slashes. In this instance, the pattern `/:$/` should be read as "match a colon followed by the end-of-line delimiter." The action for the pattern follows immediately, in curly braces: `{print $0}`. Prior examples in this book have shown that you can print a specific field by specifying its field number (for example, $3 prints the third field in each line), but here you can see that $0 is a shorthand for the entire input line.

2. Printing the matching line is sufficiently common that it is the default action. If your pattern doesn't have an action following it, awk assumes that you want `{print $0}`. We can shorten up our program like so:

```
$ awk '/:$/' /etc/passwd
bin:x:1:1:bin:/bin:
daemon:x:2:2:daemon:/sbin:
adm:x:3:4:adm:/var/adm:
lp:x:4:7:lp:/var/spool/lpd:
mail:x:8:12:mail:/var/spool/mail:
```

At this point, our awk program acts exactly like a simple call to grep (`grep -E ':$' /etc/passwd`).

3. Much of the text processing you'll be faced with in Unix is field- or column-based. awk does its best to make handling this input as easy as possible by automatically creating special variables for the fields of a line. For example, take the output from `ls -l`:

```
$ ls -l
total 24
-rwxrwxr-x    1 taylor      taylor         108 Apr  7 20:11 bytes-used
-rw-rw-r--    1 taylor      taylor        4707 Apr  7 20:16 ch22.txt
drwxrwxr-x    2 taylor      taylor        4096 Apr  7 12:48 CVS
-rw-rw-r--    1 taylor      taylor       19024 Apr  7 20:17 intro.txt
```

Fed as input, awk would see each line as a series of fields, with each field separated by a series of whitespace characters. The first line, `total 24`, has two fields, and the other four each have nine fields.

As awk reads in the lines of its input, it splits the input line into special variables $1, $2, $3, and so on, one for each field in the input. $0 is the special variable that holds the current line, and NF (notice the absence of a dollar sign variable name delimiter) holds the number of fields on the current line.

It's simple, then, to calculate the total number of bytes used by the files in the directory. Sum the values of the fifth column:

```
$ ls -l | awk '( NF >= 9 && $1 !~ /^d/ ) { total += $5 } END { print total }'
33310
```

4. A valuable improvement to this is to drop the awk commands into a separate .awk file:

```
$ cat bytes.awk
( NF >= 9 && $1 !~ /^d/ ) { total += $5}
END { print total " bytes in this directory." }
```

This can then be easily used as:

```
$ ls -l | awk -f bytes.awk
33310 bytes in this directory.
```

A further refinement would be to exploit the fact that executable scripts in Unix can specify the command interpreter they prefer as part of the first line of the file. Make sure you have the right path for your awk interpreter by using locate:

```
$ cat bytes-used
#!/usr/bin/awk -f
( NF >= 9 && $1 !~ /^d/ ) { total += $5 }
END { print total " bytes used by files" }
$ chmod +x bytes-used
$ ls -l | ./bytes-used
33310  bytes used by files
```

In this more sophisticated awk program, the pattern isn't just a regular expression, but a logical expression. To match, awk checks to ensure that there are at least nine fields on the line (NF >= 9), so that we skip that first total line in the ls output. The second half of the pattern checks to ensure that the first field doesn't begin with d, to skip directories in the ls output.

If the condition is true, then the value of the fifth field, the number of bytes used, is added to our total variable.

Finally, at the end of the program, awk runs a special block of code marked with the END label and prints the value of total. Naturally, awk also allows a corresponding block BEGIN that is run at the beginning of the program, which you'll see in the following example.

5. You're not limited to just having fields separated by whitespace. awk's special FS (field separator) variable lets you define anything as your field separator. Let's look at improving our previous example of finding entries in /etc/passwd that don't have a login shell specified. It's now called noshell:

```
$ cat noshell
#!/usr/bin/awk -f
BEGIN { FS = ":" }
( $7 == "" ) { print $1 }
```

▼

The code in the BEGIN block, executed prior to any input, sets FS to the colon. As each line is read and the seventh field is found to be blank or nonexistent, awk prints the first field (the account name):

```
$ ./noshell /etc/passwd
bin
daemon
adm
lp
mail
```

▲

There's quite a bit more you can do with awk, and there are even a few books on how to get the most out of this powerful scripting and pattern processing language. A Web site worth exploring for more awk tips is IBM's developerWorks site (www.ibm.com/developerworks/), where there's a very good tutorial on advanced awk programming at www.ibm.com/developerworks/linux/library/l-awk1.html.

Basic Perl Programming

Designed as a hybrid programming environment that offered the best of shell scripting, awk, and lots of bits and pieces stolen from other development environments, Perl has quickly grown to be the language of choice in the system administration community.

There are a couple of reasons for this, but the greatest reason for using Perl is that it's incredibly powerful, while reasonably easy to learn.

Task 22.2: Basic Perl

Perl takes the power of awk and expands it even further. Perl's abilities include the most powerful regular expressions available, sophisticated string handling, easy array manipulation, lookup tables with hashes, tight integration with SQL databases—and those are just the basics!

1. Perl doesn't automatically iterate through a file like awk does, but it's not much more difficult. Here's our noshell program in Perl:

```
$ cat noshell.pl
#!/usr/bin/perl -w
use strict;
while (<>) {
    chomp;
    my @fields = split /:/;
    print $fields[0], "\n" unless $fields[6];
}
$ ./noshell.pl /etc/passwd
bin
daemon
adm
lp
mail
```

▼

The program steps through either standard input or the files specified on the command line. Each line has the trailing linefeed removed with `chomp`, and then the line is split into individual fields using a colon as the field delimiter (the `/:/` argument after the `split`). The `my` preface to the `@fields` line ensures that the variable is only alive within its own loop (the `while` loop), and the `split` on that line breaks the line at the colon. This statement breaks down the line into separate fields, then pours those fields into the `fields` array.

Finally, we print the first field (like many programming languages, Perl indexes starting at zero, not one, so `$fields[0]` is the equivalent of the `awk` `$1` variable) if the seventh field doesn't exist or is blank.

Note that the variable `@fields` starts with an `@` sign, yet we refer to the 0th element of fields with a dollar-sign prefix: `$fields[0]`. This is one of those quirks of Perl that constantly trips up beginners. Just remember to use the `@` when referring to an entire array, and the `$` when referring to a single element.

> Most Perl scripts you see have a `-w` switch and a `use strict;` line, and for good reason. They catch about 95% of the silly typing errors that you're likely to make in a Perl program. Make the `-w` and `use strict` a reflexive way to start your Perl programs, and you'll save lots of time debugging down the road.

2. Perl uses a special variable called `$_` as the default variable for many different blocks of code. Think of `$_` as meaning *it*, where *it* is whatever the current block of Perl code is working on at the moment.

To be explicit, the preceding program can be written as

```
#!/usr/bin/perl -w
use strict;
while ( $_ = <> ) {
chomp $_;
    my @fields = split /:/, $_;
    print $fields[0], "\n" unless $fields[6];
}
```

You can also use your own variables instead of using `$_` if you find that to be more readable.

```
#!/usr/bin/perl -w
use strict;
while ( my $line = <> ) {
chomp $line;
my @fields = split /:/, $line;
print $fields[0], "\n" unless $fields[6];
}
```

▼ Which style you use depends on your needs and how you conceptualize programming in Perl. In general, the larger the program or block of code, the more likely you are to use your own variables instead of the implicit $_.

> One of the mottos of the Perl community is "There's More Than One Way To Do It." Depending on how you solve problems, you will either find this cute, or highly annoying.

3. Perl was built on Unix systems, and is specifically geared to many of the common system administration tasks you'll face. A typical problem might be checking to ensure that none of the users have a .rhosts file in their home directory with inappropriate permissions (a common security hole on multiuser systems).

Here's how we'd solve this problem in Perl:

```
$ cat rhosts-check
#!/usr/bin/perl -w
use strict;
while ( my ($uid,$dir) = (getpwent())[2,7] ) {
next unless $uid >= 100;
    my $filename = "$dir/.rhosts";
if ( -e $filename ) {
    my $permissions = (stat($filename))[2] & 0777;
    if ( $permissions != 0700 ) {
    printf( "%lo %s\n", $permissions, $filename );
    chmod( 0700, $filename );
    } # if
} # if file exists
} # while walking thru /etc/passwd
```

This script introduces quite a few Perl mechanisms that we haven't seen yet. The main while loop makes repeated calls to the Perl function getpwent(), which returns entries from the /etc/passwd file. This is safer and easier than parsing /etc/passwd yourself, and allows the code to be more graceful.

The getpwent() function returns a list of information about the user, but we're only interested in the 3rd and 8th elements, so we specify elements 2 and 7 (remember indexing starts with zero, not one), and assign those to $uid and $dir, respectively. Perl assigns these in one easy operation.

The next line skips to the next iteration of the loop if the $uid isn't at least 100. This sort of "do this unless that" way of expressing logic is one of the ways in which Perl allows flexible code. This specific line lets us automatically skip checking system and daemon accounts—user accounts should always have a UID that's

▼ greater than 100.

22

After that, we build a filename using the user's home directory and the `.rhosts` filename, and check to see if it exists with the `-e` operator[1]. If it does, we extract the file's permissions using the `stat()` function, and make sure that they're set to `0700` as desired. Finally, if the permissions aren't up to snuff, we print out a message so we can see whose files we've modified, and call Perl's `chmod()` function to set the permissions for us.

Running this script produces

```
$ rhosts-check
    711 /home/shelley/.rhosts
    777 /home/diggle/.rhosts
```

This just scratches the surface of the system administration capabilities of Perl within the Unix environment. Depending on how you look at it, the depth and sophistication of Perl is either a great boon, or an intimidating iceberg looming dead ahead.

Like any other development environment, however, Perl is malleable—but if you choose to create obscure, cryptic and ultra-compact code, you'll doubtless have everyone else baffled and confused.

Take your time and learn how to program through the many excellent examples available online and you'll soon begin to appreciate the elegance of the language.

Advanced Perl Examples

Perl's regular expressions make searching for patterns in text simple, and hashes enable us to easily create lookup tables, named numeric accumulators, and more.

Task 22.3: Advanced Perl Capabilities

There are many directions in which you can expand your Perl knowledge once you get the basics. Let's look at a few.

1. We'll combine searching and a hash-based lookup table in the following example to analyze the Apache Web server's `access_log` file.

```
#!/usr/bin/perl -w
use strict;
use Socket;
use constant NDOMAINS => 20;
my %domains;
while (<>) {
```

---

[1] *Exactly as we'd use with `test` in shell scripts. It's not a coincidence—Perl contains many best practices of this nature.*

```
        /^(\d{1,3}\.\d{1,3}\.\d{1,3}\.\d{1,3}) / or warn "No IP found", next;
        ++$domains{ domain($1) };
}

my @domains = reverse sort { $domains{$a} <=> $domains{$b} } keys %domains;
@domains = @domains[0..NDOMAINS] if @domains > NDOMAINS;
for my $key ( @domains ) {
    printf( "%6d %s\n", $domains{$key}, $key );
}
our %domain_cache;
sub domain {
    my $ip = shift;

    if ( !defined $domain_cache{$ip} ) {
    my @quads = split( /\./, $ip );
    my $domain = gethostbyaddr( pack('C4', @quads), AF_INET );
    if ( $domain ) {
    my @segments = split( /\./, $domain );
    $domain_cache{$ip} = join( ".", @segments[-2,-1] );
    } else {
    $domain_cache{$ip} = $ip;
    }
    }
    return $domain_cache{$ip};
}
```

When run, the output is quite interesting:

```
$ topdomains access_log
781 aol.com
585 cox.net
465 attbi.com
456 pacbell.net
434 net.sg
409 rr.com
286 209.232.0.86
267 Level3.net
265 funknetz.at
260 194.170.1.132
243 takas.lt
200 com.np
196 mindspring.com
186 209.158.97.3
160 uu.net
160 ca.us
155 202.54.26.98
148 att.net
146 ops.org
145 ena.net
```

▼ We're interested in domain names here, not actual hostnames. Many ISPs like Aol.com have dozens of different hosts (say, proxy-02.ca.aol.com) that generate hits, so 500 hits might be spread out over 50 different hosts. Using domains gives a more accurate view.

2. The Apache access_log file has a line for each request on the server, and the IP address is the first field on each line:

```
$ head -1 /var/log/httpd/access_log
24.154.127.122 - - [19/Apr/2002:04:30:31 -0700] "GET /house/ HTTP/1.1"
  200 769 "-" "Mozilla/4.0 (compatible; MSIE 6.0; Windows NT 5.1; .NET
➥CLR 1.0.3705)"
```

The while loop in the preceding Perl code walks through whatever file or files are specified on the command line. Specifying files on the command line instead of piping them through standard input is a good idea, because we can send many files at once.

The regular expression line checks to see whether there's an IP address at the start of the line that was just read by checking that the first four characters in the line are three digits and a period. If the match fails, the program outputs a warning to standard error and skips to the next input line.

Once we have the IP address, stored in the first field, we call the domain() subroutine, described later, to do a reverse lookup of IP address to domain name. The resultant domain name is used as a key to the hash table of domain names and either increments the value, or sets it to an initial value of 1.

> A hash is like an array, by the way, but instead of being sequentially numbered, the elements of the hash are indexed via a string value.

Once the while loop has exhausted its input, it's time to find the top 20 domains. The keys function extracts the key values from the hash into an array. We can then sort that list, but not by the domain name. We're interested in sorting by the value of the hash that corresponds to the domain. The special code block after sort specifies this. Then, the entire list of domains is reversed, so that the domains with the most hits are at the top of the list.

Now that we have a list of domains, we extract and loop over the top 20 domains. (Of course, we could have make it 10, 100, or 47 domains by changing the NDO-MAINS constant at the top of the program.) Just as in shell scripts, Perl enables us to loop through the values of an array. Inside our loop, we use the printf() function

▼ to nicely format a line showing the number of hits and the domain name.

▼ 3. What about the translation from IP address to domain name? It's complex enough
that it makes sense to wrap it in a subroutine, and the calling program doesn't need
to know about the sneakiness we pull off to speed things up, as you'll see later.

The first thing we do is check to see whether we've found a value for this given IP
address by looking it up in the hash %domains. If a value exists, there's no need to
look it up again, so we return the matched value. If there isn't a match, we do a
reverse DNS lookup by breaking apart the IP address, packing it into a special format, and using Perl's gethostbyaddr() function. If gethostbyaddr fails, we fall
back to using the IP address, or else we use the last two segments of the hostname.
Finally, the calculated domain name is stored in the %domains hash for the next
time this function is called.

4. Even given that sophisticated example, Perl's greatest strength might not lie in the
language itself, but in its huge community and base of contributed code. The
Comprehensive Perl Archive Network, or CPAN (www.cpan.org), is a collection of
modules that have been contributed, refined, and perfected over the years. Many of
the most common modules are shipped with Perl, and are probably installed on
your system.

Here's a script that uses the Net::FTP module to automatically fetch the file of
recent uploads from the CPAN:

```
#!/usr/local/bin/perl -w
use strict;
use Net::FTP;
my $ftp = Net::FTP->new('ftp.cpan.org');
$ftp->login('anonymous','myemail@mysite.com');
$ftp->cwd('/pub/CPAN/');
$ftp->get('RECENT');
```

The $ftp variable is actually an object that encapsulates all the dirty work of FTP
connections, allowing you to concern yourself only with the specifics of your task
▲ at hand.

> There's lots of interesting information about Perl modules at www.cpan.org,
> the official home of the CPAN development group. Also, don't miss
> www.theperljournal.com and www.perl.org while you're surfing around
> looking for more information about Perl!

Like many of the hours in this book, this one is the tip of an iceberg, and there's plenty
more you can learn about the powerful Perl programming language. Certainly having the
right tool at the right time can turn a major headache into a delightful victory. After all,
who's the boss? You, or your Unix system?

Summary

This hour has offered a very brief discussion of some of the most powerful capabilities of both the awk and Perl programming environments. It leads to the question: Which should you use, and when? My answer:

- Use shells for very simple manipulation, or when running many different programs.
- Use awk for automatically iterating through lines of input text.
- Use Perl for extensive use of arrays and hashes, or when you need the power of CPAN.

Q&A

Q **So which has more coolness factor, Perl or awk?**

A No question: Perl. Just pop over to somewhere like BN.com and search for Perl, then search for awk. You'll see what I mean.

Q **What alternatives are there to Perl, awk, and shell scripting for a Unix system administrator?**

A There are some other choices, including Tcl and Python, and you can always pop into C, C++, or another formal, compiled language. Remember, though, the right tool for the job makes everything progress more smoothly.

Workshop

Quiz

1. Is it true that everything you can do in awk you can also accomplish in Perl?

2. What's one of the more frustrating differences between Perl and awk (think arrays)?

3. In awk, positional variables are referenced starting with a special character, but nonpositional variables, like the number of fields in a line, don't have this special character prefix. What character is it?

4. What's the two-character prefix you can use in scripts to specify which program should interpret the contents?

5. What is the greatest advantage to using -w and use strict in Perl?

6. What's the difference between a variable referenced as $list and @list?

Answers

1. It is indeed. Something to think about when you pick which language to learn.

2. Perl indexes starting at zero, but awk uses one as its index base, so $1 is the first value in awk, but $list[1] is the *second* value in Perl.

3. The special character is $.

4. The magic two-character prefix is #! and it only works if the file is set to be executable, too.

5. Most of your typographical errors will be caught by the Perl interpreter before you try to start using your program.

6. Perl variables referenced with an @ are an array of values, whereas those prefaced with $ are considered a specific value of the array. Note that the same variable can be referenced in both ways depending on what you're trying to accomplish!

The last two hours of the book explore the important Apache Web server included with just about every version of Unix shipped. The next hour explores basic configuration and setup, and the last hour will delve into virtual hosting.

22

HOUR 23

Introduction to the Apache Web Server

I suspect that for a significant percentage of readers, this is the key chapter in the book. I might like writing about shell scripts and quotas, but if you're a Unix system administrator in the 21st century, odds are quite good that you are responsible for at least one system that operates as a Web server.

The good news is that these last two hours of the book are devoted to Web server topics (not to mention the prior visits to explore the Web log files). Not just any Web server, mind you, but the one that powers more Web sites than any other online: Apache, from the Apache Group.

In this first hour of coverage, we'll focus on ensuring that you have Apache on your system, setting it up for basic single-system use, and learning how to keep it running smoothly.

What we won't cover is the Hypertext Markup Language (HTML), or any other technologies associated with creating Web sites. If you're interested in those topics, I recommend you check out my books *Creating Cool HTML 4 Web Pages* (Hungry Minds) and its sequel *Dynamic HTML Weekend Crash Course* (Hungry Minds).

In this hour, you'll learn how to

- Set up your Web server
- Configure Apache with the `httpd.conf` file
- Test connectivity and capabilities

Setting Up Your Web Server

The first step in this journey is to see what version of Apache you might have included with your Unix OS. As of this writing, Red Hat Linux ships with Apache 1.3.20, Mac OS X includes Apache 1.3.23, and Solaris includes Apache 1.3.12 (in the somewhat odd location of `/usr/apache/`).

> To identify your version, find the `httpd` binary (use `locate`) and use the `-v` flag. For example: `/usr/sbin/httpd -v`.

The Apache 2.0 release is available through the Apache Web site (`www.apache.org`), and it's pretty stable, but you might want to stick with your current distribution of Apache if you're just serving up HTML- and CGI-based pages. What's important is that you at least have 1.3. If you have 1.2, or earlier, it's time to upgrade: Major architectural and performance changes were introduced with 1.3, most notably the inclusion of how the configuration files are laid out.

Task 23.1: Bringing Apache to Life

Before we start, a quick note: If you're wondering why we're focused on Apache versus one of the other possible servers (notably Netscape), the answer is contained in this brief quote from the Apache Web site:

> Apache has been the most popular Web server on the Internet since April of 1996. The March 2002 Netcraft Web Server Survey (`http://netcraft.com/survey/`) found that 54% of the Web sites on the Internet are using Apache, thus making it more widely used than all other Web servers combined.

1. The first and most logical test is this: Is the Web server running on your system or not? There are a couple of ways to test that, including the obvious `ps -aux|grep httpd`, but I prefer to try and connect directly to the server and see what happens:

```
# telnet localhost http < /dev/null
Trying 127.0.0.1...
telnet: connect to address 127.0.0.1: Connection refused
```

▼

It's not running. There can be three reasons for this: Apache isn't installed, Apache is installed but not enabled, or Apache was running and crashed. Hopefully it's not the last reason, but you could ascertain that by checking your syslog file (probably /var/log/messages). If you don't have Apache installed, flip back to Hour 8, "Unix Package Management," and search for and install the apache-1.3* package or its equivalent (it should take about 15 minutes total with a good network connection).

But what if the server simply isn't running? Let's look at that situation in detail.

2. As with any service, you can start Apache by hand, or you can set things up so that it's automatically launched when the system moves into a desired run state (probably run state 3 and run state 5 (multiuser/no GUI and multiuser+GUI, respectively, on Red Hat Linux. Recall, though, that different Unixes have different definitions for run levels—see Hour 13, "Changing System State.")

To start things by hand, you can use the apachectl script that's included with the Apache distribution, but I prefer to use the system control script that's in /etc/rc.d/init.d/ on Linux systems (if installed).

```
# /etc/rc.d/init.d/httpd status
httpd is stopped
```

That makes sense.

Now, we haven't touched the configuration since the Apache RPM package was installed on the system, so starting it up might have unintended consequences. So let's try it!

```
# /etc/rc.d/init.d/httpd start
Starting httpd:                              [  OK  ]
```

Hey! It worked!

```
# telnet localhost http < /dev/null
Trying 127.0.0.1...
Connected to localhost.
Escape character is '^]'.
Connection closed by foreign host.
```

3. To have Apache start up automatically each time the system is booted, we need to ensure that there's a link from the appropriate rcn.d directory to the script in init.d. A quick check reveals that the Apache RPM installs those links, but by default has the server stop, not start:

```
# ls /etc/rc.d/rc?.d/*httpd
/etc/rc.d/rc0.d/K15httpd
/etc/rc.d/rc1.d/K15httpd
/etc/rc.d/rc2.d/K15httpd
/etc/rc.d/rc3.d/K15httpd
/etc/rc.d/rc4.d/K15httpd
/etc/rc.d/rc5.d/K15httpd
/etc/rc.d/rc6.d/K15httpd
```

▼

▼

It's easy to change. Go into the appropriate directory that corresponds to the target run level and change the K in the name to an S (see Hour 13 for more details about how to work with run levels and initialization scripts).

```
# cd /etc/rc.d/rc3.d/
# mv K15httpd S15httpd
# cd ../rc5.d
# mv K15httpd S15httpd
```

That's it. For this Red Hat Linux system, the next time it boots up or otherwise switches into run level 3 or 5, it'll automatically launch the Apache Web server.

4. Getting Apache to start working in Mac OS X is a breeze: Go to the Sharing control panel from the System Preferences, and click the Start button just below Web Sharing Off, as shown in Figure 23.1.

FIGURE 23.1

Enabling the Mac OS X Web server.

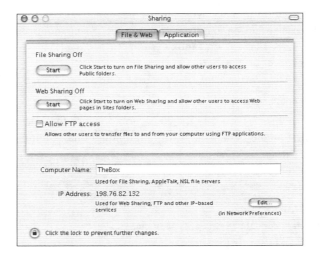

That's all there is to it!

5. The Solaris approach to turning on the Web server is a bit more convoluted, but not much. The Apache control program apachectl (apache control) is located in /usr/apache/bin:

```
# /usr/apache/bin/apachectl
usage: /usr/apache/bin/apachectl (start|stop|restart|fullstatus|status|
➥graceful|configtest|help)

start     - start httpd
stop      - stop httpd
```

▼

▼

```
restart     - restart httpd if running by sending a SIGHUP or start if
              not running
fullstatus - dump a full status screen; requires lynx and mod_status enabled
status      - dump a short status screen; requires lynx and mod_status enabled
graceful    - do a graceful restart by sending a SIGUSR1 or start if not running
configtest - do a configuration syntax test
help        - this screen
```

```
# /usr/apache/bin/apachectl start
fopen: No such file or directory
httpd: could not open document config file /etc/apache/httpd.conf
/usr/apache/bin/apachectl start: httpd could not be started
```

Surprisingly, the Solaris distribution of Apache requires us to specify the appropriate configuration before it can even launch for testing. That's what the error message about being unable to open the config file means.

Alright, we'll copy across the sample configuration file and try again:

```
# cd /etc/apache
# ls
access.conf       jserv.conf        magic          srm.conf
httpd.conf-example jserv.properties mime.types     zone.properties
# cp httpd.conf-example httpd.conf
# /usr/apache/bin/apachectl configtest
Syntax OK
# /usr/apache/bin/apachectl start
/usr/apache/bin/apachectl start: httpd started
```

This time notice that we ran the useful configuration test mode of apachectl and received no errors. Then we started up the server and all was well.

Interestingly, Solaris is shipped with the Apache server configured to launch on multiuser run levels, although the server itself cannot come up until the preceding manual step (copying the httpd.conf-example file) occurs.

```
# ls /etc/rc?.d/*apache
/etc/rc0.d/K16apache
/etc/rc1.d/K16apache
/etc/rc2.d/K16apache
/etc/rc3.d/S50apache
/etc/rcS.d/K16apache
```

▲   This means that you're ready to go after you get Apache launched by hand.

Regardless of the flavor of Unix, it's quite easy to enable a Web server on your system—certainly easier than creating a high quality Web site.

23

Exploring the `httpd.conf` File

When you get Apache running on your computer, the next step is to ensure that it's properly configured and reflects your own system configuration and setup. There are some simple changes worth making to improve the security and capabilities of the server, and we'll highlight those as we go.

Task 23.2: The Internals of the `httpd.conf` File

Earlier versions of Apache—up through 1.2—had the configuration split into three separate files: `srm.conf`, `access.conf`, and `httpd.conf`. That was useful, but it was also confusing, because there was never a clear rule on what sort of configuration statement should go in which file. As a result, starting with the 1.3 release of Apache, all the configuration is stored in a single file: `httpd.conf`.

The location of this file varies on different Unix flavors (you can use `locate`, or check the apache or httpd man page). Common locations are `/etc/apache` (Solaris), `/private/etc/httpd` (Mac OS X), and either `/etc/httpd/conf` or `/usr/local/apache/conf` (Linux).

1. Perhaps the single most important variable in the usually quite long `httpd.conf` file (expect yours to be at least 1,000 lines) is `DocumentRoot`. This tells you where in the file system the server is looking for Web pages to serve up.

   ```
   # grep DocumentRoot httpd.conf
   # DocumentRoot: The directory out of which you will serve your
   DocumentRoot "/var/apache/htdocs"
   # This should be changed to whatever you set DocumentRoot to.
   #     DocumentRoot /www/docs/host.some_domain.com
   ```

   On Solaris, Web pages are served out of `/var/apache/htdocs`. Red Hat Linux has a default directory of either `/var/www/html` or `/usr/local/apache/htdocs`, and Mac OS X has a default of `/Library/WebServer/Documents`.

2. The default file (probably `index.html`) in the `DocumentRoot` directory is what will be returned when a Web browser connects to our Web server and requests the "home" or "root" document. (Usually this is done by simply not specifying any document, as occurs when you connect to `http://www.smoothjazz.com/`, for example.)

   ```
   # pushd /var/www/html
   /var/www/html /etc/httpd/conf
   # ls -l
   total 8
   -rw-r--r--   1 root     root          2890 Sep  5  2001 index.html
   -rw-r--r--   1 root     root          1154 Sep  5  2001 poweredby.png
   # popd
   /etc/httpd/conf
   ```

By default, the Apache server has a page that says it's running, it's Apache, and that it's time to drop in personal pages. poweredby.png is the graphic file referenced in the default index.html page.

> The pushd and popd utilities are a great boon if you want to temporarily pop to another directory, then zoom back to where you were. pushd is analogous to cd, but popd knows where you were before the current directory. Very helpful!

3. The full list of possible default filenames for a given directory can be found by searching for index.html in the configuration file. Again, we'll use the *-n* to get a few lines of context around the match:

```
# grep -2 index.html httpd.conf
#
<IfModule mod_dir.c>
    DirectoryIndex index.html index.htm index.shtml index.php index.php4
➥index.php3 index.phtml index.cgi
</IfModule>
```

This rather confusing-looking statement says that if the mod_dir module is loaded (and it is, by default), Apache should try to serve up one of, in order, the following files: index.html, index.htm, index.shtml, index.php, index.php4, index.php3, index.phtml, or index.cgi.

That last file is worth a bit more exploration: Files with a .cgi filename suffix are executable programs that are written to be compatible with the Apache Common Gateway Interface. They can be quite simple, even a shell script:

```
#!/bin/sh
echo "Content-type: text/html"
echo ""
echo "Hello world!"
```

But they can also be quite complex, hook into databases, and other sophisticated programs.

4. Table 23.1 lists some of the key settings for a Web server, all found in the httpd.conf file. The default value for the Red Hat Linux 7.2 distribution of Apache 1.3.23 is also shown. Be cautious if you diverge from the standard settings: Make sure you understand the security ramifications of some of the more obscure settings before you use them!

▼

TABLE 23.1   Key Apache Configuration Fields

Name	Exemplary Value	Meaning
Port	80	Port that the Web server listens to. By default, it's always port 80, but you can actually have a Web server running on any port you'd like. SSL connections are port 443, for example.
User	apache	Account name under which the Web server runs. Do *not* use root for this!
ServerAdmin	root@localhost	E-mail address advertised as that of the server administrator.
UserDir	public_html	Wrapped by the lines <IfModule mod_userdir.c> and </ifModule>, this line defines the name of the special directory in user home directories that lets the server offer up ~*account* URLs.
ErrorLog	logs/error_log	The location of the Apache error log, rooted in ServerRoot. This is a critical snippet of information to ascertain, because keeping an eye on the error file will help you nip trouble in the bud.
LogLevel	warn	What level of transactions should be logged. If you have a busy server, keep this setting; but if you want to see how things are working, or if you are encountering errors with your Web server, ratchet this up to info or debug. If you want less, try error or alert.

There are many, many more settings in the httpd.conf file, but these will keep you busy for at least the first week.

5. One thing to be wary about is the CGI setting. By default, Apache will only let CGI scripts live in a special cgi-bin directory. Its location is, of course, defined within the configuration file. Look for the variable ScriptAlias. Here's how that snippet looks in our configuration file:

```
# ScriptAlias: This controls which directories contain server scripts.
# ScriptAliases are essentially the same as Aliases, except that
# documents in the realname directory are treated as applications and
# run by the server when requested rather than as documents sent to the
➥client.
```

▼

```
# The same rules about trailing "/" apply to ScriptAlias directives as to
# Alias.
#
ScriptAlias /cgi-bin/ "/var/www/cgi-bin/"

#
# "/var/www/cgi-bin" should be changed to whatever your ScriptAliased
# CGI directory exists, if you have that configured.
```

If you would like to give your users more latitude, where they can have CGI scripts anywhere on the system by simply ensuring that they're named .cgi, look for and uncomment out the last line of the following sequence:

```
# AddHandler allows you to map certain file extensions to "handlers",
# actions unrelated to filetype. These can be either built into the server
# or added with the Action command (see below)
#
# If you want to use server side includes, or CGI outside
# ScriptAliased directories, uncomment the following lines.
#
# To use CGI scripts:
#
#AddHandler cgi-script .cgi
```

What language can you write CGI scripts in? Just about anything that'll execute when invoked and output the proper CGI return sequence as the header before the rest of the material is returned.

Enabling CGI extends the protocol a little bit, actually. In addition to "I want/here is," we now have "Please run/Here's the output" as well. That's an essential conceptual addition if you're going to write CGI scripts of your own—make sure they output HTML!

6. Each directory that serves up Web pages, whether it's the DocumentRoot or a subdirectory, can have specific permissions or capabilities set. By default, directories inherit the permission of their parent, so setting the permissions of the DocumentRoot also sets the capabilities for everything else not otherwise specified.

This capability setting takes place within a Directory block, and most typically is in two parts. The first part specifies the permissions of / to encompass all directories in the entire filesystem, even those outside the DocumentRoot area:

```
<Directory />
    Options FollowSymLinks
    AllowOverride None
</Directory>
```

▼ This default for the entire filesystem has two permissions set: `FollowSymLinks` means that the Apache system will follow symbolic links (even if they might take the system out of the safe directory subtree specified by `DocumentRoot`), and `AllowOverride None` means that individual directories cannot contain configuration files (usually `.htaccess`) that override global access permissions.

The `DocumentRoot` block typically has a few more settings and options:

```
<Directory "/var/www/html">

#
# This may also be "None", "All", or any combination of "Indexes",
# "Includes", "FollowSymLinks", "ExecCGI", or "MultiViews".
#
# Note that "MultiViews" must be named *explicitly* --- "Options All"
# doesn't give it to you.
#
    Options Indexes FollowSymLinks

#
# This controls which options the .htaccess files in directories can
# override. Can also be "All", or any combination of "Options", "FileInfo",
# "AuthConfig", and "Limit"
#
    AllowOverride None

#
# Controls who can get stuff from this server.
#
    Order allow,deny
    Allow from all
</Directory>
```

Skipping the comments, you can see that this sets `Indexes`, repeats `FollowSymLinks` and `AllowOverride None` (which means that they don't really have to be stated because they'd inherit these permissions from the / declaration), and offers a stub that shows how to create directories that only allow (or deny) access to certain classes of users. One use for this latter feature is if you want to have an area of the Web site blocked to outside visitors. You could specify `Allow from 198.75.44.*` and `Deny from all`, and if the connecting system didn't have the matching IP address, they would receive a "permission denied" message.

There are a number of different values that `Options` can be given, most notably `ExecCGI` (specifies that CGI scripts can be run from this directory), `Includes` (enable server-side include (SSI) pages), `IncludesNOEXEC` (same as `Includes`, but prohibits the dangerous `#exec` statement), `Indexes` (show a directory listing if there's no default page available), and `None` (no features are activated). There are a ▼ few more options, but those are the most commonly used.

All documentation about Apache can be found on the Apache Group Web site, and it's well worth reading some of the tutorials and references if you're setting up a complex Web server configuration. Start at `http://httpd.apache.org/docs-project/` and pick the version number for your Apache server.

In the next hour we'll explore more about the `Directory` blocks when we learn how to extend Apache to allow virtual hosts.

That's about it for specific configuration changes you might want to make to a typical Web server.

Testing and Tuning the Configuration

Before we leave this hour, let's spend a few minutes testing some of the capabilities of the default Apache Web server, and discuss a few security considerations to ensure that you don't unwittingly leave any gaping holes open now that you're administering a full-fledged Web server. We'll address security more fully in the next hour.

Task 23.3: What Can Apache Do?

As with any Internet service, as system administrator your responsibility is to both get things up and running and to ensure that they're running safely, and aren't going to spill over and allow corruption of the system. With a service like NTP (the Network Time Protocol), it's not too dangerous, but Apache has a particularly dangerous characteristic of letting users write programs that will be run by unknown third parties—a potentially dangerous situation!

Before we get too paranoid, however, let's spend a few minutes examining the capabilities of the new Apache server that's running.

The biggest tip I'll share regarding running a Web server is that having a link to `/web` to get to the `DocumentRoot` is a tremendous timesaver. Do this by creating a symbolic link: `ln -s /var/www/html /web`.

1. The most obvious capability is that `httpd` can serve up Web pages. Go to the `DocumentRoot` directory and replace the boring default `index.html` with the following:

```
# cat index.html
<HTML>
<TITLE>Welcome to Apache!</TITLE>
```

23

▼

```
<BODY>
<CENTER><IMG SRC="poweredby.png"></CENTER>
If you need more information on Apache, please go to:
<A HREF="http://www.apache.org/">Apache.org</A> or
<A HREF="http://www.yavapai-apache-nation.com/">
The Yavalai-Apache Nation</A>.
</BODY>
</HTML>
```

The easiest way to request the page is to open up a Web browser on your Unix system and request `http://localhost/`, which should produce the page as shown in Figure 23.2.

FIGURE 23.2

Test page in KDE's Web browser, Konqueror.

2. Now that we've had some traffic, let's check the Web log file to see what happened:

```
# tail access_log
127.0.0.1 - - [10/Apr/2002:11:00:20 -0700] "GET / HTTP/1.1" 200 293 "-"
"Mozilla/5.0 (compatible; Konqueror/2.2-11; Linux)"
127.0.0.1 - - [10/Apr/2002:11:00:21 -0700] "GET /poweredby.png HTTP/1.1"
200 1154 "http://localhost/" "Mozilla/5.0 (compatible; Konqueror/2.2-11; Linux)"
127.0.0.1 - - [10/Apr/2002:11:00:22 -0700] "GET /favicon.ico HTTP/1.1" 404
295 "-" "Mozilla/5.0 (compatible; Konqueror/2.2-11; Linux)"
127.0.0.1 - - [10/Apr/2002:11:01:15 -0700] "GET / HTTP/1.1" 200 314 "-"
"Mozilla/5.0 (compatible; Konqueror/2.2-11; Linux)"
127.0.0.1 - - [10/Apr/2002:11:01:15 -0700] "GET /poweredby.png HTTP/1.1"
200 1154 "http://localhost/" "Mozilla/5.0 (compatible; Konqueror/2.2-11; Linux)"
127.0.0.1 - - [10/Apr/2002:11:01:29 -0700] "GET / HTTP/1.1" 200 314 "-"
"Mozilla/5.0 (compatible; Konqueror/2.2-11; Linux)"
127.0.0.1 - - [10/Apr/2002:11:01:29 -0700] "GET /poweredby.png HTTP/1.1"
200 1154 "http://localhost/" "Mozilla/5.0 (compatible; Konqueror/2.2-11; Linux)"
```

You can see that there were a couple of reloads when I was in the Web browser. Notice also that the first time the browser visited the page, it also requested `/favicon.ico`, an optional icon that can be used with the browser's favorites list to have a tiny logo adjacent to the link.

▼

The format of the Apache log file is actually specified in the `httpd.conf` file:

```
# grep combined /etc/httpd/conf/httpd.conf | grep -vE '^#'
LogFormat "%h %l %u %t \"%r\" %>s %b \"%{Referer}i\" \"%{User-Agent}i\""
➥combined
CustomLog logs/access_log combined
```

The second matching line shows that `logs/access_log` is a "combined" format log file, and the first line uses the `LogFormat` directive to define exactly what fields should be output, in what order, in a "combined" log file. The format and fields of this file can be changed, but do so with extreme caution, as you'll break all third-party log file analysis software.

3. The next test is to see if we can have a CGI program execute in the main directory. To do this, we'll have to whip up a succinct shell script:

```
# cat test.cgi
#!/bin/sh

echo "Content-type: text/html"
echo ""

echo "The current date and time is: `/bin/date`"
exit 0
```

A quick test while at the shell:

```
# sh test.cgi
Content-type: text/html

The current date and time is: Wed Apr 10 11:37:06 PDT 2002
```

Looks good, but when we request this CGI script to run and have its output fed to us in the Web browser, you can see the less than ideal results in Figure 23.3.

FIGURE 23.3

Instead of running the CGI, it shows us the source!

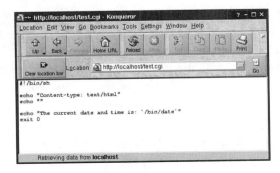

This is a very common configuration issue with Apache, and whether we want to fix it or not revolves around assumptions of security and safety on the Web server.

4. The basic question is: Do you trust your users to write good, clean, secure code? If you do, the chance that someone can exploit a hole in a CGI script still exists but isn't overwhelming, and you should add ExecCGI to the appropriate Directory block in the httpd.conf file.

If you aren't sure, one strategy commonly used is to corral all the CGI scripts and programs into a single cgi-bin directory, which is the default configuration. Where is that directory? Check the httpd.conf file:

```
# grep cgi-bin /etc/httpd/conf/httpd.conf | grep -vE '^#'
    ScriptAlias /cgi-bin/ "/var/www/cgi-bin/"
    # "/var/www/cgi-bin" should be changed to whatever your ScriptAliased
    <Directory "/var/www/cgi-bin">
<Directory "/var/www/cgi-bin">
```

The last lines are the match: /var/www/cgi-bin. Drop that very same shell script into that directory and reference it as http://localhost/cgi-bin/test.cgi, and it'll work just fine. Then you can inform users that all CGI scripts have to be mailed to you, as Webmaster, and that you'll check through them and, if they're clean, install them in the cgi-bin directory. These can be written in any language supported by your Unix system, including Perl, Python, C, and even shell scripts.

5. We are sure that on this server all the users are veritable security wizards and won't write a single line of CGI that isn't completely secure (which means that they probably won't be writing shell scripts, for one thing, but that's a bigger topic we'll address in the next hour). Therefore, we're going to enable CGI execution in the DocumentRoot.

To accomplish this, we'll need to edit httpd.conf. Find the line <Directory "/var/www/html"> (or the equivalent, depending on the configuration) and jump down a few lines to where the Options statement can be found. All we need to do is add ExecCGI to that list, so that it looks like this:

```
Options Indexes FollowSymLinks ExecCGI
```

We'll also need to tell the Web server that files with the suffix .cgi are special (they're executable programs whose output should be returned to the Web browser), and should be handled by the cgi-script module. This is done by removing the # at the beginning of the line:

```
#AddHandler cgi-script .cgi
```

It's time to restart Apache so that the server will reread its configuration file. This is most easily done with the init script:

```
# /etc/rc.d/init.d/httpd restart
Stopping httpd:                                            [  OK  ]
Starting httpd:                                            [  OK  ]
```

▼   Now when the URL `http://localhost/test.cgi` is entered, the server returns the
      current date and time, as hoped:

```
# telnet localhost http
Trying 127.0.0.1...
Connected to localhost.
Escape character is '^]'.
GET /test.cgi
The current date and time is: Wed Apr 10 12:26:36 PDT 2002
Connection closed by foreign host.
```

▲

With a configuration file that contains more than 1,000 lines of information, it should be
no surprise to you that there are a number of ways you can change Apache. The exact
needs of your site and your user community are yours to ascertain, and reading through
the documents available at the Apache.org Web site will help clarify what can be
accomplished and how.

Summary

In this hour we have figured out how to find and install (if necessary) a copy of the popular and powerful Apache Web server, bring it online, and reconfigure the OS so that it's
automatically started as one of the multiuser services. We wrapped up by looking at a few
simple capabilities, peeking into the `access_log` and learning how to enable CGI script
execution from any directory. We've only had a chance to scratch the surface of Apache. If
you'd like to learn more, one book worth seeking out is *Sams Teach Yourself Apache in 24
Hours* by Daniel Lopez. Of course, you could also try the voluminous online Apache documentation.

Q&A

**Q Why do most Unix flavors call the Apache server `httpd`, while others—notably
     Solaris—call it `apache`?**

A A good question, one that has no definitive answer. By convention, most daemons
   are named after the service they provide, so `telnetd` offers `telnet` service, `ftpd`
   offers `ftp` services, and so on. On the Solaris platform, however, service daemons
   are often named after the application that offers the service. Confusing? Oh yeah.

**Q What's your recommendation: Only allow `cgi-bin`, or let users drop CGI
     scripts wherever?**

A I think that if you're running a Web hosting firm and clients are accessing the system, my recommendation would be to either only allow a shared `cgi-bin` that only
   the administrators can access directly, or perhaps create a separate `cgi-bin` for each
   user. This way you can corral the scripts and read through them—if necessary—to
   ensure that they don't offer any obvious security holes.

Workshop

Quiz

1. If you wanted to create a separate `cgi-bin` for a user, what two statements in the `conf` file would encompass the required changes?
2. What is the standard Apache control script called?
3. Everyone knows what an HTML file is. What's a `.shtml` file, as referenced in the `config` file?
4. Summarize the HTTP protocol for both file transfers and CGI execution.
5. Where does Apache get the e-mail address for the server on its error messages?
6. What simple `grep` trick lets you avoid seeing commented-out lines when searching the Apache configuration file?

Answers

1. The `Directory` statement would explicitly allow permissions to be set in the users `/cgi-bin` directory, and `Options` would let CGI scripts become executable.
2. `apachectl`
3. A `.shtml` is an HTML file that includes server-side include directives. They look like this:

   ```
   <!--#include file="header.html"-->
   ```

   and can dramatically simplify Web site construction. A neat, newer alternative to SSI is PHP Hypertext Preprocessor, and it's well worth learning. Start at `www.php.net` to see why.
4. "I want/Here is" or "I want/Not found" are the basic file transaction dialogs, and "Please run/Here's the output" or "Please run/Failed: error" are the basic CGI dialogs.
5. The e-mail address in Apache error messages comes directly from the `httpd.conf` file. Look for `ServerAdmin`.
6. Use `grep -vE '^#'` any time you want to strip out comment lines.

In the next and final hour, we will expand upon our discussion and exploration of the Apache Web server by making the changes required to offer virtual hosting on the machine. This will have it serve up different Web sites for different domain names, even though they all point to the same IP address. Then we'll wrap up with a brief discussion of Web and system security.

Hour **24**

Virtual Hosts with Apache

In this last hour, we're going to explore a specific capability of Apache—virtual hosting—then wrap up with some discussion of Unix system security.

If you have a Web site—and odds are that you do—you know that there are two basic approaches to hosting Web sites: Each site gets its own computer, or, somehow, multiple Web sites (for example, multiple domain names) resolve to a single shared server. Because Unix is the original shared multi-user resource, it should be no surprise that sharing a Web server is easy and well within the capabilities of even the lowliest Unix box.

In this last hour, we'll explore how to

- Enable virtual hosting in Apache
- Secure your system

Enabling Virtual Hosting in Apache

The most interesting capability in Apache is its ability to deliver different Web pages for different domains, even if they all resolve to the same IP address. Of course, you can configure your domain names to have multiple IP addresses, all of which are served on a single system (you would do this with additional `ifconfig` statements; see the `man` page for more details), but that's highly inefficient because there's no reason not to have the domains share a single IP.

When `httpd` first came on the scene in the guise of the original Web server from the Center for High Energy Physics (CERN) in Switzerland and the National Center for Supercomputer Applications at the University of Illinois, Urbana-Champaign, Web servers were like other pre-Internet-boom servers—they blindly served up requests for the machine they were running on.

As the Net became more popular, the number of people wanting to have their own domain exceeded the number of discrete servers online, so it became obvious that there would need to be some sort of sharing, or *virtual hosting* capability added to Unix.

That's what the Apache team used as the inspiration for `VirtualHost` in its Web server: It's a simple mechanism that lets sysadmins set up dozens or even hundreds of different Web sites, with different domains, on the same system.

 Even `sendmail` has gotten into the act. Go to www.sendmail.org and read about virtual user tables (`virtusertable`) capabilities. You can have a single mail server appear to be dozens of different domains, so joe@hisbakerystore and jane@herclothesshop use the same system, have adjacent e-mail-boxes on the server, but are able to send mail out with different return addresses, timestamps, message IDs, and more.

Task 24.1: Configuring Virtual Hosts

▲ TASK

The first step required to configure a virtual host solution is to ensure that the DNS name servers for the domains in question are all instructed to deliver up the server IP address for any domain that should be served from the central system.

1. To check and verify that this configuration has occurred, use `dig` to confirm the IP address in the *statement of authority* record (see Hour 18, "Running Your Own Name Server" for more details on the internals of a domain name record).

   For the examples in this hour, we'll consider three domains. `staging.intuitive.com` is a subdomain that points to a staging server that's used for experimentation and

▼

development, and `sherlockworld.com` and `niftylister.com` are both Web sites available to the general public:

```
# host sherlockworld.com
sherlockworld.com. has address 10.10.2.200
# host niftylister.com
niftylister.com. has address 10.10.2.200
# host staging.intuitive.com
staging.intuitive.com. has address 10.10.2.200
```

It takes a little bit of rethinking name-to-number concepts for many sysadmins to understand how multiple domain names can resolve to the same IP address without a conflict. In a nutshell, the DNS system ensures that names resolve to a number, but you could have hundreds, nay, thousands of domains all pointing to a single box without any violation of DNS standards and usage.

> If you read the Apache documentation about virtual hosting (at `http://www.apache.org/docs/vhosts/`), realize that having a number of domains sharing an IP address is known as *name-based virtual sharing*. If each domain had a different IP address, that'd be *IP-based virtual sharing*. It's a bit confusing.

2. In a stock Apache configuration file, the virtual host directives appear within the third section, delimited by `Section 3: Virtual Hosts` in the comments.

   The configuration we're using for this server—`staging.intuitive.com`—has all the domains sharing a single IP address, so configuration consists of two basic elements: the `VirtualHost` directive and the `Directory` block that specifies what permissions and configuration directives are enabled (or disabled) for that particular directory and all below it.

   The very first step is to enable name-based virtual hosting in the `httpd.conf` configuration file. This is done by ensuring that the line

   `NameVirtualHost *`

   isn't commented out.

   Subsequent to that in the file, here are the relevant `VirtualHost` blocks:

```
<VirtualHost *>
ServerName www.niftylister.com
DocumentRoot /web/niftylister
ErrorLog /web/niftylister/error_log
CustomLog /web/niftylister/access_log
ServerAdmin webmaster@niftylister.com
```

```
</VirtualHost>

<VirtualHost *>
ServerName www.sherlockworld.com
DocumentRoot /web/sherlockworld
ServerAlias sherlockworld.com holmes.sherlockworld.com
</VirtualHost>
```

Notice that although the first virtual host definition specifies a new ErrorLog, CustomLog, and ServerAdmin, the second domain is okay inheriting the values of the overall server (for example, those values defined earlier in the configuration file). However, sherlockworld.com also has the subdomain holmes.sherlock-world.com as an alias; it'll serve up the same Web pages at the same DocumentRoot as the main sherlockworld.com site. (Of course, you still need to have a DNS record for holmes.sherlockworld.com, but that can be added to the main sherlockworld.com DNS record, if desired.)

A great feature of virtual hosting with Apache is that each virtual host can have its own copy of the access and error file automatically. This means that as system administrator, you aren't responsible for splitting out traffic for a specific domain from a central log file, a definite boon. Plus it ensures that the log traffic of other domains can remain private, because it's not always the case that Web site owners want others to see their actual traffic.

Notice that each VirtualHost has a new DocumentRoot. This is critically important, and each must be unique for virtual hosts to work properly. If you neglect this important step, you'll find that multiple domain names end up with the same home page, defeating the purpose of virtual hosts.

3. The other half of the main configuration for virtual hosts is to specify a Directory block for each of the new DocumentRoots (though technically, you could just let it default to the permissions set for / at the top of the configuration file, it's best to explicitly indicate what the owner of a specific domain can or cannot do so you can always quickly double-check security for any given user):

```
<Directory "/web/niftylister">
   Options Indexes FollowSymLinks ExecCGI
   AllowOverride None
   Order allow,deny
   Allow from all
</Directory>
<Directory "/web/sherlockworld">
   Options Indexes FollowSymLinks ExecCGI Includes
   AllowOverride None
   Order allow,deny
   Allow from all
</Directory>
```

▼ In this particular configuration, both have almost the same permissions and options set, but notice that server-side includes have been disabled for `niftylister.com` by omitting `Includes` from the `Options` line.

4. That's all that's needed! The only other step is to ensure that the new `DocumentRoot` directories exist and have at least some sort of rudimentary welcome page to avoid "page not found" error messages.

Try visiting these three domains yourself to see how different the Web sites are, even though they're all coming off the very same Web server: `staging.intu-itive.com`, `www.sherlockworld.com`, and `www.niftylister.com`.

It's worth briefly showing the organization of the `/web` directory:

```
# ls -l /web
total 12
drwxr-xr-x     2 root        root         1024 Nov 22 09:25 campusdev
drwxr-xr-x    10 root        root         1024 Dec 18 21:23 cbo
drwxr-xr-x     2 root        root         1024 Nov 22 09:35 cbofacilities
drwxr-xr-x    10 root        root         1024 Dec 18 05:20 chatter
drwxr-xr-x     8 root        root         1024 Nov 22 09:46 launchline
drwxr-xr-x     5 root        root         1024 Mar  8 22:40 niftylister
drwxr-xr-x     5 root        root         1024 Nov 22 09:58 niftyseller
drwxr-xr-x     2 root        root         1024 Nov 22 10:06 sherlockworld
drwxr-xr-x     2 root        root         1024 Dec 18 05:20 smartpage
drwxrwxr-x     6 root        root         1024 Mar 21 16:20 staging
drwxr-xr-x     5 root        root         1024 Nov 22 10:18 windward
```

24

You can see that there are actually quite a few domains being served off this system. Stepping into any one directory will show, as expected, the individual HTML files, graphics, and so on, for that Web site, neatly separated from all other Web sites on the server:

```
# ls sherlockworld
about.html                gutnavbar.js              scandal-bohemia.html
beryl-coronet.html        gutsmallprint.js          smallprint.js
blue-carbuncle.html       hmenu.js                  speckled-band.html
boscombe-valley.html      holmes.css                the-small-print.html
case-of-identity.html     how-to-access.html        topnavbar.js
copper-beeches.html       index.html                topnav.js
crashcourse.js            noble-bachelor.html        twisted-lip.html
engineers-thumb.html      originals-from gutenberg.txt
five-orange-pips.html     red-headed-league.html
```

And, as we know from the `httpd.conf` file, the default page that will be served up for sherlockworld.com is `index.html`:

```
# head sherlockworld/index.html
<!DOCTYPE HTML PUBLIC "-//W3C//DTD HTML 4.01 Transitional//EN">
<HTML>
```
▼

▼
```
<META HTTP-EQUIV="content-type" CONTENT="text/html; charset=iso-8859-1">

<META NAME="keywords" CONTENT="Sherlock Holmes,Arthur Conan Doyle,Dr.
➥Watson,John
Watson,Sherlockian,Baker Street,221b,Moriarty,detective,mystery,London,
England,Jeremy Brett,Christopher Plummer,Scotland Yard">
<META NAME="description" CONTENT="A reader-friendly library of some
of the best Sherlock Holmes  stories, as written by Arthur Conan Doyle and
➥narrated
by Dr. Watson. Inspired by the work of Project
Gutenberg. Note: Site won't work with Netscape 4.x">
<META NAME="ROBOTS" CONTENT="ALL">
```
▲
```
<TITLE>The Adventures of Sherlock Holmes, by Arthur Conan Doyle</TITLE>
```

Simple in concept, and simple in execution, virtual hosts are a "killer app" for Unix as an Internet server. As a system administrator, it's your job to configure and maintain this sort of setup if you're with an ISP or any other firm that serves up Web sites, and as such, it should be a relief that it's so straightforward.

Having run different Web hosting servers for almost 10 years now (rather amazing, really!), my experience leads me to two strong recommendations:

1. Put all the Web sites on a different partition or different physical disk. It helps manage disk space and maintain quotas for customers (see Hour 12, "Managing Disk Quotas," for more details on how you might set up a simple Web hosting disk usage quota).

2. Set up aliases so that when users connect to the server, they're either dropped directly into their Web hosting account (not a bad strategy, all in all—just set the home directory to /web/sherlockworld, for example), or so that they have a link directly in the home directory that takes them to the appropriate place on the filesystem (perhaps public_html, to be consistent with other hosting firms).

If you can avoid it, don't let people have telnet or ssh access to the system. Set them up with ftp (see Hour 19, "Running Internet Services") and, again, have their home directory be their Web directory, too.

A few minutes of organization and proper setup and you can easily manage a server hosting hundreds of Web sites.

Keeping Your System Secure

The preceding comments about trying to sidestep granting your users telnet or ssh access to the system is the tip of a much bigger iceberg: Unix system security.

Although we clearly do not have sufficient space (or time) left to discuss this topic in any extensive manner, it is worthwhile to wrap up *Teach Yourself Unix System Administration in 24 Hours* with a brief foray into the world of system and server security.

There are two basic categories of security—keeping people out and keeping people contained. I always think about security by remembering that it's a study in trade-offs: The more secure you make your system, the less accessible it is. Make it too secure, and no one can use it. Make it too insecure, and anyone—including a bad guy—can do anything they want.

Clearly, it's finding the happy medium, the middle ground, that is the goal of computer security. The exact balance of security and capability for a given system is a function of its purpose and the sophistication, capabilities, trustworthiness, and type of its user community.

If you are managing a shared Unix system for the undergraduate computer science majors at a local university, I'd say that you're at ground zero for trouble: smart, curious computer types who will unquestionably look around and experiment. The greatest danger in this situation will most likely be from within the user community, not outsiders.

If, on the other hand, you are managing a set of collocated servers that only a half dozen screened and bonded company administrators will be even accessing, you can ratchet up the security quite a bit and know that your greatest danger will be unauthorized outsiders.

So how does Unix let you manage these security issues? Through a combination of specific security tools, third-party software, and implementation of your specific site policies regarding security and usage.

Passwords

The first, and simplest, level of security is passwords. Yes, it sounds obvious and dopey, but the most common method for cracking into a system is through poorly selected passwords. It used to be the case that passwords that were names or dictionary words were easy targets (for example, if Joe has the password `eoj` or `joseph`). Nowadays, computers are so fast that if a cracker can get a copy of the encrypted password string, he can encrypt all the words in the dictionary and lots of common variations (for example, `jump!` or `?jump`) within an hour or two. As a result, the simplest step towards ensuring system security is simply to ensure that your users change their passwords with some frequency, and that the resultant passwords are complex and sufficiently varied that it would take days, not seconds, for a cracker to match guesses.

Oh, and don't write your password down. You just never know...

rlogin

There's also a Unix facility called `rlogin` that combines a simple login-not-necessary mechanism for accessing trusted remote systems with the software necessary to access this capability. This is not a good idea, and smart crackers immediately search for `.rhosts` or `/etc/hosts.equiv` files on the system (which contain a list of trusted hosts;

if the cracker has broken into one system, he's then therefore broken into the entire trusted set). Disable rlogin by removing the rlogin and rshd binaries.

Unnecessary Network Services

This leads to a general observation: Shut off all services that are unnecessary to the day-to-day use of your system. You probably don't need to run the rwho daemon, for example, or talkd or fingerd. Shut them off in xinetd (or an equivalent—see Hour 19 for details).

Speaking of unnecessary network services, turn off telnet and ftpd now. If your users need to log in to the system, instruct them to use ssh and point them to some ssh-compliant client programs (check at www.download.com). The ssh system also supports secure file transfers, and there are ssh-compliant FTP clients available online, too.

When you're done turning things off, run the useful nmap utility to scan your ports and inform you what's still running:

```
# nmap -sT localhost

Starting nmap V. 2.54BETA22 ( www.insecure.org/nmap/ )
Interesting ports on localhost.localdomain (127.0.0.1):
(The 1536 ports scanned but not shown below are in state: closed)
Port       State       Service
22/tcp     open        ssh
25/tcp     open        smtp
111/tcp    open        sunrpc
1024/tcp   open        kdm
1025/tcp   open        listen
6000/tcp   open        X11


Nmap run completed -- 1 IP address (1 host up) scanned in 3 seconds
```

Here you can see that it might be smart to disable kdm (the KDE desktop manager), sunRPC (the SunOS remote procedure call mechanism), and X11 (the X Window System server).

Keep Your Operating System Up-To-Date

One of the most important security measures you can take as a system administrator is to ensure that your Unix operating system is always up-to-date. It's common for sysadmins to run old operating systems that have all sorts of known—and fixed—security problems, and that's clearly a bad idea.

Regardless of which Unix you have, your vendor's Web site should have any patches and updates, and most have e-mail lists you can join that notify you proactively of any security holes and how to fix them. Pay attention to this!

Join the Computer Emergency Response Team

One U.S. government-funded group that does a great job of keeping an eye on security problems and promptly issuing warnings and notifications across a wide variety of different operating systems is CERT, the Computer Emergency Response Team at Carnegie-Mellon University. You can find it online at `www.cert.org`, then sign up for their mailing list.

Other Useful Web Sites

There are a couple of other sites worth exploring if you want to learn more about securing your Unix systems: The Computer Incident Advisory Capability (`www.ciac.org`), Rootshell (`www.rootshell.org`), Security Focus (`www.securityfocus.com`), and the System Administration, Networking and Security group (`www.sans.org`) are all well worth spending time exploring.

Useful Tools

There are a number of third-party security tools available that help you batten down the hatches and keep an electronic eye on what's happening. Chief among them are `swatch`, an elegant and simple system logfile watchdog; `tripwire`, a tool that snapshots all the system binaries and informs you of any change (for example, a cracker trying to sneak a Trojan horse onto the system); `crack`, an effective password guesser that lets you enforce a "non-guessable" password policy; and `ipchains`, a firewall that's included with many modern flavors of Unix. Other tools worth exploring if you want to really ratchet up your protection include COPS, SATAN, SAINT, `tcpd`, and TCT.

Start your search for these sophisticated security tools at an appropriate package management archive Web site (see Hour 8, "Unix Package Management"), or search at the Usenix System Administration Guild (SAGE) Web site (`www.usenix.org/sage/`) for details.

Summary

The most important security strategy is to be paranoid, circumspect, suspicious, secretive, and open and friendly at the same time. Seriously, be conscious of security and security issues, teach your user community simple steps—like picking good passwords—and do your best to create an open and productive work environment, while still doing regular backups, rotating your backup media to ensure you always have at least one "spare" backup image.

And So Our 24 Hours Come to an End...

This marks the end of the 24th hour of *Teach Yourself Unix System Administration in 24 Hours*. It's been quite a journey, and there's been a remarkable amount of material covered, much of which takes some time to digest and understand properly. So, whether you've slammed through in 24 hours, or whether you've taken a few weeks to slowly step through and understand each topic, it's time to *use* what you've learned in this book. It's only through use that you'll truly learn how to think and work like a top Unix system administrator, comfortable in front of a command line and able to convince your systems to jump through hoops of your own making.

Good luck!

Remember, if you encounter any errata in this book, any examples that you cannot duplicate, typographical mistakes, or other problems, please let us know! Go to `www.intu-itive.com/tyusa/` and you'll find an errata report form there.

And stay in touch.

Dave Taylor

`taylor@intuitive.com`

INDEX

A

Acceptable Use Policy (AUP), 402
access
  accounts, 108
  CERT, 481
  crontab, 286-291
  /etc/passwd file, 86-90
  groups
    /etc/group, 73-76
    security, 77-79
  hackers, 307-311
  inetd, 379-381
  passwords, 91-94, 479
  Red Hat Linux, 14
  rlogin, 479
  strings, 67
    /etc/passwd, 70-73
    files, 68-70

  unnecessary network services, 480
  updating, 480
  Web sites, 481
access.log file, 316
accounts
  Darwin password files, 91-94
  deleting, 112-114
  Linux management tools, 114-121
  passwords, 126-129
  re-enabling, 111
  Red Hat Linux, 14
  Solaris management tools, 121-126
  suspending, 108-111
  user, 89
actions, init, 250
adding
  drives, 208-212
  users, 94-103
addresses
  IP, 333
  ranges, 328

How can we make this index more useful? E-mail us at indexes@samspublishing.com

G

GID (group ID), 70. *See also* **permissions**
gpasswd command, 78
grep command, 444
groups
   permissions, 68-70
      /etc/group, 73-76
      security, 77-79
   users, 95-99
GRUB (GRand Unified Boot loader),
  223-226
gunzip command, 141
gzip tool, 138-144

H

hackers, tracking log files, 307-311. *See also*
  security
hard limits, 235
hash tables, 34
Help, 16-17
   Apache Web servers, 464
   disks, 182-193
   DNS, 364-370
   dual-booting, 218-219
      GRUB, 223-226
      LILO, 220-223
      partitioning disks, 219-220
      virtual machines, 226-228
   fink, 172
   init processes, 248, 250-253
   installation, 8-10
   Mac OS X, 336-343
   named application, 359-362

   networks, 327
      connecting Linux to Internet, 328-335
      Mac OS X/Solaris, 336-343
      testing, 343-349
   passwords, 95-99
   Red Hat Linux, 16-17
      keyboards, 10
      network connections, 13
   rndc application, 362-364
   RPM, 162-167
   reloading, 362
   run levels, 254-259
   Solaris, 336-343
   tools
      artsd, 273-275
      at command, 296-298
      compress, 134-138
      crontab, 286-291
      dig, 364-370
      du command, 47-52
      fsck, 182-193
      gzip, 138-142, 144
      host, 364-370
      ifconfig, 343-349
      management, 114-121, 121-126
      netstat, 343-349
      passwords, 126-129
      ping, 343-349
      popd, 463
      pushd, 463
      rotation, 320-323
      virtual hosts, 474-478
     virtual hosts, 474-478
home directories, creating, 95-99
host tool, 364-370
hosting Apache Web servers, 474-478
hosts command, 313
httpd log files, navigating, 312-316
httpd.conf files, navigating, 462-467

T